# Gendering Nationalism

"The impressive range of case studies included in this collection highlight the complex but intimate relationships that exist, in variable ways, in different nationalist political projects. The book points out how notions of masculinity and femininity, and sexuality and belonging, construct—in shifting and contested ways which vary temporarily and spatially—the boundaries of these nationalisms. An important contribution to the field of nationalism studies."
—Professor Nira Yuval-Davis, *Director of the Centre for Research on Migration, Refugees and Belonging (CMRB), University of East London*

"In the critical juncture of the Great Regression, nationalist types of identification have increased in spread and intensity. From Brexit to the Catalan crisis, renewed calls for separatism, national symbols and narratives have acquired relevance, challenging the expectations of a linear trend towards cosmopolitan visions. Focusing on the interaction between gender and nationalism, this very timely volume contributes to our understanding of the diversity and fluidity of various nationalist projects."
—Professor Donatella della Porta, *Professor of Political Science, Dean of the Institute for Humanities and the Social Sciences and Director of the PD program in Political Science and Sociology at the Scuola Normale Superiore, Florence*

Jon Mulholland
Nicola Montagna
Erin Sanders-McDonagh
Editors

# Gendering Nationalism

Intersections of Nation, Gender and Sexuality

*Editors*
Jon Mulholland
School of Health and Social Sciences
University of the West of England
Bristol, UK

Nicola Montagna
School of Law
Middlesex University
London, UK

Erin Sanders-McDonagh
School of Social Policy, Sociology
and Social Research
University of Kent
Kent, UK

ISBN 978-3-319-76698-0     ISBN 978-3-319-76699-7  (eBook)
https://doi.org/10.1007/978-3-319-76699-7

Library of Congress Control Number: 2018944259

© The Editor(s) (if applicable) and The Author(s) 2018
This work is subject to copyright. All rights are solely and exclusively licensed by the Publisher, whether the whole or part of the material is concerned, specifically the rights of translation, reprinting, reuse of illustrations, recitation, broadcasting, reproduction on microfilms or in any other physical way, and transmission or information storage and retrieval, electronic adaptation, computer software, or by similar or dissimilar methodology now known or hereafter developed.
The use of general descriptive names, registered names, trademarks, service marks, etc. in this publication does not imply, even in the absence of a specific statement, that such names are exempt from the relevant protective laws and regulations and therefore free for general use.
The publisher, the authors, and the editors are safe to assume that the advice and information in this book are believed to be true and accurate at the date of publication. Neither the publisher nor the authors or the editors give a warranty, express or implied, with respect to the material contained herein or for any errors or omissions that may have been made. The publisher remains neutral with regard to jurisdictional claims in published maps and institutional affiliations.

Cover image © Blend Images / Alamy Stock Photo

Printed on acid-free paper

This Palgrave Macmillan imprint is published by the registered company Springer International Publishing AG part of Springer Nature.
The registered company address is: Gewerbestrasse 11, 6330 Cham, Switzerland

# Foreword

*Gendering Nationalism* makes an important intervention at a critical time in global politics in which nationalism is resurgent in a variety of places, from Russia to Europe, the USA and elsewhere. Its contribution builds on a first wave of studies of gender and nationalist projects that convincingly identified a gender subtext within the practices and ideologies of nationalist and national liberation movements, parties and political cultures. Such research demonstrated that gender inclusivity tends to be more pronounced in emerging nationalist movements than in settled nationalist states and that gender matters in nationalist projects on the political left as well as the political right. From these first-wave studies, we also learned how hegemonic notions of femininity and masculinity can become foundational elements in the construction of nations, national belonging, and citizenship.

*Gendering Nationalism* builds as well on a second wave of scholarship that focused on contextual differences. These studies added a more precise sense of the relationship between nationalism and gender over time, and across and within national borders. Second-wave research also showed the complex ways that ideologies of gender and nationalism are constructed differently depending on specific geo-political, social and historical factors. The chapters collected in this volume are exemplars of a third wave of scholarship that illuminates the entanglement of gender in nationalist projects. These studies move forward our understanding of gender and nationalism by identifying patterns across contextually embedded cases that vary across national boundaries and historical periods. Put more simply, these chapters highlight general trends in gendered nationalism without losing sight of its specific manifestation in particular times and places. These third-wave works also productively locate sexuality in the nexus of gender and nationalism. They show that nationalist projects differ in how they highlight or ignore sexual issues such as interracial sexuality, and the extent to which they include or exclude lesbians, gay men, transgendered persons and other sexual minorities from social life, the economy or politics. As well, this research points to how movements and states vary in whether or not they treat sexuality as an aspect of gender, as, for instance, by defining women but not men by their sexual practices.

Perhaps the most significant contribution of this new wave of research on gendered nationalism is its attention to the fluidity and contradictions of nationalist projects. These studies show how modern nationalism both centers national interests and draws on transnationally circulating ideologies and rhetoric. Indeed, nationalist states and movements, especially in recent years those on the far right, engage in transnationally coordinated efforts such as summits of nationalist politicians and alliances among nationalistic states. These chapters also reveal the fragility of political categories, with instances of both far-right and left-oriented nationalist projects that include women and support gender rights as well as instances in which nationalisms across the political spectrum exclude women and oppose gender equality. The same is true for LGBT and other sexuality minority rights. In contrast, the treatment of racial-ethnic minorities is less variable, with leftist nationalism generally supportive of equity and inclusion and rightist nationalism generally opposed; this pattern is particularly pronounced with respect to the treatment of Muslim residents in modern nationalist states. The chapters in this volume thus deepen our understanding of these complexities and open new questions about the conditions under which nationalist projects become intensely masculinist or heterosexual.

Kathleen Blee

# Acknowledgments

We would firstly like to thank the commissioning editor for the opportunity to publish this book with Palgrave Macmillan. The catalyst for this book came from the International Symposium, *Gender and Nationalism*, organized by the editorial team at Middlesex University in September 2014, and thanks in turn go to all the delegates at that event and in particular to the keynote speakers, Professors Floya Anthias, Nira Yuval-Davis and Kathleen Blee. The symposium was itself a platform for the dissemination of the findings of our British Academy/Leverhulme Trust-funded project (SG121452) exploring women supporters of the nationalist Right in the UK. Thank you to the research participants in this project, to Sylvia Moon for a diligent and engaged effort in transcribing the (not always easy) interviews, and to Agnieszka Kowalska for support in coding interview data. Thanks also must go to our respective institutions, Middlesex University, the University of the West of England and the University of Kent for supporting the production of this text. Of course, a thank you goes to all our contributors, without whom there would be no book. As with all things, it would not be possible to be productive without the support of significant others, and particular thanks goes to Agnieszka Kowalska for all her help.

# Contents

1 Introduction                                                                    1
  *Jon Mulholland, Erin Sanders-McDonagh,*
  *and Nicola Montagna*

Part I  Deploying Sexuality for a Gendered Nationalism        29

2 Mining, Masculinity, and Morality: Understanding
  the Australian National Imaginary Through Iconic Labor     31
  *Nick Skilton*

3 Inventing a Muscular Global India: History, Masculinity,
  and Nation in *Mangal Pandey: The Rising*                  49
  *Sikata Banerjee*

4 Homophobia as Geopolitics: 'Traditional Values'
  and the Negotiation of Russia's Place in the World         67
  *Emil Edenborg*

5   The Formation of an Israeli Gay 'Counterpublic':
    Challenging Heteronormative Modes of Masculinity
    in a 'Nation in Arms'                                             89
    *Yoav Kanyas*

6   "Tampering with Society's DNA" or "Making Society
    Stronger": A Comparative Perspective on Family, Religion
    and Gay Rights in the Construction of the Nation                  109
    *Bronwyn Winter*

Part II   Women Supporting Nationalist Movements                      127

7   Women, Gender, and the Puerto Rican Nationalist Party             129
    *Margaret Power*

8   Overcoming the Nation-State: Women's Autonomy
    and Radical Democracy in Kurdistan                                145
    *Dilar Dirik*

9   Gendering the 'White Backlash': Islam, Patriarchal
    'Unfairness', and the Defense of Women's Rights Among
    Women Supporters of the British National Party                    165
    *Jon Mulholland*

10  Feminism and Nationalism in Québec                                187
    *Diane Lamoureux*

11  Women's Support for UKIP: Exploring Gender,
    Nativism, and the Populist Radical Right (PRR)                    203
    *Erin Sanders-McDonagh*

## Part III  Nations, Borders, and the Gendered Signification of Migration    221

**12** Policing the Intimate Borders of the Nation: A Review of Recent Trends in Family-Related Forms of Immigration Control    223
*Paola Bonizzoni*

**13** 'Subaltern Victims' or 'Useful Resources'? Migrant Women in the *Lega Nord* Ideology and Politics    241
*Sara R. Farris and Francesca Scrinzi*

**14** The Media Framing of Migration in Sending and Receiving Countries: The Case of Romanians Migrating to the UK    259
*Bianca-Florentina Cheregi*

**15** The British Nationalist Right and the Gendering of Anti-migration Politics    281
*Nicola Montagna*

**16** 'Narrations of the Nation in Mobility Life Stories: Gendered Scripts, Emotional Spheres and Transnational Performativity in the Greek Diaspora'    299
*Anastasia Christou*

## Part IV  Institutional Mediations Past and Present: Understanding the Conditions for Women-Friendly Nationalisms    315

**17** 'Gender Diversity' and Nationalisms in Multiple Contexts    317
*Jill Vickers*

18  Territorial Autonomy, Nationalisms, and Women's Equality and Rights: The Case of the Hong Kong Special Administrative Region 337
*Susan J. Henders*

Index 357

# Notes on Contributors

**Sikata Banerjee** is Professor of Gender Studies at the University of Victoria, Canada. She works on gender and nationalism, with a specific focus on India. Her published works include *Warriors In Politics: Hindu Nationalism, Violence, and The Shiv Sena In India* (Westview 2000); *Make Me a Man! Masculinity, Hinduism, and Nationalism in India* (SUNY 2005); and *Muscular Nationalism: Gender, Empire, and Violence in India and Ireland* (NYU 2012) as well as articles in *Women and Politics, Asian Survey, Women's Studies International Forum, Gender and History* and *International Feminist Journal of Politics*.

**Paola Bonizzoni** is an Associate Professor at the Department of Social and Political Sciences at the University of Milan, where she teaches Sociology. Her research explores different sub-themes of migration studies and immigration policymaking, with a prominent interest in gender and intergenerational familial relationships. Her recent publications include *The shifting boundaries of (un)documentedness: a gendered understanding of migrants' employment-based legalization pathways in Italy* (2016, in *Ethnic and Racial Studies*) and *Uneven paths. Latin American women facing Italian family migration policies in Journal of Ethnic and Migration Studies* (2015, in *Journal of Ethnic and Migration Studies*).

**Bianca-Florentina Cheregi** holds a PhD in Communication Sciences, with a dissertation entitled "The media construction of nation branding in post-communist Romania. A constructivist-semiotic perspective". She teaches *Semiotics* and *Ethics in Communication* seminars at the National University of Political Studies and Public Administration, Bucharest. Her research interests include nation branding, cultural semiotics, social semiotics, framing, national identity and discourse analysis. Scientific articles and presentations from international conferences revolve around themes such as Romania's country image as a public problem, the media discourse on nation branding and interactive media campaigns on Romanian migration.

**Anastasia Christou** is an Associate Professor of Sociology, member of the Social Policy Research Centre and founding member of the FemGenSex research network at Middlesex University, London, UK. Anastasia has engaged in multi-sited, multi-method and comparative ethnographic research in the USA, the UK, Denmark, Germany, Greece, Cyprus, France, Iceland and recently in Switzerland. Anastasia has widely published research on issues of diasporas, migration and return migration; the second generation and ethnicity; space and place; transnationalism and identity; culture and memory; gender and feminism; home and belonging; emotion and narrativity; aging/youth mobilities, care, trauma, race/racisms and intersectionalities, embodiment, sexualities, women/men/masculinities, motherhood/mothering. Her most recent book is a jointly authored research monograph entitled, Christou, A. and King, R., *Counter-diaspora: The Greek Second Generation Returns "Home"*, appearing in the series Cultural Politics, Socioaesthetics, Beginnings, distributed by Harvard University Press (2014).

**Dilar Dirik** is currently a PhD researcher at the Department of Sociology, University of Cambridge.

**Emil Edenborg** is a postdoctoral researcher at Södertörn University, Sweden, working on a project entitled "Sexuality and the everyday bordering of Europe". He finished his PhD in Political Science at Lund University in 2016 and has worked as a senior lecturer in International Relations and Political Science at Malmö University. His publications have appeared in *International Journal of Cultural Studies*, *Sexuality & Culture*, *East European Studies* and *Postcolonial Studies*, and he recently published the book *Politics of Visibility and Belonging: From Russia's "Homosexual Propaganda" Laws to the Ukraine War* (Routledge, 2017).

**Sara R. Farris** is a Senior Lecturer in the Sociology Department at Goldsmiths, University of London. She works on sociological and political theory, "race"/racism and feminism, migration and gender, with a particular focus on migrant women and their role within social reproduction. She is the author of *Max Weber's Theory of Personality: Individuation, Politics and Orientalism in the Sociology of Religion* (Haymarket, 2015), and *In the Name of Women's Rights: The Rise of Femonationalism* (Duke University Press, 2017). She is a member of the *Critical Sociology* and *Historical Materialism* Editorial Boards.

**Susan J. Henders** is Associate Professor of Political Science at York University, Toronto, Canada. Her current research concerns the politics of exclusion and vulnerability in minority autonomy arrangements and the diplomatic roles of non-state actors. Among her recent publications are a special issue of the *Hague Journal of Diplomacy* (2016) on "other diplomacies" in Canadian-Asian relations (co-editor and contributor with Mary M. Young); *Human Rights and the Arts in Global Asia* (2014) (co-editor and contributor with Lily Cho); and "Internationalized Minority Territorial Autonomy in Early Post-WWI Europe" (2015) in *International Approaches to Governing Ethnic Diversity*, Will Kymlicka and Jane Boulden, eds.

**Yoav Kanyas** completed his PhD at the Department of Communication and Journalism at the Hebrew University of Jerusalem in 2018. His main research interests focus on the cultural and social aspects, relations and struggles associated with sexuality, gender and media discourse. His submitted dissertation, entitled "Sex – Science – Media: Analyzing Public Aspects of Sexual Advice and Sexology in Hebrew Journalism", demonstrates the ways in which a scientific professional knowledge field is shaped and constructed through the media, focusing on an analysis of public expressions of the sexual knowledge field. Yoav teaches courses in communication culture and media studies at the Department of Sociology, Political Science and Communication at the Open University of Israel. His media and advertising career included the general management of the Israeli gay and lesbian magazine, *Hazman Havarod*.

**Diane Lamoureux** is now retired and was Professor in the Department of Political Science at Laval University, where she taught political philosophy. She has written extensively on the feminist movement in Quebec, including a book on feminism and nationalism, *L'Amère patrie* (Montréal, Remue-ménage, 2001) and, more recently, *Les possibles du féminisme* (Montréal, Remue-ménage, 2016). Her research interests concern citizenship and democracy in contemporary Western societies from the standpoint of marginalized or subaltern groups.

**Nicola Montagna** is a Senior Lecturer in Sociology at the Middlesex University, School of Law, Department of Criminology and Sociology. He has extensive experience in carrying and coordinating research on migration, ethnicity and social movements. He has widely published on international migration, skilled migration and migration policies in Britain, Italy and Europe, social movements and the politics of protest. Some of his recent publications include "The contestation of space in Milan's Chinatown" (2016, *City: analysis of urban trends, culture, theory, policy, action*), "Dominant or subordinate? The relational dynamics in a protest cycle for undocumented migrant rights" (2018, *Ethnic and Racial Studies*) and a co-edited (with Nick Dines and Elena Vacchelli) issue on "Migration and crisis in Europe" for *Sociology* to be published in Spring 2018.

**Jon Mulholland** is an Associate Professor in Sociology and Associate Head of Department (Sociology and Criminology), at the University of the West of England (Bristol). With Professor Louise Ryan, and drawing on data derived from an Economic and Social Research Council grant, Jon has recently published widely in the field of highly skilled migration. With Nicola Montagna and Erin Sanders-McDonagh, he has recently completed a British Academy/Leverhulme Trust-funded project on women supporters of the nationalist right in the UK.

**Margaret Power** is a Professor of History at the Illinois Institute of Technology in Chicago, USA. She is the author of *Right-Wing Women in Chile: Feminine Power and the Struggle Against Allende* (2002) and co-editor of *Right-Wing Women Around the World* (2002) and *New Perspectives on the Transnational Right* (2010). She co-authored *Hope in Hard Times: Norvelt and the Struggle for Community During the Great Depression* (2016). Her current research focuses on the Puerto Rican Nationalist Party, about which she has published several articles. She is currently working on a book about the Nationalist Party and trans-Latin America solidarity.

**Erin Sanders-McDonagh** completed her PhD in Sociology at the University of Nottingham and is a Lecturer in Criminology in the School of Social Policy, Sociology and Social Research at University of Kent. She researches and publishes on gender and sexuality. Her monograph *Women and Sex Tourism Landscapes* was published by Routledge in 2016.

**Francesca Scrinzi** is a Senior Lecturer in Sociology at the University of Glasgow, UK. She is Marie Sklodowska-Curie fellow at the European University Institute, with the project "Migrant Christianity. Migration, Religion and Work in Comparative Perspective". She was Principal Investigator of the ERC Starting Grant "Gendering activism in populist radical right parties. A comparative study of women's and men's participation in the Northern League (Italy) and the National Front (France)". Her publications include *Migration, Masculinities and Reproductive Labour* (co-authored with Ester Gallo), Palgrave Macmillan, 2016, and articles on *Sociology, Feminist Review, Men and Masculinities* and *West European Politics*.

**Nick Skilton** is a PhD candidate at the University of Wollongong and an archivist at NSW State Archives. He is interested in how labour and juridico-political technologies of power reinforce or challenge privilege in the Australian national imaginary.

**Jill Vickers** is Distinguished Research Professor and Emeritus Chancellor's Professor in Political Science at Carleton University in Ottawa, Canada. A former president of the Canadian Political Science Association, and a fellow of the Royal Society of Canada, she has written and edited ten books and many articles and book chapters about: interactions between gender and national phenomena; how gender relates to state architectures, notably federalism; and women's movements' participation in constitution-making, and in efforts to achieve legislative and policy changes in central and regional politics.

**Bronwyn Winter** is Deputy Director of the European Studies program at the University of Sydney, Australia, where she also teaches International and Global Studies. Her publications include *September 11, 2001: Feminist Perspectives* (Hawthorne and Winter eds., Spinifex 2002), *Hijab and the Republic: Uncovering the French Headscarf Debate* (Syracuse University Press 2008), and *Women, Insecurity, and Violence in a Post-9/11 World* (Syracuse University Press 2017). She is a contributing advisory editor of the *Wiley Blackwell Encyclopedia of Gender and Sexuality Studies*, ed. N. Naples et al. (2016), and contributing co-editor of *Institutionalizing Same-Sex Marriage: Between Globalization and Path Dependency* (Palgrave 2017, forthcoming).

# List of Figures

Fig. 14.1　Frame frequencies in the British and Romanian press　　268
Fig. 14.2　The visual framing of Romanian migrants in three Romanian national newspapers　　274

ID# 1

# Introduction

Jon Mulholland, Erin Sanders-McDonagh, and Nicola Montagna

A cold and gray September 2017 afternoon in Bristol (the principal city of England's greater southwest region) and the 80 attendees of the *Gays Against Sharia* march shuffled their underwhelming way through the city center's peripheral streets, on a route configured by the authorities to ensure the least possible inconvenience to the city's throngs of weekend shoppers. Organized by former English Defence League (EDL) activist Tommy English (aka Thomas Cook) under the joint banners of the fledgling micro-movements *Gays Against Sharia* and *British and Immigrants United Against Terrorism*, the march sought to build on the momentum

---

J. Mulholland (✉)
School of Health and Social Sciences, University of the West of England, Bristol, UK

E. Sanders-McDonagh
School of Social Policy, Sociology and Social Research, University of Kent, Canterbury, UK

N. Montagna
School of Law, Middlesex University, London, UK

© The Author(s) 2018
J. Mulholland et al. (eds.), *Gendering Nationalism*,
https://doi.org/10.1007/978-3-319-76699-7_1

established by the much larger, and more eventful, demonstration in Manchester in the wake of the Islamist terror attack in the same city (killing 22 people). The Manchester demo had in fact also been organized by Tommy English under the same *Gays Against Sharia* banner, but looked set for a pitifully low attendance until organizationally hijacked by Tommy Robinson[1] (aka Stephen Lennon), now leader of *UK Against Hate* and *Pegida UK*. As the *Gays Against Sharia* branding of the Manchester demo progressively succumbed to the more forceful banner of Tommy Robinson's *UK Against Hate*, the demonstration ultimately became a catalyst for re-uniting many of the (largely violent) activists and leaders associated with the now dissolved EDL. Estimated as being attended by up to 2000 people, the Manchester demonstration evidenced the still potent force of extreme nationalist protest, at the same time as its descent into violence and chaos gave ample voice to its unruly masculinist energies.

For the Bristol event, no doubt mindful of the chaos in Manchester, and aware of the scheduled presence of a number of "celebrity" figures from the anti-Islamic radical right in the UK,[2] the police: deployed some 250 officers; enacted special powers banning face coverings, masks, banners, and flags "that might incite hatred"; and barricaded the attendees into the grandeur of Queen Square for collective address on the threats presented by the "Evil and Hateful Ideology of Sharia Law". Attendees were promised representation on topics such as female genital mutilation, homophobia within Islam, and the perils of Sharia Law. With hindsight, the police needn't have worried. The counter-demonstration, organized by Bristol Stand Up To Racism, and supported by diversity and anti-fascist groups, local politicians, and a coalition of unions, had little to get its teeth into with a mere 80 marchers on the rally. Undoubtedly, the *Gays Against Sharia* organizers would have felt bitterly disappointed with the pitifully low turnout, and for an event so clearly seeking to work the

---

[1] Tommy Robinson is an ex-Luton Town football hooligan and founder of the violent anti-Islamist street protest movement, the *English Defence League*.
[2] Named speakers included: Anne Marie Waters, UKIP Leader Candidate founder of *Sharia Watch UK* and ex-leader of the anti-Islam Pegida UK; Paul Weston and Jack Buckby, previously members of the *British National Party* and now leaders of the Alt-Right organization Liberty GB; Annie Greek, founder of *British and Immigrants United Against Terrorism*; and Lucy Brown and Caolan Robertson of *The Rebel Media*.

political capital of potentially fruitful conflations of sexual cosmopolitanism, liberalism, and anti-Islamic politics. If the Bristol march represented something of an acid test of how much grassroots traction had been secured through the deployment of sexual cosmopolitanism as a recruiting sergeant for a radical anti-Islamic politics, then it would appear as though recruitment had not been going particularly well. For the anti-Islamic political entrepreneurs who would seek to build alliances between sexual minorities and the broader interests of the radical and extreme right, the Bristol march appears suggestive that such alliances remain tenuous, at least in the context of organized street-level political action in the UK.

In that same year, the long Italian summer had been marked by a series of incidents that had served to bring the linkages of nationalism, gender, and sexuality to the forefront of public debate. Two principal events drew the attention of media and public alike. On the night of 26 August 2017, a group of young men, identified by the victims as North-African, attacked two Polish tourists (a heterosexual couple) on a Rimini beach, one of the most popular destinations on the Adriatic coast for young tourists and revelers alike. What at first appeared a friendly approach from the group quickly turned into a violent and sexual assault, with the man being knocked unconscious and the woman repeatedly raped. After attacking the Polish couple, the group of young men would continue their night of violence under the influence of alcohol and drugs, heading to Miramare, on the border with Rimini, where they sexually abused a transsexual of Peruvian origin.

Changing scene to Florence, a regional city attracting millions of tourists every year, in addition to thousands of overseas students (particularly from the USA), the night of 7 September saw two 21-year-old American students sexually assaulted. Approached outside a club in central Florence by two on duty *carabinieri*[3] patrolling the area after receiving a call from the owner of the premises, journalistic reports account for how the two women were raped by the two *carabinieri* in the lift and on the stairs of the women's place of residence. CCTV footage showed that the two *carabinieri* used their police vehicle to take the American students home, an illegal act according to Italian law.

---

[3] The *carabinieri* is one of Italy's oldest military forces, charged with police duties under the authority of both the Ministry of Defense and Ministry of the Interior (with public order functions).

The two cases elicited quite different responses from both public opinion and the media. The rape in Rimini was treated from the outset as a confirmed case of sexual violence and was associated with a general outcry against asylum seekers, refugees, "do-gooder" (*buonisti* in Italian) advocates of migrant interests, and an overly tolerant and permissive immigration policy. Media headlines accounted for the rape in Rimini in terms implying the certain guilt of the accused. The main Italian newspaper *Corriere della Sera*, for instance, entitled its Bologna online edition, "Rimini, gang rapes a tourist on the beach, and a transsexual", and added in the summary, "A group of foreigners attacked the couple last night: first beating the man and then abusing the woman. Then they would move to State 16, and also abused a transsexual" (26 August 2017).

In contrast, in the Florence case, though the government soon realized that the American students' claims were fully grounded, the general public appeared more reluctant to accept the possibility that the two *carabinieri* were capable of committing rape. Media presentations of the case clearly stressed that the students' allegations were yet to be proven. In fact the *Corriere della Sera* entitled its online edition: "Florence, the allegation of two American students: 'We were raped by two *carabinieri*'" (07 September 2017). Following confirmation of their guilt, the two officers were quickly reconstructed as "rotten apples" in an otherwise healthy barrel of national masculinity, thus protecting the national body from implication in such sexual crime. Media defense of the *carabinieri*, as representatives of the nation itself, here became a mechanism for defending national masculinities.

Our final case concerns a quite different continental context and one for that matter not substantively addressed in this text. In February of 2014, Yoweri Museveni, the president of Uganda signed the Anti-Homosexuality Act into law. The Act criminalizes any sexual contact between persons of the same sex, where the initial bill (introduced in 2009) originally included the death penalty for certain homosexual acts. Karimi and Thompson (2014) note that capital punishment was rescinded after the UK and many other European nations threatened to withdraw millions of dollars of aid to the country. However, the bill includes a provisional of life imprisonment for several specific crimes and includes prison sentences for groups that work with or counsel the LGBT community, essentially criminalizing many organizations and individuals who seek to support or otherwise work with an already vulnerable group.

In an interview with CNN, President Museveni was asked if he was worried whether the new laws were a step backwards for the people of Uganda. He replied:

> Worried? Not at all. If the West doesn't want to work with us because of homosexuals then we have enough space here to live by ourselves and do business with other people. We see how you do things, the families, how they're organized. All the things, we see them, we keep quiet. It's not our country, maybe you like it. So there's now an attempt at social imperialism – to impose social values of one group on our society. (Karimi and Thompson 2014: online)

In August of 2017, the Ugandan government canceled a week of activities scheduled for Gay Pride in the capital city of Kampala. Simon Lokodo, the state minister of ethics and integrity, accused organizers of recruiting, exhibiting, and promoting homosexuality. A *Guardian* report suggested that police officers were sent to hotels and specific venues where events had been scheduled in order to "arrest anyone participating in activities" (Okiror 2017: online). While police had granted permission for the pride celebrations in 2015, it is clear that the president and the government were intent on ensuring that the LGBT community was actively silenced. Reports from Reuters (Lykke Lind 2016) suggest that gay men had been dragged from their homes by police and subjected to painful anal examinations to determine whether they may be guilty of sodomy. The murder of LGBT activist David Kato in 2011 was also indicative of the levels of violence that anyone who is openly gay may face, not just from official state actors but from the local community as well.

## Some Strands, and their Unpicking

In their own ways, these three vignettes bring to the fore some important and contemporaneous themes pertaining to the shifting relations between nationalism, gender, and sexuality. In the case of the *Gays Against Sharia* march, we see captured here some of the most salient and pressing features of extreme nationalism's amended relationships to some of its core associations. Firstly, we see at least some degree of dis/re-placement of a once central reference point in extreme nationalist discourses, namely, "race". Islam, and Muslims, have emerged as absolutely pivotal reference points within nationalist narratives in the West and, in fact, beyond. Anti-Islam and Anti-Muslim sentiment has come to predominate as *the* key nodal point for nationalist mobilizations, and in a manner that conflates civilization, ethnicity, and religion in complex and uncertain ways. In this refrain, the Western nation itself becomes constructed as a social body conjoining civilizational, ethnic and religious elements, though still commonly under-written by the whispered subtext of race. In this way, the gendered and sexed subjects of nationalist discourse and practice become, at least in part, reconfigured (Zúquete 2008).

Secondly, and always perplexingly in this context of extreme nationalistic antipathy toward the presence of Islam and Muslims in "our national homes" in the West, the category of the nation itself somewhat gives way to the broader category/boundary of the West and/or Europe (Bunzl 2007). Western and European nations become firmly located in an extended civilizational family that despite its internal heterogeneities is rendered ever more homogenous by the socio-cultural and political consequences of its common "Muslim colonization" (Zúquete 2015).

Thirdly, in this alignment of extreme nationalism with what might at least appear to be an inclusive orientation toward non-normative sexual and gender identities, we are reminded that nationalism operates in a context-specific political-cultural landscape. In national settings where political culture has shifted to normatively incorporate at least some basic premises and practices associated with gender equality, nationalism's "inherent" gender conservatism must be understood as relative to the gendered political culture of the broader context in which it is located (Mudde and Kaltwasser 2015). Populist Radical Right (PRR) organizations across multiple European nation-states have variably but increasingly deployed rhetoric associated with gender egalitarianism and sexual cosmopolitanism (Spierings et al. 2017; Akkerman 2015). At the same time, we are brought to question the sincerity of extreme nationalism's apparent embracing of a gendered and sexualized politics of inclusion.

Evidence clearly indicates the Janus-faced nature of the extreme and Populist Radical Right's deployment of gender and sexual liberalism, where such deployments appear much more about their functional utility in rendering Islam and Muslims other to the West than reflecting any authentic and extra-contextual ideological positioning (Akkerman 2015). However Janus-faced, there is nevertheless evidence to show that the extreme and populist right have become increasingly influential among European LGBTQ constituencies. Spierings et al. (2017), in a study of European Social Survey data linked to 29 elections, found that "sexually modern nativists are more likely to vote for PRRs than sexually traditional nativists" (230).

However, it becomes clear from the *Gays Against Sharia* vignette that strategic deployments of gender and sexual liberalism by multifarious nationalisms are in no sense destined to succeed. The forces of masculinism, that so readily, and one might say inevitably, imbue nationalism (see Nagel 1998), may place a very real limit on how fruitful such strategic deployments can be in capturing the hearts and minds of men within extreme nationalist movements. In the case of the Manchester demonstration, it was only at the point when Stephen Lennon (aka Tommy Robinson and ex-leader of the EDL) hijacked and redirected the focus of the public demonstration away from the specific matter of "gay rights" that the demonstration was able to attract a large and impassioned audience. Finally, we might also reflect upon the ideological and relational precarities of those interests, genuinely allied to gender and sexual nonconformity, who choose to make ideological bed-fellows out of (extreme) nationalists.

The Italian rape case vignettes pick up on themes that resonate powerfully with contributions found within this edited collection. Firstly, both vignettes illustrate something of the dynamics of racialization and sexism in the context of nationalistic accounts of sexual crime. In both cases, media and public/political discourses had mobilized what Farris and Scrinzi define as the "racialization of sexism" (this volume and also Farris 2017; Scrinzi 2014a, b), where racism functions to produce differential applications of sexism, in this case, two categories of rapists. In the first category are refugees and migrants, who are rendered "culturally" and "biologically" more prone to rape, in turn confirming our fears about "uncontrolled migration". In the second category are those rapists who undeniably belong to the "national body" (in this case indigenous, white police officers). In this latter case, their sexual violence becomes reconstructed as an individual pathology, insulating the broader national body from any equivalent accusations of ethno-national culpability in respect of violent misogyny. It is notable that in both these cases the victims were in fact non-nationals. In the case of the Polish couple, their positioning here might be imagined to be complex. On the one hand the couple are white, European, and on vacation (and as the latter, desired visitors with a legitimate reason for their presence). On the other hand, the accession of Poland to the EU has itself been associated with mass immigration to Western Europe in a context of variably hostile media and popular-political anti-Eastern immigration sentiment. As such, the status of Poles, as "belonging" in a Western European context, and as such being "one of us", should not be assumed to be secure. However, set against the racialized and immigrant otherness of the attackers, who as non-white immigrants are routinely subjected to racialized exclusion from the national body, the Polish tourists become functionally included. In the context of the American students, their racial and national identity might be expected to firmly locate them within a Western collectivity within the public imaginary, but their juxtaposition to the emblematic legitimacy of white, masculine servants of the nation-state (here in the form of the *carabinieri*) in fact located them in a position of conditionality.

So, and this is the second theme emerging from the two rape case vignettes, what is going on here is not just a war between the sexes, where women pay the price for their freedom, but more immediately, a war between men played out with and through women's bodies, and in ways that are both material and symbolic (Dominijanni 2017). The former category of war is fought anytime a woman is abused and raped or becomes a victim of violence. The latter is waged through the meanings assigned to the former. As feminist literature on nationalism and gender has shown, women, and their reproductive capacity, are inextricably identified with community, territory, ethnicity, and national identity (Anthias and Yuval-Davis 1989). For this reason, women are framed as the future of the nation, and in a manner that authorizes their dominaiton and the control of their reproductive capacity. The national "community" is under threat where the rapist is a foreigner. In the Florence case, the victim's allegations are doubted, the rape is downplayed, and the community is left safe in its national-cultural reproduction. As the feminist lawyer and activist Tatiana Montella (Cecchini 2017) argued in the aftermath of these events: "What happened this summer is something very serious. A scandalous and racist game has been played: when the rapists are migrants, women become a property to defend against the invader. But if the rapist is an Italian, then it is always the woman's fault".

The example of Uganda's passing of the Anti-Homosexuality Act of 2014 provides an illuminating case of the ways in which gender, sexuality, and nation are bound together by different ideological tropes that govern different geographical regions and in turn broader differences of political culture. Uganda is one of many African countries that seeks to outlaw homosexual practices, and many of these nation-states are heavily influenced by religious doctrines that prohibit homosexuality. As seen with the quotation from President Museveni, there are other ideological lines drawn here—in this instance, for the West to mandate tolerant approaches to LGBT communities becomes tantamount to "social imperialism". While much of the contemporary social science and political studies literature has focused on the inclusion/exclusion of certain minority communities within nationalist discourses, it is clear that emerging nations in the Global South are grappling with the legacy of colonialism. What makes the Ugandan case so interesting is that President Museveni is a member of the National Resistance Movement (NRM). The NRM was originally founded as part of liberation movement that sought to seize power from fascist regimes (propped up by the West in an attempt to maintain "stability" in the region and keep the threat of communist or socialist movements at bay). The NRM introduced meaningful democratic processes for the people of Uganda and sought to re-enfranchise the population, particularly focusing on traditionally marginalized groups (i.e. the impoverished, women, young people, disabled people, etc.). Museveni was part of the movement that deposed Idi Amin in 1979 (estimated to have killed hundreds of thousands of Ugandans during his rule from 1971 to 1979). While the NRM brought some measure of economic and political stability to Uganda, several scholars and international organizations (Oliver 2013; African Women 2014; Amnesty International

2014; Vorhölter 2017) have argued that the continuing influence of the USA on Ugandan politics has created a situation where religious, right-wing Conservatives have overtly influenced particular policies and suggest that anti-gay legislation is shaped by the US Christian Right. This raises questions about the extent to which political decisions about the inclusion of the different minority groups, especially the LGBT community, are influenced by imperialist, Christian Right forces.

## Aims and Scope of the Book

The principal objective of this text is to provide a multidisciplinary and comparison-rich platform for both established and newly emerging researchers to bring to bear their latest empirical research, and critical thinking, on the question of nationalism's complex and shifting relationships to gender and sexuality. More specifically, the book seeks to address a number of key aims. Firstly, the text looks to advance our theoretical and conceptual understandings of how variable expressions of nation/alism intersect with gender and sexuality. Secondly, it brings to the table a range of contemporaneous empirical accounts, drawn from across the globe, to inform comparative, context-specific understandings of the interactions taking place at the interface of nation/ism, gender, and sexuality. Thirdly, the book offers a multi-sited exploration of the fluid, and always "productive", dynamics of inclusion and exclusion associated with the nationalist project, mapping and explaining the shifting contours of belonging and otherness generated in the context of multitudinous particular nationalisms. Fourthly, and challenging a scholarly legacy that has overly focused on the masculinist character of nationalism, the book seeks to pay particular attention to the people and issues less commonly considered in the context of nationalist projects, namely, women, sexual minorities. Finally, the book endeavors to propose an agenda for theoretically informed, empirical research fit for the uncertainties and instabilities of the twenty-first century.

The text covers an impressive empirical scope. Geographically, European case studies focus on the UK, Italy, Russia, Greece, and Romania. North America is represented by papers engaging with Canada and the US, and Latin America by a focus on Puerto Rico. The South and Southeast Asian contexts are represented by chapters on India and Hong Kong, the Middle East by papers focusing on the context of Israel and Kurdistan, and Oceania by two chapters concerned with Australia itself. The book covers a broad spectrum of linkages between nation/alism, gender, and sexuality. Multiple modalities of nationalism are addressed, ranging from the nationalisms of the "modernizing great powers", to extreme and populist nationalism, to anti- and post-colonial nationalisms. A particular strength of this collection lies in the manner in which it engages with the multiple, shifting, and deeply ambivalent articulations that form between these many modalities of nationalism on the one hand and gender and sexuality on the other. The diverse and context-specific positionings of men and women, masculinities and femininities, and hegemonic and non-normative sexualities, vis-à-vis nation/alism, are fully illuminated across the spectrum of case studies comprising this text.

The text productively engages with a vibrant array of contemporary theoretical lenses. Historical and feminist institutionalism, post-colonial theory, critical race approaches, transnational and migration theory, and semiotics contribute to the theoretical breath of the text. The collection also engages critically with some of the key conceptual tools available to an understanding of nationalism's contemporaneous interactions with gender and sexuality. Muscular nationalism, femonationalism, homonationalism, state-sanctioned homophobia, the gendering and sexualization of Islamophobia, racialization and nativism, and the performativities of gendered national identities provide some of the most important conceptual resources deployed within this volume. Drawing on these and other theoretical and conceptual tools, and across the full spectrum of international case studies, the text engages with some of the most pressing questions associated with nationalism's dynamic interactions with gender and sexuality. Nationalism's symbolic deployments of gender and sexuality; men and women's involvement in, and support for, nationalist movements; nationalism's shifting configuration of gender and sexuality rights; the increasing centrality of questions pertaining to the presence of Islam and Muslims in Muslim-minority nations; the role played by international mobilities in supporting and challenging the gendered and sexualized borders so constitutive of contemporary nationalisms all feature prominently within this volume. In this way, *Gendering Nationalism* offers an empirically rich, theoretically informed, and sustained engagement with the complex, shifting, and "productive" intersections of nation/alism, gender, and sexuality.

## The Composition of the Book

Part I of the book focuses on the ways in which sexuality becomes variably deployed in the formulation of gendered nationalisms. Nick Skilton discusses mining and masculinity in the context of Australia. His historical account explores the importance of working-class masculinities in relation to the development of the Australian national imaginary; mining, he argues, is an example *par excellence* of an industry whose lineage has served to underpin contemporary understandings of the nation. Working-class miners were able to exploit the raw materials of the Australian land to claim both economic status and political enfranchisement. By asserting their rights in the face of opposition from the landowning middle class, and celebrating the grit and hard work associated with their profession, Skilton argues that mining came to occupy an important place in Australia's history, and continues to this day to be celebrated as a unique cultural, political, and financial institution.

Sikata Banerjee offers an important reading of masculinity within the Hindu Indian state. Using the 2005 film *Mangal Pandey: The Rising* as a way to explore popular understandings of masculinity in relation to the Hindu nation-state, she introduces the concept of "muscular nationalism" to develop her argument, which centers on the ascendancy of a particular hegemonic mode of masculinity that has accompanied the rise of the right-wing Bharatiya Janata Party (BJP). Her analysis of the film offers insights into the ways in which the male body becomes an important signifier in media representations of India, and signals a move away from colonial and post-colonial cultural artifacts to new modalities that can be seen with the rise of the Indian middle class, and India's emergence as a force in global geopolitics.

Emil Edenborg provides a compelling account of LGBT rights in Russia and Chechnya, arguing that nationalist discourses that champion "traditional values" have been mobilized as a means to maintaining the hegemonic Russian nation-state. Edenborg documents the rise of state-sponsored violence, directed particularly at gay men living in the Chechen region, and suggests the conservative religiosity of the Muslim majority in that region are often seen as motivating these attacks. He argues that these vicious assaults have more to do with homophobic Russian sentiments, initiated and extended by Vladimir Putin's regime. This chapter offers a persuasive analysis of the role of the Russian media, exploring its framing of an anti-gay agenda, arguing that this agenda serves to reinforce cultural boundaries that mark out the geopolitical distance and differences between Russia and the West.

In his chapter on gay men's use of public parks in Tel Aviv, Yoav Kanyas charts important moments in Israel's nation-building process. Like the chapter from Banerjee, this chapter also explores the importance of a particular type of masculinity to the post-colonial process—Israel's image as a nation-state relies on heteronormative ideas about the place of the family. Masculinities are constructed around very particular ideas that allow Israel to see itself as dominant, partly through the role that such renderings of masculinity play in distancing past accounts of the Jewish community as weak and in exile, and partly through strengthening their martial stand against the perceived threats from their Arab (and particularly Palestinian) neighbors. This chapter provides archival material that makes clear how gay men were able to fight for rights in the face of political and religious conservatism tied to nationalist ideas about "appropriate" forms of masculinity in Israel.

Bronwyn Winter's chapter offers an insightful exploration of the nature, meaning, and implications of contemporary liberal democratic nations' inclusion of "rainbow families" via the legalization of same-sex marriage. Winter skillfully elucidates the ambivalences and precarities associated with such inclusion, highlighting how what may be seen by some as a game-changing modernization of the family as a gender-neutral structure may in fact constitute a mode of homonormativity that further consolidates the exclusive institutional boundaries of the martial family at the very point of gay and lesbian inclusion. Such national homoprotectionism readily serves the twin purpose of rendering the non-West Rest (in particular Muslims) as antithetical to such necessary, diversity-driven, modernization, and also disguises the partialities of the West's own commitments to inclusion. Winter calls for further research to explore what the legalization of gay marriage actually means, both on the ground and on the inside, but also on how such families are incorporated into national socio-economic organization and symbolism, and to what effect.

With examples drawn from across four continents, Part II of the book examines the complex, yet pivotal, realities (certainly for a text such as this) of women as supporters of nationalist movements. Margaret Power's chapter invites us to question the masculinism inhering not only within popular-political accounts of the nature and logic of nationalism but also within the multitudinous academic renditions that effectively collude in giving authorial primacy to men's accounts of national struggle. Asserting the political and methodological standpoint of women's own experiences of active engagement in the nationalist project, Power raises important questions about how we might re-consider, and significantly complicate, our understanding of women's actual and potential relationships to nationalism. She also brings to the fore our need to reflect upon what the implications might be for women, in their active involvement in nationalist struggle, in their relationship to nationally sanctioned, and conventional, readings of womanhood and femininity.

Bringing directly into question a host of assumptions about the inherent masculinism of nationalism, and of women as nationalistically inactive, or even victims, Dilar Dirik offers a powerful account of the role of Kurdish women's active liberatory resistance to the feminicidal forces of ISIS in Kobane. In this sense, Dirik illuminates the potential and accomplished links between women's military self-defense, direct forms of democracy, and liberation. Dirik asserts the possibility of forms of "nationhood", in this case the democratic nationhood espoused by Öcolan and the Kurdish Freedom Movement, that takes as its central premise the permanent and substantive liberation of women, supported by an autonomous women's movement. In this context, the ideology and practice of *democratic nation* ensures grassroots self-determining structures for women to define and enact their self-defined political priorities. *Democratic nation* provided a context in which patriarchy and masculinism could be understood as the antithesis of democratic forms of social coherence and citizenship. While brining to our attention the capacity of liberatory (non-)nationalisms to be movements supportive of gender equality and liberation, Dirik calls for further research to explore how the accomplishments of such exceptional times (in the form of inclusive social cohesion) can be sustained.

In drawing attention to the centrality of Islam and Muslims to the "othering" practices of contemporary Western nationalisms, Jon Mulholland's chapter draws on rich qualitative interview data with women supporters of the extreme British Nationalist Party (BNP) to explore how Islam and Muslims are signified and pathologized as a direct threat to gender-related justice and equality in the UK. The chapter illuminates the ways in which women supporters of the BNP utilize gender and sexuality to fix the nature of, and relationship between, four discursively constructed collective subjectivities, and to infuse the respective natures of, and relations between, these subjectivities, as locked into a social drama marked by a gender injustice wrought by the pathology of Muslim patriarchy. In their particular accounts of Muslim men as *oppressors*, Muslim women and vulnerable non-Muslim women as *victims*, the BNP as *saviors*, and liberated non-Muslim women as the *saved*, Mulholland goes on to demonstrate how resentful invocations of "unfairness" inform and lend coherence to women BNP supporters' claims of the wholescale oppression of non-Muslims at the hands of Muslim patriarchy.

Diane Lamoureux analyzes the links between feminism and nationalism in Québec from the late 1960s to the middle of the 1990s that is from the creation of the *Front de libération des femmes* to the 1995 referendum. She shows that initially, feminism and nationalism seemed united, where Quebec feminists defined themselves as actively involved in the project of Quebec's national liberation. Subsequently, the voices of ethnic women of long-standing and recent immigration made themselves heard and known to a francophone majority that had tended to ignore their existence. More recently, Aboriginal women have forced a reconfiguration of the nation and have questioned Quebec's stance toward Aboriginal nations. Lamoureux examines how the neoliberal turn of the nationalist movement, and the social justice turn of the feminist movement, opened up a space that made audible other voices in the feminist movement, and principally those of an immigrant, racialized, or Aboriginal status. She concludes by insisting on the gendered nature of the nation.

Drawing on qualitative interview data with women supporters of the UK Independence Party (UKIP), a particularly prominent Populist Radical Right Party in Britain, Erin Sanders-McDonagh builds on existing debates about the gendered nature of women's support for PRR parties by examining expressions of nativism. Sanders-McDonagh explores the ways in which women supporters of UKIP link their support for this political party with nativist ideas; she argues that for the women in this sample, they clearly see Islam and Muslims (as a "non-indigenous" presence in the UK) as a threat to native culture and lives. Understanding UKIP as one example of a broader resurgence of Populist Radical Right (PRR) parties throughout Europe, Sanders-McDonagh illuminates the ways in which women supporters of UKIP construct representations of the "native" women in the UK as liberated vis-à-vis Muslim women, who, by being victims to Islamic patriarchal norms, are a threat to "British values". This process of othering becomes key to the formulation of patriotic renditions of the UK as characterized by an accomplished condition of gender equality. This chapter resonates with the chapter from Mulholland, which explores women in the far-right and their relationship to Muslim Others.

Part III of the book explores the nature and roles of migration-related border crossings, specifically in respect of how these crossings become signaled in gendered and sexualized terms. Borders function as powerful markers, or containers, of nationness, and by gendering and sexing the salience of border crossings, particular expressions of nationness become enabled, just as they become threatened. Paola Bonizzoni's chapter critically reviews a range of themes arising from different streams of literature engaging with nation-states' efforts to actively reproduce their national identities through the regulation of intimate cross-border lives of their aspiring citizens and residents. Family migration management embodies the public-political tensions associated with culturally problematized immigrant social reproduction: "excessive" fertilities, "backward marriages" and gender relationships, low-quality human capital, and welfare dependency. The chapter explores how different aspects of social reproduction—love and marriage, parenthood, fertility and childbearing, care and dependency among adult relatives—are implicated in issues of migration control, showing how matters of legitimacy and veracity have triggered an emerging set of controls centered on the intimate and bodily life of citizens. Bonizzoni concludes that the realm of the intimate delineates a porous zone between insiders and outsiders. Defining the family proves critical for understanding what immigration means for the nation, and she calls for a deeper exploration of the nexus between the governance of national reproduction, citizenship, and mobility.

By focusing on the gendered dimensions of anti-immigration ideology, policy, and politics in the case of the Lega Nord (*Lega Nord*, hereafter LN), Farris' and Scrinzi's chapter aims to address the gaps in the scholarly literature relating to how gender impacts on activism in Populist Radical Right (PRR) Parties, particularly in respect of the LN in Italy. They draw on the empirical findings of two research projects to analyze the instrumental mobilization of women's rights by the LN to stigmatize migrant, and particularly, Muslim communities. By combining ethnographic and documentary data, Farris and Scrinzi shed light on what they call the "sexualization of racism" (Farris 2017) and the "racialization of sexism" (Scrinzi 2014a, b) in the LN discourse. These concepts refer to the application of a sexualized double standard to migrant men and women, where the former are treated as "oppressors" and the latter as "victims". The former concept draws our attention to the different racist registers applied to migrant men and women, respectively. The latter refers to the processes through which sexism is treated as a problem affecting only migrant communities within allegedly liberated European societies. In their chapter, Farris and Scrinzi reconstruct both the ways in which the LN has publicly presented the issue of gender equality among migrants and the party's depictions of migrant women. They then analyze the LN agenda on gender and the family as well as its seemingly "contradictory" policy with regard to female migrants, and conclude by showing how LN activists negotiate the party's treatment of migrant caregivers.

Bianca Cheregi shifts the focus toward the role of the media—particularly the British and Romanian media—to explore the ways in which the media frame issues associated with Romanian immigrants in Great Britain in the context of the free movement of labor in the EU. Her chapter is structured in three main parts. In the first part, Cheregi comparatively examines how frames of migration are employed in the British and Romanian media. In the second part she analyzes British media stereotypes of Romanian people. In the third part, she explores the visual framing of Romanian migrants in the national press. The results illustrate how the Romanian press reproduce the frames developed and deployed by British journalists, with seven key media frames emerging: the *economic, educational, political, social benefits, employment, public security*, and *EU policy*. Of particular importance was the manner in which Romanian migration was visually and discursively constructed through the trope of the Roma, reproducing dominant anti-Roma discourses found in Romanian society more generally.

Nicola Montagna investigates how immigration has become a key topic in right-wing nationalist parties, contributing to the framing of their political agenda and their success. These parties prioritize immigration as a pressing political issue, regarding it as a cause of economic competition and a threat to national identity and security. His chapter, which is based on 36 in-depth, semi-structured interviews with female members and supporters of UKIP, the BNP, and the EDL carried out between September 2013 and December 2014, examines how women on the nationalist right frame migration and construct it as a primary political issue. In particular, Montagna looks at three dimensions: the perception of migration as "mass migration", and the associated threat it is deemed to pose to national identity; the pressure such migration is deemed to have on the welfare system; and the impact of migrants on the national labor market. These dimensions are examined through the lens of a gendered perspective, as women nationalists signify the implications of mass immigration with particular regard to its constructed impact on women across these three domains.

Anastasia Christou's chapter offers a welcome, and direct engagement, with the question of transnationalism, and of its uncertain relations with gender and sexuality, via a focus on the diasporic experiences of second-generation Greek migrants. Christou brings into view the emotional and performative aspects of gender and sexuality, understood as social constructions that literally and metaphorically move in the case of diasporic mobilities. Her chapter shows how second-generation Greeks navigate the challenging and at times constraining contours associated with hegemonically configured national renderings of gender and sexuality. The inherent disruptions that come with transnational, translocal mobilities introduce liminality, fragility, and fracture, into the gendered and sexualized lives of diasporic migrants. In turn, these liminal spaces and subjectivities necessitate negotiations of gendered and sexualized identities, but in a place never entirely removed from the overbearing "nationness" of the national home, and the hegemonic heteronormative and patriarchal norms associated with that home. But such diasporic experiences also promise the possibility of plural, intersected identities that challenge primordial understandings of the national self.

Part IV concludes the book with an exploration of how contemporary nationalisms, in all their profoundly gendered ways, become differentially mediated by institutional structures and forces. Jill Vickers makes a decisive case for placing a comparative approach at the hearts of our endeavors in understanding the complex and shifting relationships between nation and gender. By adopting a triple comparative model (theoretical, historical, and ideological), and deploying a feminist institutionalist framework, Vickers brings to the fore the profoundly context-specific nature of how differential national legacies go on to frame the trajectories and parameters of nation/gender interactions. Through such an approach Vickers is able to demonstrate how diversity in gender/nation relations emerges as the necessary outcome. Considering colonial versus anti-colonial contexts, and comparing stages in the development of the nation-state, Vickers illuminates the variable determinants, natures, and impacts of women's roles in national projects.

Offering the reader a fruitful companion to Vickers comparative account of nation-gender interactions, and drawing on a firm institutionalist framework, Susan Henders' chapter offers a detailed and nuanced account of the implications of transition to meso-level autonomy arrangements in the context of the Hong Kong Special Administrative Region (HKSAR). Henders goes on to illuminate the uncertainties that may characterize such devolution projects, in particular in respect of the interests of women. Whether women's rights are enhanced or impeded in such contexts is shown to depend on a host of context-specific structural, institutional, and ideational variables. While Henders insists that democracy is no guarantee of equality for women, the Hong Kong case clearly indicates that non-democracy (in this case characterized by a concentration power in the hands of a state-business elite), allied to neoliberalism, provides a fertile ground for the advance of a patriarchal nationalist agenda unsupportive of women's individual and collective struggle for inclusion and participation. Henders calls for more research to explore the conditions in which democratization in such contexts might lead to more woman-friendly outcomes.

## An Agenda for Research

On the basis of our reading of existing research, and on the conclusions drawn by our own contributors, we propose some features of a necessarily selective research agenda to address what remain important deficits in the contemporary literature.

An important, yet remarkably under-developed trajectory of research, relates to the systematic comparative analysis of men and women's respective relationship to the key issues that populate the nationalist agenda, such as migration, Islam, globalization, and national identity. Research has mainly centered either on gender-undifferentiated participation in nationalist and far-right politics, with an implicit focus on male activism (Klandermans and Mayer 2006; Mammone et al. 2012, 2013) or on female participation (see the seminal works by Blee 2003 and more recently Blee 2008). Research explicitly concerned with exploring the similarities and differences in how such issues are thematized by female and male supporters and activists remains surprisingly scarce.

An emergent and increasingly influential trajectory of research and writing has sought to counter enduring assumptions, both of a scholarly and popular nature, that nationalism remains so much a masculinist project that we can afford to render consideration of women's active engagement in, and support for, nationalism, as something of a sideshow. Seminal theoretical contributions have offered powerful and fruitful (re)framings of our understandings of nation/alism's relation to gender and sexuality (Puar 2007; Anthias and Yuval-Davis 1989, 2005; Yuval-Davis 1997; Dhruvarajan and Vickers 2002). Important contributions have been made to our appreciation of the historically important role played by women in early twentieth-century "great power" nationalisms (see Vickers, this volume (Chap. 17), Blee 2008; Jeansonne 1997).

Relationships between nation, gender, and sexuality have been explored in the post-colonial context (see Vickers, this volume (Chap. 17), Mcclintock 1997). The increasingly significant presence of women as supporters and activists in extreme nationalist movements has also become a focus of influential research (Köttig et al. 2016; Blee 2003). But it stands as testimony to the strengths of such masculinist assumptions, that a further "shout-out" remains so urgently needed for more empirical research that takes as its focus women's active involvement in, and support for, nationalist movements. Though hardly scientific, a mere cursory search reveals that the internet is currently awash with popular and mainstream accounts of nationalism's, and in particular extreme nationalism's, increased effectiveness in capturing the hearts and minds of young women. *The Statesman* invites us "to talk about the online radicalisation of young, white women" (Tait 2017); *The Guardian* accounts for the transformation of the Polish Far Right under the heading "'More girls, fewer skinheads': Poland's far right wrestles with changing image" (*The Guardian* 2017); and *Marie Claire* (2017) asks of "far-right millennials: what drives young women to extreme politics?". Never before has the need to understand women's involvement in, and support for, nationalism been more necessary. Such research, wherever possible, should take as its primary objective, the adoption of methodologies concerned to give voice to the women themselves, as a necessary bulwark against masculinist paradigms that assume men are both the natural objects and speaking subjects of nationalism.

There has been recent, and buoyant, interest in the connections between nationalism and sexuality. Jasbir Puar's seminar text Terrorist Assemblages: Homonationalism in Queer Times, published in 2007, was one of the first texts that sought to provide a theoretical approach to deconstructing the complicated ways in which some Western nations embraced homosexuality as a way to demonstrate their "tolerance" vis-à-vis the new Muslim threat that emerged post-9/11. While the LGBT population, and gay men in particular, have long been seen as a threat to hegemonic modes of masculinity, particularly in the case of the US, the AIDS crisis of the 1980s and 1990s only served to further disenfranchise an already vilified and vulnerable population. To have the LGBT community championed, less than a decade after members of the US Senate tried to initiate the Defense of Marriage Act in 1996, as part of a movement that saw gay marriage as immoral and a stain on the American "Way of Life", remains a remarkable move. In the wake of 9/11 (and perhaps not coincidentally, with the advent of antiretroviral therapy that meant HIV was no longer a veritable death sentence), there was a notable discursive shift in the direction of inclusion—with many politicians and public figures welcoming the LGBT community in an effort to demonstrate the open and tolerant nature of liberal democracy.

Puar argues persuasively that this move was not based on any real or meaningful concern for LGBT rights but rather served a politically expedient end: to justify the invasion of Afghanistan and later Iraq. Politicians who had frequently worked against women's rights in the USA now found themselves needing justification for attacks on Afghanistan and Iraq, and found fertile ground in the construction of narratives alleging Islamic opposition to "women's rights" as demonstrative of a "backward" unenlightened civilization. Fekete (2006) provides evidence of a similar trend taking hold across many northern European countries, and suggests that the "war on terror" focuses specifically on Islam as the enemy par excellence. In order to extend the sense of menace that the uncivilized Muslim Other is constructed as posing, highlighting Europe's commitment to equality for the LGBT community became a useful way of underpinning a "clash of civilizations" thesis. While a number of contemporary social science and political studies scholars are beginning to explore these connections (c.f. Gerhards 2010; Akkerman 2015; Mulholland this volume), there is more to be done here. Several of the chapters in this collection make some headway in trying to explore new directions and complications that come with the ways in which LGBT communities are either embraced or disavowed at different times in different geopolitical contexts. Chapters from Edenborg, Kanyas, and Winter in particular explore the ways in which religion in two very different national contexts (respectively, the Russian Federation, Israel, and Australia) intersects with masculinity and sexuality in quite variable ways, and extends existing scholarship from critical race scholars and feminists on how masculinity and the nation are intertwined (c.f. Nagel 1998), and augments still emergent literature on the complex role of queerness in nationalist politics (c.f. Sharp 2007; Talburt and Matus 2014; Brubaker 2017; Mackie 2017).

Even more recently, we have witnessed what promise to be influential developments in the morphology of nationalism, with the emergence of the so-called Alt-Right. Though it is undoubtedly true that there is much yet to untangle in some of nationalism's contemporaneous inclusions of non-normative expressions of gender and sexuality, and that this untangling remains as important and productive as it is incomplete, the recent emergence of the Alt-Right movement suggests some influential countering of these now important developments. The Alt-Right, while closely associated with the USA, has extended its influence throughout the world, with groups such as the Australian *Nationalist Alternative*, the UK-based *Hope Not Hate* and *National Action*, the French *Bloc Identitaire and Génération Identitaire*, and German *Identitäre Bewegung*. According to Hawley (2017), "the Alt-Right is unlike any racist movement we have ever seen. It is atomized, amorphous, predominantly online, and mostly anonymous" (3). Though fluid and uncertain in its nature, reach, traction, and trajectory, the Alt-Right is most commonly associated with a certain revival of ultra-conservative positions on race purity and relatedly gender and sexual traditionalism, within a broader anti-libertarian and anti-egalitarian frame (Hawley 2017). Though notoriously difficult to pin down, conceptually and empirically, the Alt-Right has been strongly linked to biological racism, anti-Semitism, nativism, and masculinism.

Unlike expressions of nationalism that have strategically sought to include ethnic and sexual minorities, and even to embrace liberal democratic renditions of diversity, as pivotal devices for constructing cleavage vis-à-vis the "Muslim Other", the Alt-Right is premised on forms of white supremacism that see practically all forms of non-white, non-gender-normative, and non-heterosexual difference as a threat. Its successful usage of social media has also supported its influence among the young (Hawley 2017). The infancy of the Alt-Right, allied to its remarkable influence, at least on-line, render it an urgent focus for critical research attention. Indications clearly suggest that the Alt-Right may be linked to a rolling back of nationalism's (circumscribed and strategic) engagement with non-normative expressions of gender and sexuality (via homonationalism), and the interests of gender and sexual equality more generally, via an insistence on a return to more traditional readings. Kelly

(2017) argues that the Alt-Right can be understood as a "new brand of masculinity politics…[and more specifically as]…a digital coalition of identity politics for straight white American men" (68). Kelly (2017) goes on to claim that,

> the alt-right's positions on race and national security are linked to their more implicit anxieties about the evolving nature of American masculinity…It has created an idealised avatar of white masculinity in opposition to what they perceive as the inherent savagery of Islam and the emasculated figure of the Millennial

Tracking the development of Alt-Right nationalisms, in all their gendered and sexualized dynamics and manifestations, presents itself as a pressing need.

## Conclusion

The complex, fluid, and increasingly uncertain relations between nationalism, gender, and sexuality require us to adopt a careful, nuanced, and deeply contextual approach to their understanding. Embracing the latest theoretical and conceptual developments, and deploying these in the context of grounded empirical research, offers invaluable opportunities to problematize what have become established as academically hegemonic assumptions about the nature of nationalism's intersections with gender and sexuality. The chapters in this book offer a diverse but consistently engaged exploration of these intersections, raising important questions, challenging prevailing assumptions, and suggesting fruitful avenues for future investigation.

## References

African Woman. 2014. How the Anti-Pornography Act Validated Violence Against Women. Available at: http://africanwomanmagazine.net/features/anti-pornography-act-uganda/. Accessed 11 Jan 2018.

Akkerman, Tjitske. 2015. Gender and the Radical Right in Western Europe: A Comparative Analysis of Policy Agendas. *Patterns of Prejudice* 49 (1–2): 37–60.
Amnesty International. 2014. *Rule by Law—Discriminatory Legislation and Legitimized Abuse in Uganda*. London: Amnesty International.
Anthias, Floya, and Nira Yuval-Davis. 1989. *Woman-Nation-State*. Basingstoke: Palgrave Macmillan.
———. 2005. *Racialized Boundaries: Race, Nation, Gender, Colour and Class and the Anti-Racist Struggle*. London: Routledge.
Blee, Kathleen M. 2003. *Inside Organized Racism: Women in the Hate Movement*. Berkeley: University of California Press.
———. 2008. *Women of the Klan: Racism and Gender in the 1920s*. Berkeley: University of California Press.
Brubaker, Roger. 2017. Between Nationalism and Civilizationism: The European Populist Moment in Comparative Perspective. *Ethnic and Racial Studies* 40 (8): 1191–1199.
Bunzl, Matti. 2007. *Anti-Semitism and Islamophobia: Hatreds Old and New in Europe*. Chicago: Prickly Paradigm Press.
Cecchini, Chiara. 2017. "Ve la siete cercata": donne in piazza per il diritto all'aborto e contro ogni violenza. Today. http://www.today.it/donna/storie/non-una-di-meno-manifestazione-28-settembre-2017.html. Accessed 13 Jan 2018.
Dhruvarajan, Vanaja, and Jill Vickers. 2002. *Gender, Race, and Nation: A Global Perspective*. Toronto: University of Toronto Press.
Dominijanni, Ida. 2017. Solo uno stupro, solo una lapidazione. *Internazionale*, September 14. https://www.internazionale.it/opinione/ida-dominijanni/2017/09/14/stupro-lapidazione-lecce-firenze.
Farris, Sara R. 2017. *In the Name of Women's Rights. The Rise of Femonationalism*. Durham: Duke University Press.
Fekete, Liz. 2006. Enlightened Fundamentalism? Immigration, Feminism and the Right. *Race and Class* 48 (1): 1–22.
Gerhards, Juergen. 2010. Non-discrimination Towards Homosexuality. The European Union's Policy and Citizens: Attitudes Towards Homosexuality in 27 European Countries. *International Sociology* 25 (1): 5–28.
Hawley, George. 2017. *Making Sense of the Alt-Right*. New York: Columbia University Press.
Jeansonne, Glen. 1997. *Women of the Far Right: Mothers' Movement and World War II*. Chicago: University of Chicago Press.

Karimi, Faith, and Nick Thompson. 2014. Uganda's President Museveni Signs Controversial Anti-gay Bill into Law. *CNN* [Online] http://edition.cnn.com/2014/02/24/world/africa/uganda-anti-gay-bill/index.html. Accessed 9 Jan 2017.
Kelly, Annie. 2017. The Alt-Right: Reactionary Rehabilitation for White Masculinity. *Soundings* 65: 68–78.
Klandermans, Bert, and Nonna Mayer. 2006. *Extreme Right Activists in Europe: Through the Magnifying Glass*. London: Routledge.
Köttig, Michaela, Renate Bitzan, and Andrea Petö. 2016. *Gender and Far Right Politics in Europe*. Basingstoke: Palgrave Macmillan.
Lykke Lind, Peter. 2016. In Uganda, Gay Men Say Police Use Torturous Method to 'Prove' Homosexuality. *Reuters*. https://www.reuters.com/article/us-uganda-lgbt/in-uganda-gay-men-say-police-use-torturous-method-to-prove-homosexuality-idUSKBN12X0WJ. Accessed 9 Jan 2017.
Mackie, Vera. 2017. Rethinking Sexual Citizenship: Asia-Pacific Perspectives. *Sexualities* 20 (1–21): 43–55.
Mammone, Andrea, Emmanuel Godin, and Brian Jenkins, eds. 2012. *Mapping the Extreme Right in Contemporary Europe: From Local to Transnational*. London: Routledge.
———, eds. 2013. *Varieties of Right-Wing Extremism in Europe*. London: Routledge.
Marie Claire. 2017. Far-Right Millennials: What Drives Young Women to Extreme Politics? http://www.marieclaire.co.uk/reports/far-right-millennials-507601. Accessed 18 Dec 2017.
Mcclintock, Anne. 1997. *Dangerous Liaisons: Gender, Nation and Postcolonial Perspectives*. Minneapolis: University of Minnesota Press.
Mudde, Cas, and Cristóbal Rovira Kaltwasser. 2015. Vox Populi or Vox Masculini? Populism and Gender in Northern Europe and South America. *Patterns of Prejudice* 49 (1–2): 16–36.
Nagel, Joane. 1998. Masculinity and Nationalism: Gender and Sexuality in the Making of Nations. *Ethnic and Racial Studies* 21 (2): 242–269.
Okiror, Samuel. 2017. No Gay Promotion Allowed: Uganda Cancels Pride Event. *The Guardian* [Online] https://www.theguardian.com/global-development/2017/aug/21/no-gay-promotion-can-be-allowed-uganda-cancels-pride-events-lgbt. Accessed 9 Jan 2017.
Oliver, Marcia. 2013. Transnational Sex Politics, Conservative Christianity, and Antigay Activism in Uganda. *Studies in Social Justice* 7 (1): online.
Puar, Jasbir K. 2007. *Terrorist Assemblages: Homonationalism in Queer Times*. Durham: Duke University Press Books.

Scrinzi, Francesca. 2014a. Gendering Activism in Populist Radical Right Parties. In-Progress Preliminary Report, ERC Starting Grant. http://www.gla.ac.uk/schools/socialpolitical/research/sociology/projects/genderingactivisminpopulistradicalrightparties/publications/preliminary%20report/. Accessed on 11 Nov 2014.

———. 2014b. Rapporti di Genere e Militanza nella Lega Nord. In *Attraverso la Lega*, ed. Anna Curcio and Lorenza Perini, 163–184. Bologna: Il Mulino.

Sharp, Joanne. 2007. Geography and Gender: Finding Feminist Political Geographies. *Progress in Human Geography* 31 (3): 381–387.

Spierings, Niels, Marcel Lubbers, and Andrej Zaslove. 2017. 'Sexually Modern Nativist Voters': Do They Exist and Do They Vote for the Populist Radical Right? *Gender and Education* 29 (2): 216–237.

Tait, Amelia. 2017. We Need to Talk About the Online Radicalisation of Young, White Women: Alt-Right Women Are Less Visible Than Their Tiki Torch-Carrying Male Counterparts—but They Still Exist. *New Statesman*, August 18. https://www.newstatesman.com/science-tech/internet/2017/08/we-need-talk-about-online-radicalisation-young-white-women.

Talburt, Susan, and Claudia Matus. 2014. Confusing the Grid: Spatiotemporalities, Queer Imaginaries, and Movement. *Gender, Place & Culture* 21 (6): 785–801.

*The Guardian*. 2017. 'More Girls, Fewer Skinheads': Poland's Far Right Wrestles with Changing Image. https://www.theguardian.com/world/2017/nov/18/more-girls-fewer-skinheads-polands-far-right-wrestles-with-changing-image. Accessed 18 Dec 2017.

Vorhölter, Julia. 2017. Homosexuality, Pornography, and Other 'Modern Threats'—The Deployment of Sexuality in Recent Laws and Public Discourses in Uganda. *Critique of Anthropology* 37 (1): 93–111.

Yuval-Davis, Nira. 1997. *Gender and Nation*. Thousand Oaks: Sage Publications.

Zúquete, José Pedro. 2008. The European Extreme-Right and Islam: New Directions? *Journal of Political Ideologies* 13 (3): 321–344.

———. 2015. The New Frontlines of Right-Wing Nationalism. *Journal of Political Ideologies* 20 (1): 69–85.

# Part I

## Deploying Sexuality for a Gendered Nationalism

# 2

# Mining, Masculinity, and Morality: Understanding the Australian National Imaginary Through Iconic Labor

Nick Skilton

## Introduction

The twenty-first century in Australia opened with a decade-long boom, with miners dominating the national imaginary. Miners have long been heralded by leaders of Australian states as "modern-day heroes" (Australian Associated Press 2013, 1). Furthermore, historians have noted the importance of mining as part of Australia's national identity, with Pearse (2009, 1) arguing that "From every direction, Australians are told that their current and future prosperity depends on what we dig, drill and smelt for the world". However, this celebratory vision of mining is a relatively recent phenomenon. In the mid-nineteenth century, as gold fever gripped the fledgling Australian colonies, colonial governments were forced to enact repressive legislation designed to suppress the rush of labor to the goldfields, and saw mining as a potential threat to the emerging Australian

---

Special thanks to: Scarlet Alliance, Chris Gibson, Leah Gibbs, and Erin Sanders-McDonagh

N. Skilton (✉)
Australian Centre for Cultural Environmental Research (AUSCCER), University of Wollongong, Wollongong, NSW, Australia

nation-state. This chapter will explore the ascendancy of mining in Australia—charting its development as a nascent industry that was originally curtailed and regulated in an attempt to stymy upwardly mobile miners drawn to the lure of the gold rush—to a respected and highly visible sector that is now validated and legitimized by the Australian Government. I will argue that it is not just the mining industry that is now celebrated as part of Australia's national imaginary but also the nostalgically rendered, rugged, working-class mining men who forged this industry and who ground the identity of the contemporary Australian nation-state.

Central to understanding how mining became a dominant part of the emergent Australian national imaginary is a description of the shift that occurred in the understanding of miners themselves, so that their key qualities and defining characteristics, once a source of anxiety for Victorian-era middle-class moralists, could be integrated into the emergent Australian national imaginary. The national imaginary may best be understood as "the myths of the nation [that] are forged, transmitted, reconstructed and negotiated constantly" (Bell 2003, 75). The aim of this chapter is to draw attention to these multifaceted shifts in the social landscape that provided the opportunity for mining to be elevated and privileged in the national imaginary. The primary mechanism for this change in understanding was the juridico-political system, employing legislation as a technology of power that at first attempted to suppress mining, alongside other unruly and morally objectionable working-class industries, during a distinctive phase in the creation of the Australian state. As Foucault (1982, 791) argues, to understand the workings of technologies of power, we must consider "their historical formation, [and] and the source of their strength or fragility."

An examination of historical labor legislation, as a key governmental technology of power, provides the empirical and theoretical core of this chapter. Theorizing how the middle-class wielded their power through acts of parliament in a time of concentrated nation-building enables a better understanding of the historical antecedents of the Australian national imaginary in the twenty-first century. By paying attention to this relationship between national myths and the classed and gendered aspects of labor history, the ascendant position of the mining industry can be seen to be part of a deliberate regime of control through hegemonic heteronormative middle-class morality. The following section explores the historical antecedents of privilege and marginalization experienced by the iconic industry of mining in Australia.

## The Middle-Class, Federation, and Nation-Building

Australia, during the Victorian era, was a collection of individual British (predominantly penal) colonies, with governors who were appointed by, and answerable to, the British parliament. The colonies were New South Wales, Western Australia, South Australia, Tasmania, Victoria, and Queensland, and each had their own governments, military, customs houses, tariffs, and so on. The birth of the Australian nation came in 1901, when the six colonies federated by a peaceful act of parliament and became the original states of present-day Australia. Federation was needed, according to an anxious and insecure middle-class, to unite the colonies against "'undesirable' immigration" (Osborne 2002, 41). To galvanize public opinion behind Federation, a campaign was initiated by the Australian middle-class, including political leviathans such as Henry Parkes (commonly referred to as the "Father of Federation") and future Prime Minister Alfred Deakin, to promote national pride. The key tenets of this national pride included the exclusion of non-Anglo ethnicities and an intrepid, heroic, and all-conquering masculinity (Osborne 2002).

Such nationalistic themes could be found in *The Bulletin*, an influential colonial-era business, political, and literary magazine, which was instrumental in shaping an emergent national imaginary. Important literary figures in *The Bulletin* and other sources in this pre-Federation era, such as Banjo Paterson and Henry Lawson (whose father was a gold fossicker), wrote in the 1880s and 1890s nostalgic poetry and stories about the early Australian frontier and outback for an increasingly urbanized and geographically removed public. Their writing romanticized the purported origins of a defining Australian character in "the bush" and its male heroes and anti-heroes (bushrangers, swagmen, drovers, and rebellious miners). Non-Anglo male laborers important in Australian bush life, including Afghan cameleers (Gibbs et al. 2015), Chinese miners (Curthoys 2001), and the female sex workers who followed the miners out to the digs (Davidson 1984), did not feature at all. Importantly, while many of these characters written into the Australian national imaginary were ratbags and rabble-rousers from convict or other insalubrious backgrounds, they were all hardy white men, and these qualities were then taken to represent all Australians in an emergent national imaginary (and will be discussed in greater detail in following sections).

Grattan (1947, in Barcan 1955, 64) argues that the Australian middle-class condition pre-Federation could be described as a "buffer between the contemporary group with oligarchical tendencies [the landed gentry], and the working class … thus affecting the social balance, but not defining what it shall be". The Australian pre-Federation middle-class social stratum was relatively weak, and commanded no position of imagination and influence in a burgeoning national identity. The middle-class therefore had to be content with using existing romanticized working-class symbols from the Australian literary canon, such as the "noble bushman"— "a heroic race endowed with special democratic, Australian qualities"—to further their own populist agenda for a federated Australia (Blackton 1961, 353; Ward 1966; Lawson 1980). In this regard, there is a distinct parallel to the US myth of the frontier on which the American national "character" was made, via heroic male archetypes such as the iconic cowboy figure (Gibson 2013b). Thus, both the media and politics were dominated by middle-class men of European origin, whose nationalistic and insular values came to dominate national myth-making (Blackton 1961). *The Bulletin* was so committed to these values that, in 1886, the editor changed its tagline from "Australia for the Australians" to "Australia for the White Man", further embedding these values in a pre-eminent media source of the time (AustLit 2017).

Convergent with this emphasis on rural, masculinist symbolism by the Australian middle-class were the broader manifold social relations of the Victorian era. The dominance of Victorian-era morality and gender relations punctuated politics, public discourse, and class dynamics, largely due to the population dynamics that saw the great majority of the Australian population born from British descent. Even in 1881, according to the census of that year, 30 percent of the population in the two most populous colonies of New South Wales and Victoria were born in the UK, bringing with them such Victorian-era values (Historical Census and Colonial Data Archive n.d.). Embedded in these values were clearly separated gender roles, where men were placed "firmly in the newly defined public world of business, commerce, and politics; women were placed in the private world of home and family" (Hall 1992, 133). Masculinity and femininity, so defined, could therefore be attributed to specific labor types and the qualities they represented. Thus, for women, domestic service was respectable, feminine work, but factory or sex work was amoral or disreputable. This pre-Federation intersection of labor, gender, and morality is therefore crucial in understanding how the middle-class perceived itself, and the myths that it created in the process of nation-building. The next section explores this intersection in greater detail.

## Mining, Morality, and Gender in the Victorian Era

It was with the gold-rushes of the mid-1850s that the mining industry burst forth in Australia, establishing a movement so important that it became ingrained in the national imaginary. Independent alluvial miners traveled from goldfield to goldfield in search of the nugget that would make them rich. This included both new arrivals fresh off the boat, and men absconding from their labor elsewhere in the country, all hoping to strike it rich. This was a provocation to the land-owning upper-class, and emerging middle-class, who suddenly found their supply of labor contracting, and was occurring at a time when the middle-class was attempting to control and define values on the path to Australian Federation in 1901. Despite the chaos caused by the gold-rushes, and the lawlessness and immorality that was perceived to accompany miners in frontier towns, mining was eventually elevated to the position of "nation-builder" (*Dirty Business: How mining made Australia* 2013; Gibson 2013a; House of Representatives Standing Committee on Regional Australia 2013; Knox 2013; Jensen 2014).

The gold-rushes saw Australia's population significantly increase in a very short space of time. The population in the Victorian colony where much of the extractive activity was taking place rose from 77,000 in 1851 to 538,000 in 1857 (Knox 2013). Many of these migrants arrived from Britain, which was in the midst of its great global empire-building project at the time, but large numbers also arrived from China to work the goldfields (Curthoys 2001). The population growth in the Victorian colony affirmed its capital Melbourne as the largest city in Australia, and the traffic in gold secured it as the nation's financial center (Blainey 1993). While the goldfields provided opportunities for working-class men to gain financial affluence and provided opportunities to ascend classed expectations, there was, however, always the looming possibility of destitution for those who wagered everything in their quest for riches (Blainey 1993; Wright 2016). As the alluvial gold dried up and the rushes ended, men who remained on the fields chose (or were forced by the changing nature of the new capital-intensive form of extractive mining) to relinquish the mercurial fortunes of prospecting for less independent but more financially secure company jobs. Mining towns consolidated, and wives and families began to arrive in mining towns such as Ballarat (Victoria), Broken Hill (New South Wales), Queenstown (Tasmania), and Kalgoorlie (Western Australia). It was around this time that "working-class family life … shifted a little further towards the style of family life cherished by the middle-class" (Grimshaw et al. 1994, 202). Other industries central to the mining boom, such as sex work, had until this time been "widely accepted as an essential part of a frontier community … so long as the rollicking atmosphere of the boom years prevailed" (Davidson 1984, 169). However, the changing nature of mining towns, from chaotic and hyper-masculine frontier mining outposts, to places of burgeoning heteronormativity with the family as the center of Australian life (with attendant "appropriate" gender roles for women), explains the "increasing resistance" to sex work and other morally suspect labor in said towns (Davidson 1984, 170). The relationships between miners, sex workers, their families, and the community were fraught, with tensions around new modes of gendered and classed relations. As mining became more "respectable", pre-existing middle-class, Victorian-era ideas about apposite morality (including notions about the family, class, and gendered expectations) were also introduced to an already complex shifting social milieu.

As amplified gender divisions in the industrializing and urbanizing Victorian-era were separating the male, public sphere of work and politics, from the apolitical female, private sphere of home, the subtle ways that women "were central" to the formation of classed and gendered expectations were largely ignored (Grimshaw et al. 1994, 121). Ubiquitous middle-class conceptions of women being confined to the home, and embodying a particular style of femininity, were fantasies precluding the necessity of working-class women laboring to sustain themselves or their families (Grimshaw et al. 1994). Women's positions in the labor market were "the result of a 'negotiated outcome' between the forces of capitalism and patriarchy" (Digby 1992, 205). At the very bottom of the labor market were women working in increasingly large industrial clothing factories, where wages typically failed to cover the cost of living for a widow with three children (Grimshaw et al. 1994). Gold transformed these existing middle-class social relations, becoming a dominant and disruptive presence in the colonies. The wealth flowing through the Victorian colony saw existing gendered power structures challenged by assertive and morally transgressive women (Wright 2016). Women enjoyed "flash dresses better than making butter and cheese" (Read 1853, 100), which was a serious enough problem that a meeting was convened in Melbourne to decide how "the ever-increasing fickleness of women could be most quickly and safely remedied" (Wright 2016, 1). Gold, by upsetting the pre-eminent social order and emergent middle-class hegemony on cultural and social values, particularly the dominant Victorian-era gendered, moral values, demonstrated its importance in shaping the social discourse of the time.

These examples suggest an emergent hegemonic ideal of masculinity that stood in contrast to new norms of respectable femininity for women, both of which began to structure both work and home life during the nation-building period. The following section delves more deeply into the legislation that elevated mining from its transgressive origins into the middle-class presentation and widely understood imaginings of Australia by Australians.

## Mining and the Pre-federation Middle-Class

Minerals, at the time of the first gold-rushes, were considered "Royal Minerals" as Australia was beholden to England as a colony. Minerals were, in effect, the property of the Crown rather than the owner of the land (be they Indigenous or non-Indigenous), and any person who conspired to keep their finds for themselves was doing so illegally (Birrell 1998). People of all backgrounds were irrepressibly drawn to gold, and saw in it a way of "bettering themselves, of gaining independence, of storing money for old age or sickness, of teaching their children to read or write" (Blainey 1993, 38). Working-class people could rise up the social ladder with one modest claim. This class transgression of working-class miners, combined with the general state of social flux on the goldfields (such as the aforementioned challenge to gendered social structures), was an affront to the middle-class and their attempts to impose social order. Thus, mining became a source of anxiety for the middle-class and colonial governments of the mid-nineteenth century. In what may signal a return to such classed anxieties, the accumulation of wealth by working-class miners is causing consternation among the Australian middle-class, exemplified by the antipathy toward the "cashed-up bogan" (Pini et al. 2012, 142).

Accepting that the lure of gold would be too strong to suppress after witnessing the madness of the California Gold Rush in 1849, and the subsequent rush at Ophir in New South Wales, the New South Wales government gazetted the Provisional Regulations of the goldfields in May 1851 (Birrell 1998). These regulations, although not an official law of the colony, provided for the appointment of commissioners, mostly young British men educated at private and military schools, to issue licenses that endowed prospectors to keep any gold they found. They were also charged with ensuring each miner had a certificate of discharge from their previous employer, without which a license would not be issued, a measure designed to regulate the labor market and address the soaring rate of men absconding from their general trades. Considering that a gold-rush by its very nature involves beating out others to the rich claims, most men did not obtain such certificates before leaving, nor would employers likely issue them. The obvious difference in class between the commissioners and miners, and the attempted suppression of mining by the commissioners, ensured the commissioners were unpopular with the miners (Birrell 1998).

These Provisional Regulations were an obvious example of how the upper- and middle-classes viewed gold as a harbinger of transgressive class mobility and a disruption to well-entrenched forms of labor exploitation. It was thus inevitable that these they would become law, and in 1852, the first law to regulate mining in Australia—the Victorian *Act to Restrain by Summary Proceedings Unauthorised Mining on Waste Lands of the Crown*—was passed. New South Wales followed suit with a *Gold Fields Management Act* in December of that same year. The tone of the middle-class anxiety toward this transgressive male working-class labor was set for the next half-decade. Yet, despite mining's precarious legal status and the hard work required, "for most [men] it was the first time in their lives they were independent and they cherished this" (Birrell 1998, 18). The lure of gold encouraged prospectors to trespass on agricultural land where they encountered resistance from land owners and local Aboriginal people (O'Hare 1971). In the *Gold Fields Management Act* 1852, New South Wales attempted to mitigate any conflict by granting permission to mine on private lands, which was later repealed in the *Gold Fields Management Act* 1857, demonstrating some of the political ebbs and flows of the era, and dynamics between the middle- and upper-class positions toward mining (O'Hare 1971). It was however a violent event (the Eureka Rebellion) on the Victorian goldfields that acutely transformed the legislative environment and national imaginary around mining.

The Eureka Lead was a seam of gold just outside Ballarat in the colony of Victoria. The infamous Eureka Rebellion there in 1854 violently dragged Victoria and the rest of the colonies of Australia into the democratic age. Blainey (1993, 56) recounts the scene of the Rebellion:

> On Saturday evening, 2$^{nd}$ December, more than a thousand men were in the stockade at Eureka, and more than four hundred soldiers and police were in their camps on the hills two miles away … In the pale light before the sunrise, soldiers and police attacked the stockade … The fighting lasted

less than half an hour but killed an uncounted number of miners, perhaps thirty, and five soldiers … and by breakfast that Sunday morning the rebellion was bleeding … Eureka became a legend, a battlecry for nationalists, republicans, liberals, radicals, and communists, each creed finding in the rebellion the lessons they liked to see.

Eureka became known not only as a defining moment in the history of mining but also in Australian history more generally. The retelling of this traumatic event through the poems of prominent figures in the national imaginary, such as Henry Lawson,[1] and the elevation of miners into the political class, eventually ensured the events of the uprising pushed mining into the forefront of Australian national mythology. This elevation into the political class occurred through both political and economic channels.

The increasing legitimation of mining as labor and industry through official political means occurred primarily after a *Victorian Royal Commission on Goldfield Problems and Grievances* (Victoria, Parliament 1855), which gained urgency after the Rebellion, and in 1855, handed down its recommendations. The recommendations proposed the establishment of the "Miners Right" to replace the existing gold license system, which was essentially a tax on mining. The introduction of the *Miners Right* enabled its holders to be elected to local courts, where they were empowered to create by-laws for the working of claims, and resolve disputes between miners, doing away with the power of the unpopular commissioners. The *Miners Right* further allowed holders to vote in the Victorian Legislative Assembly. By the end of 1855, 50,000 *Miners Rights* had been issued (Heritage Council Victoria 2007). *Miners Rights* were, for all intents and purposes for the holders, a pre-cursor to universal manhood suffrage in 1857 (Birrell 1998). Blainey (1993, 57) called this "the high tide of Australian democracy", and as representation of the miners in the court system in Victoria grew, the balance of power shifted away from the dominant, pastoral upper-class that largely controlled politics at the time.

The legitimation of mining from an economic perspective came despite the calamity of the Eureka Rebellion and ensuing loss of life.

According to Blainey (1993, 62), the gold-rushes gave "California and then Australia … such purchasing power that they largely revived the sick economy of Britain". This in turn stimulated prosperity throughout the developed world. At home, in Australia, gold mining was understood to be bringing Australia to the international stage, and elevating its station from a colonial backwater and dumping ground for Britain's criminals, to a cosmopolitan destination. But this situation required a continuing supply of gold, and as the easily accessible alluvial gold began to dry up, colonial governments began to welcome investment and capital in extractive mining ventures because of the revenue that could be generated from taxes. So began the shift from repressive colonial governments that wished to limit mining activity, to ones willing to encourage mining. Miners themselves saw extractive mining as a threat to their independent way of life, but they were fighting against the tide of history and the changing demands of gold mining, which were increasingly capital-centric.

Thus, as miners were increasingly incorporated into middle-class power structures, such as the Victorian courts and parliament, and critically, as they embraced heteronormative family values (as described in the previous section), the mining middle-class could seriously challenge the pre-existing social structures and values of the landed gentry that had been in place since settlement began in 1788. Barcan (1955, 69) thus concluded that without the legitimation of miners, "it is doubtful whether the middle-classes of town and country (the farmers and merchants) would have been strong enough to impose political democracy" on Australia's landed gentry. Mining laws were amended at various points from the mid-1850s after Eureka, but did not substantially change again until another Royal Commission, the *Gold Fields Royal Commission of Enquiry* (Victoria, Parliament 1862), was instituted in 1862. The recommendations from this Commission included the need for a uniform code of mining law, abolition of Mining Boards, and creation of a Minister for Mines with a Mining Affairs Department (most of which was incorporated into the *Victorian Mining Statute* of 1865) (c.f. Birrell 1998). This statute shaped the development of mining legislation in all the other Australian colonies. More importantly, however, the mining statutes rendered mining as a fully legitimate industry, indeed *necessary* for the economic prosperity of the colonies, and ensured that mining need no longer be a source of anxiety for the middle-class. Over the course of this transition from anxious, amoral labor, to a legitimate and necessary industry, the heroic hetero-masculinity and symbolism of the miners was the key enabler of change and will be discussed in the following section.

# Discussion

During the early part of the 1850s, mining occupied a place of anxiety in the imagination of the Australian upper- and middle-classes. The previous section identified that this anxiety increasingly found its way into legislation that attempted to suppress working bodies that were Othered, primarily working-class women and men, including sheep-shearers, sex workers, publicans, miners, Aboriginal domestic workers and farmhands, any other non-Anglo laborers, and any workers that were antagonistic to social order, or considered abject. Yet, as mining became increasingly important to the wealth and prosperity of the colonies and global capital, and as the gold-rushes continued to edge their way around the continent (expanding the frontier as they went), the "miner" was incorporated into the masculine, heroic signifiers of the national imaginary. Significant portions of the national imaginary were cemented in the decades before Federation by a middle-class that, although nostalgic for a romanticized, frontier past, was also increasingly urban, industrialized, and in control of political power and the power to legislate (Blackton 1961). Mining mobilized the popular imaginary to reify hegemonic masculinities as a way of creating space for working-class men as they moved from a no- or low-waged labor, into a more clearly defined middle-class position as a result of changing political structures, largely attributed to Eureka and the increasing importance of gold for the prosperity for the colonies. In fact, mining was such a powerful force, that the values of Victorian society imported wholesale from England had to be renegotiated to accommodate this new stratum of mining men.

Mining was originally a lottery, initially raising many men from impoverished working-class precarity, to a more solidly middle-class wage and way of life. Unlike the hyper-masculine "noble bushman" of Australian folklore, heteronormative middle-class ideals, such as waged work, separation of gender roles, and the nuclear family, do not fire the imagination. In the fledgling Australian nation, those attempting to build a national identity closely aligned with British values and unified by the desire to "protect" the nation from unwelcome migration from China and other non-Anglo countries, were impelled to develop and embrace a national myth powerful enough to inspire the population (in circumstances that seem doomed to repeat themselves in Australian immigration policy). Thanks to writers like Henry Lawson and Banjo Paterson, Australian folklore was populated with such ready-made myths, and in *The Bulletin*, there was a ready-made mechanism for distribution to the middle-class audience. Miners, embodying the noble bushman character as they helped "open up" the frontier during the gold-rushes, eventually transitioned to waged workers in company mining towns, where family life was valued in alignment with more hegemonic, heteronormative middle-class ideals. So tamed, the hyper-masculine miner could be incorporated into the moral economy of the time, and increasingly epitomized as a heroic masculine figure within the developing Australian imaginary.

The development of the mining industry was and is vitally important to understanding the Australian national imaginary, because it essentially shifted normative and rigid ideals about "appropriate" standards that dictated ideals about class, nation, and gender. Whereas many miners in developing contexts continue to be understood as dirty, backward, and degenerate, the Australian mining industry, and the rugged, individualistic, and hegemonic masculinity of the miners themselves, is now memorialized and valorized in the Australian national imaginary.

# Conclusions

This chapter has interrogated shifting perceptions of mining, through a dominant middle-class technology of power—legislation—during a time of concentrated nation-building. Legislation, implemented by an anxious middle-class determined to protect their social status (by keeping working-class men and women on the periphery), was formative during the colonial period production of mining. Over time, legislation shifted according to the corresponding increased social privilege experienced by miners, as they rose to prominence in politics, and gravitated towards the genteel, refined archetype of a gentile British nobleman. Rather than competing against an ideal figure, and an insular society that was impossible to penetrate without requisite amounts of social and cultural capital, the pioneers of Australia forged their own unique national identity and character. This rugged form of masculinity permeated (and still permeates) the Australian national imaginary.

This chapter attempts to rectify the narrow, masculinist frame of the Australian national imaginary by drawing attention to mining, and to an important modality of one key historical technology that gave rise to a stable and enduring representation of the heroic mining figure. This chapter adds to existing debates on the foundations of the Australian nation-state by looking at masculinity, mining, and the regulation of (women's) respectability. Female dominated industries such as factory and sex work, and other forms of precarious employment (c.f. Sanders-McDonagh 2010, 2017), were previously obscured by masculinist frames of the national imaginary, in no small part due to the influence of mining, and deserve to have a more prominent position in our reading of Australian history (Frances 1999). In other words, the persistence of stable or enduring national imaginaries welded to heteronormative masculinist forms of work problematically precludes reimagining the nation in more plural ways.

# Note

1. Excerpt from *Eureka* by Henry Lawson (1889). About the streets of Melbourne town the sound of bells is borne That call the citizens to prayer that fateful Sabbath morn; But there upon Eureka's hill, a hundred miles away, The diggers' forms lie white and still above the blood-stained clay. The bells that toll the diggers' death might also ring a knell For those few gallant soldiers, dead, who did their duty well. The sight of murdered

heroes is to hero-hearts a goad, A thousand men are up in arms upon the Creswick road, And wildest rumours in the air are flying up and down, 'Tis said the men of Ballarat will march on Melbourne town. But not in vain those diggers died. Their comrades may rejoice, For o'er the voice of tyranny is heard the people's voice; It says: "Reform your rotten law, the diggers' wrongs make right, Or else with them, our brothers now, we'll gather to the fight." 'Twas of such stuff the men were made who saw our nation born, And such as Lalor were the men who led the vanguard on; And like such men may we be found, with leaders such as they, In the roll-up of Australians on our darkest, grandest day!

# References

Gold Fields Management Act 1852 (NSW).
——— 1857 (NSW).
Mining Statute 1865 (VIC).
Act to Restrain by Summary Proceedings Unauthorised Mining on Waste Lands of the Crown 1852 (VIC).
AustLit. 2017. The Bulletin. Last modified June 13, 2017. https://www.austlit.edu.au/austlit/page/C278241.
Australian Associated Press. 2013. FIFO Workers Nation's Heroes: Premier. *The West Australian*, March 6. https://thewest.com.au/news/pilbara/fifo-workers-nations-heroes-premier-ng-ya-280696?r=1.
Barcan, A. 1955. The Development of the Australian Middle Class. *Past and Present* 8 (1): 64–77.
Bell, Duncan. 2003. Mythscapes: Memory, Mythology, and National Identity. *British Journal of Sociology* 54 (1): 63–81.
Birrell, Ralph W. 1998. *Staking a Claim: Gold and the Development of Victorian Mining Law*. Carlton South: University of Melbourne Press.
Blackton, Charles S. 1961. Australian Nationality and Nationalism, 1850–1900. *Historical Studies: Australia and New Zealand* 9 (36): 351–367.
Blainey, Geoffrey. 1993. *The Rush That Never Ended: A History of Australian Mining*. Melbourne: University of Melbourne Press.
Curthoys, Ann. 2001. 'Men of All Nations, Except Chinamen': Europeans and Chinese on the Goldfields of New South Wales. In *Gold: Forgotten Histories and Lost Objects of Australia*, ed. I. McCalman and A. Cook, 103–123. Cambridge: Cambridge University Press.

Davidson, Raelene. 1984. Dealing with the 'Social Evil': Prostitution and the Police in Perth and on the Eastern Goldfields, 1895–1924. In *So Much Hard Work: Women and Prostitution in Australian History*, ed. K. Daniels, 162–191. Sydney: Fontana/Collins.

Digby, Anne. 1992. Victorian Values and Women in Public and Private. In *Victorian Values: A Joint Symposium of the Royal Society of Edinburgh and the British Academy December 1990*, ed. T.C. Smout, 195–216. New York: Oxford University Press.

*Dirty Business: How Mining Made Australia*. 2013. DVD, Special Broadcasting Service, Artarmon, NSW, directed by J. Hickey and S. Tiefenbrun.

Foucault, Michel. 1982. The Subject and Power. *Critical Inquiry*. 8 (4): 777–795.

Frances, Raelene. 1999. Sex Workers or Citizens? Prostitution and the Shaping of 'Settler' Society in Australia. *International Review of Social History* 44 (Supplement S7): 101–122.

Gibbs, Leah, Jennifer Atchison, and Ingereth Macfarlane. 2015. Camel Country: Assemblage, Belonging and Scale in Invasive Species Geographies. *Geoforum* 58: 56–67.

Gibson, Chris. 2013a. 'Muting' Neoliberalism? Class and Colonial Legacies in Australia. *Human Geography: A New Radical Journal* 6 (2): 54–68.

———. 2013b. The Global Cowboy: Rural Masculinities and Sexualities. In *Sexuality, Rurality, and Geography*, ed. A. Gorman-Murray, B. Pini, and L. Bryant, 199–218. Plymouth: Lexington Books.

Grattan, Hartley. 1947. *Australia*. Berkeley: University of California Press.

Grimshaw, Patricia, Marilyn Lake, Ann McGrath, and Marian Quartly. 1994. *Creating a Nation*. South Yarra: McPhee Gribble.

Hall, C. 1992. *White, Male and Middle Class: Explorations in Feminism and History*. Hoboken: Wiley.

Heritage Council Victoria. 2007. Miners Right Collection. Last modified September 13, 2007. vhd.heritagecouncil.vic.gov.au/places/13628.

Historical Census and Colonial Data Archive. n.d. HCCDA Document 'VIC-1881-census_01' Page 29. http://hccda.anu.edu.au/pages/VIC-1881-census_01-03_29. Accessed 26 Aug 2017.

House of Representatives Standing Committee on Regional Australia. 2013. *Cancer of the Bush or Salvation for Our Cities? Fly-in, Fly-out and Drive-in, Drive-out Workforce Practices in Regional Australia*, 1–237. Canberra: The Parliament of the Commonwealth of Australia.

Jensen, Lars. 2014. Giving Diggers a Rest or Resurrecting Them? (Under) Mining the Australian National Narrative. *Australian Cultural Studies* 1 (1): 118–133.

Knox, Malcolm. 2013. *Boom: The Underground History of Australia, from Gold Rush to GFC*. London: Penguin Australia.
Lawson, Henry. 1889. Eureka (A Fragment). *The Bulletin* 10 (472): 12.
Lawson, Ronald. 1980. Towards Demythologizing the "Australian Legend": Turner's Frontier Thesis and the Australian Experience. *Journal of Social History* 13 (4): 577–587.
O'Hare, C.W. 1971. A History of Mining Law in Australia. *The Australian Law Journal* 45: 281–289.
Osborne, George. 2002. We Have Enemies to Oppose: Communication, Class and the Federation of Australia. *Media History* 8 (1): 35–47.
Pearse, Guy. 2009. Quarry Vision: Coal, Climate Change and the End of the Resources Boom. *Quarterly Essay* 33: 1–129.
Pini, Barbara, Paula McDonald, and Robyn Mayes. 2012. Class Contestations and Australia's Resource Boom: The Emergence of the 'Cashed-up Bogan'. *Sociology* 46 (1): 142–158.
Read, C.R. 1853. *What I Heard, Saw, and Did at the Australian Gold Fields*. London: T. & W. Boone.
Sanders-McDonagh, Erin. 2010. Situating the Female Gaze: Understanding (Sex) Tourism Practices in Thailand. In *New Sociologies of Sex*, ed. Kate Hardy, Sarah Kingston, and Teela Sanders. Surrey: Ashgate.
———. 2017. *Women and Sex Tourism Landscapes*. London: Routledge.
Victoria, Parliament. 1855. *Royal Commission on Goldfield Problems and Grievances* (W. Westgarth, Chairman). Melbourne: The Commission.
———. 1862. *Gold Fields Royal Commission of Enquiry* (Commissioners: J.B. Humffray, Frederick McCoy, Crawford Mollison). Melbourne: The Commission.
Ward, Russel. 1966. *The Australian Legend*. Melbourne: Oxford University Press.
Wright, Clare. 2016. Emancipated Wenches in Gaudy Jewellery: The Liberating Bling of the Goldfields. *The Conversation*, June 14. http://theconversation.com/emancipated-wenches-in-gaudy-jewellery-the-liberating-bling-of-the-goldfields-60449.

# 3

# Inventing a Muscular Global India: History, Masculinity, and Nation in *Mangal Pandey: The Rising*

Sikata Banerjee

Released in 2005, *Mangal Pandey: The Rising* directed by Ketan Mehta was both a commercial and critical hit. It ranked sixth in terms of domestic box office returns as well as being nominated for the prestigious International Indian Film Academy and Film Fare Awards. This film draws together masculinity, militarism, and a self-confident nationalism in the context of a globalizing India.

*Mangal Pandey* joins a host of historical films that have been released in the past decade which aim to configure Indian history in light of present national aspirations to occupy a dominant space in the international system. These cultural interpretations of a glorious Indian history have struck a chord among middle-class viewers who are at the forefront of imagining an economically dominant India (Farooqui 2006; Khan 2011; Majumdar and Chakrabarty 2007; Srivastava 2009). I unpack the construction of manhood and nation in *Mangal Pandey*. There has been much work on the intersection of femininity and globalization in the Indian cultural milieu but similar theoretical attention has not been

---

S. Banerjee (✉)
Department of Gender Studies, University of Victoria, Victoria, BC, Canada

© The Author(s) 2018
J. Mulholland et al. (eds.), *Gendering Nationalism*,
https://doi.org/10.1007/978-3-319-76699-7_3

49

focused on masculinity (Munshi 2001; Oza 2006; Parameswaran 2004). This chapter addresses this lacuna by underlining the manner in which masculinity and nation intersect in the film to provide an eloquent cultural depiction of an ascendant vision of aggressive national triumphalism mediated through a particular male embodiment.

My analysis is informed by McClintock's argument that popular film as spectacle is an important vehicle for the circulation of dominant visions of nation (McClintock 1993). I argue that India's imagining of its location in the global order is expressed through muscular nationalism, defined as an intersection of a specific vision of armed masculinity with the political doctrine of nationalism, which has become ascendant in India in the context of neoliberal globalization and the increasing dominance of right-wing, majoritarian Hindu chauvinism. Muscular nationalism expressed in popular Hindi film through powerful male bodies is a gendered signifier of India's desire to be seen as a serious player on the global stage. Nationalism in this era of globalization is a gendered affair.

I begin by tracing the cultural and economic contexts that frame my analysis of *The Rising* including neoliberal globalization in contemporary India which has shaped the emergence of a new global middle class. I then turn to a theorization of muscular nationalism, followed by a discussion of precedent filmic conceptions of Indian masculinity that *Mangal Pandey* responds to and reconfigures. Finally, before moving on to my analysis of the film, I set the stage by outlining two dominant variations of muscular nationalism in India.

## Globalization and the Middle Classes in India

The key turning point for globalization in India came in 1991 with a series of economic liberalization policies to implement structural reforms in response to a fiscal and balance of payment crisis. These changes sparked the growth of a consumer goods economy dominated by multinational companies and a new, growing globalized urban middle class which displays a taste for cosmopolitan consumption that marks a significant shift away from the years of early independence. Then, the tenets of Gandhi and Nehru emphasized social responsibility and the notion of refinement associated with a muted material desire and restraint on consumption (Fernandes 2000). In contrast, the new global middle class perceives conspicuous consumption as the signifier of a new India that is no longer a marginal player in the international political economy. Earning annual salaries that are unprecedented because of the entry of international capital, they usually work for Indian subsidiaries of multinational corporations, educate their children in Western universities, and vacation abroad (Farrell and Beinhocker 2007). Specifically, for my argument it is important to note that given structural changes to the film industry (specifically distribution and box office returns), Hindi films that used to cater to a wide section of society cutting across caste and class are not only geared to appeal to the global tastes of this middle class but can remain profitable through high ticket prices by mainly focusing on this class-based audience (Athique and Hill 2010). An important component of this appeal centers on gender.

The robust scholarship on the intersection of femininity and globalization in the Indian context provides a point of departure for studying masculinity. Focusing on the global ideas of beauty that have foregrounded the slim and toned bodies of actresses and models, these studies discuss the shifts in norms of dominant feminine desirability sparked by the entry of international cultural capital via Western magazines such as *Cosmopolitan*, *Elle*, and *Glamour* into the Indian market. The constitutive corollary to slim feminine bodies signaling the introduction of international feminine beauty ideals, I argue, is the rising dominance of muscular male bodies, indicating that ideas of "proper" manhood along with idealized femininity are changing in the new Indian context. Global magazines such as *Men's Health* (e.g. the cover of the July 2013 issue) offering advice on how to achieve "six-pack abs", as well as the exponential growth in gyms and personal trainers, track the rising dominance of a finely chiseled and fat-free male body (Balaji 2009; Yardley 2012). These male bodies intersect with an unprecedented number of films in Bollywood (referring to the dominant film industry located in Bombay, later re-named Mumbai) centering tales of martial prowess, military courage, and athletic glory (Desai 2007; Fazira-Yaccobali 2002). When these muscular bodies in Bollywood films intersect with a contemporary national triumphalism that is associated with the new Indian middle classes whose cultural values are strongly influenced by globalization, specifically the rise of consumer capitalism, it becomes clear that a particular masculinized nationalism is becoming ascendant in India. A theoretical exploration of the underpinnings of this image of nation—which I term muscular nationalism—follows.

## Muscular Nationalism

Like other forms of identity, masculinity is historically, politically, and culturally constituted. However, one form becomes dominant or hegemonic in setting the norms for male action (Connell 1995). In the nineteenth, twentieth, and early twenty-first centuries, Anglo-American hegemonic masculinity is defined by physical strength, aggression, action, strategic use of violence, courage, and martial prowess (Hooper 2001). These traits congeal in a muscular male body. This notion of hegemonic masculinity—that entered the Indian milieu through historical processes of British imperialism as well as the contemporary influence of American cultural consumerism introduced through global capital—underlines my vision of nationalism. British imperial effeminization of Indian men ignited nationalist responses which challenged this "gendering" and used cultural and historical examples to prove Indian manhood in terms of British hegemonic masculinity. Indeed, this historical legacy provides a cultural background for *Mangal Pandey* (and other contemporary films) as they turn to history to challenge the discourse of effeminization that still haunts the Indian polity as well as to affirm India as it seeks international recognition at this particular global moment of neoliberal capitalism and consumerism. Opening India to foreign investment has enabled the entry of Hollywood films (rarely screened in India before liberalization) and global fashion magazines such as *Glamour, Men's Health, Vogue,* and *Cosmopolitan* which have introduced a particular type of muscular male body associated with handsome Hollywood celebrities and advertisements encouraging consumer spending required to achieve this ideal.

My focus on the intersection of manhood and nation builds on the significant existing scholarship on the importance of the male body as signifying particular nationalisms (Banerjee 2005; Mayer 2000; Mosse

1996; Nagel 2003). Briefly put, muscular nationalism is the intersection of the traits of hegemonic masculinity with nation. Examples of muscular nationalism center an adult male body poised to kill and sacrifice for the nation. Some scholars have argued that this particular construction of manhood became prominent in certain dominant visions of colonial nationalism in India (Banerjee 2005; Sinha 1995). Contemporary muscular nationalism has reconfigured this colonial legacy and global cultural forces offer a rich milieu for the emergence of this image of manhood.

However, although this interpretation of nationalism focuses on manhood, it also relies on certain imaginings of the feminine. Images of womanhood symbolizing nation can take multiple forms: suffering mother as expressed by Mother India or the vulnerable virgin signified by nationalist icons such as the Irish Cathleen ni Houlihan or the warrior goddess embodied by Brittania or the Indian Durga. However, regardless what form of femininity is embodied in muscular nationalism, chastity is a constant trait of the female body which both symbolizes national honor and provides a moral code for the lives of women in the nation. Put another way, muscular nationalism generally centers a gendered binary, martial man/chaste woman. This means that one test of/rationale for the martial man's masculinity is his ability to protect chaste women, who in turn nurture/support the "martial" man as wife, mother, and sister.

The hegemonic notion of masculinity that informs the contemporary view of muscular nationalism as well as the muscular male body was not always dominant in Bollywood filmic narratives. The following section discusses the three major archetypes that have dominated Hindi popular film, before the arrival of the new "muscular national" hero found in *Mangal Pandey*. This discussion aims to highlight that dominant tropes of masculinity are not static, but shifting, hence providing the cultural history culminating in the male hero found in *Mangal Pandey*.

## Shifting Masculine Ideals

I would like to briefly discuss three archetypes—the effete self-destructive hero, the Five Year Plan hero, and the angry young man—to begin the discussion of masculinity and male body portrayed in *Mangal Pandey*.

Ashis Nandy points to the depiction of Devdas by actor Pramathesh Barua in the 1935 film of the same name as a particular type of colonial masculinity located in the borderlands of India's transition from a dominant rural landowning middle class to a middle class rooted in urban centers. As Nandy argues, Barua fitted middle-class India's especially Bengal's idea of a romantic hero, handsome but fragile and androgynous with a penchant for big game hunting and womanizing as if "…he were constantly trying to affirm his masculinity"(Nandy 2001, 142).The self-doubt that informed this need for constant affirmation led to self-destructive behavior such as addiction to alcohol and gambling.

In the years following Devdas, we had the emergence of what Sanjay Srivastava calls the Five Year Plan hero, who embodies a manliness that is attached "…not to bodily representations or aggressive behaviour but rather to being 'scientific' and 'rational'" and was associated with the Nehruvian vision of collective action and planned economy which was based on Soviet-style five year plans (Srivastava 2006, 141). Further, male bodies in films during the heyday of the effete self-destructive and Five Year Plan heroes tended to be soft and androgynous. However, the hegemonic image of manhood shifted with the making of *Zanjeer* in 1973 starring Amitabh Bachchan who dominated Bollywood films until recently and introduced what Karen Gabriel (2010) calls the macho melodrama during a period of political instability and an emerging economic crisis. Bachchan's lean body represented a subaltern struggle against the unfulfilled promises of the postcolonial state (specifically to the middle class) (Nandy 2001). It is also worth noting that by and large the masculinities which inhabit these films are Hindu (although actors playing them may be Muslim), and although decidedly shaped by middle-class aspirations, there is an attempt to erase internal caste and class divisions to create a unified India (which was also Hindu). The only deviation from this narrative was Bachchan's subaltern manhood which highlighted class (not caste) divisions, and in his iconic film, *Coolie*, (1983) he played a Muslim working class hero.

However, the rise of the global middle classes in a period of ascendant Hindu nationalism or Hindutva (claiming that India is a Hindu country and minorities may remain only if they accept Hindu dominance) has marginalized the stories of the subaltern.

I would argue that the muscular nationalism embodied by the chiseled male bodies in a recent outpouring of Bollywood films that emphasize Indian national valor and glory retains the aggression of Bachchan but moves onto portraying a self-confident, assertive nationalism that was not evident in the angry young man character. The muscled bodies of contemporary Bollywood stars—distinct from the angry young man's lean angularity—are a physical embodiment of a new national self-confidence among certain sections of the urban middle classes who have benefitted from globalization. This self-confidence relies on pushing internal divisions—caste and class—to the background in an attempt to project an unambiguous national strength.

Two variations of Indian muscular nationalism illuminate the context against which *Mangal Pandey* projects its national vision.

## India Poised to Rise: National Triumphalism

A 2007 Pew Global Attitudes Survey of urban middle classes in India revealed that not only was this social group emphatically supportive of global investment in India but 93% of the respondents agreed with the statement, "Our people aren't perfect but our culture is superior to others," (Pew Research Center 2007, 97). This national triumphalism is reflected in the India Poised Campaign which was launched in the same year by India's prominent English-language paper, *The Times of India*, the primary readership of which is the global middle class. It is fitting that the campaign was inaugurated by a two-minute video featuring an aging but fit Bollywood superstar Amitabh Bachchan, who proclaims:

> And quietly while the world is not looking a pulsating, dynamic new India is emerging…An India that no longer boycotts foreign-made goods but buys out the companies that makes them instead…. (Bachchan 2007)

As it unfolded throughout the month, this campaign was punctuated by articles titled "Why are We Embarrassed to Show Love for India?" and "We love India and Will Say It Out Aloud!" (Sharma 2007, 2007a). The male body embedded in muscular nationalism represents this new boldness through its physical expression of muscularity.

## Hindu Nationalism

Hindu nationalism provides a more explicit interpretation of this vision of the nation. When in power at the center (1999–2004, 2014 to present), the Hindu nationalist Bharatiya Janata Party (BJP) led a coalition which, although wary of the cultural impact of globalization, unabashedly embraced India's integration into the global economy. Given the discussion of the increasing "Hindu tinged" globalization and perceived ties between Hindu nationalist (Hindutva) ideals and Bollywood, this vision of muscular nationalism is an important component of the cultural context of today's India (Fazira-Yaccobali 2002; Khan 2011).

In the Hindutva articulation of muscular nationalism, ideas of manhood are animated by a fear of a hypermasculine enemy, which necessitates the recovery of a lost manhood to resist the erosion of Hindu political presence, even dominance, in India. The tone of Hindu nationalism is not modest, but aggressively self-confident and heavily influenced by Hindu nationalist V.D. Savarkar's vision of Indian history, especially of the 1857 uprising. Defining it as the first war of Indian independence, he saw his martial interpretation of Mangal Pandey as well as other icons of this uprising—Peshwa Nana Saheb and his general Tantia Tope—as the first step toward national glory which depended on militarizing Hinduism and Hinduizing the military. Additionally, although Bachchan's India Poised text is not agitating for Hindu power, it is assertive in its articulation of national pride. The depiction of manhood and nation in *Mangal Pandey* needs to be read against both these visions: the confident nationalism echoing the global middle-class triumphalism of the India Poised Campaign and the emergence of an aggressive *Hindutva* movement and my methodology acknowledges these dual cultural factors.

My gendered interdisciplinary analysis of this filmic text relies on the "presentist" use of history in popular film (Jaikumar 2006; Lichtner and Bandyopadhyay 2008). By this I mean that the needs of the present in today's India center on the imagination of a historical legacy of muscular nationalism that will challenge any trace of imperial effeminization that may linger in the modern polity, and furthermore this film also infuses this putative legacy with notions of secularism and individual freedom.

This potent mixture creates a "proper" lineage for a modern, strong, globally powerful, muscular India reflecting the triumphalism revealed by the Pew survey. Although, the film makes reference to "secularism," it centers the Hindu male body as the representation of India's power and it is no coincidence that this Hindu masculinity is embodied by Mangal Pandey, a popular Hindu nationalist icon and the putative hero of the war of 1857 validated by Savarkar, the acknowledged Hindutva interpreter of cultural history, as the first instance wherein Hindu masculinity proved its martial prowess.

## Mangal Pandey

Narrating the martial exploits of Mangal Pandey, a sepoy (or foot soldier) in the British Indian army and an iconic historical figure who has become central to the glorious failure narrative of the 1857 uprising against the British, this film provides a valuable insight into the manner in which a particular masculinized nationalism is unfolding in modern India. Although, suppressed brutally by British forces, this armed resistance was historically and culturally crucial. In its aftermath, India was put under direct British imperial rule, dislodging the power of the East India Company, while in the Indian popular—especially the Hindu nationalist—imagination, this conflict has come to signify (masculine) courage in the face of oppression.

In this film, the story of the 1857 uprising in India is narrated from the perspective of Mangal Pandey, a Brahmin Hindu, who is transformed through circumstances from a loyal servant of the East India Company to a rebel who realizes British oppression, reaching for the idea of a united Indian nation. In first sequence of scenes, the camera pans onto Barrackpore prison, the venue where Pandey will be hanged. He walks—the camera revealing his muscular body—up to the noose, which then frames his face with his eyes gazing defiantly ahead. The British commander asks if Pandey has any last wishes. He replies, "You cannot grant me my last wish, but one day it will be fulfilled."

This statement—which leaves Pandey's wish a mystery—is the cue for the film to dissolve into flashback. As it does so, a battle scene emerges.

In the aftermath of a bloody skirmish, Mangal saves William Gordon, a British officer, who acknowledges this debt by presenting Pandey his pistol. We then move forward four years to a New Year's Eve party in the governor general's palace. Events during this party evoke Pandey's rebellious nature. An Indian servant serving champagne trips and spills it on Emily Kent, the daughter of an imperial dignitary; horrified, he tries to sop up the liquid which has stained her blouse. Captain Hewson—a British officer standing nearby—immediately hits the servant for daring to touch a white woman. When he throws the servant on the ground outside the palace, Pandey—on guard duty by the front entrance—intervenes, setting the tone for his continuous defiance in the film. Pandey's defiance is the first hint of an Indian challenge to British manhood.

Indeed, this film traces a slightly transgressive path through ideas of "proper" manhood. The friendship between Gordon and Pandey has definite homoerotic tones. However, simultaneously, Pandey always embodies hegemonic masculinity, and any possibility of transgressive sexuality is foreclosed by Gordon's desire for Jwala (a woman he snatches from her husband's funeral pyre) and Pandey's for Heera (a courtesan he saves from Captain Hewson's violent lust). In one of the film's most provocative scenes, an interaction between Mangal and William simultaneously affirms the power of Indian manhood and hints at homoeroticism. In a way, this tension reveals that, in the nation, it is the relationship between men that is central, with women playing supporting roles.

The day after the New Year's Eve party, Gordon rides into village in search of Pandey. He finds him wrestling in the dirt. Wrestling is an indigenous Indian expression of male athletic and muscular prowess (Alter 1992). Mangal challenges William to a match, he accepts. The dynamic between the two half-naked bodies grappling on the ground seems almost sexual especially since Gordon asks Mangal—as they wrestle—why he didn't come to visit him last night. Mangal replies that he was angry, and the match becomes almost an expression through physical power of Gordon's attempt to appease—like a lover—Mangal's anger.

Having hinted at this transgression, the film then retreats into a tried and true colonial trope to mute any homoerotic undertones. In a later scene as Mangal and William chat by the river, they spot a funeral procession in the horizon; William Gordon immediately, from a distance (without any visual clues), identifies it as a sati in process and rushes to save the chaste middle-class Indian woman about to be burned on her husband's funeral pyre. Jwala, the woman William rescues, deflects the homoerotic turn in the narrative by becoming the object of Gordon's desire.

In contrast, Heera, Mangal Pandey's love interest, is not an embodiment of middle-class respectability but rather a courtesan trafficked by men who kidnapped her as a child. Mangal rescues the spirited and beautiful Heera, from the clutches of the violent Captain Hewson, hence winning her love and trust. It should be noted that Hewson was the officer who physically assaulted the Indian servant for daring to touch Emily Kent. In a symmetrical parallel Pandey now engages Hewson in a violent confrontation to protect Heera. This is an illustration of the martial man/chaste woman binary within muscular nationalism with the woman's body representing masculine honor.

The expression of masculinity in this film—embodied by Mangal Pandey—certainly highlights a muscular, martial bravery and defiance that is in direct contrast to British effeminization of Indian men. It sets out to imagine—echoing nationalist narratives made popular by Hindu nationalism—a proper history of the restoration of manhood that seems most fitting for India's desire to be a "muscular nation."

A clear break in the film occurs when Mangal along with his fellow sepoys are provided with evidence—a visit to a cavernous space dotted with boiling vats of animal fat—that confirms the rumor that the cartridge of the Enfields being used by the sepoys were indeed greased by pig and cow fat.[1] It is in this second half that we begin to see the contours of a vision of a proper nation emerging. But this vision of nation is expressed through the images of manhood sketched in the first part of the film. Mangal returns the pistol Gordon gifted him and declares, "We are no longer brothers." Symbolically, the Indian man sheds his reliance on British masculinity. After this scene, the filmic narrative shifts to events that construct a historical lineage appropriate for a secular and powerful India.

---

[1] In popular narratives about 1857, the rumor of the British use of animal fat to grease cartridges is seen to be a catalyst for the uprising. There is little scholarly evidence of this.

This begins with a fateful meeting. While Mangal together with his friend Bakht Khan and other fellow sepoys are attending a Sufi performance, they are called outside to meet the emissaries of Peshwa (King) Nana Sahib, one of whom is General Tantia Tope. They invite the sepoys to join their uprising. Mangal explodes with anger at the request declaring, "Rajahs and nawabs have gambled away their kingdoms…as the company's army we have seen you grovel and lay down your arms in front of us—You are nothing. We are Hindustan, the company rules based on our strength." In response to this outburst Tantia Tope asks who will rule if the rebellion is successful. Mangal replies, "The people. Even in England, the Queen may be on the coin, but the rule is of the people. Do you want us to spill your blood so that we can become your slaves? No! This is a fight for freedom—freedom from our past…." Whether or not in reality, an uneducated sepoy would have so eloquently expressed such a notion of democracy is irrelevant, what is relevant is that a contemporary India imagines him as having articulated these ideas and hence creating a historical lineage of indigenous democratic ideals.

This ideological trajectory is further enhanced in a conversation between Pandey and Gordon toward the end of the film. In terms of muscular nationalism, this dialogue can be situated within the context of competing masculinities; Mangal is representing the voice of a muscular India as he declares, "Gordon sahib our fight is no longer against grease on a cartridge, it is for our dignity and our freedom—India is rising, nothing and nobody can stop it." This sentence about India rising can be interpreted not only in the historical context of nationalism but also in the present moment as India flexes it muscles as a potential economic powerhouse.

Although, the film expresses its image of nation through masculinized tension linking Pandey and Gordon, corresponding images of femininity illustrate what I have termed the martial man/chaste woman dichotomy. Chaste Jwala throws into relief Gordon's chivalry while Heera underlines Mangal's courage and muscular prowess as he takes on four British officers to defend her honor. These two Indian women are situated to highlight the main gendered dynamic expressed by competing masculinities embodied by William Gordon and Mangal Pandey. It is also worth noting that while he awaits his death sentence in prison, Heera visits

Mangal. Clothed in the simple cotton sari of a middle-class, Hindu wife, rather than the colorful, provocative clothing of a courtesan, she asks Mangal to put sindoor—a vermillion powder worn by married women—in the parting of her hair; thus symbolically married, she blesses Mangal by performing simple Hindu rites. She does not beseech him to abandon his fight but rather she supports his sacrifice for the nation's freedom.

In the last sequence of the film, Mangal Pandey's portrait is juxtaposed with images of Gandhi and popular demonstrations against the British presence. The film ends with Nehru raising the tri-color national flag. Deftly, Mangal Pandey and his uprising have been inserted in the origin story of nationalism in India. However, it is a nationalism that may not necessarily be "secular." The film makes gestures toward Hindu-Muslim unity through Pandey's friendship with Bakht Khan and an appreciation of Sufi music, but the fact remains that a Brahmin Hindu—embodying hegemonic masculinity—is constructed as launching the legacy of nationalist resistance. It also should be noticed that this film has somehow erased both castes—by emphasizing Pandey's realization of the evils of caste hierarchy with his claims of brotherhood with the village untouchable (the lowest caste, a Brahmin becomes polluted through touch or sharing meals with this caste) Nainsukh and class divisions—there is no reference to any socio-economic divisions among Hindus. Such erasure of internal differences not only creates a monolithic Hindu community but foregrounds it with no discussion of the multiplicity of religions, castes, and classes dividing India even in 1857. Further, the masculinity embodied by Pandey is constructed to appeal to a contemporary audience comprising the global middle classes. In the language of the "presentist" use of history, this uniform vision of India shores up this middle class's desire to project a powerful, united presence on the world stage.

## Conclusion

I have argued that the critically acclaimed Bollywood movie *Mangal Pandey* constructs a vision of Indian nationalism that can best be captured and theorized through the framework of muscular nationalism—the intersection of the political doctrine of nationalism with armed masculinity. I argued that this vision of nationalism has emerged in the broader historical and political context of India's economic opening and liberalization after 1991 and its entry into the neoliberal global order. These changes and changed contexts have spurred several critical developments, the most pertinent of which for my analysis are two: first, the development of a nationalist triumphalism linked to an economically robust global middle class, and second, structural changes in the Indian, specifically Mumbai-based, Hindi film industry. As a result of these changes, Indian and particularly Hindi-language films are now geared to appeal more to the globalized middle classes rather than the masses of poorer Indians—indeed, Bollywood films now can be highly successful financially by appealing only to the former audiences and virtually ignoring or erasing the latter.

The muscular nationalism that sustains and fulfills these globalized/globalizing aspirations is substantively and substantially different than precedent popular conceptions of Indian masculinity portrayed in films from the 1950s on. Today's muscular nationalist hero portrays an aggressive masculinity, rooted in martial prowess and athletic strength, proclaiming a strident confidence in himself and in the place of India in the world.

My argument is that *Mangal Pandey* mirrors all these aspects of muscular nationalism perfectly. *Mangal Pandey* illuminates the manner in which modern India—eager to establish itself as a powerful global actor—uses history to imagine a legacy of muscular nationalism and secular democratic values. The nation's present aspirations are shored up by a history based on the recovery of a tradition of national manhood expressing strength, martial prowess, and defiance. By locating itself in a historical lineage shaped by muscular nationalism, India can indeed express a contemporary strength. It should be noted that national masculinity is conflated with individual heroic action. This film centers a muscular hero as the locus of nationalist expression in keeping with the ethos of neo-liberal capitalism. This focus on individual heroism signals a move away from ideas of collective action (hinted by the Five Year Plan hero) and although Pandey rises up against British imperialism, there is no discussion of class and caste inequities and social justice (highlighted in earlier films by the subaltern anger of the Amitabh Bachchan character). Furthermore, secularism occupies a contested position in this nationalist origin story; despite gestures toward an acknowledgment of India's religious diversity and tolerance, a muted unified Hinduism steadfastly colors the vision of nation shaping the filmic narrative.

## Explaining the Context

**1857 Uprising** Refers to the armed conflict resulting from a group of Indian foot soldiers rising up against East India Company's rule. The causes for this are complex and still under debate. This uprising ended the East India Company's dominance in India, and the country was brought under direct rule of Queen Victoria and the Parliament.

**BJP** Bharatiya Janata Party (literally, Indian people's party). A Hindu right party which fights for Hindu dominance in India. India's present prime minister, Narendra Modi, belongs to the party.

**India Poised Campaign** Launched in 2007, the 60th anniversary of Indian independence, initiated and run by *The Times of India*, the premier English-language newspaper in this country. The campaign was aimed at encouraging citizens to express the myriad ways in which they could help India progress.

**Jawaharlal Nehru (1889–1964)** First prime minister of India. He implemented a moderate socialist economy which was marked by five year plans aimed at accelerating industrialization based on manufacturing. Against the background of the Cold War, he favored a policy of non-alignment for India, refusing to ally with either the USA or the Soviet Union. Usually, the adjective Nehruvian refers to these ideological perspectives.

**Mohandas Karamchand Gandhi (1869–1948)** Pre-eminent leader of the Indian independence movement. Popularized the political doctrine of non-violence. Believed India should focus on small village-based industries (not a fan of Nehruvian-style development). Both Gandhi and Nehru were opponents of rampant consumer capitalism.

**Vinayak Damodar Savarkar (1883–1966)** A famous Indian nationalist who advocated for the Hindu religion to be militarized and emphasized the need for Hindus to emphasize the glorious martial past which would provide the inspiration for a present powerful India. The BJP and other Hindu nationalist organizations revere his work. His historical vision of the 1857 is contained in his book *The Indian War of Independence* first published in 1909.

# References

Alter, Joseph S. 1992. *The Wrestler's Body*. Berkeley: University of California Press.
Athique, Adrian, and Douglas Hill. 2010. *The Multiplex in India: A Cultural Economy of Urban Leisure*. London: Routledge.
Balaji, Murali. 2009. Exporting Indian Masculinity. *Technoculture: An Online Journal for Technology Studies* 14: 1–12.
Banerjee, Sikata. 2005. *Make Me a Man: Masculinity, Hinduism, and Nationalism in India*. Albany: State University of New York Press.
Connell, Rae Wynn. 1995. *Masculinities*. Berkeley: University of California Press.
Desai, Radhika. 2007. Imagi-nation: The Reconfiguration of National Identity in Bombay Cinema in the 1990s. In *Once Upon a Time in Bollywood*, ed. Gurbir Singh Jolly, Zenia B. Wadhwani, and Deborah Barretto, 43–61. Toronto: Tsarbooks.
Farooqui, Mahmood. 2006. Bollywood and the Middle-Class Nation. *Himal Magazine*, July. www.himalmag.com. Accessed 16 June 2016.
Farrell, Diana, and Eric Beinhocker. 2007. Next Big Spenders: India's Middle Class. *McKinsey and Company Global Institute*. http://www.mckinsey.com/mgi/overview/in-the-news/next-big-spenders. Accessed June 2016.
Fazira-Yaccobali, Vazira. 2002. Yeh Mulk Hamara Ghar: National Order of Things, and Muslim Identity in John Mathew Mattan's Sarfarosh. *Contemporary South Asia* 11 (2): 183–198.
Fernandes, Leela. 2000. Restructuring the New Middle Class in Liberalizing India. *Comparative Studies of South Asia, Africa and the Middle East* 20 (1): 88–112.

Gabriel, Karen. 2010. *Melodrama and the Nation: Sexual Economies of Bombay Cinema 1970–2000*. New Delhi: Women Unlimited.

Hooper, Charlotte. 2001. *Manly States: Masculinities, International Relations, and Gender Relations*. New York: Columbia University Press.

Jaikumar, Priya. 2006. *Cinema: At the End of Empire*. Durham: Duke University Press.

Khan, Shahnaz. 2011. Recovering the Past in *Jodha Akbar*: Masculinities, Femininities and Cultural Politics in Bombay Cinema. *Feminist Review* 99 (1): 132–146.

Lichtner, Giacomo, and Sekhar Bandyopadhyay. 2008. Indian Cinema and the Presentist Use of History: Conceptions of "Nationhood" in *Earth* and *Lagaan*. *Asian Survey* 48 (3): 431–452.

Majumdar, Ruby, and Dipesh Chakrabarty. 2007. Mangal Pandey: Film and History. *Economic and Political Weekly* 42 (19): 1771–1778.

Mayer, Tamer. 2000. Gender Ironies of Nationalism: Setting the Stage. In *Gender Ironies of Nationalism: Sexing the Nation*, ed. Tamer Mayer, 1–24. London/New York: Routledge.

McClintock, Anne. 1993. Family Feuds: Gender, Nationalism and the Family. *Feminist Review* 44: 61–80.

Mosse, George. 1996. *The Image of Man: The Creation of Modern Masculinity*. New York: Oxford University Press.

Munshi, Shobha. 2001. Marvellous Me: The Beauty Industry and the Construction of the 'Modern' Indian Woman. In *Images of the 'Modern Woman' in Asia: Global Media, Local Meanings*, ed. Shobha Munshi, 78–93. Richmond: Curzon.

Nagel, Joane. 2003. *Race, Ethnicity, and Sexuality: Intimate Intersections, Forbidden Frontiers*. New York: Oxford University Press.

Nandy, Ashis. 2001. Invitation to an Antique Death: The Journey of Pramathesh Barua as the Origin of the Terribly Effeminate, Maudlin, Self-Destructive Heroes of Indian Cinema. In *The History, Politics, and Consumption of Public Culture in India*, ed. Rachel Dwyer and Christopher Pinney, 39–161. New Delhi: Oxford University Press.

Oza, Rupal. 2006. *The Making of Neoliberal India: Nationalism, Gender, and the Paradoxes of Globalization*. New York: Routledge.

Parameswaran, Radhika. 2004. Global Queens, National Celebrities: Tales of Feminine Triumph in Post Liberalization India. *Critical Studies in Media Communication* 21 (4): 346–370.

Pew Research Center. 2007. *Pew Global Attitudes Report*. Washington DC: Pew Research Centre. http://www.pewglobal.org/files/2007/10/Pew-Global-Attitudes-Report-October-4-2007-REVISED-UPDATED-5-27-14.pdf. Accessed June 2016.

Sharma, Jyoti. 2007. Why Are We Embarrassed to Show Love for India? *Times of India*, January 24. http://timesofindia.indiatimes.com/bombay-times/Why-are-we-embarrassed-to-show-love-for-India/articleshow/1434862.cms? Accessed 16 June 2016.

———. 2007a. We Love India and Will Say It Aloud. *Times of India*, January 25. http://timesofindia.indiatimes.com/bombay-times/We-love-India-and-will-say-it-aloud/articleshow/1459986.cms? Accessed 16 June 2016.

Sinha, Mrinalini. 1995. *Colonial Masculinity: The 'Manly Englishman' and the 'Effeminate' Bengali in the Late Nineteenth Century*. Manchester: Manchester University Press.

Srivastava, Sanjay. 2006. The Voice of the Nation and the Five-Year Plan Hero: Speculations on Gender, Space, and Popular Culture. In *Fingerprinting Popular Culture: The Mythic and the Iconic in Indian Cinema*, ed. Vinay Lal and Ashis Nandy, 122–155. New Delhi: Oxford University Press.

Srivastava, Neelam. 2009. Bollywood as National(ist) Cinema: Violence, Patriotism and the National-Popular in *Rang De Basanti*. *Third Text* 23 (6): 703–716.

Yardley, Jim. 2012. A Quest for Six Packs Inspired by Bollywood. *New York Times*, July 12. http://www.nytimes.com/2012/07/19/world/asia/on-screen-abdominals-send-indias-men-to-gym.html?_r=0. Accessed June 2016.

# 4

# Homophobia as Geopolitics: 'Traditional Values' and the Negotiation of Russia's Place in the World

Emil Edenborg

In early spring 2017, a state-initiated campaign of homophobic violence was unleashed in Chechnya, a war-torn and authoritarian republic on the southern border of the Russian Federation. According to several media reports, the wave of persecution started when the local police arrested a man suspected of using narcotics in late February. After finding information in his telephone suggesting he was engaging in sexual relationships with other men, the police started rounding up and detaining large numbers of men suspected of being homosexual. Although at the time of writing this chapter some details are still unclear, several Russian news sources and LGBT organizations as well as international HR groups have published concurrent witness reports painting a very gruesome picture (Ekho Moskvy 2017; Kost'uchenko 2017; Milashina 2017a, b; Milashina and Gordinenko 2017). According to these stories, during the weeks following

E. Edenborg (✉)
Swedish Institute of International Affairs, Stockholm, Sweden

Södertörn University, Huddinge, Sweden

the first arrest, more than a hundred men from different sectors of Chechen society were arrested and brought to secret prisons (targets including a wide range of people, e.g. a well-known television personality and religious leaders close to the government). The existence of such prisons (where suspected extremists, Salafists and drug addicts are unlawfully detained) is already well-documented, as is the common use of torture by the Chechen authorities, led by President Ramzan Kadyrov with implicit approval from the Federal Russian government. Suspected homosexual men who had been brought to these detentions centers reported experiencing both physical violence and emotional torture. While some were released, several were confirmed to have been killed—among them a 16-year-old boy. In some cases, the authorities transferred these men to male family members with instructions to kill them, a process called "prophylactic work". Witness stories, photos and videos gave clear indications that high-ranking Chechen officials, among them the Speaker of the Parliament and the Leader of the Chechen Interior Ministry, were directly involved in the campaign. At the same time, President Kadyrov's spokesperson called the reports an "absolute lie" and denied even the existence of homosexuals in Chechnya: "you cannot detain and oppress what does not exist".

For those in the West watching these scenes of homophobic violence unfold, the reports from Chechnya may have been seen as yet another confirmation of Russia as an essentially and categorically homophobic place. However, Chechnya is a distinct geographical space and must be distinguished from other parts of the Russian Federation. For many Russian observers these events were interpreted as evidence of the Chechen Muslim-majority Republic's archaic, tribal and intrinsically homophobic character. Already in 2013, when asked by journalists about Russia's "homosexual propaganda" law,[1] President Vladimir Putin used the specter of Chechen homophobia as one of the reasons for why the law was necessary, claiming that if same-sex marriage were to be allowed in Chechnya, "it would result in casualties" (Blagoi 2013). For some, the 2017 events in Chechnya appeared to confirm Putin's warning. Whether interpreted as indicative of a "homophobic Russia" or a "homophobic

---

[1] The Russian Propaganda Law was unanimously approved in the State Duma in 2013 and seeks to "protect children from information advocating for a denial of traditional family values" and makes the distribution of "propaganda of non-traditional sexual relationships" to minors a criminal offense.

(Muslim) Chechnya", for many it was tempting to interpret the anti-gay wave as a problem of the Other's culture, narrated in terms of religious, civilizational and cultural difference, intolerant popular attitudes and persistence of "traditional values".

While not denying the significance of religion, culture or attitudes, this chapter departs slightly from these discourses to argue that such explanations may obscure the politics of homophobia. As Wendy Brown (2006: 15ff.) argues, the culturalization of intolerance, that is, to understand prejudice as essential to and inherent within specific cultural and religious groups, is a depoliticizing discourse which glosses over the historical, social and economic context as well as the power relations within which, for example, homophobic politics emerges. In the case of Chechnya, reports suggest that the anti-gay campaign unleashed in 2017 cannot be reduced to cultural explanations. While anti-gay and patriarchal attitudes are no doubt widespread and institutionalized in Chechen society (the practice of "honor killings", for example, is well-documented), what happened was not a spontaneous eruption of popular homophobia. In fact, the campaign was initiated and coordinated by Chechen authorities, with direct involvement of leading state officials. These violent attacks on gay men follow a pre-existing pattern that was reinforced in the 2010s, where the Putin-supported Kadyrov government harasses, tortures and murders perceived enemies of Chechnya with impunity (Amnesty 2016). Crucially for the aims of this chapter, the anti-gay campaign in Chechnya must also be seen in the political context of publicly sanctioned homophobia across the Russian Federation and a climate of aggressive search for internal enemies.

In the twenty-first century sexual rights and the politics of sexual citizenship are increasingly framed as a question with global repercussions, entangled in contestations over geopolitics, influence and security, and often at the heart of discourses of "tradition" and "modernity" (Altman and Symons 2016). This is particularly true for LGBT politics, and in the rhetoric of states and non-state actors in many parts of the world, gay rights have emerged as a form of symbolic border guard (Yuval-Davis 1997) marking civilizations and their boundaries, though in multiple and contradictory ways. In certain political discourses in Western Europe and North America, LGBT inclusion is represented as a marker of national, European or Western advancement and superiority vis-à-vis "intolerant" and "backward" Others, a tendency which Jasbir Puar has labeled "homonationalism" (2007). Simultaneously, projects of "state homophobia" in some countries in Africa, Asia and Eastern Europe are motivated by discourses depicting homosexuality as a Western import and local LGBT activists as proxies of US or European imperialism (Weiss and Bosia 2013). In both modalities of this discourse, sexual politics is situated according to a polarized, essentialist and historically inaccurate dichotomy of a "gay-friendly West" confronting a "traditional non-West".

With this conversation as a theoretical backdrop, this chapter explores the transnational and geopolitical dimensions of contemporary state-supported homophobia in Russia. Whereas previous research on the increasingly repressive policies and rhetoric on gays and lesbians in Russia in the 2010s has stressed how homophobia constitutes part of a biopolitical project of ensuring the nation's survival (Stella and Nartova 2016), or the role of sexual Otherness in producing a narrative of national belonging (Persson 2015), little attention has been devoted to global political dimensions of the current anti-gay wave in Russia (however, see Moss 2017). Drawing on a media analysis of the Russian framing of the 2013 ban on "propaganda for non-traditional sexual relationships", this chapter analyzes how dominant narratives of homosexuality in Russia are articulated in relation to domestic perceptions of Russia's role in global politics. Arguing that political homophobia in Russia must be understood within the larger project of negotiating Russia's geopolitical identity, I make two specific arguments: firstly, that Russia's recent (re)turn to "traditional values" is a boundary-making move, delineating Russia from the West and seeking to restore Russia's place in world politics by positioning the country as a leader in a transnational conservative alliance. This effort must be seen against the background of the ways in which sexual politics have emerged as a symbolic battlefield in an imagined clash of civilizations and competing conceptions of modernity. Secondly, at the heart of this geopolitical project is a contradiction which stems from Russia's historically ambivalent relation to Western modernity. Dominant Russian narratives on homosexuality are undercut by overlapping and contradictory schemas of cultural differentiation, where Russia on the one hand is positioned as a counterhegemonic force opposing Western-imposed gay rights and, on the other hand, as a force of order and civilization in relation to "Muslim homophobia" within Russia's borders.

The empirical material presented in this chapter provides an analysis of Russian media reporting on the ban on "propaganda for non-traditional sexual relations" and LGBT issues more widely. Data was collected from 25 January to 11 June 2013 (corresponding to the time the law was under consideration of the Duma and the moments when public discussion was most intense). News items, op-eds and columns were collected from two Kremlin-close newspapers: the official government publication *Rossiyskaya Gazeta* and the tabloid *Komsomolskaya Pravda*. Clips from the news program *Vrem'a* on state-aligned *Channel One* were also collected and analyzed. In addition, a more extensive but less structured analysis of the reporting on these issues was carried out and looked at discourses in the wider mainstream media. Deploying a form of narrative analysis (Patterson and Monroe 1998), I sought to identify and analyze the process of emplotment, that is, how disparate events and phenomena (such as "homosexuality" and "the West") were selected and organized into storylines and thereby rendered meaningful. Importantly, this process involves the linking of the temporal to the spatial, for example, the construction of certain places as "modern" and others as "backward". The specific quotes and examples included in the chapter were chosen because they illustrate larger patterns in the media reporting which were relevant to the analytical concerns of the text (i.e. because they implicitly or explicitly tied the issue of sexual politics to Russia's global and geopolitical standing).

## Russian Sexuality Politics in Historical Perspective

In all societies, efforts to regulate sexuality and categorize certain forms of sexual behavior as deviant and others as normal have been crucial, setting standards and norms for how a proper citizen should act, and thereby seeking to govern and secure the well-being and prosperity of the population as a whole (Foucault 1990). The delineation between "respectable" and "dangerous" sexualities has historically been closely tied to processes of nation building,[2] as the border between "good" and "bad" sexuality has also symbolically marked the border between domestic and foreign (Mosse 1985). This suggests that in addition to the biopolitical function of regulating sexuality identified by Foucault, such discourses also perform a certain geopolitical function.

Historically in Russia, the regulation of sexual deviance has been closely related to perceptions of Europe and to ideas of modernity and progress. Historians of sexuality have shown how both liberalizing and repressive measures have been entangled in negotiating Russia's relation to Western modernity. The first sodomy ban was introduced by Peter the Great in 1706 as part of his military code, which was based on the Swedish model, expressing an attempt to discipline the Russian army in accordance to European standards (Kon 1998). The sodomy ban was removed by the Bolsheviks in 1917 as part of their efforts to get rid of what they considered to be antiquated bourgeois morality. In 1934, however, the ban was re-introduced by Stalin based on fears that "hidden homosexual networks" would turn into Western espionage cells (Healey 2001). In post-war Soviet society, homosexuality was a taboo and rarely talked about in public discourse (Banting et al. 1998). The sodomy ban was removed in 1993 to enable Russia to enter the Council of Europe, which again demonstrates the intertwinement of governing sexuality and Russia's geopolitical orientation.

The recent upsurge of anti-LGBT politics in Russia is related to both domestic and global dynamics. Since the mid-2000s, there has been an intense discussion about the rights and place of homosexuals in the national community, as public visibility of queers and LGBT issues has increased dramatically in Russian mass media, social media and popular culture. A factor which contributed to this new visibility were the Pride marches organized yearly in Moscow, starting in 2006, each of which were officially banned by the authorities but still took place, albeit under tumultuous circumstances which were widely reported in domestic and international media. These marches, often with a significant share of Western

---

[2] C.f. Nick Skilton's chapter on nation building in this collection for an interesting perspective on similar issues in the Australian context.

activists among the participants, have also been controversial in Moscow's local LGBT community, with some arguing that the Western model of visibility-enhancing identity politics is not necessarily the best way of improving the situation for queers in Russia (cf. Stella 2015). In the 2010s, there were massive reactions to LGBT visibility from the state and various societal actors, ranging from the Putinist party United Russia, parental organizations, nationalists, communists (whose emphasis on Soviet nostalgia and great power revanchism make them very unlike leftist parties in many other countries) and the Orthodox Church, the influence of which has grown significantly under Putin. The 2013 law on "propaganda for non-traditional sexual relationships among children" was introduced along with a hysterically aggressive homophobic campaign of stigmatization and scapegoating in state-aligned media. The wider political context was an increasingly authoritarian and repressive society, which included an atmosphere of aggressive anti-Westernism, official searches for internal enemies and a general move toward promoting "traditional values"—all tendencies which are not new but have been reinforced after the re-election of Putin in 2012 (Edenborg 2017).

The anti-gay atmosphere in Russia should be seen against an international trend of state homophobia (Weiss and Bosia 2013) in the 2010s, which can be observed in countries as diverse as India, Egypt, Hungary, Indonesia and Uganda. In these contexts, homophobic discourses merge with anti-Western (or anti-European) rhetoric and are deployed in projects of national belonging and state legitimization. The securitization and policing of queers is interwoven in counterhegemonic, anti-imperialist politics and inform efforts to entrench unique national identities in communities seen as menaced by globalization and Westernization (Amar 2013; Altman and Symons 2016). In many cases, local religious associations as well as globalized religious movements play important roles in legitimizing homophobic politics. Importantly, instances where political and religious leaders use anti-Western discourses to justify persecution of LGBT people seem to be on the rise at the same time as some movements in the West are using pro-gay rhetoric to justify anti-Muslim politics (Puar 2007). This attests to the growing significance of sexual politics as a powerful political signifier in global struggles over influence, belonging and modernity. The next section will explore in more detail the role of homophobia in current efforts to position Russia in global politics as a leader in "traditional values".

## The Geopolitics of "Traditional Values"

> There is a war going on between Russia and the West. About the human being and what he should be like (…). The West is legalizing homosexual marriage. Russia prohibits even propaganda for homosexuality. The ban is really about the West and its gay laws. (Shevchenko 2013)

The above quote from the tabloid *Komsomolskaya Pravda* encapsulates a narrative that was repeatedly articulated in Russian mainstream discourses. The curbing of gay liberation in Russia had, according to this storyline, a larger symbolic meaning, indicating the civilizational choice that Russia would not (and should not) become like the West. Underlying this narrative was a geopolitical imaginary of an innocent Russia cherishing "traditional values", confronting a degenerate West characterized by sexual immorality and dissolution of gender norms (Riabov and Riabova 2014). According to Michael J. Shapiro (1997), communities create "violent cartographies" which delineate geographical space by imagining the homeland as innocent and good, and the spaces of Others as disordered, threatening and thus legitimate objects of violence. Such landscapes of danger, he argues, help to naturalize and depoliticize relations of domination and violence, by representing them as necessary for ensuring safety at home. The figure of enemies imperiling the community, and the mobilization of emotions of fear and hatred toward them, is central to narratives of collective identity and belonging.

Sara Ahmed's theory of the cultural politics of emotions (2014) provides a helpful point of reference for understanding the work of emotions in producing and reinforcing such imaginaries. Ahmed does not view emotions as residing within or originating from pre-defined individuals or collectives. Rather than asking what emotions are, she investigates what they do. According to her, the circulation of emotions produces the very effect of the surfaces and boundaries that make it possible to distinguish between inside and outside. For example, the experience of pain when an object touches or penetrates the skin allows us to experience the boundedness of the body itself: "it is through this violation that I feel the border in the first place" (Ahmed 2014: 27). When applied not to the individual but collective body, this suggests that the experience of a border violation, while it demonstrates the penetrability of the community, simultaneously reproduces the community and reminds us of its existence (Kuntsman 2009). Violent cartographies, that is, ideas of an innocent home being threatened by outside violation, depend on the invocation of fear and disgust of Others, and of love and care for the homeland. Thus, the circulation of emotions imbues spaces with particular affective dispositions, constructing certain places as object of love, and others as objects of fear or hate. Ahmed's theory allows us to take into account how geopolitical imaginaries may be produced not by explicit statements but in more implicit ways. She suggests that emotions work by the creation of "sticky associations". Through repetition and proximities in speech, different discursive figures stick together so that when people hear the one they will think of the other. Certain words can evoke historical narratives and past associations so that explicit allegations become unnecessary, as Ahmed puts it: "the undeclared history sticks" (2014: 47). These links are often not articulated by substantial arguments or coherent narratives; they do not need to "make sense" because they work on an emotional rather than cognitive level. In some cases, even when a connection is explicitly denied, sticky associations may still be reproduced.

Much Russian media reporting on LGBT issues relied on precisely such sticky associations. The figure of the homosexual was put in proximity to various negatively connoted figures, implicitly suggesting a link between them and making homosexuality appear as dangerous and worthy of contempt. The visual imagery, that is, the sequencing or combination of certain images, and the interrelation between texts and images, was often crucial in the production of stickiness. One example was a news clip on *Channel One* (Blagoi 2013), first showing Putin at a press conference in the Netherlands answering questions from Western journalists about LGBT issues in Russia, and was then immediately followed by a clip about the founding of a pedophile party in the Netherlands, the reporter sarcastically remarking that this was "a wonder of Dutch tolerance". The clip was illustrated by images of bearded men with children in their laps. The final clip returned to the press conference, with Putin saying: "I find it difficult to believe that any court in Moscow would allow an organization that propagandizes pedophilia to continue working. In Holland it is possible, there is such an organization". In this clip, it was not explicitly stated that LGBT people are pedophiles, or have anything to do with pedophiles, but the association was established nonetheless, by placing the two 'deviant' figures close to each other.

A similar stickiness was produced by Russian media reporting on Ukraine during the 2013–14 Maidan protests and the following war, where links between homosexuals and various suspicious political figures were made. Under the headline "Gay fuel on the Maidan bonfire: Ukraine is invited to Europe by nationalists, anti-Semites, neo-Nazis and homosexuals", *Komsomolskaya Pravda* (2013) wrote about the German Foreign Minister Guido Westerwelle visiting Ukraine in support of the Maidan protesters. In the article, it was repeatedly emphasized that the minister was accompanied by his husband. No open allegations were made about homosexual activists cooperating with Ukrainian neo-Nazis, but by mentioning the figures together, a link was suggested. A possible effect of such representations was a transfer of emotion, that the hatred and disgust associated with Nazism among the Russian public, fueled by the collective trauma of the Second World War (which affected nearly every Russian family), would somehow stick to the figure of the homosexual.

Moreover, the reporting about homosexuals involved in the Maidan revolution could function as a confirmation of the fear that also in Russia, domestic LGBT activists sponsored from abroad might come to undermine political stability. The Kremlin-friendly newspaper *Izvestiya*, citing a report by Russian political scientists, warned about the prospect of a "sexual gay-revolution, accompanied by the collapse of an already weakening societal morality" that would throw Russia back to the "chaos of the 1990s" (Podosenov 2013). Thus, in the geopolitical imaginary of the dominant narrative, lesbians and gays were ambivalently located on what Didier Bigo (2001) calls the "Möbius ribbon" of internal and external security. Symbolically placed both outside and inside the community, homosexuals were narrated as ominous reminders of an unsafe external world. Given this framing, it is not surprising that international criticism of the LGBT rights situation was interpreted through a geopolitical lens in Russian media. Russia's ambassador to the EU said that criticism of the propaganda law from EU leaders was a way to distract attention from the economic crisis in Europe (RIA Novosti 2013). Western criticism against Russia's LGBT politics before the Sochi Olympics was interpreted as an aggressive attack on Russia's sovereignty (Grishin 2013).

As mentioned previously, global contestations of sexual politics often revolve around temporal notions such as "tradition" and "modernity". According to Homi Bhabha (1994: 140), the practice of imagining communities necessitates the enforcement of one hegemonic temporality, a narrative of a shared past and common future, superseding possible competing and contradictory histories. People imagined as Others are then associated with other temporalities and represented as existing in another time. Not surprisingly, political efforts to define what constitutes normal sexual practices "here" and "there" reproduce and rely on certain notions of time and history. Today, in the rhetoric of many Western politicians and activists, LGBT rights (as well as gender equality) are represented as intrinsically bound up with modernity, as a measure of the advancement of a society (Puar 2007). States not respecting LGBT rights are claimed to be "on the wrong side of history", a phrase expressing a unidirectional and deterministic view on the relation between sexual liberation and time. The dominant Russian anti-gay narrative challenged the idea of a uniform modernity following the Western example. European modernity was represented as derailed: a telling parallel was made in a radio interview with a Russian politician who compared same-sex marriages to nuclear energy, once considered the peak of modernity but now being closed down (gayRussia.com 2013a). The idea that Russia, for historical, cultural and religious reasons, should not imitate the Western model of modernity but must follow a "special path" constitutes, according to Pain and Verkhovskii (2012), the closest that post-Soviet Russia comes to a state ideology.

However, the search for an alternative modernity is far from unique to Russia. In today's world, there is an intensified struggle over the content and ownership of modernity. Calhoun (2007: 170) argues that we should talk of modernities in plural, and Appadurai (1996) has famously claimed that modernity is "at large". Contestations around modernity are more than a question of competing cultural preferences about how to lead the "good life"; they are at the heart of global power politics. The claim to represent modernity is a powerful political resource, which has historically justified control and violence against colonized populations as well as domestic minority groups. In the words of Judith Butler: "…power relies on a certain taken-for-granted notion of historical progress to legitimate itself as the ultimately modern achievement" (2008: 21). Similarly, the repeated invocation of "traditional values" in contemporary Russian discourse should be seen in this light. Craig Calhoun (2007) points out that tradition is a political project, something that is continually reproduced, rather than a fixed, pre-determined cultural reality. Tradition is not only about the past but is both backward- and forward-looking and should not be understood as existing in opposition to modernity, but rather as a way to negotiate modernity. Russia's narrative of an alternative modernity and the turn toward "traditional values" is thus a political struggle over identity and modernity, which makes sense only in the context of globalization and contentious global geopolitics.

In the Russian media reporting about the ban on "homosexual propaganda", the issue of lesbian and gay rights was repeatedly linked to the question of Russia's influence and standing in the world. To understand this framing, one must take into account the increased global polarization and heated international debates around LGBT rights that have emerged in the twenty-first century (Altman and Symons 2016). The material on which this study is based indicates that in Russian public discourse, the LGBT issue has become intertwined in the negotiation of what should be Russia's geopolitical role in a post-Cold War world order. In a speech to the Federal Assembly in December 2013, Putin lamented what he described as the erasure of moral norms and national traditions in many countries, instigated "from above" against the will of the people. Fortunately, however, he had observed that more and more people in the world were supporting Russia's position in defending "traditional values" regarding family, religion and a "genuine human life" (Channel One 2013). More explicitly, Pavel Danilin, well-known political scientist ideologically close to the Kremlin, articulated a similar idea:

... the experiments of political correctness regarding sexual minorities, going on all over the world, provoke disgust and contempt. Russia could of course attain a high-profile position in relation to such progressive legislations, and become a landmark for many intellectuals who enjoy seeing the decadence in Western Europe (...) Thus, Russia could clearly and unambiguously delineate its position and become a moral leader. (Baev 2013)

The idea of Russia as an international beacon of "traditional values" echoes of older missionary narratives of Russia's role in the world, such as the pre-revolutionary idea of Moscow as a "Third Rome" embodying true Christianity after the fall of the Roman and Byzantine empires, as well as the Soviet rhetoric of liberating workers across the world (Duncan 2002). The above suggests that the Russian state's turn to "traditional values" does not merely represent a defensive and inward-looking reaction to globalization and perceived threats to established norms of gender and sexuality. On the contrary, this move constitutes an element of an activist and revisionist foreign policy, a soft power initiative that sends a message about Russia's importance in world affairs, as a purported leader in a transnational conservative axis.

## An Ambivalent Mapping

Though the dominant discourse appears to produce a clear-cut and binary geography of a "gay-friendly" West versus a Russia defending "traditional values", at closer scrutiny, this mapping was neither rigid nor monolithic. Historically, narratives of Russia's geopolitical identity have been characterized by ambivalence, contradiction and dramatic shifts. The Russian self has been imagined in relation to two significant Others—Europe and Asia—providing a tripartite scheme for identification and dis-identification. Dostoevsky described this experience: "in Europe we were hangers-on and slaves, while in Asia we shall be masters. In Europe we were the Tatars, while in Asia we are the Europeans" (Shkandrij 2001: 16). Madina Tlostanova characterizes Russia as a Janus-faced "subaltern empire" which feels itself a colony in the presence of the West. On the one hand, Russia is the center of an empire and imagined as a provider of law and modernity. On the other hand, there is a sense of inferiority vis-à-vis the West, a form of implicit acceptance of the "epistemic bondage" of global coloniality, which posits the Western trajectory as a universal model of development.

> The subaltern empire, even when claiming a global spiritual and transcendental superiority, has always been looking for approval/envy and love/hatred from the west, never questioning the main frame of western modernity, only changing the superfluous details. (2012)

Russia's cultural subjection to global coloniality is, according to Tlostanova (2012), expressed by a historical vacillation between excessive mimicry of the West and nativist rejection of all things considered Western.

The dominant discourse on the 2013 ban on "homosexual propaganda" was characterized precisely by this awkward relation to the West. On the one hand, by framing the ban in counterhegemonic terms, as a defense against perceived Western incursions on Russia's sovereignty in the form of promoting universal gay recognition and same-sex marriage across the world, Russian politicians legitimated the ban using the West as a constant point of reference, a measure and standard. These motivations for introducing the ban were meaningful only in relation to the figure of the West; in consequence, that figure functioned as a constitutive Other, necessary to the idea of Russian "traditional sexuality", and to Russian identity more broadly.

On the other hand, when Putin defended the ban in 2013, his reference to homophobia in Chechnya (where he claimed that same-sex marriage would "result in casualties" if introduced in this region) deployed another logic within the complex scheme of overlapping self-Other relations which informs rhetoric on gay rights in Russia. This was not the only example where Russian officials justified the 2013 ban by claiming that increased LGBT visibility would provoke violence among Russia's Muslim citizens. The chairman of the Constitutional Court of Russia, Valery Zorkin, used the hypothetical example of an imagined gay parade in Dagestan, a Muslim-majority republic neighboring Chechnya, suggesting that the violent reactions such a march would provoke indicated the impossibility of allowing LGBT recognition in Russia (gayRussia.com 2013b). An official from the republic of Udmurtia said, on the topic of gay rights: "...don't forget that Islam is strong here. Therefore, such things are not acceptable" (gayRussia.ru 2013c). In contrast to the arguments supporting the ban that invoke anti-Western sentiments, this second form of reasoning does not position Russia as the injured "subaltern" assailed by the West but rather as an "empire" with a responsibility to uphold law and order and accommodate a multi-confessional population by respecting their religious and cultural demands, in this case preventing presumably anti-gay and violence-prone Muslims from being provoked by homosexuals.

According to historian Dan Healey, the tripartite geographical imaginary of Russia situated in-between Europe and Asia enabled Russians in the late nineteenth and early twentieth century to imagine their nation as sexually pure and innocent, by contrasting it to the depraved sexual habits of "civilized" Europe on the one hand and to the uninhibited sexuality of a "primitive" Orient (embodied by Muslim-dominated regions in the Caucasus and Central Asia) on the other (Healey 2001: 251f). The Russian media discourse in 2013, in comparison, produced a sexual geography where Russia was awkwardly positioned between a "gay-friendly" West aggressively promoting sexual liberation, and an "anti-gay" Muslim Other, perceived as aggressively intolerant and hostile to cultural change. Curiously, the idea of the need to restrict gay rights out of respect for Russia's Muslims both mirrors and reverses the Western homonationalist narrative that Islam endangers the freedom and security of gays (Puar 2007). In both cases, the repression of one minority population is justified (by representatives of the majority) by the need to protect and respect another minority population. Thus, the sliding in dominant Russian discourse between the idea that gay rights contradict Russian "traditional values" and the idea that they are a security threat as they risk provoking Russia's Muslims, indicates that the LGBT question is entangled in multiple contradictory logics of cultural differentiation, and the dominant discourse less fixed and coherent than it may appear.

The reports of an anti-gay persecution wave in Chechnya in early 2017 appeared to confirm the fears expressed by Putin and others about homophobia among Russia's Muslims. Especially so since, according to the first reports, the events had, apparently, been provoked by applications filed by a Russian LGBT organization to organize Pride marches in several cities in the North Caucasus, although it was soon revealed that the anti-gay campaign had been initiated several weeks before those applications were made (Milashina and Gordinenko 2017). The contradiction at the heart of sexuality discourse in Russia made possible an externalization of homophobia, allowing Russian officials to disavow anti-gay violence and position Russia as a force of order and civilization vis-à-vis "backwards" Chechnya. Crucially, such a disavowal conceals the political context in which the purges in Chechnya occurred. It overlooks that the events fit well into the pattern of how the Putin-supported Kadyrov regime represses groups perceived as threatening with silent approval from the Kremlin, as well as the general climate of searching for internal enemies in contemporary Russia, bolstered by projects such as the ban on "homosexual propaganda".

## Conclusion: Beyond the "Gay Divide"

This chapter has examined how political regulations of "normal" and "deviant" sexualities are enmeshed in state projects of geopolitical boundary-making. It complements a literature that has hitherto often regarded homophobia from a more biopolitical perspective, that is, as tied to efforts to govern a national population and its future reproduction. Drawing on Russian media material about the 2013 law on "propaganda for non-traditional sexual relationships", and discussing the findings in light of the 2017 anti-gay campaign in Chechnya, I have made two claims. Firstly, that Russia's rejection of LGBT rights is a vital dimension of its efforts to profile Russia as a global leader of "traditional values", in the context of increased international polarization around sexuality politics. Secondly, that this project is characterized by an internal split produced by overlapping contradictory self-Other relations, positioning Russia as simultaneously a counterhegemonic actor resisting the West's enforcement of gay rights, *and* as a source of order and modernity in relation to Russia's own, purportedly homophobic, Muslim population.

Thus, despite the staunch and categorical anti-gay rhetoric of its political leaders, narratives on sexual rights in Russia are contradictory, unstable and subject to change. This has implications for global sexual politics, where the conflicts are often articulated in binary and civilizational terms by both proponents and opponents of LGBT rights, as Russian rhetoric on a gay war between Russia and the West is mirrored by Western accounts such as *The Economist*'s (2014) identification of a "gay divide" between countries that are "friendly to gays" and "parts of the world where it is not safe to be homosexual". The latter kind of model not just overlooks gray zones and internal stratifications of sexual politics but provides an unhelpful ground for global solidarity. As Joan Scott (2007: 19) argues, a worldview organized in simple oppositional terms is one we inhabit at our risk, because dichotomies blind us to complexities but also create their own realities, leaving no room for change or self-reflection. While providing assistance to local activists on the terms that they request is essential, international polarization and highly pitched condemnation campaigns may prompt further entrenched positions around sexual rights, closing avenues for dialogue and keeping queers as hostages in global power politics (Altman and Symons 2016: 157). As an alternative to viewing homophobia as indicative of cultural backwardness, we should, as suggested by Puar and Rai (2002), "disrupt the neat folding of queerness into narratives of modernity, patriotism and nationalism". Although popular attitudes to sexual diversity undoubtedly vary in different parts of the world, the recent upsurge of political homophobia in Russia (and most likely elsewhere) cannot be explained and addressed as simply a result of "lingering traditional attitudes" but as a decidedly *contemporary* negotiation of identity, security and political influence in a contested and unequal global order. If we regard fault lines of sexual politics not as primarily existing between, but *within* and *across* cultures, nation-states and regions, we will more likely be able to perceive similarities as well as differences between various local patterns of domination and resistance, which forms a firmer and more relevant starting point for political analysis and global solidarity.

# References

Ahmed, Sara. 2014. *The Cultural Politics of Emotion*. 2nd ed. Edinburgh: Edinburgh University Press.

Altman, Dennis, and Jonathan Symons. 2016. *Queer Wars: The New Global Polarization over Gay Rights*. Cambridge: Polity.

Amar, Paul. 2013. *The Security Archipelago: Human-Security States, Sexuality Politics and the End of Neoliberalism*. Durham/London: Duke University Press.

Amnesty International. 2016. Russian Federation: The Federal Authorities Must Respond Immediately and Decisively to Latest Threats Against Human Rights Defenders, Journalists and Political Activists. Amnesty International Public Statement. https://www.amnesty.org/en/documents/eur46/3255/2016/en/. Accessed 19 May 2017.

Appadurai, Arjun. 1996. *Modernity at Large. Cultural Dimensions of Globalization*. Minneapolis/London: University of Minnesota Press.

Baev, Nikolai. 2013. Gomofobnuyu Rossiyu khotyat sdelat' 'moralnym liderom' mira. *GayRussia.ru*, June 8. http://www.gayRussia.eu/Russia/5800/. Accessed 12 June 2013.

Banting, Mark, Catriona Kelly, and James Riordan. 1998. Sexuality. In *Russian Cultural Studies. An Introduction*, ed. Catriona Kelly and David Shepherd, 311–351. Oxford: Oxford University Press.

Bhabha, Homi. 1994. *The Location of Culture*. London/New York: Routledge.

Bigo, Didier. 2001. The Möbius Ribbon of Internal and External Security(ies). In *Identities, Borders, Orders: Rethinking International Relations Theory*, ed. Mathias Albert, David Jacobson, and Yosef Lapid, 91–116. Minneapolis: University of Minnesota Press.

Blagoi, Ivan. 2013. Obnazhennye feministki i demonstratsii geev stali fonom vizita Vladimira Putina v Niderlandy. *Channel One*, April 14. http://www.1tv.ru/news/polit/230800. Accessed 23 May 2017.

Brown, Wendy. 2006. *Regulating Aversion: Tolerance in the Age of Identity and Empire*. Princeton: Princeton University Press.

Butler, Judith. 2008. Sexual Politics, Torture, and Secular Time. *British Journal of Sociology* 59 (1): 1–23.

Calhoun, Craig. 2007. *Nations Matter: Culture, History, and the Cosmopolitan Dream*. London: Routledge.

Channel One. 2013. Vystupleniye Prezidenta RF V. Putina s poslaniyem Federal'nomu sobraniyu (polnaya versiya), December 12. http://www.1tv.ru/news/polit/248171. Accessed 13 June 2014.

Duncan, Peter J.S. 2002. *Russian Messianism: Third Rome, Holy Revolution, Communism and After*. London: Routledge.
Edenborg, Emil. 2017. *Politics of Visibility and Belonging. From Russia's "Homosexual Propaganda" Laws to the Ukraine War*. London: Routledge.
Ekho Moskvy. 2017. LGBT-aktivisty rasskazali o sotn'akh presleduyemykh v Chechne geyakh, April 22. http://echo.msk.ru/news/1967850-echo.html. Accessed 19 May 2017.
Foucault, Michel. 1990. *The History of Sexuality. Vol. 1: The Will to Knowledge*. Harmondsworth: Penguin.
GayRussia.ru. 2013a. Vladimir Milov sravnil odnopolye braki s atomnymi stantsiyami. *GayRussia.ru*, May 10. http://www.gayRussia.eu/Russia/6463/. Accessed 26 June 2013.
———. 2013b. Valerii Zorkin razreshil rossiiskim regionam zapreshchat publichnye aktsii seksmenshinstv. *GayRussia.ru*, March 22. http://www.gayRussia.eu/Russia/6097/. Accessed 26 June 2013.
———. 2013c. Glava komiteta ZAGS Udmurtii rada, chto v Rossii zapreshcheny gei-braki. *GayRussia.ru*, May 15. http://www.gayRussia.eu/Russia/6512/. Accessed 26 June 2013.
Grishin, Aleksandr. 2013. Missis' Frai id'et na voinu s Rossiyei. *Komsomolskaya Pravda*, August 8.
Healey, Dan. 2001. *Homosexual Desire in Revolutionary Russia. The Regulation of Sexual and Gender Dissent*. Chicago/London: The University of Chicago Press.
Komsomolskaya, Pravda. 2013. Gei-drovishki v koster Maidana. *Komsomolskaya Pravda*, December 5. http://www.kp.ru/daily/26168.4/3055033/. Accessed 31 Mar 2015.
Kon, Igor. 1998. *Moonlight Love*. http://www.gay.ru/english/history/kon/index.htm. Accessed 19 May 2017.
Kost'uchenko, Elena. 2017. Vy ego ub'ete ili my ego ub'em. Monolog gomoseksuala, sbezhavshego iz Chechni. *Meduza*, April 16. https://meduza.io/feature/2017/04/16/vy-ego-ubiete-ili-my-ego-ubiem-vybirayte-chto-luchshe. Accessed 19 May 2017.
Kuntsman, Adi. 2009. *Figurations of Violence and Belonging. Queerness, Migranthood and Nationalism in Cyberspace and Beyond*. Oxford: Peter Lang.
Milashina, Elena. 2017a. Ubiistvo chesti. *Novaya Gazeta*, April 1.
———. 2017b. V Chechne idut profilakticheskie raboty. *Novaya Gazeta*, April 24.
Milashina, Elena, and Irina Gordinenko. 2017. Raspravy nad chechenskimi geyami. *Novaya Gazeta*, April 4.

Moss, Kevin. 2017. Russia as the Savior of European Civilization: Gender and the Geopolitics of Traditional Values. In *Anti-Gender Campaigns in Europe: Mobilizing against Equality*, ed. Roman Kuhar and David Patternotte. London: Rowman & Littlefield.

Mosse, George L. 1985. *Nationalism and Sexuality: Respectability and Abnormal Sexuality in Modern Europe*. New York: Howard Fertig.

Pain, Emil, and Aleksandr Verkhovskii. 2012. Civilizational Nationalism. The Russian Version of the 'Special Path'. *Russian Politics and Law* 50 (5): 52–86.

Patterson, Molly, and Kristen Renwick Monroe. 1998. Narrative in Political Science. *Annual Review of Political Science* 1 (1): 315–331.

Persson, Emil. 2015. Banning 'Homosexual Propaganda'. Belonging and Visibility in Contemporary Russian Media. *Sexuality & Culture* 19 (2): 256–274.

Podosenov, Sergei. 2013. Politicheskie eksperty predrekayut Rossii gei-revolyutsii. *Izvestiya*, June 24.

Puar, Jasbir K. 2007. *Terrorist Assemblages: Homonationalism in Queer Times*. Durham/London: Duke University Press.

Puar, Jasbir K., and Amit S. Rai. 2002. Monster, Terrorist, Fag: The War on Terrorism and the Production of Docile Patriots. *Social Text* 20 (3): 117–148.

RIA Novosti. 2013. Chizhov: Diskussiya po otmene viz mezhdu Rossiei i ES na finalnom etape. *RIA Novosti*, May 24. http://ria.ru/interview/20130524/939280140.html. Accessed 19 June 2013.

Riabov, Oleg, and Tatiana Riabova. 2014. The Decline of Gayropa? How Russia Intends to Save the World. *Eurozine*. http://www.eurozine.com/the-decline-of-gayropa/. Accessed 23 May 2017.

Scott, Joan W. 2007. *The Politics of the Veil*. Princeton: Princeton University Press.

Shapiro, Michael J. 1997. *Violent Cartographies: Mapping Cultures of War*. Minneapolis: University of Minnesota Press.

Shevchenko, Maksim. 2013. My ne Evropa? I slava bogu!. *Moskovskii Komsomolets*, February 11.

Shkandrij, Myroslav. 2001. *Russia and Ukraine: Literature and the Discourse of Empire from Napoleonic to Postcolonial Times*. Chesham: Combined Academic Publishing.

Stella, Francesca. 2015. *Lesbian Lives in Soviet and Post-Soviet Russia: Post/Socialism and Gendered Sexualities*. New York: Palgrave Macmillan.

Stella, Francesca, and Nadya Nartova. 2016. Sexual Citizenship, Nationalism and Biopolitics in Putin's Russia. In *Sexuality, Citizenship and Belonging: Trans-National and Intersectional Perspectives*, ed. Francesca Stella, Yvette Taylor, Tracey Reynolds, and Antoine Rogers, 17–36. London: Routledge.

The Economist. 2014. The Gay Divide, October 11. http://www.economist.com/news/leaders/21623668-victories-gay-rights-some-parts-world-have-provoked-backlash-elsewhere-gay. Accessed 15 Jan 2015.

Tlostanova, Madina. 2012. Postsocialist≠ Postcolonial? On Post-Soviet Imaginary and Global Coloniality. *Journal of Postcolonial Writing* 48 (2): 130–142.

Weiss, Meredith L., and Michael J. Bosia. 2013. *Global Homophobia: States, Movements, and the Politics of Oppression*. Urbana/Chicago/Springfield: University of Illinois Press.

Yuval-Davis, Nira. 1997. *Gender and Nation*. London: Sage.

# 5

# The Formation of an Israeli Gay 'Counterpublic': Challenging Heteronormative Modes of Masculinity in a 'Nation in Arms'

Yoav Kanyas

This chapter argues that normative ideas about "appropriate" modes of masculinity are deeply embedded in the Israeli national imaginary; the inclusion of gay men is particularly challenging for the militarized Israeli government whose nationalism seeks to reify hegemonic and heteronormative forms of masculinity as part of the nation building process (Melamed 2004; Sasson-Levi 2006). This chapter provides a case study that demonstrates the struggles gay men have faced in obtaining recognition and legitimacy from both the Israeli government and Israeli society. Using archival material, I explore media coverage of a controversy related to gay men's right to public space; specifically, I will look at Tel Aviv's Independence Park. I maintain that this historical struggle, which lasted through the 1990s and the beginning of the twenty-first century, as well as the media coverage of it (in both the mainstream and gay and lesbian press), helped to strengthen LGBT activism in Israel and has

Y. Kanyas (✉)
Department of Communication and Journalism, Hebrew University of Jerusalem, Jerusalem, Israel

extended some of the rights afforded to gay men (and the LGBT[1] public more widely).[2]

While much of the literature on gay men in Israel employs the commonly used term "gay community", I suggest that Michael Warner's term "counterpublic" (Warner 2002) is more appropriate, as this definition extends beyond communal ties and explores how gay people organize themselves independently of state institutions, law, or formal frameworks of citizenship. Further, "counterpublics" are formed through a conflictual relation to dominant discourses, and counterpublics are able to use different dispositions and maintaining conscious or unconscious awareness of its subordinate status (*ibid*). In my media analysis, the case of Israeli gay men fits this meaning, as the consumption of gay media played the central role in their emergence as a social and political force. In order to discuss the process of forming a gay men's counterpublic in Israel's heteronormative modes of masculinity, I will first explore the sources of the states' national and gender characteristics.

## The Israeli Nation and Masculinity

Israel was established in 1948 on dominant masculine values, such as physical and emotional strength and sexual potency, which were cultivated within Zionism (the major Israeli national ideology, originating in the nineteenth century) as the antithesis to the image of the feminine, passive, and physically weak Jew in exile (Boyarin 1997; Gilman 1993; Weininge 1906). Like many other national movements, Zionism preserved traditional family values and norms concerning fertility, sexuality, and gender roles (Mosse 1985; Nagel 1998). For instance, Maxwell (2005) shows how in the Habsburg Empire female sexuality was associated with cultural concepts of nationality, while male sexuality reflected statehood and political nationalism. Massad (1995) argues that although

---

[1] Due to the limitations of this chapter, I have chosen not to discuss Israeli society's and government's relation to lesbians, which is subtle and complex and deserves a separate discussion.

[2] However, the complexity of Israeli nationalism means that the underlying issues here about "appropriate" modes of masculinity are still problematic, as is the meaningful inclusion of gay men as citizens of Israel (e.g., recent legislation that forbids LGBT couples to adopt).

masculinity was always the identitarian pole of European nationalist thought, Palestinian nationalism endorsed Western and colonial gendered narratives, which included the metaphor of the nation as a mother- or fatherland. It also included the practice of defending and administering these narratives with homosocial institutions like the military and the bureaucracy, as well as gendered strategies of reproducing. Norms around sexual decency were also inherited in part from the Jewish pioneers' European past, as most of them were brought up in religious families, which sanctified conservative Jewish values. An ethos of asceticism was thus cultivated, including practices that limited sexual contact and highly rigid, normative rules that governed expressions of sexuality in heterosexual courtship (Almog 1998) (and concurrently further disenfranchised LGBT people as well).

The role of military service in Israel, and for young men in particular, was a result of hegemonically masculine nation building, which fits sociologists' (Lissak 2007; Sasson-Levi 2006) references to the state as a "nation in arms". This characteristic means that the army has a central role in the formation process of Israeli society's national identity. Moreover, the army functions as a melting pot for Jewish immigrants, who come from all over the globe to the Jewish state, as well as being an entrance ticket into Israeli civil society. According to the 5709-1949 Defense Service Law, Israeli military service is mandatory for every citizen, so that every 18-year-old boy is drafted for three years of service and every girl for two years.[3] As every Israeli citizen has to pass through the army, Levy (2003) and other sociologists (c.f. Kimmerling 1993) see it as an organization standing apart from Israeli society's other divisions (political, class, ethnicity), and as such it is considered an objective product of a universal sorting system, under the influence of no particular social or political group. Consequently, military service has become a significant criterion for evaluating a social, personal, or group activity, even in the civilian sphere. Militarism has also penetrated the education system and created a socialization mechanism, which cultivated a martial culture.

---

[3] It is important to note that Israel is one of the few nations in the world in which women are conscripted to the army. This fact makes the issue of how "appropriate" femininities fit into the national imaginary more complex; however, this is beyond the scope of this chapter. For useful reading on this issue, see Brownfield-Stein 2012, Izraeli 1999, and Sasson-Levi 2006.

The Israeli government in the nation's first decades cultivated heteronormative modes of masculinity by enhancing the importance of heteronormative family values and birth rate. Motivated by the demographic race against Israel's Arab citizens (Melamed 2004), this policy strengthened the state's endorsement of heteronormative values, which implicitly resent homosexuality.[4] Religion is also vital to the discussion of homosexuality in Israeli society, as Orthodox Jews held, and hold, central positions in Israel's parliament and government offices. They have always resented any liberal approach toward homosexuality, maintaining that the Bible explicitly forbids homosexuality (according to Leviticus 18:22). As a result, it was almost impossible for a long period to effect any change concerning gay men's issues either in Israeli law or in public opinion.

## Gay Legislation in Israel

When the State of Israel was established in 1948, it adopted some of the legislation enacted by the British Mandate, which had ruled the country prior to independence. One of these laws was Section 152 of the criminal law, which included a sub-section prohibiting sodomy. One can interpret this act as a product of the long colonialist regime in the land of Israel (or Palestine). Consequently, the European Jewish settlers, while rising up against the British authority, still saw themselves as superior to the native Arabs, and this orientalist perspective (Said 1978) was maintained by the Zionist government. Thus, the Zionist rulers saw themselves as successors to the British, who had to restrain the natives' uninhibited sexuality (which alludes to orientalist myths such as Sodom and Gomorrah). The sodomy legislation therefore appears to have been formed as part of a colonial discourse, which was in turn based on an orientalist knowledge of cultural and racial differences between Western Jewish citizens and Eastern Arab ones (Bhabha 1996).

---

[4] This policy was ultimately changed in response to the high birth rate in the ultra-Orthodox population, whose children are exempted from military service for the sake of learning in the Torah "yeshivot". However, this is an issue in its own right, which again is beyond the scope of this chapter.

The punishment for breaking the sodomy law was a ten-year prison sentence. However, in 1953, the legal advisor to the Israeli government instructed the Director of Public Prosecutions to avoid filing charges for violating this law; he also instructed the police in 1956 not to investigate suspects of this felony, as to do so was immoral in his opinion (Yonay and Spivak 1999). This policy shows the diversity of Israel's society and legislation, which combines liberal (democratic) with conservative (religious) elements. Israeli sociologists explain this diversity via the contradictory self-definition of the state in its Declaration of Independence (1948) as the land of the Jewish people while sanctifying democratic values such as equal rights, justice, and liberty for citizens of all religions.[5] This duality was also manifested in the failure of a number of attempts to repeal homophobic legislation in the 1960s and 1970s. Nevertheless, it was not until 1988 that this section of the sodomy law was abolished, thanks to liberal members of parliament who promoted this change in the face of opposition from the religious and conservative parties.

However, this change in the law was also part of the wider changing social and political atmosphere in Israeli society during the 1980s, which brought civil rights discourse to the public sphere, including LGBT rights. From a political perspective, the outbreak of the first Lebanon war (1982–1985) provoked an unprecedented public debate about the necessity of the war and its consequences for Arab and Jewish citizens. This controversy shook Israeli hegemony and undermined the consensual national loyalty among Jewish citizens. Thus, Israeli society became more divided between citizens who supported a conservative national military agenda and those who were concerned about the state's civic and democratic foundations, which were jeopardized by the ongoing occupation of the Palestinian territories (Shafir and Peled 2002). This discourse became even more radical when the first Intifada started in 1987 (it ended in 1993 with the Oslo Accords), when Palestinians rose up against Israeli military rule in the West Bank (Hechter 2014).

I argue that by this time, as the Israeli government was dealing with the implications of the Palestinian occupation, it became easier for the internal discussion concerning LGBT rights to proceed. As the left-wing

---

[5] For further reading about this duality, see Neuberger 1997, Smooha 2002, and Ram 2000.

protest movement against the occupation grew in the 1990s, gay activists began to recruit these activists for their struggle too. Thus, gradually, the legal system and Israeli society were becoming increasingly tolerant of LGBT rights—at the expense of the continued denial of those rights of the Palestinians in the occupied territories (c.f. Puar 2013). Homophobic policies and attitudes forced Israeli gay men to socialize outside the prying eyes of the public, and Tel Aviv's Independence Park provided an important public space for these men. The following analysis charts the transformation of the park's image in the media, and considers how this particular example can reveal the social and political dynamics that attempt to regulate normative modes of sexuality.

## Methodology

Analyzing a range of media texts about Independence Park, and the appropriation of this space by gay men using critical discourse analysis (CDA) (c.f. Wodak and Meyer 2001), this chapter examines both the diachronic dimensions and the socio-political context in which these texts were produced and distributed. CDA is a practical tool to deconstruct and interpret media representations and constructions of reality, and to identify how these relate to broader societal debates (Nickels et al. 2012). The research corpus is based on an extensive survey of the documents concerning Tel Aviv's Independence Park, originated in the city council's archives. The search included references to the park from 1952 to 2004 in the main daily newspapers *Haaretz*, *Maariv*, *Yediot Ahronoth*, *Al HaMishmar*, and *Davar*; the local newspaper *Yedioth Iriat Tel Aviv*; and the gay and lesbian magazines *Hazman Havarod* and *Magaim*.

## The Symbolic Significance of Independence Park and Its Uses by Gay Men

Independence Park was established as part of the "green urbanism agenda" (Olmsted 2003; Schultz 1989). This agenda originated in the nineteenth century "American Park movement", which defined the parks' main goal as serving as a safe public space for middle-class women, whose daily life was limited to the private sphere as it was deemed unsafe for them to walk the city's streets (Evelev 2014). Thus, public parks' design as neutral calm spaces refuted the commercialized, overcrowded, male-dominated inner-city streets. Furthermore, public parks' original aim was to be a gathering place for relaxation and enjoyment of the working- and middle-class family (Olmsted 2003). However, the liminal nature of urban parks often enabled their visitors to deviate from their intended social and sexual public behavior (Hirsch 1999). In the era before gay bars or clubs, "cruising" became popular in many urban spaces (Chauncey 1994; Delph 1978; Higgs 1999; Warren 1999) and gave gay men the opportunity to meet in public spaces to arrange and negotiate sexual and social encounters.

Tel Aviv's Independence Park is particularly interesting to consider, given its national symbolic meaning: the park was planned, and planting after the War of Independence (1948) and its opening included a military ceremony followed by the erection of a monument to pilots killed in combat. Thus, the sexual and social uses of the park by gay men, excluded from other public places, subverted the park's nationalistic, heteronormative order. In order to demonstrate these changes in the park's symbolic public image, I first examine the media coverage of gay men's activity in Independence Park as represented in both mainstream and gay print media. In my analysis, firstly, I will show how the gay press transformed the image of the public park from a degrading symbol of gay men into a symbol of social power. Secondly, I will demonstrate how this social power formed a politically active LGBT counterpublic, in turn strengthening the status of LGBT people within Israeli society.

## Independence Park's National Symbolic Transformation

Independence Park's establishment by Tel Aviv city council marked it as a national symbol for Israel's independence, as well as a relaxation place for the heteronormative family (Mozes 2002). On the park's opening day (2.11.1952), the chairman of the city's "planting committee" stated in the local newspaper that planting public parks in the city was part of a national goal to turn the wasteland into a blossoming area, and to reinforce the Jewish people's grip of its land (Shoshani 1952). Building the park on the remains of a Muslim cemetery—part of an Arab settlement which had been destroyed during the British Mandate period and Israel's War of Independence—reinforced its national meaning. The park's establishment was therefore part of the process of erasing the city's Arab history (Rotbard 1978) under the guise of the "green agenda". On the park's launch day, the city council distributed a pamphlet explaining the park's planning and history. Above the picture of the planting area was the headline *Park = Independence*, which enhanced the symbolic analogy between the park's planting and the independence of the Jewish people.[6]

However, this national image changed, as an article in the Ministry of Environment's magazine indicates: the park used to be a center of social and cultural activities, but nearly 30 years later, "its glow has been dimmed" (Yahav 1981). This was due to its transformation from a leisure spot designated for families in the honeymoon years of the birth of the Israeli state in the 1950s, to a more insidious location in the 1980s, when the park became a space that attracted "deviant visitors (partly criminal), who made it impossible for 'normal' men, women, and children to have a routine walk in the park" (ibid.). This description signifies a warning for both the heteronormative citizens and the city council about the deteriorating national image of the park and its invasion by deviant visitors. Although Yahav did not name the "deviant visitors", it was clear to his readers, who were familiar with the mainstream media coverage, that he was mainly referring to gay visitors to the park.

The mainstream media did not begin to focus on the "deviant activity" taking place in the park until the end of the 1970s, but when they did, news articles consistently represented gay men's presence in the park as either immoral and deviant or criminal. The media frequently conflated being gay with criminality and prostitution, and the park was increasingly seen as space of deviance. The coverage of this "problematic" activity in mainstream new outlets perpetuated the image of the park as dangerous (particularly for women and children) (c.f. Azulay 1979; Bashan 1983).

---

[6] On the pamphlet it says that the area of the park is 70 dunams, but it would subsequently be expanded to 110 dunams when the Muslim cemetery was removed and incorporated into the park.

The AIDS crisis that erupted globally in the 1990s meant that this already deviant space was relabeled as "AIDS Park" (Gilboa 1990), in an attempt to create a script that painted gay men and gay spaces as dangerous. Global media coverage focused on the promiscuity of gays as the main cause of the spread of the virus (Albert 1986), and despite having very few cases of AIDS in Israel, national media coverage incorporated the same discourses. Labeling the park in such a way allows gay men to be constructed as a dangerous Other. One reporter describes the atmosphere in the park:

> It's 2.00am … Here, life has just begun … I look around terrified of seeing a familiar face. Maybe my neighbor will see me and think that I am one of those…You see everything, beatings, even with knives. Occasionally, the police come and everyone runs like mad to hide. (Gilboa 1990)

The reporter feared being seen and identified as one of the "promiscuous visitors", endangering his heterosexual masculinity. He justified his fears by describing the park as a battlefield and mentioning police persecution of the visitors for their unacceptable use of public space (police were constantly present in the park at this time). Therefore, although homosexuality was not a criminal offense anymore in Israel, when the article was published, gay men were still persecuted by the police, in their role as guardians of the national image of masculinity.

As Independence Park became a dominant gay symbol in Israeli mainstream media and society, the gay and lesbian press used it as a trope for the LGBT social struggle with the Israeli heteronormative national apparatus, by reporting extensively on incidents in the park. However, while the mainstream press tried to represent the park's gay image as menacing, the LGBT press embraced its alternative image, presenting it as a crucial site for gay men, which should be fought for and preserved for the sake of its visitors. My analysis of these alternative texts shows writers' intention to evoke readers' social and political consciousness, to stand up for their rights for social and sexual expression.

For instance, one issue of Israel's main gay magazine, *Hazman Havarod* (Pink Times), dedicated its cover story to the reconstruction work in the Park area, featuring the headline "Independence Park's extermination".

The term *extermination* presented an irreversible, drastic action and meant to invoke its readers to take action against the city council's oppression of the visitors. This term resonates with the Jewish national imaginary and collective memory of the Holocaust, in which Jews were "exterminated", as well as to the gay social identity of the readers, since the Nazis also sent homosexuals to their deaths. Therefore, this headline has a double meaning, which enhances on one hand the common national destiny of Jewish gay men with their nation and on the other their inferior social and citizenship status. In other words, the magazine editor insinuates that the Tel Aviv city council was acting like the Nazis, in persecuting their own people.

Two years later, however, Tel Aviv city council did in fact recognize the park's significance to gay men by inviting representatives of the LGBT Association to the city council's conference concerning a construction project near the park. This was the first official step of recognition and toward normalizing the link between a national symbol and gay men, thereby acknowledging them as citizens who had the right to have their social needs taken into consideration in urban planning. The LGBT Association's representatives' point of view was cited thus in the gay press coverage of the deliberation:

> One half of the park has already been plundered by the Hilton Hotel, the other half by the Hyatt…if no organized group cares about the flora… there won't be a park…Gays are its main users. The city council should deal with the residents' rights. For many men the park is all they have…Now, finally, we can speak for them. (Kesler 2000: 9)

These representatives defended the subversive use of the park for sexual encounters. Even though it is a public space owned by the city council and designated for all residents' use, the LGBT Association's representatives claimed to have priority and therefore interpreted building a hotel as an invasion of their territory. Gay men's struggle became political as the visitors—who were previously defenseless—had someone (albeit not appointed by them) who represented their needs. By covering the debate, the LGBT magazine's editorial board showed its readers that their subversive use of the park had an impact on the city council's strategic actions.

Therefore, gay men's presence in the park despite police harassment had actually a performative effect (Butler 1993), which helped change gay men's citizenship status.

Another piece of evidence demonstrating the rising social and political power of gay men and the symbolic transformation of Independence Park was manifested by the collaboration between gay representatives and the municipal establishment in organizing LGBT events in the park. One of these events was Wigstock, a 1998 AIDS benefit event, which ended in clashes after the police closed it down as it overran into Friday night, the Jewish Sabbath. This case demonstrates the collision between a principal signifier of the Jewish nation and gay men's desire for public sexual expression. It was also interpreted as a threat to Jewish Israeli masculinity by the policemen who were familiar with "the gay scene of the crime". The police wore rubber gloves during the evacuation of participants. This act enraged the participants, who responded with a spontaneous march in the streets of Tel Aviv protesting against such degrading treatment.

The protest was the first significant, large-scale, expression of social and political power by the LGBT counterpublic, and constituted a provocation to heteronormative modes of Israeli sexuality and gender, since it was led by drag queens confronting the macho aggression of police officers. The change of atmosphere at the following year's event was reported in *Hazman Havarod* magazine:

> A group of policemen stands [guarding the event] in Independence Park...a year after the battle...Blood and tears will not be shed here...Dozens of volunteers are hanging huge Aids ribbons, decorating the trees with safe sex advice.... (Ohana 1999: 16)

The writer's use of war terminology ("battle", "bloodshed") presents the park as a battlefield, in which people fought for their lives and their freedom. His focus on the police officers guarding the event highlights their acceptance of the park's norm breaking and shows they were actually protecting it. Thus, by sponsoring an AIDS event in Independence Park, both the municipal establishment and the police force acknowledged the park's non-normative nature, and accepted gay men's civic right to express their sexual and social identity in the public space, alongside heteronormative families.

While the Wigstock riots were a significant step in the LGBT counter-public's social and political struggle for recognition of their civil right to self-expression in public spaces, police officers continued to harass the gay "cruisers" in the park at night. The LGBT press therefore kept intensifying the signification of the public struggle over Independence Park by its consistent coverage of police interactions with the park's gay visitors. However, as opposed to the mainstream press coverage of the police actions as protecting "normative visitors", the gay and lesbian press focused on the police's deliberately violent treatment of the visitors to the park:

> For months Tel Aviv's "Blues" have been leaving blue marks on our friends at the park...none of the complaints about gay abuse have ended with prosecution, or any meaningful action against the cops involved. The cases were closed...due to lack of interest to the public. (Horowitz 2003: 8)

The writer argues that the police abused visitors intentionally as part of a mission to oppress their rights of movement and expression. Consequently, it did not investigate gay men's cases of abuse, although they occurred on a daily basis, as testified by the Gay and Lesbian Association Chairman in another article (Bogayski 2003a, b: 10). This appears to represent a deliberate policy of the police to ignore these cases for homophobic reasons.

Furthermore, *Hazman Havarod* magazine covered the abused victims' testimonies in addition to the response of the LGBT Association[7] Chairman, Alon Stricovsky: "We see a declaration of war by the police, so we are fighting back" (Ibid.). He announced the formation of a team of volunteers to defend visitors from police violence. This performative act of protest demonstrates the social and political ability of the gay counter-public to stand up to the agents of the state who were assigned to patrol the heteronormative boundaries of the public space. The use of war and

---

[7] The LGBT Association was established in 1975 under the undercover name: "The Association of Individual Rights" by a group of 12 gay men and one lesbian. For the first ten years they acted secretly from a member's home and only after the sodomy law was abolished (1988) did they start to take public action promoting LGBT rights, changing their name officially only at the beginning of the twenty-first century.

army terminology in Stricovsky's response resonates with the dominant masculine and martial nature of Israeli social discourse (Sasson-Levi 2006), deliberately aiming to break the stereotype of gays as effeminate and victimized. Consequently, this coverage entreated gay readers to fight against their own oppression by proving their masculinity.

This coverage of the alternative gay press helped to transform the park's image from a deviant forbidden space into a site of physical, political, and existential struggle for the gay counterpublic against the national heteronormative surveillance establishment. The gay visitors' representatives felt betrayed by the police, who, instead of looking out for their safety, chose to harm them. In response, they organized an autonomous unit to defend themselves. These actions signified a declaration of war over the national public space, on behalf of gay citizens' freedom to use it. The gay magazine emphasized the struggle's success in legitimizing the non-normative use of the public park through its reporting of a meeting between the LGBT Association representatives and police leaders, in which they discussed the severity of the situation, and reached an agreement to address it (Bogayski 2003a, b). This meeting was unprecedented, as gay men finally stood equally before a police force representing a national heteronormative establishment, and in doing so, asserting their official status as citizens entitled to police protection as they freely and safely use public space for their needs.

## Implications of Independence Park: On Israeli Nationalism, Masculinity, and Gay Men

This analysis of the social and political struggle over Tel Aviv's Independence Park reveals a complex discourse, conducted on three distinct levels: the physical level, concerned with the friction between gay "cruisers" and the police; the political level, focusing on the negotiations between LGBT representatives and the municipal and surveillance authorities; and the public discourse level, relating to the mainstream and gay press's function in the production of this discourse, which assisted in the formation of a gay counterpublic through the medium of coverage of the park. Through this layered discourse, which involves ideologies, norms, and values, one can learn about the abundance of meanings that are produced in the process of negotiations among different social groups concerning civil rights, citizenship, sexuality, and masculinity in the nation of Israel. This discourse also invoked national meanings, concerning Israel's image, history, and relations with its own varied groups of citizens as well as with its international enemies and allies.

I argue that these subversive performative actions, along with the 1998 Wigstock clashes, had a broad and immediate effect on gay men and the LGBT struggle toward obtaining recognition and legitimacy from both Israeli government and Israeli society. In the same year as the Wigstock troubles, openly gay and lesbian activists were elected for the first time to public positions such as membership of Tel Aviv city council (Michal Eden in 1998) and even membership of the Israeli parliament (Uzi Even in 2002).

However, this recognition would not have happened without the coverage of Independence Park controversy in both the mainstream and gay press, which produced various representations of both the park and gay men. This symbolic reality (Adoni and Mane 1984) produced a battle over the heteronormative national image of the park, as the mainstream press portrayed gay men as the park's dangerous enemy. Consequently, not only did heteronormative park visitors abstain, this representation also burnished the symbolic meaning of the park as "the gay men's park". The gay press adopted this ascription, adopting it as a banner in the LGBT fight for equal rights. Accordingly, it consistently covered the park's incidents, as well as published opinion and personal columns (Gaby 1999; Onger 2002), enhancing the park's centrality in readers' consciousness as well as reinforcing their emotional and political attachment to it.

This coverage played a major role in forming a strong infrastructure for a powerful and conscious gay counterpublic that could walk the streets and public parks of Tel Aviv as well as other cities in Israel more confidently and express their social and sexual identity more freely. This is evident, as ever since the successful negotiations between the LGBT Association representatives and police leaders concerning Independence Park, the cases of police and other harassments of gay men became numerous. Moreover, LGBT cooperation with the city council can be seen in the latter's enabling and support of the gay pride parade's overt presence in the public heteronormative space, which has taken over the streets of Tel Aviv annually since 1998. Every year the number of participants increases. For example, this year (2017) approximately 200,000 people participated in the event, as the city council promoted it around the world as a tourist attraction, and organized various gay events that same month (June). The gay-friendly concept, which started in Tel Aviv, has reached a national level, as the Ministry of Tourism and even the Ministry of Foreign Affairs have used the gay-friendly image in their international campaigns for promoting Israel's liberal spirit. While some researchers (Puar 2013; Hochberg 2010) have interpreted this move as "pinkwashing",[8] it also demonstrates the merging of the gay counterpublic with the dominant social and political national discourse while broadening the boundaries of the deeply rooted martial and macho Israeli masculinity.

Thus, one cannot ascribe the recognition and social status of the LGBT counterpublic in the Israeli nation to "Homonationalism" alone (Puar 2013), since this counterpublic stands strongly against conservative and regressive forces as well as against militaristic heteronormative modes of masculinity which still exist in national public affairs and even dominate large segments of Israeli government and formal institutions.

In conclusion, although the social reality of LGBT people in Israel has undergone a major transformation over the last 30 years, their struggle is far from over, given the conservative and regressive forces that still prevail among the Israeli public and institutions. However, through their struggle, gay men have made Israeli heteronormative society face its deepest fear of homosexuality, firmly established as it has been both in Jewish family values and in the image of Zionist national masculinity still cultivated by the Israeli government. Consequently, a struggle for free sexual expression in public spaces served to open a door to more fluid concepts of sexuality and gender.

---

[8] "Pinkwashing" is defined as a national discourse strategy which is meant to present Israel as a liberal state and society, using its tolerant policy toward its LGBT citizens. This discourse is aimed at gaining the liberal Western world's support in the Israel-Palestinian conflict vis-à-vis the homophobic policy of the Palestinian authorities (Puar, "Introduction", 32–35).

# References

Adoni, Hana, and Sherril Mane. 1984. Media and the Social Construction of Reality. *Communication Research* 11: 323–340.

Albert, Edward. 1986. Illness and Deviance: The Response of the Press to Aids. In *The Social Dimension of Aids: Method and Theory*, ed. Douglas A. Feldman and Thomas M. Johnson, 163–177. New York: Prager Publishers.

Almog, Oz. 1998. *The Sabra: A Profile*. Tel Aviv: Am Oved Publishers.

Azulay, Orly. 1979. Gvarim bamikzoa [in Hebrew]. *Yediot Aharonot: seven Yamim*, August 3, [in Hebrew].

Bashan, Tal. 1983. Erim baafela. *Maariv: Sof Shavua*, March 11, [in Hebrew].

Bhabha, H. K. 1996. The Other Question: Difference, Discrimination and the Discourse of Colonialism. In *Black British Cultural Studies: A Reader*, ed. Houston A. Baker Jr., Manthia Diawara, and Ruth H. Lindeborg, 87–107. Chicago/London: University of Chicago Press.

Bogayski, Yuval. 2003a. Zehiroot shotrim. *Hazman Havarod*, October, [in Hebrew].

———. 2003b. Haruchut nirgaot. *Hazman Havarod*, November, [in Hebrew].

Boyarin, Daniel. 1997. *Un Heroic Conduct: The Rise of Heterosexuality and the Invention of the Jewish Man*. Los Angeles: University of California Press.

Brownfield-Stein, Chava. 2012. *Fantasy of the State: Photographs of IDF Female Soldiers and the Eroticization of Civil Militarism in Israel*. Tel Aviv: Resling Publishing. [in Hebrew].

Butler, Judith. 1993. Critically Queer. *GLQ: A Journal of Lesbian and Gay Studies* 1 (November): 17–32.

Chauncey, George. 1994. *Gay New York: Gender, Urban Culture, and the Making of the Gay Male World, 1890–1940*. New York: Basic Books.

Dayan, Daniel, and Elihu Katz. 1994. *Media Events: The Live Broadcasting of History*. Cambridge, MA: Harvard.

Delph, Edward Williams. 1978. *The Silent Community*. Sage, London/Beverly Hills.

Evelev, John. 2014. Rus-Urban Imaginings: Literature of the American Park Movement and Representations of Social Space in the Mid-Nineteenth Century. *Early American Studies* 12 (1, winter): 174–201.

Filc, Dany. 2010. *The Political Right in Israel: Different Faces of Jewish Populism*. London: Routledge.

Gaby. 1999. Ad haoneg haba. *Hazman Havarod*, September, [in Hebrew].

Gilboa, Nir. 1990. Et Shoshi kvar lo roim po. *Al Hamishmar: Hotam*, March 23, [in Hebrew].
Gilman, Sander L. 1993. *Freud, Race, and Gender*. Princeton: Princeton University Press.
Hechter, Tirza. 2014. *The Yom Kippur War: Trauma, Memory and Myth (1973–2013)*. Ramat Gan: Tirza Hechter. [in Hebrew].
Higgs, David. 1999. *Queer Sights: Gay Urban Histories Since 1600*. London: Routledge.
Hirsch, Dafna. 1999. Independence Park: Homosexual Domain. *Architecture& Internal Design Quarterly* 36: 60–68. [in Hebrew].
Hochberg, Gil Z. 2010. Introduction: Israelis, Palestinians, Queers: Points of Departure. *A Journal of Lesbian and Gay Studies* 16 (4): 493–516.
Horowitz, Nizan. 2003. Al hasakin [in Hebrew]. *Hazman Havarod*, October, [in Hebrew].
Izraeli, Dafna. 1999. Gendering Military Service in the Israeli Defense Forces. *Theory & Criticism* 14: 85–109.
Kesler, Ron. 2000. Gan Hatzmaut mehapes adrichal nof. *Hazman Havarod*, October, [in Hebrew].
Kimmerling, Baruch. 1993. Patterns of Militarism in Israel. *European Journal of Sociology* 34 (2): 196–223.
Levy, Yagil. 2003. *The Other Army of Israel- Materialist Militarism in Israel*. Tel-Aviv: Yedioth Ahronoth Books. [in Hebrew].
Lissak, Moshe. 2007. The I.D.F. Between National and Communal Identities. In *Army, Memory and National Identity*, ed. Moshe Naor, 13–26. Jerusalem: The Hebrew university Magnes Press. [in Hebrew].
Massad, Joseph. 1995. Conceiving the Masculine: Gender and Palestinian Nationalism. *Middle East Journal* 49 (3): 467–483.
Maxwell, Alexander. 2005. Nationalizing Sexuality: Sexual Stereotypes in the Hapsburg Empire. *Journal of the History of Sexuality* 14 (3): 266–290.
Melamed, Shaham. 2004. Motherhood, Fertility and the Construction of the "Demographic Threat" in the Marital Age Law. *Theory and Criticism* 25 (Fall): 69–96. [in Hebrew].
Mosse, Gorge L. 1985. *Nationalism and Sexuality*. Madison: University of Wisconsin Press.
Mozes, Alon, T. 2002. *Text, Culture and the Meaning of the Hebrew Vernacular Garden in Israel: Tel Aviv and Its Surroundings*. Phd. dissertation, Technion-technological institute of Israel, Haifa [in Hebrew].

Nagel, Joane. 1998. Masculinity and Nationalism: Gender and Sexuality in the Making of Nations. *Ethnic and Racial Studies* 21: 242–269.
Neuberger, Benyamin. 1997. *Religion and Democracy in Israel*. Jerusalem: The Floersheimer Institute for Policy Studies.
Nickels, Henry C., Lyn Thomas, Mary J. Hickman, and Sara Silvestri. 2012. De/constructing "Suspect" Communities. *Journalism Studies* 13 (3): 340–355.
Ohana, Etay. 1999. Mizad hadivot hagdolot. *Hazman Havarod*, October, [in Hebrew].
Olmsted, Fredrick Law. 2003. Public Parks and the Enlargement of Towns. In *The City Reader*, ed. Richard T. Legates and Fredric Stout, 3rd ed., 302–308. London: Routledge.
Onger, Richie. 2002. Hameshtet. *Hazman Havarod*, February, [in Hebrew].
Puar, Jasbir K. 2013. Homonationalism as Assemblage: Viral Travels, Affective Sexualities. *Jindal Global Law Review* 4 (2): 23–43.
Ram, Uri. 2000. National, Ethnic or Civic?: Contesting Paradigms of Memory, Identity and Culture in Israel. *Studies in Philosophy and Education* 19 (5–6): 405–422.
Rotbard, Sharon. 1978. *White City Black City*. Tel Aviv: Babel. [in Hebrew].
Said, Edward. 1978. *Orientalism*. New York: Pantheon Books.
Sasson-Levi, Orly. 2006. *Identities in Uniform: Masculinities and Femininities in the Israeli Military*. Jerusalem: Hebrew University Magnes Press. [in Hebrew].
Schultz, Stanley K. 1989. *Constructing Urban Culture*. Philadelphia: Temple University Press.
Shafir, Gershon, and Yoav Peled. 2002. *Being Israeli: The Dynamics of Multiple Citizenship*. Cambridge: Cambridge University Press.
Shoshani, David. 1952. Tel Aviv: eir gamin [in Hebrew]. *Yediot Iriat Tel Aviv*, November.
Smooha, Sami. 2002. The Model of Ethnic Democracy: Israel as a Jewish and Democratic State. *Nations and Nationalism* 8 (4): 475–503.
Warner, M. Publics and Counterpublics. 2002. *Quarterly Journal of Speech* 88 (4): 413–425.
Warren, Carol A. 1999. Space and Time. In *Social Perspectives in Lesbian and Gay Studies*, ed. Peter M. Nardi and Beth E. Schneider, 183–193. New York/London: Routledge.
Weininge, Otto. 1906. *Sex & Character*. London: William Heinemann.
Wodak, Ruth, and Michael Meyer. 2001. *Methods of Critical Discourse Analysis*. London: Sage Publications.

Yahav, Dan. 1981. Gan hatzmaut—riat avir yeruka. *Habiosphera*, May, [in Hebrew].

Yonay, Yuval, and Dori Spivak. 1999. Between Silence and Damnation: The Construction of Gay Identity in the Israeli Legal Discourse, 1948–1988. *Israeli Sociology* 1 (2): 257–293. [in Hebrew].

# 6

# "Tampering with Society's DNA" or "Making Society Stronger": A Comparative Perspective on Family, Religion and Gay Rights in the Construction of the Nation

## Bronwyn Winter

The family is encoded in the Universal Declaration of Human Rights (UDHR) as "the natural and fundamental group unit of society ... entitled to protection by society and the State" (UN 1948, Article 16[3]). Similar articles appear in subsequent treaties: International Covenant on Civil and Political Rights (ICCPR), 1966; International Covenant on Economic, Social and Cultural Rights (ICESCR), 1966; and Convention on the Rights of the Child (CRC), 1989. Article 10(1) of ICESCR even

---

"The court has tampered with society's DNA, and the consequent mutation will reap unimaginable consequences for Massachusetts and our nation". Brian Fahling, senior attorney for the American Family Association Centre for Law and Policy, reacting to the Massachusetts Supreme Court ruling in favour of gay marriage in 2003, cited in *WND* 2003.

British Prime Minister David Cameron, in arguing for the gay marriage law in parliament, stated that it would "make our society stronger" (Cameron 2013).

B. Winter (✉)
School of Languages and Cultures, Faculty of Arts and Social Sciences, The University of Sydney, Sydney, NSW, Australia

insists on the need for the "widest possible protection and assistance [to] be accorded to the family". Both the European Convention on Human Rights (Council of Europe 1950) and the Charter of Fundamental Rights (CFR) of the European Union (2000) similarly articulate marriage and the family as rights of individuals and the state's duty to protect the family, as do several national constitutions. That of the Republic of Ireland goes even further: its article 41(1), paragraph 1, stipulates that the family is "a moral institution possessing inalienable and imprescriptible rights, antecedent and superior to all positive law". In this case, a cultural and legal *institution* (rather than actual people) is endowed with inalienable rights. The wording is all the more bizarre in that the notion of imprescriptible and inalienable rights comes to us directly from the French Declaration of the Rights of Man [sic], which, along with the US Constitution and Bill of Rights, forms the basis for our modern conceptions of the human rights of *individuals*.

The family thus appears as the bedrock of the modern nation. The battle for the nation is also the battle for the family: for its definition as absolute *value* in cultural, social and economic terms, and for the political and moral *values* that are considered to underpin the family institution. This chapter considers the role played by debates over same-sex couples and so-called rainbow families in these battles for the national family. Same-sex marriage advocates, who base their arguments on equality, rights and social justice claims, have maintained that same-sex marriage will revolutionize or at least modernize the family, recasting it as a more egalitarian and gender-neutral structure, and in doing so, strengthen the family as an institution of liberal states. Liberal states or political families (e.g. Green parties) supporting same-sex marriage also do so in the name of equal rights and social justice, such that same-sex marriage has become framed as *a key barometer of the modernity and human rights credentials of a nation*. Those opposing same-sex marriage, whether conservative states or conservative minorities within liberal states, invariably invoke "nature"—including appropriate gender roles—social order and religiously informed values, along with *concern for the future cohesion of the nation*, as the basis of their opposition.

These debates have lent weight to a "West vs the Rest" polarization within international politics, where the "West" and Western-aligned capitalist democracies, such as Argentina or South Africa, position themselves as champions of gay rights against the non-West, which is demonized as religiously conservative and as an abuser of human rights. This self-positioning by Western and Western-aligned nations has been criticized as "pinkwashing", notably albeit not exclusively in relation to the Israeli occupation of Palestine (Baum 2006; Daniel 2007) or as "homonationalism" (Puar 2007), in which defense of gay rights becomes a mechanism by which the (Muslim) Other becomes more effectively demonized. It has even been criticized as a hypocritical "homoprotectionism", in which the state positions itself as protector of homosexuals but, in doing so, claims the right to define what such protection constitutes and obscures the ways in which it might also be homophobic: "political authorities often rely on a complex interplay of both approaches in order to mobilize consent" (Keating 2013: 248). More generally, the assimilation of gay minorities within the national political economy of capitalist democracies has been denounced as "homonormativity" (Duggan 2002), or as "selling out" (Chasin 2000). Such critiques have extended to same-sex marriage as an expression of this homonormativity or as in fundamental contradiction with feminist critiques of the family (see, e.g. Donovan 2004; Bernstein and Taylor 2013).

Moreover, "homoprotectionist" Western states, whether they have legalized same-sex marriage or not, often have a less than stellar record as concerns their willingness or ability to protect their own LGBTI populations from abuse, and as concerns their treatment of LGBTI asylum seekers (see, e.g. Millbank 2009; Winter 2012, 2015). In addition, vocal Christian and (extreme) right-wing groups across the democratic world have either succeeded in blocking proposed same-sex marriage legislation or made sure its passage into law has been very bumpy indeed. The "West vs the Rest" polarization is thus less clear-cut than may be assumed in the area of gay rights, and even homoprotectionist state intervention in favor of same-sex marriage is as much if not more about preserving the institution of marriage and the dominance of the nuclear family model, anchor of the nation and thus of the state that gives it political form, as it is about supporting gay rights.

I will begin this discussion by considering the idea of family as *value* and briefly reviewing feminist critiques thereof. In doing so, I will also consider "femoprotectionist" institutionalization of some feminist understandings through women's rights treaties and state measures to protect the individual rights of married women, notably as concerns economic independence and bodily integrity. I will then examine the various ways in which different political and moral *values* attached to the "family" as anchor of the nation are mobilized either for or against same-sex marriage across various national sites. In discussing these case studies, I will also interrogate the assumption that same-sex marriage and family are by definition gender-neutral.

## Family as Value

In all nations, the bases of positive law concerning marriage, filiation, personal status and inheritance are religious and endogamous in origin. One marries within one's own tribe and within one's own faith. The family, that "natural and fundamental unit of the State", is—however secularized the state in question may be—steeped in religious tradition and religious beliefs about what is natural and moral. That tradition is deeply patriarchal and even modern accommodations to family that incorporate some understandings of women's rights have not managed to transform it.

At least since the Enlightenment if not before, well-known feminists have plurally and vociferously denounced the infantilization (both culturally and legally) of women in marriage (e.g. Gouges 1791; Beauvoir 1949; Millett 1969; Pateman 1988). They have recognized this infantilization as being ideologically enabled in supposedly egalitarian (post-)Enlightenment liberal societies by the sociopolitical division of society into public and private spheres, with the family and its supposedly male head being posited as guardian of the latter and women within the family being ruled legally incompetent. It is only relatively recently that liberal democracies stopped requiring married women to obtain their husband's permission to take out loans, purchase property or work outside the home, and marital rape was unthinkable as a concept until less than half a century ago: submitting to men's sexual impositions was legally part of the conjugal duty of wives. Tellingly, even the UN Convention on the Elimination of all forms of Discrimination Against Women (CEDAW, 1979), although it does spell out a range of women's rights and equality within marriage, is silent on violence against women and rape. It is not until the 1993 General Assembly Declaration on the Elimination of Violence Against Women that marital rape is formally recognized by the UN as a form of violence against women.

Yet feminists have long pointed out not only that most violence against women occurs in the home but also that the protection of the family as the privileged site of "private life" depends on women's unpaid reproductive, domestic and sexual labor: a form of modern enslavement that Colette Guillaumin ([1980]1992) referred to as *sexage*, a term she coined to echo the French words for slavery, *esclavage*, and serfdom, *servage* (see also Delphy and Leonard 1992).

Debates around same-sex marriage may seem to be light years away from these considerations, but, like the homoprotectionism/homophobia dichotomy to which Cricket Keating drew attention in 2013, femoprotectionism and misogyny also go hand in hand in the way governments handle women's rights within and outside the family. Structural inequities and stereotyped attitudes about women's role, how much women count and what sorts of entitlements men should have continue to inform government policies in areas concerning the family, even "rainbow families". One particularly worrying same-sex re-expression of male entitlement within the family, and access to women's bodies—to *sexage*—in order to service that entitlement, has come to the fore through gay men's demands for access to parenting by surrogacy. While surrogacy is not my core concern here, what is of interest for our discussion is the idea of *biological* family, and by extension matrilineality and patrilineality, as value. Although transnational research on the demographics of same-sex-couple-headed families remains to date relatively thin on the ground, anecdotal evidence suggests that, given the choice, same-sex couples, like heterosexual couples, prefer to have children containing the DNA of at least one of the parents who will rear them. In the case of gay male parents, this demand translates into a new form of instrumentalization of women's bodies, which feminist research critical of surrogacy has characterized not only as a new form of prostitution but also as a new form of trafficking in children (see, e.g. Ekman 2014). Interestingly, this critique lends some weight to the long-standing European materialist feminist and radical lesbian critique of marriage and prostitution as different sides of the same patriarchal coin (Tabet 2004).

Not only does family as value remain largely tied to biological parentality within "rainbow families", but both social movement campaigns and government discourse on same-sex marriage reinforce the heterosexual ideological framing of families in which the romantically attached couple is the moral and ideological basis and the socioeconomic core. It is this modern bourgeois understanding of marriage and the family that also underpins the statements concerning family contained in the human rights treaties outlined in the first paragraph of this chapter.

This understanding of the family, composed of couple-plus-(preferably) biological children, as forming "society's DNA" is not undermined by state recognition of same-sex unions but reinforced by it, and governments openly acknowledge this. Former British Prime Minister David Cameron, for example, famously said, in his defense of the legalization of same-sex marriage, that families are the "ties that bind us" as a society and a nation, and that he was in favor of gay marriage not *in spite of* his Conservative values but *because* of them (cited in Winter 2014). The homoprotected family is thus fully integrated into the nation and becomes a new expression of national values.

## The Values of Family

The debate over gay marriage, then, has been a battle for the meaning of family and the ways in which this meaning is institutionalized within the nation. Among the opponents, religion has never been very far from the conversation, although there have been some interesting hybrid expressions. The following discussion will draw on examples from France, Ireland, Argentina, Brazil, Colombia, Taiwan, the USA and Australia.

All countries where same-sex marriage has been furiously debated in the context of potential and/or subsequent legalization are, with the exception of Taiwan, Christian-majority countries, even when constitutionally secular. It is thus unsurprising that it is Christianity and its perceived relationship to national culture and natural social relations that most deeply inform oppositions to homosexuality and most particularly to state initiatives to assimilate homosexuals into heterosexual family laws and social arrangements. Even in Taiwan, the anti-same-sex marriage campaign has been largely fueled by Christian organizations, although fewer than five percent of Taiwanese are of Christian faith or culture. At the same time, the values mobilized by opponents of same-sex marriage are strongly national ones, and the religious and the secular are in some cases strangely hybridized within their discourse, while states legalizing same-sex marriage invariably defend that action in the name of the values of the nation and the cohesion of the state (but almost never in the name of religion).

In France, the massive demonstrations against gay marriage in 2012 and 2013 blended Catholic normative imagery of the family with Republican symbols such as the Civil Code (which covers family law among other things) and various revolutionary accoutrements such as the tricolor rosette or Phrygian cap (Winter 2014). In Taiwan, where in May 2017 the Constitutional Court ruled against restricting marriage to heterosexuals, Christian militancy against same-sex marriage—and the wealth of several powerful Christian sects and individuals—have, according to some observers, been a key element of the opposition movement "The Happiness of the Next Generation Alliance" (Cole 2013). Concern about Taiwan's declining birth rate has also been a key element (hence the movement's name). This element is in itself an interesting aspect of opposition to same-sex marriage: it is, within a heterosexual conservative moral frame, assumed to be a sterile union incapable of producing families. Once again, the importance of biological offspring is foregrounded, and this biological offspring must be produced without intervention of third parties—although, paradoxically, "unnatural" reproductive technologies are generally admissible when used by "natural" heterosexual couples.

In Brazil, opposition to same-sex marriage and to homosexuality more generally has been mixed up with the impeachment process of left-wing President Dilma Rousseff and the self-positioning of new would-be presidential candidates representing markedly different values. In an opinion poll taken in October, 2016, on Brazilians' confidence in the nation's institutions, the army and the Catholic Church were the highest, with a close to 60 percent confidence rate, and the Presidency and the Congress were the lowest, with 11 percent and 10 percent, respectively (cited in

Douglas 2016). In a poll on potential 2018 Brazilian presidential candidates taken in the wake of Donald Trump's win in the USA, ultra-right evangelical Christian congressman Jair Bolsonaro, who had previously polled fourth, moved to second place (Douglas 2016). Apart from his sexist and tough-on-crime attitudes, not to mention his alleged past actions as a torturer, Bolsonaro has stated that he would rather his son be dead than gay, has compared same-sex marriage to pedophilia, and has advocated "corrective" physical abuse of gay children (Avery 2016). He is perceived as the extreme tip of a growingly conservative and anti-LGBTI iceberg in Brazil, which in 2014 elected its most conservative Congress in 50 years.

In all of these scenarios, opposition to same-sex marriage (and by extension, at least in Brazil's case, to any sort of gay rights) has been based on a combination of Christian and national(ist) values. The future of the family and indeed of masculinist heterosexuality is posited as central to the future of the nation. On the pro-same-sex marriage side, however, the imbrication of family and nation is equally strong, but it is framed as a nation that is forward-looking and guarantor of equality for all. Above all, the nation is framed as modern and progressive precisely because it has ceased to be governed by religious tradition, replacing it with a strong *civil* tradition. During the lead up to the vote legalizing same-sex marriage in Argentina, President Cristina Kirchner stated that the tone of the Christian opposition, with its references to "God's battle" and "the Devil's work", was worrying in that it took Argentina back to medieval times, the times of the Inquisition. She directly referred to the historical evolution of marriage in Argentina from canonical law to civil law, as different ethnic and religious groups migrated to the country, and posited same-sex marriage as a logical continuation of the egalitarianism and pluralism of the civil law (Kirchner 2010). Similarly, in France, Justice Minister Christiane Taubira, in presenting the same-sex marriage bill to parliament, placed it within the history of the introduction of civil marriage, which, citing celebrated French jurist Jean Carbonnier, she characterized as the "hidden glory of the Republic". She went on to state that "civil marriage carries the imprint of equality…it was a veritable founding conquest of the Republic…carried by a general movement of secularization of society" (Taubira 2013, my translation). Taubira thus firmly linked civil marriage, and by extension gay marriage, to the fourth pillar of the French republic: *Laïcité* (secularism), the invisible but ever-present and constantly vocalized partner of *Liberté, Egalité, Fraternité*.

Across the Channel in the very Catholic Republic of Ireland, where as we have seen the family benefits from "imprescriptible and inalienable" constitutional rights, the opposition between religious and civil understandings of family was not anywhere near as clear-cut. The Irish Constitution, notwithstanding some amendments over the years, remains resolutely Catholic, and, before the May 2015 referendum, stipulated that marriage must be between a man and a woman. It is the only country discussed here in which a referendum on constitutional change was required in order to legalize same-sex marriage, although others (Brazil and Colombia) required a Court decision.

If in France or in Argentina the legalization of same-sex marriage and by extension a redefinition of the family is framed by the government as the triumph of modern egalitarian and secular national values over the "medieval" attitudes of many in the Catholic Church, in Ireland, by contrast, the debate has occurred very prominently *within* as well as *outside* the Church. A number of priests—albeit already considered dissident by the Vatican in some cases—spoke out in favor of same-sex marriage, and following the victory of the "Yes" vote (by a 62 percent majority), the Archbishop of Dublin, Diarmuid Martin, stated to the press that "We [the Catholic Church] have to stop and have a reality check, not move into denial of the realities" (cited in Kelly 2015). Former Irish President Mary McAleese, a practicing Catholic, had argued during the campaign, along with dissident priest Tony Flannery, that a "Yes" vote was "the Christian thing to do" and that she was voting "Yes" not in spite of her faith but because of it (Kelly 2015).

In Ireland, then, the battle for the meaning of the family as the basis of the national community was concurrently a battle for the meaning of the Catholic faith. If the Irish result, like David Cameron's "conservative" defense of same-sex marriage in the UK, can seem surprising, it becomes less so in the context of a push by Pope Francis—who nonetheless led the fight *against* same-sex marriage when he was still Cardinal Jorge Bergoglio in Argentina—to modernize the Church and make it both more accountable (as regards sexual abuse of children by priests in particular) and more socially inclusive. Although as Pope Francis, Bergoglio remains opposed to same-sex marriage, he has openly advocated a more inclusive attitude to gay and lesbian Catholics, famously telling the press "Who am I to judge?" (*BBC News* 2013).

The legalization of same-sex marriage in Ireland further needs to be placed in a context of social liberalization and embracing of egalitarian values notably as concerns women's rights (e.g. through the legalization of divorce via the 1995 Fifth Amendment to the Constitution). In any case, it has proven popular there: between May 2015 and May 2016, 412 same-sex marriages were registered in Ireland, and unlike Brazil, there appears to have been little backlash to date.

Yet it does not follow that where same-sex marriage goes, gender equality will automatically go also. In Ireland, as in Argentina, abortion is illegal except when the mother's life is endangered. The redefinition of the family as embracing the rainbow thus does not always translate into redefinition of the rights of the female individuals within families more generally. Moreover, cultural norms, even "homonorms", continue to favor the couple over single parents, most of the latter being women—a situation to which lesbian scholars have drawn attention (e.g. Lapidus 2008). In any country in the world, including those discussed here, single mothers, their children and the elderly are likely to be among the poorest people. This situation is exacerbated as states retreat from welfare provision and make benefits increasingly difficult and complex to access. Indeed, women's reproductive rights, economic rights and rights to freedom from violence lag well behind gay rights, including the rights of gay couples, in many parts of the liberal democratic world. This is so either because there is insufficient legislation to protect women's rights, the legislation is not applied, or women's services are woefully underfunded.

Of course, in some countries, such as Colombia, neither women nor gay couples are doing particularly well—and this is the case *despite* ostensibly progressive laws. Colombia shares with Brazil current political instability, following the October 2016 failure of the peace agreement with the rebel organization FARC (*Fuerzas Armadas Revolucionarias de Colombia*); very high homicide rates; and an anti-gay and anti-feminist backlash. Colombia also, like Brazil, has extremely high rates of violence against women, notwithstanding the fact that it has one of the most advanced legal and policy frameworks on violence against women in Latin America. Unfortunately, application of these laws is patchy: an estimated 80 percent of acts of male violence against women, whether in public or in the home, go unreported (Wentz n.d.)

This is not, however, the only Colombian contradiction: gay rights and same-sex marriage constitute another. In April 2016, the Constitutional Court voted six to three against a proposed ruling that would impose heterosexual-only marriage. This comes five years after another ruling that recognized same-sex couples as families that would automatically benefit from the same rights as heterosexual married couples if Congress failed to pass an enabling law within two years. However, the wording of the ruling was vague, and Congress did fail to pass such a law. Following the registration of a number of same-sex spouses by some civil court judges, the Inspector General brought the matter once again before the Constitutional Court, advocating that existing same-sex marriages be annulled and that the Court stipulate that marriage must be between a man and a woman, which led to the 2016 ruling. As with the situation concerning violence against women, the apparently progressive legal and political framework has not been reflected in a more gay-friendly society. In fact, some observers have suggested that an anti-gay backlash was part of what fueled popular opposition to the FARC peace deal. President Juan Manuel Santos was accused by a national soccer hero of practices that were "not of God", and during 2016 there were demonstrations and parliamentary accusations against the openly lesbian education minister, Gina Parody, who had taken the lead on the "Yes" campaign. She resigned in October 2016 following the failure of the peace agreement and "months of political bullying" because of her sexual orientation (Alsema 2016). Conservative former president Álvaro Uribe, who led the opposition to the peace deal, did so in the name of religion and "family values" (Casey 2016). Given Colombia's appalling statistics on violence against women, one can easily infer what sorts of "values" might underpin Uribe's conception of the family: conservative, Catholic and deeply patriarchal.

Beyond these material realities, men also seem to be favored over women in the media focus on same-sex marriage. In the first, highly orchestrated, and nationally televised same-sex marriages in both Argentina in 2010 and France in 2013, the chosen couple was male, approaching middle age (or already arrived there), white and professional. Similarly, the plaintiff in the 2015 US Supreme Court case that resulted in the nationwide legalization of gay marriage, Jim Obergefell, was a 49-year-old white male IT consultant and realtor from Ohio, who was even dubbed the "poster boy" for gay marriage by CNN daytime presenter Michaela Pereira, much to the disgust of anti-liberal online publication *mrcNewsBusters* (Balan 2015). More generally, however, the US press has featured more images of lesbians than gay men getting married, which corresponds to the reality. Married lesbians are also far more likely to be raising children, which confirms the foregrounding of family in same-sex marriage (O'Neill 2014). And it is quite a normative family: a 2013 survey by the US Census bureau found that same-sex married couples are more likely to be white (and more likely to be so than heterosexual couples as well) and are more well off financially than unmarried couples (see Gates 2015 for analysis of the survey).

Last, we come to Australia, which may be the most paradoxical case of all. It is a secular, multicultural, relatively egalitarian and relatively safe country with a high standard of living, and fourth behind Finland, Denmark and Canada on the 2016 Social Progress Index.[1] Unfortunately, it joins the rest of the liberal capitalist democratic pack in the importance it accords to family as couple-plus-children. Even on the left, the bizarre term "working families" became a rallying cry for greater economic equality during the 2000s, and "family-friendly" workplaces a desirable goal. And until December 2017, that family remained, legally, heterosexual. Marriage in Australia, unlike Ireland, is not a constitutional matter, nor is it under state jurisdiction as it is in the USA, but regulated by national legislation. In 2004 the then Liberal-National coalition government (conservative) led by Prime Minister John Howard adopted the Marriage Amendment Act, which stipulated that marriage was between a man and a woman. (The Act had hitherto been silent on the sexual orientation of married couples.) Australia thus bucked an international liberal democratic trend by regressing on the matter of same-sex marriage. In 2013, the Australian Capital Territory (ACT), where the capital Canberra is located, passed the Marriage

---

[1] Table available at http://www.socialprogressimperative.org/global-index/#data_table/countries/dim3/dim1,dim2,dim3, accessed 9 December 2016.

Equality Act and 31 same-sex couples got married in the ACT on 7 December that year, when that Act came into effect. Those marriages, however, were annulled only five days later when a challenge mounted by the conservative Federal government was upheld by the High Court of Australia, as the 2004 Act was still in place and Federal law trumps state law.

Most recently, a move by the Federal government to organize a national plebiscite on same-sex marriage was defeated in the Senate, and in August 2017 the government proceeded to organize a postal survey of voters instead. The broad left along with gay rights groups opposed both as unnecessary, particularly in the light of the well-over AU$100 million cost involved. The postal ballot returned a 61.6 percent "yes" vote in November, 2017 and the Parliament voted to legalise same-sex marriage the following month. At the time of writing in March 2018, there are no available statistics on the number of same-sex weddings to date.

One of the most ardent defenders of same-sex marriage in Federal parliament has been Australian Labor Party Senate leader and shadow foreign minister Penny Wong, who is raising two daughters with her partner Sophie Allouache, the children's birth mother. Wong and her partner are the very public political face of multicultural gay married Australia, thus feminizing and de-whitening the media face of "marriage equality" there, contrary to what has been the case in many other countries, as we have seen. However, Wong is also a practicing Christian: she is a member of the progressive protestant Uniting Church.

## Conclusion: The Family Is the Family Is the Family

In all of the cases discussed in this chapter—notwithstanding some varied and sometimes surprising outcomes—battles over the meaning of "family" and its supposedly intrinsic relationship to marriage have been paramount. For some, the family is yet more firmly cast as anchor of the modern nation by the legalization of same-sex marriage, and even, for some progressive Christians, religious underpinnings of marriage receive a modernizing fillip. For others, the consequence of legalizing same-sex marriage is to cast the family loose from its sociocultural moorings, leaving it adrift at risk of drowning in an "unnatural" or worse, heathen sea. The fervor with which same-sex marriage campaigns have been waged, and opposed, are indicative of the stakes involved in assimilating gay men and lesbians into the "family" model of social relations. There remain dissenting voices, which suggest that societies and polities should both re-evaluate their relationship with, and reliance on, "the family" as fundamental *value* and question the *values* overtly or tacitly presumed to underpin that institution. However, in a global environment where legalization of same-sex marriage is constructed as some sort of endpoint of liberal campaigns for social justice and equality, and its most vociferous opponents are deeply reactionary, it is increasingly difficult to raise such questions in a constructive way. Yet, one might do well to raise them: statistics on heterosexual marriage rates in liberal capitalist democracies show that they are in sharp decline, which begs the question of why gay men and lesbians want to be part of this institution. On the other hand, the tendency among heterosexuals to abandon the institution perhaps explains why some states are so eager to introduce new populations to prop it up.

Early days yet, however: the legalization of gay marriage remains as young as our millennium. The first law came into effect in the Netherlands in April 2001, and most legalizations were less than ten years ago. With these increasing legalizations come new research agendas, such as more comparative work on the process of institutionalization of same-sex marriage (e.g. Winter et al. 2018). Another area that as yet has been sparsely explored, with some notable exceptions (e.g. Badgett 2009; Rydström 2011), is what happens next. What are the demographics of same-sex marriage? Are certain social classes and ethno-racial groups marrying more than others, as some early US research suggests? What are the main motivating factors for marriage? Do lesbians and gay men marry for the same reasons? What about the same-sex divorce rate? Is it following similar patterns to the heterosexual divorce rate? How are states responding to this new addition to the marriage-and-family demographic: for example, have there been policy shifts in other areas, such as workplace rights or welfare regimes? One area as yet underexplored, and one to which I am now turning my own attention in my current work, is the political economy of same-sex marriage and rainbow families in relation to both the state and the market.

Although, as suggested above, empirical studies on how lesbians and gay men "do" family remain for the moment relatively thin on the ground, existing data does little to fulfill the oft-made claim that same-sex marriage will "revolutionize" the family. On the contrary, the current image of the "rainbow family" reinforces family as value and the values of family within national socioeconomic organization and national symbolism. Rainbow families are not Indigenous, they are not working class, they are not unemployed. They speak the national language in middle-class voices without a trace of foreign accent and what is more, they are highly photogenic. Wherever else they may have led us, debates on same-sex marriage have confirmed that the nation is still very much wedded, if the pun may be excused, to the family. By its very definition, same-sex marriage is a homonormative idea, which continues to align with that of family as bedrock of the nation, that great extended "family" to which the allegiance of all citizens is demanded.

# References

Alsema, Adriaan. 2016. Colombia's Education Minister Resigns After Months of Political Bullying over Her Sexual Orientation. *Colombia Reports*, October 4. At http://colombiareports.com/colombias-education-minister-resigns-months-political-bullying-sexual-orientation/. Accessed 10 Dec 2016.
Avery, Dan. 2016. Why Brazil Could Soon Be the Worst Place on Earth for LGBT People. *Newnownext*, April 26. At http://www.newnownext.com/why-brazil-could-soon-be-the-worst-place-on-earth-for-lgbt-people/04/2016/. Accessed 7 Dec 2016.
Badgett, M.V. Lee. 2009. *When Gay People Get Married: What Happens When Societies Legalize Same-Sex Marriage*. New York: New York University Press.
Balan, Michael. 2015. CNN's Pereira Gushes over 'Poster Boy' for Same-Sex 'Marriage'. *mrcNewsBusters*, April 28. At https://www.newsbusters.org/blogs/matthew-balan/2015/04/28/cnns-pereira-gushes-over-poster-boy-same-sex-marriage. 9 Dec 2016.
Baum, Dalit. 2006. Women in Black and Men in Pink: Protesting Against the Israeli Occupation. *Social Identities* 12 (5): 563–574.
BBC News. 2013. Pope Francis: Who Am I to Judge Gay People?, July 29. At http://www.bbc.com/news/world-europe-23489702. Accessed 8 Dec 2016.

de Beauvoir, Simone. 1949. *Le Deuxième sexe*. Paris: Gallimard.
Bernstein, Mary, and Verta Taylor, eds. 2013. *The Marrying Kind? Debating Same-Sex Marriage Within the Lesbian and Gay Movement*. Minneapolis: University of Minnesota Press.
Cameron, David. 2013. Televised Statement on Gay Marriage, February 4. Available online at Channel 4, https://www.channel4.com/news/senior-tories-rally-round-same-sex-marriage-bill. Accessed 9 Dec 2016.
Casey, Nicholas. 2016. Colombian Opposition to Peace Deal Feeds Off Gay Rights Backlash. *The New York Times,* October 8. At http://www.nytimes.com/2016/10/09/world/americas/colombian-opposition-to-peace-deal-feeds-off-gay-rights-backlash.html. Accessed 8 Dec 2016.
Chasin, Alexandra. 2000. *Selling Out: The Gay and Lesbian Movement Goes to Market*. New York: Palgrave Macmillan.
Cole, J. Michael. 2013. Who Is Behind the Happiness of the Next Generation Alliance? *The Far Eastern Sweet Potato* blogspot, December 11. At http://fareasternpotato.blogspot.com.au/2013/12/who-is-behind-happiness-of-next.html. Accessed 7 Dec 2016.
Daniel, Tallie Ben. 2007. Ani Geh Bisrael: Zionism and the Paradox of Gay Rights. UCLA Center for the Study of Women. At https://escholarship.org/uc/item/43s5k7nf. Accessed 20 Mar 2015.
Delphy, Christine, and Diana Leonard. 1992. *Familiar Exploitation: A New Analysis of Marriage in Contemporary Western Societies*. Cambridge: Polity Press.
Donovan, Catherine. 2004. Why Reach for the Moon? Because the Stars Aren't Enough. *Feminism & Psychology* 14 (1): 24–29. https://doi.org/10.1177/0959353504040298.
Douglas, Bruce. 2016. Trump Victory Prompts Brazil to Review Risk of Mavericks. *Bloomberg News*, November 23. At https://www.bloomberg.com/news/articles/2016-11-23/trump-victory-prompts-brazil-to-review-risk-of-mavericks. Accessed 7 Dec 2016.
Duggan, Lisa. 2002. The New Homonormativity: The Sexual Politics of Neoliberalism. In *Materializing Democracy: Toward a Revitalized Cultural Politics*, ed. Russ Castronovo and Dana D. Nelson, 175–194. Durham: Duke University Press.
Ekman, Kajsa. 2014. *Being and Being Bought: Prostitution, Surrogacy and the Split Self*. Melbourne: Spinifex Press.
Gates, Gary J. 2015. Demographics of Married and Unmarried Same-Sex Couples: Analyses of the 2013 American Community Survey. UCLA, Los

Angeles: The Williams Institute. At http://williamsinstitute.law.ucla.edu/research/census-lgbt-demographics-studies/demographics-of-married-and-unmarried-same-sex-couples-analyses-of-the-2013-american-community-survey/. Accessed 9 Dec 2016.

Gouges, Olympe de. 1791. Declaration des droits de la femme et de la citoyenne. At https://fr.wikisource.org/wiki/D%C3%A9claration_des_droits_de_la_femme_et_de_la_citoyenne. Accessed 10 Dec 2016.

Guillaumin, Colette. 1992. Pratique du pouvoir et idée de Nature. In *Sexe, Race et Pratique du pouvoir: L'idée de Nature*, ed. Colette Guillaumin, 15–82. Paris: côté-femmes.

Keating, Christine (Cricket). 2013. Conclusion. In *Global Homophobia: States, Movements, and the Politics of Oppression*, ed. Meredith L. Weiss and Michael J. Bosia, 246–254. Champaign: University of Illinois Press.

Kelly, Michael. 2015. How Same-Sex Marriage Won Out in Ireland. *The Catholic World Report*, May 26. At http://www.catholicworldreport.com/Item/3902/how_samesex_marriage_won_out_in_ireland.aspx. Accessed 8 Dec 2016.

Kirchner, Cristina. 2010. Televised Statement in Support of Marriage Equality Bill, July 12. At https://www.youtube.com/watch?v=ixVrmrQg9AM. Accessed 7 Dec 2016.

Lapidus, June. 2008. All the Lesbian Mothers Are Coupled, All the Single Mothers Are Straight, and All of Us Are Tired: Reflections on Being a Single Lesbian Mom. *Feminist Economics* 10 (2): 227–236. https://doi.org/10.1080/13545700420002177784.

Millbank, Jenni. 2009. 'The Ring of Truth': A Case Study of Credibility Assessment in Particular Social Group Refugee Determinations. *International Journal of Refugee Law* 21 (1): 1–33. https://doi.org/10.1093/ijrl/een040.

Millett, Kate. 1969. *Sexual Politics*. New York: Doubleday.

O'Neill, Luke. 2014. Do Lesbians Get Married More Than Gay Men? *Boston.com*, October 11. http://www.boston.com/news/national-news/2014/10/11/do-lesbians-get-married-more-than-gay-men. Accessed 9 Dec 2016.

Pateman, Carole. 1988. *The Sexual Contract*. Stanford: Stanford University Press.

Puar, Jasbir. 2007. *Terrorist Assemblages: Homonationalism in Queer Times*. Durham: Duke University Press.

Rydström, Jens. 2011. *Odd Couples: A History of Gay Marriage in Scandinavia*. Amsterdam: Amsterdam University Press.

Tabet, Paola. 2004. *La grande beffa. Sessualità delle donne e scambio sessuo-economico*. Soveria Mannelli: Rubbettino.

Taubira, Christiane. 2013. Le discours de Christiane Taubira pour le mariage pour tous, January 29. Texte intégral. *Le Figaro*, 27 March 2014. At http://www.lefigaro.fr/politique/le-scan/2014/03/27/25001-20140327ART-FIG00079-le-discours-de-christiane-taubira-pour-le-mariage-pour-tous.php. Accessed 7 Dec 2016.

Wentz, Sarah. n.d. Combating Domestic and Sexual Violence in Colombia. *Vital Voices*. At https://www.vitalvoices.org/blog/2016/07/combating-domestic-and-sexual-violence-colombia. Accessed 8 Dec 2016.

Winter, Bronwyn. 2012. Sûr de rien: les demandeurs/euses d'asile homosexuels et lesbiennes face à l'idée des 'pays sûrs'. *Australian Journal of French Studies* 49 (3): 280–294.

———. 2014. The Ties That Bind Us: The Hidden Knots of Gay Marriage. *Portal: Journal of Multidisciplinary International Studies* 11 (1): special issue on "Stigma." http://epress.lib.uts.edu.au/journals/index.php/portal/article/view/3296.

———. 2015. The 'L' in the LGBTI 'Alphabet Soup': Issues Faced by Lesbian Asylum Seekers and Other Non-Western Lesbian Exiles in France. *Contemporary French Civilization* 40 (2) (special issue on immigration). https://doi.org/10.3828/cfc.2015.11.

Winter, Bronwyn, Maxime Forest, and Réjane Sénac, eds. 2018. *Institutionalizing Same-Sex Marriage: Between Globalization and Path Dependency*. Basingstoke: Palgrave Macmillan.

WND. 2003. 'Gay' Marriage Ruling's Consequences 'Dire', November 19. At http://www.wnd.com/2003/11/21865/. Accessed 9 Dec 2016.

# Part II

## Women Supporting Nationalist Movements

# 7

# Women, Gender, and the Puerto Rican Nationalist Party

## Margaret Power

Lolita Lebrón led the Puerto Rican Nationalist Party's March 1, 1954, attack on the US Congress to bring world attention to US colonialism of the island.[1] She recounted, "[Pedro] Albizu Campos [Nationalist Party president] named Lolita Lebrón … leader of the attack. He named me and I was Albizu Campos' top delegate in the New York chapter. No one was above me. That's how it was." She added, "I don't want to say I was a victim, but I was affected by machismo." The other members of the commando unit were male Nationalists, Rafael Cancel Miranda, Andres Figueroa Cordero, and Irvin Flores. For Lebrón, being a woman leader "was difficult. My compañeros were men and I was the only woman …. They felt under so much pressure thinking they were men; they were the ones who gave the orders. That really affected me. We just never agreed

---

I gratefully thank Jill Vickers for her help in editing and shortening this chapter.

[1] A New York City-based unit of the Nationalist Party attacked the US Congress to alert the world that Puerto Rico was a US colony. They timed the assault to coincide with the OAS meeting in Caracas, Venezuela. Power, interview with Lebrón, Chicago, September 9, 2004.

M. Power (✉)
Illinois Tech, Department of Humanities, Chicago, IL, USA

© The Author(s) 2018
J. Mulholland et al. (eds.), *Gendering Nationalism*,
https://doi.org/10.1007/978-3-319-76699-7_7

on anything. I love these men. They are magnificent…[but] they were from a time when men ruled supreme."[2]

Most literature on gender and nationalism assumes nationalism is fundamentally a masculine project. It ascribes secondary, gendered roles to women in the movements and struggles to liberate or create nations (Chaterjee 1993; Yuval-Davis and Anthias 1989; Anderson 1983). These presumptions reflect an overreliance on men's perspective and a failure to consider women's viewpoint. By accepting men's version of how the nation is formed and who contributes to its formation, the literature replicates a masculine vision and overlooks how women understand their participation in national liberation movements, the creation of nationalist rhetoric, and the development of nations.

In this chapter, I explore how Puerto Rican women members of the Nationalist Party conceived their roles in the struggle against US colonial rule. I draw on my interviews with them, newspaper accounts, their statements and writings, and FBI documents. This chapter examines the understanding of what nationalism meant to these women, why they were nationalists committed to securing national sovereignty, and what actions they engaged in to attain this goal. Far from considering nationalism a male endeavor, they voluntarily and forcefully entered and even led the struggle for national independence.

Most literature on the Puerto Rican Nationalist Party focuses on the thought and life of party president Pedro Albizu Campos. Whether it extols (see Rosado 2006; Bruno 1950; Torres 1975) or criticizes (Briggs 2002; Ferrao 1990) Albizu Campos' roles, it generally ignores or minimizes Nationalist women's roles and overlooks gender relations in the party. Olga Jiménez de Wagenheim's (2016) new book represents a notable and welcome exception. She tells the stories of 15 Nationalist Party women and demonstrates their critical role in the anti-colonial movement.

Albizu Campos unquestionably wielded enormous influence over the thoughts and actions of party members. Yet, I argue in this chapter that conflating the party with the male leader and ignoring the thoughts and

---

[2] Ibid. Capitol police arrested the four, who were found guilty of various charges. After serving 25 years in US prisons, President Jimmy Carter released them in 1979.

actions of female members is a mistake. The most prominent women members were and understood themselves to be important participants in the Nationalist Party.[3] They dedicated their life to it and the independence fight, despite the risks this meant for their well-being. By participating in the Puerto Rican independence struggle, they transgressed prescribed gender roles, but as *independentistas* and Nationalists, not as feminists. Neither publicly nor, possibly, even consciously, did they challenge established ideas regarding womanhood, but they certainly did in practice. Prescribed gender roles dictated that women should be wives and mothers, or at least connected to a man. However, the Nationalist Party women I discuss chose politics over domesticity and dedicated themselves to their nation's freedom not the well-being of a husband or partner or the raising of children.

Albizu Campos, the unassailable leader of the Nationalist Party, called on women to join the party and work for Puerto Rican independence. He proclaimed (1930), "Establishing the homeland is the duty of all, [both] women and men. We salute the woman liberator. The homeland wants to immediately incorporate her strength [into the struggle for independence]."

Instead of challenging patriarchal assumptions about women and politics, these nationalist women cited Albizu Campos' words to justify their political involvement. In a patriarchal society, such as Puerto Rico during the 1930s, 1940s, and 1950s, a powerful male leader's encouragement of women's participation, as members or leaders, carried significant weight with both women and men followers. But does it stimulate women's political participation or shift women's subservience from fathers or husband to the male party leader? The Nationalist women I examine in this chapter used Albizu Campos' public declarations and personal backing to empower themselves and to engage fully in the struggle to free their homeland. I suggest that my understanding of women's role in the Puerto Rican nationalist movement offers new insights into women's participation in nationalist movements elsewhere.

---

[3] I focus on prominent women Nationalists because there are sources available about them and I interviewed three of them.

## Puerto Rico and the Puerto Rican Nationalist Party

Puerto Rico has been a US colony since 1898, when the United States acquired it following the Spanish-American war. Albizu Campos was president of the party, founded in 1922, from 1930 until his death in 1965. The party enjoyed its greatest support in the 1930s, when the Great Depression intensified Puerto Ricans' poverty and revealed the hollowness of US promises to improve their standard of living. The 1930s also were a period of increased US repression against the Nationalists: the 1937 imprisonment and exile in US prisons of the party's top leadership (Paralitici 2004) and police killing of 19 and wounding of 115 during a peaceful Nationalist march in Ponce (Randall 1979). The US strategy of jailing leaders and repressing party members had its desired effect. Nationalist Party membership and activity declined during the 1940s.

The United States emerged from World War II as one of the two superpowers, determined to portray itself as leader of the Free World and eager to extend its political and economic rule across the globe. Aware that maintaining Puerto Rico as a colony undercut its claims to champion anti-colonial movements and newly independent nations, the United States worked with Luis Muñoz Marín and the Popular Democratic Party (PPD) to change Puerto Rico's status. The process included: the 1948 victory of Luis Muñoz Marín as the first elected governor; Puerto Ricans' 1952 vote to pass a new constitution that President Truman hastily approved; and the 1953 declaration of Puerto Rico as a Free Associated State; and the United States' successful petition to the United Nations to no longer consider Puerto Rico a colony.

## Women and the Nationalist Party

During the 1920s, women attended Nationalist Party events, but men led the party, determined its policies, spoke at events, and were its public face.[4] After Albizu Campos assumed the presidency in 1930, the politics and

---

[4] I have found no records of the number or gender of people in the party. But newspaper accounts and photos of the party's activities mention or show their presence.

strategy of the party changed. Instead of the party's earlier approach of promoting cultural identity, political and intellectual discussions, electoral politics, and an ambivalent but fundamentally friendly relationship with the United States, henceforth it demanded independence and used various means, including armed struggle, to obtain it (Ferrao 1990). Large numbers of Puerto Ricans responded favorably to the call for sovereignty, attended party activities, and sought membership. The party, eager to increase its membership, actively recruited women supporters, as exemplified in the 1930 opening of the *sección femenina* (women's section).

The first *sección femenina* started in Vieques, an island off Puerto Rico's east coast. Albizu's speech at the inaugural ceremony predates Yuval-Davis and Anthias' (1989) now classic description of women's relationship to nationalism but bears a startling resemblance to it. Yuval-Davis and Anthias (1989) maintain that women "biologically and culturally reproduce members of the nation; actively transmit, reproduce, and produce national culture" (p. 26). Some 60 years earlier Albizu proclaimed, "women are the physical and moral mothers of the nation. When men forget their patriotic duty and play the game of illegitimate politics, then it is the role of women to call them to fulfill their duty; women need to remind their husbands and brothers to carry out their debt of honor."[5]

However, women did not join the party at men's behest, define themselves in accordance with male expectations, or see their role limited to urging their men folk to act. Anti-colonial women worked with the Nationalist Party because they wanted to secure the independence of their homeland and believed they could and should play a part in doing so. Women stated why they should join the party. One wrote, "Women should join the Nationalist Party because it is seeking their contribution, not for [personal] advancement but for ideals."[6] Another stated her understanding of women's role in the movement. "Women need to join the nationalist movement so that they will fulfill women's sacred duty and unify the homeland. Not only men are called upon to define the homeland, women are too. Women's [traditional] abnegation and sacrifice must contribute to the formation of our Puerto Rican nationality."[7]

---

[5] "Los actos nacionalistas de Vieques y Naguabo," *El Mundo*, November 15, 1930.
[6] "Pareceres," *El Mundo*, November 1930.
[7] "Adhesión nacionalista," *El Mundo*, June 1, 1931.

The writer affirmed the importance of women and their responsibility to "define the homeland," and, drawing on a gendered definition of women's "nature" and role, their "sacred duty" to do so. While she doesn't deny women should be *abnegada* or self-sacrificing, a valued attribute for women in a Catholic society, she redirects that quality from household duties to the struggle for the homeland. Instead of challenging the traditional attributes of femininity, she draws on them to assert women's role in the anti-colonial, nationalist movement.

Women's sections opened in towns throughout the island.[8] Sixteen women served as officers in the Nationalist Party Juntas, the local units of the party set up across the island.[9] Some women were featured speakers at Nationalist Party events. That same year the party established two parallel, gender-distinct organizations: *Los Cadetes de la República* (the Cadets of the Republic) and *Las Enfermeras de la República* (the Nurses of the Republic).[10]

Angelina Torresola, who was an *Enfermera*, recalled: "We conducted exercises in the plaza dressed in white. A young man from the town trained us and we followed his orders. We dressed in white because we were supposed to be the nurses for the army. In a war there is an army and if blood is shed you need nurses for the wounded." Torresola added, "we received military training, but that only lasted a little while."[11] Blanca Canales, like Torresola, was from the small interior town of Jayuya and also an *Enfermera* in the 1930s. She led the uprising against US colonial

---

[8] "Una Junta Nacionalista de Damas," *El Mundo*, September 19, 1931; "Una sección femenina de la junta nacionalista," *El Mundo*, October 3, 1931; "Grandioso Mítin Nacionalista en Rio Piedras," *La Nación*, December 30, 1932. I have been unable to determine how many women's sections existed or how many women belonged to them.

[9] I thank Luis Ferrao who shared his list of municipal officers between 1931 and 1934. For the names of women activists, see "Los Nacionalistas de Barranquitas," *El Mundo*, May, 20, 1932; "Candidaturas del Partido Nacionalista," *El Mundo*, September 20, 1932; "Candidaturas del Partido Nacionalista," *El Mundo*, September 22, 1932; "Lares, Puerto Rico, 23 de Septiembre," *El Mundo*, September 28, 1934.

[10] Ferrao, *Pedro Albizu Campos*, p. 129. For a history of the Cadetes, see José Manuel Dávila Marichal, "Atención, firmes, de frente, marchen! Historia del Ejército Libertador del Partido Nacionalista de Puerto Rico," Master's thesis, University of Puerto Rico, Rio Piedras, 2011.

[11] Angelina Torresola, interview with author and Janine Santiago, Guaynabo, Puerto Rico, October 26, 2013.

rule in Jayuya in 1950. In her memoirs she recalls that the group "raised money for the party's work and to send delegations to carry out international work." While gender divisions existed in the party, Canales circumvented them: "I never officially attended a party assembly, nor did I feature publicly in it since men made up the Juntas Municipales at that stage of the struggle. But, I conspired in other aspects of the struggle, about which I cannot speak at this time. No one ever forced me to do so. I acted on my own free will" (Canales 1997, p. 12).

These two organizations reflect typical assumptions about women and men's gender roles. Men are the protagonists; they do the fighting and represent the vanguard. Women are their supportive helpmates; they take care of wounded men. Yet, the formation of these two organizations, the inclusion of women in an official and important capacity, albeit in a gender-defined position, represented a step forward for women, who saw themselves as Puerto Ricans who contributed to securing the independence of their homeland. Moreover, the party defined women as more than wives and mothers and formally recognized women as an important component of the anti-colonial, nationalist movement.

One task many women in the Nationalist Party performed was fundraising, as Canales noted. Angelina Torresola maintained that Nationalist women went "from business to business asking [for money]." They would approach the owner and "ask for a small amount of money for the party." She explained their willingness to contribute this way: "Maybe because in the small pueblos we all knew each other, everyone liked me and the others [Nationalists], and we were honest." (Angelina Torres). This brings to mind women's fundraising for charity (see O'Connor 2014). Does it matter that these women were seeking funds for a political cause rather than for charity? Yes. Instead of fulfilling their Christian duty to help the unfortunate, these women chose to solicit contributions for a radical change in the political status of Puerto Rico. Instead of perpetuating the image of women succoring the poor, they worked as political actors whose mission was to end US colonial rule. In the process, they defined themselves as women responsible for the destiny of Puerto Rico and its inhabitants.

## The 1950s

By the 1950s membership in the Nationalist Party and support for independence had fallen from its high point in the 1930s for four interrelated reasons.[12] First, the absence of party leadership (due to imprisonment and exile) from 1937 to 1947 and heightened repression against activists by the US government and Puerto Rican police took a toll. Puerto Ricans were fearful about belonging to or associating with the Nationalist Party, because it could lead to their imprisonment, loss of a job, or constant surveillance (Bosque-Pérez 2006). Second, more money flowed into Puerto Rico during World War II due to the higher prices paid for Puerto Rican products and remittances from Puerto Ricans in the US military or working in US mainland factories (Jiménez de Wagenheim 2016, p. 23). The Popular Democratic Party (PPD), with US backing, encouraged US manufacturers to set up factories on the island, for which they received substantial tax exemptions. The efforts proved successful, for a time. As Ayala and Bernabe note, "By 1950, 80 new industrial plants were in operation; by 1952…150" (Ayala and Bernabe 2007, p. 190). Increased government spending also boosted the standard of living for most Puerto Ricans from the late 1940s to the 1960s (Ibid, p. 181). These changes lowered dissatisfaction with US rule and undercut the demand for independence. Third, rural Puerto Ricans relocated to cities, then to the United States, in search of work during the 1940s and 1950s. In 1940, 100,000 Puerto Ricans lived in the United States; by 1960, 800,000 did (Jiménez de Wagenheim 2016). This unprecedented migration disrupted social and political networks presenting the Nationalist Party with new challenges, such as organizing in new locales and contexts, and opportunities, such as establishing or building bases in Chicago and New York City.

Fourth, the growing popularity of the PPD reflected and caused declining support for independence. The party promised enhanced sovereignty

---

[12] No membership lists exist, so I cannot quantify how many people belonged to the Nationalist Party. According to the FBI, however, "3000 people belonged to the party in 1936," but only "approximately 500" did in 1950. These figures underestimate popular support for the party but reveal the decline in support. FBI Files, "Nationalist Party of Puerto Rico" (NPPR) SJ 100–3 Volume 23, Report made at San Juan, July 31, 1952, 6, 42–44, 120.

and social, political, and economic reforms. The economic improvements mentioned above along with modernization projects, such as the building of hospitals in all of Puerto Rico's municipalities, convinced a majority of Puerto Ricans that life with Muñoz Marín as governor and as a Free Associated State offered hope for a better future. One indicator of this was that "life expectancy ... increased from forty-six to sixty-nine years between 1940 and 1960" (Ayala and Bernabe 2007, p. 181). It was in this context that the Nationalist Party launched the 1950 insurrection to tell the world that Puerto Rico was still a US colony and to prevent it from becoming a Free Associated State.

## Women, Gender, and the Nationalists in the 1950s

After Albizu returned to Puerto Rico in 1947, he divided the party into military and political wings. He appointed seven military commanders, all men; men also led the party's political organizations, with a few exceptions (Rosado 2006). This reflected both his and prevailing ideas regarding appropriate gender divisions. Yet actions before and during the 1950 uprising and the 1954 attack on the US Congress suggest a more complicated reality.

Blanca Canales was one woman who rose to a prominent position in the party. A college-educated social worker, she was a political activist from an early age (Canales 1997). In her memoir she recounted, "One of my favorite things ...when I was between nine and eleven years old was to go up on the big balcony behind our house and make a podium out of a chair. From there I would make political speeches to the kids in the family and my young neighbors, imitating the [speeches] I had heard in meetings" (Canales 1997, p. 5). Canales joined the Nationalist Party in 1931, becoming an important member of the Jayuya branch. She raised funds, was active in the Enfermeras, and participated in both the military and political wings (Canales 1997). "Albizu organized a body of men and women willing to engage in armed struggle. This group replaced the

Cadetes, only we didn't wear uniforms and we worked in secret."[13] Political commitment and choice, not gender, determined who joined this clandestine organization that formed the military core of the 1950 revolt against US colonial rule.

The rebellion began on October 30, when Nationalists attacked seven towns in Puerto Rico, the Governor's House in San Juan, and, on November 1, Blair House in Washington, D.C. where President Truman was staying.[14] It ended on November 1, after the United States National Guard strafed Jayuya and Utuado and the Puerto Rican police and the National Guard retook Jayuya. Of the 140 Puerto Ricans who participated, three were women (Seijo Bruno 1950). Twenty-five Puerto Ricans, 16 of them Nationalists, were killed, dozens wounded, and 1106 arrested (Ayala and Bernabe 2007; Seijo Bruno 1950).[15]

From a prominent family, unlike many Nationalist women, Canales had a large house where she stored party munitions in her basement and launched the 1950 uprising in Jayuya. After the Nationalists took over the town, she mounted the stairs to the balcony of the main hotel, "unfurled the [Puerto Rican] flag … waved it many times, shouted Viva Puerto Rico Libre, and invited the people gathered below to join the revolution" (Canales 1997, p. 39). She later recounted, "I had been reading stories of heroines and imagined myself off to a crusade" (Zwickel 1988, p. 26).[16] She carried a medallion with a picture of Joan of Arc and the words "Saint Joan of Arc, intercede for the independence of Puerto Rico."[17] Canales was arrested, convicted of burning the Jayuya Post Office, and given a life sentence, commuted in 1967. Her jailers wrote, "we give up with her," and "she is impossible to rehabilitate" (Zwickel 1988, p. 27).

---

[13] Candida Cotto, "Entrevista a Blanca Canales," *Claridad*, October 30–November 5, 1987, p. 17.
[14] Griselio Torresola died in the attack on Blair House and Oscar Collazo spent the next 29 years in prison. *El Mundo* November 1 and 2, 1950; *New York Times* November 2, 1950. For a detailed description, see Seijo Bruno, *La Insurrección Nacionalista*.
[15] José Enrique Ayoroa Santaliz, "La Insurrección Nacionalista del año 1950," unpublished, October 29, 2000, p. 51. Different sources cite different numbers of wounded. See Paralitici, *Sentencia Impuesta*, pp. 106–07.
[16] Canales identified with Joan of Arc because she too was a Catholic woman who fought to free her nation from the Protestant invaders.
[17] Ayoroa Santaliz, "La Insurrección Nacionalista," p. 26.

Blanca Canales was not the only woman involved in the 1950 uprising. Isabel Rosado also played an important role in the days before and during it. Isabel Rosado, like many members, was from a poor, rural family. Nonetheless, she obtained a college education and worked as a social worker.[18] Atypically for most Puerto Rican women, she never married, nor did she have a partner or children. Instead, she dedicated herself to the independence movement, defying gender expectations.

Rosado joined the Nationalist Party following the 1937 Ponce Massacre.[19] She subsequently obtained a position of high trust and responsibility within the party. According to FBI reports, she was a member of the national leadership.[20] In 1950 she called on Nationalists to prepare for the coming insurrection. She was arrested in 1951 and convicted of violating Law #53, which made it a crime to belong to a subversive organization, which the US government considered the Nationalist Party, or to call publicly for independence.[21] Despite 13 months in prison and the loss of her job, she continued to participate in Nationalist activities after her release (Jiménez de Wagenheim 2016, p. 171).

Rosado, Albizu Campos, and three other Nationalists, Doris Torresola, Carmín Perez, and José Pepe Sotomayor were in Nationalist Party headquarters in San Juan on March 6, 1954, two days after the Nationalists, led by Lolita Lebrón, attacked the US Congress.[22] When the police arrived, Rosado and the other Nationalists exchanged fire with them but were subdued when the police lobbed tear gas into their room. Rosado was convicted of attempted murder, violation of Law #53, and the illegal possession of arms.[23] She served ten years in prison.[24]

Like Rosado, Nationalists Carmín Pérez and Doris Torresola never married nor had children, instead they worked to end US colonial rule.

---

[18] Isabel Rosado, interview with author, Ceiba, Puerto Rico, March 20, 2006.
[19] Isabel Rosado, interview with author, Ceiba, Puerto Rico, May 16, 2008.
[20] FBI, File Number 105–11898, Section XI, "Pedro Albizu Campos," p. SJ 3–1.
[21] For more on Law #53, see Ivonne Acosta 1987.
[22] Mildred Rivera Marrero, "Un siglo de lucidez," *El Nuevo Día*, January 30, 2007.
[23] According to FBI reports, Rosado had delivered Albizu Campos' message to Lolita Lebrón and two other US-based Nationalists that the party should attack the US Congress, Jiménez de Wagenheim, *Nationalist Heroines*, p. 173; 174–175.
[24] José E. Ayoroa Santaliz, "Doña Isabel Rosado Morales," *Claridad*, August 6–12, 1993, pp. 24–25.

They were, like Rosado, part of Albizu Campos' inner circle. Pérez joined the Nationalist Party in 1949, at age 20 (Jiménez de Wagenheim 2016). Torresola was from Jayuya, a cousin of Blanca Canales, and part of the Torresola family.[25] Like Rosado, they were in the Nationalist Party headquarters when the police arrived to arrest Albizu Campos in 1950. Torresola was shot, "the only Nationalist woman ... injured during the Nationalist uprising."[26] Both she and Pérez were arrested and imprisoned.[27]

By 1954, the Free Associated State was a fait accompli, Muñoz Marín was a popular governor, and the economy improved. Support for independence and membership in the Nationalist Party plummeted. Although most of the Nationalists arrested in 1950 had been released, US government surveillance of the party and harassment of its members continued. Increasingly isolated yet as determined as ever to end US colonialism in Puerto Rico, Lolita Lebrón led three members of the New York Nationalist Party to attack the US Congress on March 1, 1954.

After the Washington D.C. police arrested them, a reporter asked a very self-possessed Lebrón whose idea it was to carry out the assault. She replied, "it's my idea, and our idea, the four of our[s] idea" nodding at Rafael Cancel Miranda, one of the male Nationalists who accompanied her. Another reporter asked her if the four had "shot to kill" the Congressmen. She replied, "not to kill." To the question, "Are you sorry for what you did?" Lebrón answered, "I am not sorry to come and ask freedom for my country any place."[28] Lebrón, and the three men, spent 25 years in US prisons.

While the lives, actions, and thoughts of these women do not represent all women Nationalists, they do offer insights into women, gender, and the Nationalist Party. None of the most active Nationalist Party women married or cohabited with a man while politically active. Lebrón,

---

[25] Her brother, Elio, led the 1950 uprising in Jayuya and another brother, Griselio, attacked Blair House. See Seijo Bruno, *La insurrección nacionalista*, pp. 121; 207–209.

[26] FBI, File Number 105–11898, Section XI, "Pedro Albizu Campos," p. SJ 3–1; "La Secretaría de Albizu en Hospital Municipal," *El Mundo*, November 1, 1950.

[27] Paralitici, *Sentencia Impuesta*, p. 129.

[28] YouTube, "Lolita Lebrón ataca el Congreso 1954," www.youtube.com/watch?v=Pom5iJlVLrk, accessed August 3, 2016.

who had two children, was divorced. Isabel Rosado had had a fiancé, but he left the struggle to work in Mexico. When he asked her to accompany him, she refused; instead she dedicated her life to freeing Puerto Rico.[29]

Ideas about gender in 1940s and 1950s Puerto Rico consigned married women to the home as wives and mothers. It would have been difficult if not impossible for these women to both marry and have children and commit themselves full time to the Nationalist Party. Nor would it have been easy for them to lead the relatively independent lives they did.[30]

## Conclusion

This chapter examines nationalism from the perspective of women nationalists, not male leaders, activists, or scholars who have adopted men's viewpoints of nationalism. It examines how women nationalists understood and performed their role in the anti-colonial movement. In so doing, it presents a new and useful way of understanding the relationship between women, gender, and nationalism. Although male Nationalists occupied most leadership positions, female Nationalists carved out significant roles for themselves in the struggle to end US colonialism of the island, albeit with the backing of Albizu Campos. Wanting an independent nation, they transgressed gender ideas about proper female behavior. They eschewed marriage or cohabitation and the more conventional life most of their countrywomen experienced. They largely ignored gendered ideas about womanhood, dedicated their lives to securing Puerto Rican independence, and secured for some women prominent roles in the Puerto Rican nationalism movement.

Although many scholars have studied women's involvements in nationalist movements, many scholars as well as much of the general public retain the idea that both the nation and nationalism are masculine constructs. To challenge and counter this erroneous assumption, it is critical

---

[29] Isabel Rosado, interview, March 20, 2006.
[30] Another possibility is that some were not heterosexual and had no desire to marry or live with men.

that future research include a study of women's understanding of their roles, participation in, contributions to, and impact on nationalist movements. We can no longer accept an analysis of nationalism that relies on the study of men's involvement and perceptions, even if they are the leaders, major ideologues, public voices, or record keepers. Their interpretation is inevitably skewed and precludes the development of an accurate understanding of how and why women belong to, contribute to, lead, or reject nationalism.

One unsavory and extreme example that cries out for analysis is women and ISIS, which is simultaneously a national, transnational, and religious movement. Despite the perception shared by many around the world that ISIS is a masculine movement par excellence, one, in fact, based on the oppression of women, women are part of ISIS. Certainly, many women have had no choice because they live in areas ISIS has conquered. But other women have voluntarily joined. Why have they? What difference has it made to them or to ISIS or to women in ISIS-controlled areas to have women in it? The fact that these questions are seldom asked reflects the ongoing assumption that it is possible to comprehend a movement without assessing women's involvement in it. I hope this chapter contributed to demonstrating why, in fact, it is not possible.

# References

Acosta, Ivonne. 1987. *La Mordaza: Puerto Rico 1948–1957*. Río Piedras: Editorial Edil.

Anderson, Benedict. 1983. *Imagined Communities. Reflections on the Origins and Spread of Nationalism*. London: Verso Press.

Ayala, César J., and Rafael Bernabe. 2007. *Puerto Rico in the American Century. A History Since 1898*. Chapel Hill: University of North Carolina Press.

Bosque-Pérez, Ramón. 2006. Political Persecution Against Puerto Rican Anti-Colonial Activists in the Twentieth Century. In *Puerto Rico Under Colonial Rule. Political Persecution and the Quest for Human Rights*, ed. Ramón Bosque-Pérez and José Javier Colón Morera, 13–48. Albany: State University of New York Press.

Briggs, Laura. 2002. *Reproducing Empire. Race, Sex, Science, and U.S. Imperialism in Puerto Rico*. Berkeley: University of California Press.
Campos, Albizu. 1930. La mujer libertadora. *El Mundo*, May 4.
Canales, Blanca. 1997. *La Constitución es la Revolución*. San Juan: Congreso Nacional Hostosiano.
Chaterjee, Partha. 1993. *The Nation and Its Fragments*. Princeton: Princeton University Press.
Ferrao, Luis Angel. 1990. *Pedro Albizu Campos y el Nacionalismo Puertorriqueño*. San Juan: Editorial Cultural.
Jiménez de Wagenheim, Olga. 2016. *Nationalist Heroines. Puerto Rican Women History Forgot, 1930s–1950s*. Princeton: Markus Wiener Publishers.
O'Connor, Erin E. 2014. *Mothers Making Latin America. Gender, Households, and Politics Since 1825*. Chichester: Wiley Blackwell.
Paralitici, Che. 2004. *Sentencia Impuesta: 100 años de encarcelamientos por la independencia de Puerto Rico*. San Juan: Ediciones Puerto.
Randall, Margaret. 1979. *El pueblo no sólo es testigo. La historia de Dominga*. Rio Piedras: Ediciones Huracán.
Rosado, Marisa. 2006. *Pedro Albizu Campos. Las llamas de la aurora*. San Juan: Ediciones Puerto.
Seijo, Bruno. 1950. *La Insurrección Nacionalista en Puerto Rico*. Rio Piedras: Editorial Edil.
Torres, Benjamín J. 1975. *Pedro Albizu Campos. Obras Escogidas, 1923–1936*. Vol. 1. San Juan: Editorial Jelofe.
Yuval-Davis, Nira, and Floya Anthias, eds. 1989. *Woman-Nation-State*. New York: St. Martin's.
Zwickel, Jean. 1988. *Voices for Independence*. Pittsburg: White Star Press.

# 8

# Overcoming the Nation-State: Women's Autonomy and Radical Democracy in Kurdistan

Dilar Dirik

On August 3, 2014, the so-called Islamic State (ISIS) launched a devastating attack on the predominantly Yezidi-Kurdish city Sinjar (*Shengal* in Kurdish) in Iraq, killing thousands of men and raping and selling thousands of women into sex slavery. The brutal atrocities on the Yezidis, especially women, was referred by the United Nations as "genocide"[1] and constituted one of the main arguments to launch the US-led Global Coalition against ISIS.

A month after, ISIS was met with an astonishing response when it started its raid on Kobane, the predominantly Kurdish city in Northern Syria. As the jihadists that previously captured Mosul, the second largest city of Iraq, within days besieged Kobane, the residents organized and armed themselves, singlehandedly resisting for one month before any outside intervention. Kobane's historic resistance received international admiration, mobilized millions of people around the world, and was

---

[1] See report of OHCHR, "They came to destroy: ISIS Crimes Against the Yazidis", published in July 2016.

D. Dirik (✉)
Department of Sociology, University of Cambridge, Cambridge, UK

© The Author(s) 2018
J. Mulholland et al. (eds.), *Gendering Nationalism*,
https://doi.org/10.1007/978-3-319-76699-7_8

145

described as "heroic" and "unbelievable".[2] Upon freeing the city in January 2015, Kobane became "the city that defeated ISIS", the "Kurdish Stalingrad".

The most remarkable element of the battle for Kobane was the army of Kurdish women who took the fight to the explicitly feminicidal jihadist group. The Women's Defense Units (YPJ), formed in 2013 as an autonomous unit out of the People's Defense Units (YPG), counts tens of thousands of women among their ranks. Not only do they make up a strong dynamic in the anti-ISIS military resistance but also strike out for their political struggle—a women's revolution. Their fight transcends the battlefield and is being implemented since 2012 in the "Rojava Revolution",[3] as an alternative self-governance system, based on a grassroots-democratic, ecological, and women's liberationist paradigm. This system, *democratic confederalism*, was proposed by the imprisoned leader of the Kurdistan Workers' Party (PKK), Abdullah Öcalan.

The impact of the gendered events in Shengal and Kobane on the collective Kurdish psyche cannot be underestimated. The Shengal massacre perpetuated the notion of women as the eternally helpless objects of war on whose behalf decisions are being made—the battlegrounds of patriarchal violence. Kobane's resistance with its women's liberation-based self-defense and freedom concept, however, proposed a model of the "free woman", who liberates and determines herself by turning herself into an autonomous subject against the dominant rapist male. Perceived as a historical feud, Kobane challenged traditional political notions of militarism, state, and male domination and illustrated the relationship between self-defense, direct democracy, and women's freedom in practice. This narrative was widely used in Kurdish media, popular culture, and politics and further reinforced women's gains in the Kurdish freedom movement.[4] As Narîn Afrîn and Meryem Kobane, two female commanders of the

---

[2] This eventually led the international coalition to reconsider its priorities and to aid the fighters on the ground through air strikes, which enabled the—until then failing—coalition to finally claim some victory against ISIS by capitalizing on the resistance on the ground.

[3] Rojava (Kurdish: "west", referring to western Kurdistan, i.e. Northern Syria). For a detailed description of the "Rojava Revolution", see "Revolution in Rojava: Democratic Autonomy and Women's Liberation in Syrian Kurdistan", 2016, by Michael Knapp, Anja Flach and Ercan Ayboğa.

[4] The term Kurdish freedom movement refers here to the social and political movement loosely affiliated with Öcalan's ideology and organized within the democratic confederal system.

Kobane resistance told me in interviews, their victory was a result of their women's liberationist ideology and autonomous women's struggle.

The following chapter outlines the ideological underpinnings of the Kurdish freedom movement concerning women's liberation, by focusing on its shift from Marxist-Leninist national liberation to articulating novel concepts of identity and experimenting with grassroots politics that function in opposition to the nation-state ideal. I introduce the *democratic nation* concept as proposed by Öcalan as an attempt to redefine notions of identity and belonging in favor of democratic and liberatory rather than ethnic ideals. While the Kurdish freedom movement is explicitly committed to women's liberation,[5] further, an autonomous women's movement defines itself as the guarantor for social change and revolution, positions itself as the pioneering force of democratization, and actively creates own organizational mechanisms and practices. A radical democratic polity beyond kinship associations, which makes women's liberation conditional to its principles and identity, has a liberating effect on people's everyday lives.[6]

## The Struggle Between Struggles: National and Women's Liberation in Tension

It has long been a subject of discussion in critical feminist studies and activism that women are often decisive in national liberation or revolutionary struggles, but once "liberation" (e.g. statehood, power seizure, autonomy, revolution, reforms, etc.) is perceived to be achieved, they experience a backlash, because many movements subordinate the so-called

---

[5] Women were among the founders of the PKK and among the first guerrilla fighters since the 1980s. The first women's body within the PKK was the Union of Patriotic Women in Kurdistan (YJWK) in 1987. Women actively led prison uprisings and people's revolts in Kurdish villages in Turkey throughout the 1980s. Later, encouraged by Öcalan, in 1993, women formed their own army (today called YJA Star), in 1999 their first autonomous party (today called PAJK), and since 2005, began their autonomous self-organization in all spheres of life. In 2003, the previously formed women's academy initiated educations for the "transformation of the man". Today, all militants undergo educations on sexism, women's history, and women's liberation, taught by women. The KJK is the umbrella women's democratic confederal system.

[6] My observations are a result of my ethnographic fieldwork in the region.

women's issue to an alleged larger cause (Mies 1998). Presumably, post-struggle societies often revive traditional gender roles in an attempt to return to conservative normality (Hipkins and Plain 2007). This seems to apply especially in post-colonial contexts, where the nation is perceived as having been "emasculated", which can lead to the commitment to re-establish the nation's "honor" through patriarchal narratives (Hipkins and Plain 2007). Women's status, despite its transnational dimensions, is conceptualized as a matter that belongs to the "private" sphere, domesticated as a national matter and hence stripped off of its political status.

According to Yuval-Davis (1997) cultural decolonization processes resort to redefinitions of gender relations and myths to signify modernity and change. At the same time, as Hannah Papanek claims, women are expected to be the carriers of traditionalist, essentialist notions of culture (1991). Nationalist politics often mobilize gender for their agendas, especially by portraying women as patriotic mothers, housewives, or the country's honor that needs to be protected (see Grayzel 1999; Vickers 1993). When women enter traditionally male spheres (such as the military), the nationalistic discourse, often uncomfortable with gender deviance itself, uses such exceptional historic moments for political narratives that "emasculate" the enemy and feminize weakness. At the same time, feminists often subscribed to an essentialist ideal of women being incapable of carrying agency that may subvert a perceived notion of gender interest (Eisenstein 2007; Meyers 2002; Morrissey 2003). Polemics aside, empirical studies often expose women's political behavior within national contexts through a variety of interplaying and counteracting factors. As Lily and Irvine's (2002) insights from the gender dynamics of ethnic mobilization in Croatia and Serbia reveal, women who may participate in nationalist projects often do so as women and as members of communities, sometimes selectively, sometimes simultaneously, while their respective positions, identities, and interests clash and contradict each other.

Thus, due to the negative associations between gender and nationalism, feminists were often reluctant to acknowledge any feminist credentials that the Kurdish freedom movement could have (see, e.g. Mojab 2001; or Açık 2014), even though Kurdish women have long been leading, visible actors of different political processes in the Middle East, while often actively rejecting nationalism (Flach 2007; Demir 2014; Knapp et al. 2016; Genç 2002; Cenî 2012; Solina 1997; and Westrheim 2008). Especially feminist literature on militarism and violence often limited itself to statist notions of violence, thus rejecting any liberating aspects that women's armed struggle could have on the societal level. In fact, debates around Kurdish women fighters have often uncritically repeated the trope of the "post-war backlash of women" in an almost fatalistic manner, without engaging with these women's politics, ideologies, and modes of organization.

Within the relationship between co-existing struggles, such as women's and national liberation, there seems to be, both conceptually and practically, a conflict over concepts of identity, as well as over notions of wider social transformation in favor of justice that exceed the singularity of one objective. Contested are the sets of values, practices, and principles that inform and articulate imagined models, visions, and organization of alternative society projects, especially concerning the relationship between democracy, government, and power and their respective source of legitimacy (see, for instance, Laclau and Mouffe 1985). One way to critically engage with the question over the potentiality of radical liberation and democratic politics within a national or anti-colonial context however is perhaps to investigate the value of seeking new meanings in the "community" part of the Andersonian concept of nations as "imagined communities" (Anderson 1983) through new sets of terms. Anti-colonial feminism contributed much to our understanding of identity, raced and sexed bodies, and the intersectionality of struggles. Especially black feminism sheds light on the links between resistance against racial, sexual, and economic violence and the role of embodied identity within this power matrix. Hardt and Negri (2009) argue that "revolutionary politics has to start from identity but cannot end there" and believe that revolutionary thought "must work through it and learn from it" (p. 326). If one considers Stuart Hall's reflections on "cultural identity" and its potential utility for political mobilization (Hall 1995), especially in areas like the Middle East, is it not possible to fill categories that define very human feelings of belonging, meaning, and worth, with radically democratic meanings, especially in context of war and conflict?

Along this line of reasoning, departing from his earlier thought, Abdullah Öcalan analyzes the national liberationist context of the Kurdish struggle merely as a vehicle for a larger multi-front struggle for radical democracy. His proposal for an anti-nationalist, yet identity-based, sense of community is a concept that he calls *democratic nation*—an internationalist yet deeply communal re-articulation of identity not based on ethnic terms but radical democratic values and participatory practices, with women's liberation at its core.

Öcalan analyzes not class but patriarchy as the main contradiction of society and prioritizes women's liberation over other struggles. He calls feminism "the uprising of the oldest colony" (Öcalan 2009b, p. 317) and believes dominant masculinity to be at the core of societal problems. "Killing the man", thus, becomes a primary objective and raison d'être for the Kurdish struggle. "To kill the dominant man is the fundamental principle of socialism. This is what killing power means: to kill the one-sided domination, the inequality and intolerance. Moreover it is to kill fascism, dictatorship and despotism" (Öcalan 2013, p. 51).

Women's liberation thus serves as both reason and method of freedom. "The solutions for all social problems in the Middle East should have woman's position as focus […]. The most permanent and comprehensive component of democratization is woman's freedom" (Öcalan 2010, p. 296).

## From National Statehood to Feminist Radical Democracy

Officially formed in 1978 as a Marxist-Leninist organization to abolish "colonialism in Kurdistan" through an "independent, united, and democratic Kurdistan" in the form of a socialist state, the Kurdistan Workers' Party (PKK) nevertheless always actively resisted the "nationalist" label. Deeply influenced by Turkish revolutionaries such as Deniz Gezmiş[7] and

---

[7] Deniz Gezmiş, often described as the "Turkish Che Guevara", one of the founders of the People's Liberation Army of Turkey (THKO), was a revolutionary Marxist-Leninist, who became an iconic hero of the left for his role in the 1968 revolutionary movement and later due to his execution by the state. Along with his comrades Hüseyin Inan and Yusuf Aslan, he was hanged by the state on May 6, 1972.

Mahir Çayan,[8] the PKK counts members of Turkish origin among its founders. In her memoirs, Sakine Cansız,[9] one of the female co-founders of the party, explains that although the PKK never used chauvinistic-nationalist language and always committed to internationalism with reference to the legacy of Turkish revolutionaries, the Turkish left generally failed to address the specific nature of the Kurdish question and dismissed a separate Kurdish leftist organization in a hostile manner as "nationalist" (Cansiz 2015). For the PKK, nationalism was always a "backward" idea and simultaneously a tool of the bourgeoisie, while "national liberation" in the socialist fashion in the service of the international proletarian revolution was the primary goal. Öcalan's conceptualization of "the Kurd" denotes a theoretical category by which he aims to analyze the sociology of colonialism, degradation, exploitation, and historic denial in a specific geography.

Scholars of Kurdish studies across the spectrum agree on the qualitatively different appeal that the PKK posed to the Kurdish masses in contrast to traditional political leaders (see Allsopp 2015; Güneş 2012; Marcus 2007; Romano 2006). Unlike urban intellectuals, early twentieth-century nationalist Kurdish political groups, or traditional tribal authorities with collaborative links to states, the PKK initially appealed to leftist students, women, and youth, and later increasingly to the rural masses and workers. As Anja Flach describes, the PKK does not follow the pattern of classical *kurdayetî* ("Kurdishness") movements that developed since the 1930s, which follow the concept of a national party that represents all social classes, but rather attracted the marginalized: women, youth, peasants, and workers. It deliberately chose to position itself as the enemy of a Kurdish national bourgeoisie (Flach 2007, p. 28, see also Westrheim 2008).

---

[8] Mahir Çayan was one of the leaders of the People's Liberation Party-Front of Turkey (THKP-C). Kidnapping two NATO officials to pressure the Turkish state into reverting the death sentence for Deniz Gezmiş and his friends, Cayan and nine other activists were attacked and killed by the army on March 30, 1972.

[9] Sakine Cansız nom-de-guerre Sara co-founded the PKK and famously led the uprisings in Diyarbakir prison in the early 1980s. She spent years in the mountains as a guerrilla and is considered a hero for the Kurdish freedom movement. On January 9, 2013, she was murdered along with two other Kurdish women activists, Fidan Doğan and Leyla Şaylemez, in Paris. It is suspected that the Turkish intelligence service was behind the assassination.

Although nationalism was denounced as reactionary, the state was upheld as necessary. Written in a language reminiscent of Marxist-Leninist national liberation struggles, the PKK manifesto of 1978 dismisses any solution other than an independent Kurdish state as reformism in the face of imperialism and colonialism, as betrayal to the international proletarian revolution (Öcalan 1993, p. 195). Not having achieved the level of adequate nationhood is seen as the main reason for the "backward" status of the Kurds. Civilization was understood in a Hegelian dialectical manner, as a gradual linear chain of developments, which necessitates the state as a signifier of modernity and progress. According to this modernist assumption, to be a proper Kurdish nation then requires an own state. Even though it is acknowledged as the "strongest vehicle for the realization of exploitation" (ibid, p. 55), the state, like capitalism, is nevertheless a necessary evil on the way to socialism. In other words, "the societies that achieve a nation-state are closer to a classless society" (Ibid, p. 29). For decades, a "revolutionary people's war" was waged in the name of statehood, and authoritarian mentalities established a dogmatic organizational style.

Already in the mid-1990s PKK, after the collapse of the Soviet Union, early quests for alternative concepts of freedom outside of the state system began, but especially after his capture in 1999, the declaration of the Kurdistan Regional Government in Iraq, and a rupture in the PKK in 2004, Öcalan wrote several books at a time when the end of the PKK was predicted, only to surprisingly come up with a paradigm that would turn his early writings regarding the state on their head and put women at the center of his analysis. Along came a radical investigation of the historical origins of patriarchy, the state, and hierarchy-based civilization and a general deconstruction of concepts as "nation", "class", "modernity", and "democracy". Criticizing his own organization's dogmatism and violence in the name of statehood, the same institution that lies at the root of oppression, domination, enslavement, and exploitation, Öcalan announced "democratic confederalism" in 2005, as an anti-nationalist, anti-statist, women's liberationist, ecological, radical democratic political system. Ever since, the movement's language, organizational practices, and political proposals saw a remarkable turn in favor of regional democratic autonomy and decentralization through the creation of people's councils, communes, cooperatives, and academies.[10]

Öcalan traces the roots of the Middle East crisis to the emergence of the state, especially the nation-state, arguing that "another state would only be the creation of additional injustice and would curtail the right to freedom even more" (Öcalan 2010, p. 19). By referring to the transition from communal life organizations in the Neolithic age to the beginning of civilization in Ancient Sumer, Öcalan believes the rise of the state to be the original tragedy of humanity, resulting in the deep institutionalization of hierarchy in thought, politics, religion, economy, and family.

Accordingly, a "dominant civilization", based on enslavement, oppression, hierarchy, exploitation, rape, and control institutionalized itself over 5000 years. At the same time, an alternative stream of resistance, the "democratic civilization" continued to flow in history—embodied by the groups outside of the system: women, oppressed peoples, artists, peaceful cultures, workers, and so on, who protected their existence through self-defense and creativity (Öcalan 2009b, p. 207). In a Gramscian counter-hegemonic manner, Öcalan believes these to be the protagonists of "democratic modernity", a cosmology opposed to "capitalist modernity", which eliminated and colonized peoples, enslaved and degraded women, and devastated the environment through industrialism and consumerism.

Öcalan, by prosing democratic confederalism as a political system based on radical democracy, ecology, and women's revolution, implemented in practice through democratic autonomy, with the communes as the most radical and essential units of the democracy practice, introduces the concepts of *moral-political society* and *democratic nation* as referents for legitimacy and identity. Through education and active citizenship, values like justice and equality ought to be internalized and practiced by society, instead of the state through coercion and law. Political literacy, consciousness, and constructions of participatory alternatives give such values meaning by expressing them in practice.[11]

---

[10] For detailed accounts on these structures, see "Democratic Autonomy in Kurdistan", 2013, by TATORT Kurdistan and "Revolution in Rojava", 2016, by Knapp, Flach, and Ayboğa.

[11] Öcalan's emphasis on ecology as well as some of his ideas on direct democratic politics owes to Murray Bookchin's concept of "Social Ecology". See Jongerden and Akkaya for these intellectual links.

The most radical site of the democratic autonomy project is the commune. Here, ordinary people of the same street/neighborhood organize everyday life and collectively solve social problems. Instead of deriving its legitimacy from statist coercion, law, and bureaucracy, the envisioned "moral-political" society is based on free and voluntary participation of a politically literate collective and of conscious individuals, who reclaim politics from authorities and take up responsibility in everyday "face-to-face democracy" (see above). And so, according to Akkaya and Jongerden (2012), democratic confederalism constitutes a "radical conception of democracy aiming at the dissociation of democracy from nationalism by excluding state and nation from it and considering democracy as an unrestricted and unmediated form of people's sovereignty rather than a form of government" (Akkaya and Jongerden, p. 12).

Öcalan's opposition to the state system is connected to the latter's fundamental linkage to patriarchy. Drawing on Maria Mies' concept of "housewifization", he argues that with women's subordination to men, the entire society was subject to housewifization under the state (Öcalan 2015, p. 116). Beneath all other forms of social hierarchies and domination lies the fall of woman in the history of civilization (Öcalan 2010, p. 189). Real socialists, social democrats, and national liberation movements failed due to their prioritization of statehood over democracy (Akkaya and Jongerden 2012). Looking at history not through class or nations, but from the lens of women's freedom, the argument goes, the premises of liberation struggles, the meaning of autonomy and self-determination change. The "women's question" becomes humanity's "freedom problem". Today, a more ideological system of women's confederalism positions itself on the radical side of the democratic confederalism project, along with the youth, and sometimes even acts in opposition to the own movement—a revolution within the revolution.[12] For those affiliated with the democratic confederal model, women's liberation is not a distant aim but something to be implemented in the here and now, as the very method of liberation, the guarantor of democracy.

---

[12] See *Widerstand und Gelebte Utopien: Frauenguerrilla, Frauenbefreiung und Demokratischer Konföderalismus in Kurdistan*, 2012, by Cenî Kurdisches Frauenbüro für Frieden. Also *Democratic Autonomy in Kurdistan*, 2013, by TATORT Kurdistan and *Revolution in Rojava*, 2016, by Knapp, Flach, and Ayboğa.

The purpose of this rough sketch of the PKK's paradigm shift was to illustrate the ways in which the movement's justifications for liberation changed. This transformed the movement's identification of the subject of liberation and thus replaced national ideals with modes of identity and belonging based on liberationist ideals, practiced through self-management structures. Woman, as the first colony, becomes the central agent of the liberation struggle.

## Democratic Nation Against the Nation-State

The national state-centered identity had to be artificially created in the Middle East after the collapse of the Ottoman Empire, especially in Kurdistan, where tribal affiliation, village communities, and regional cultural units have traditionally been and often continue to be more meaningful frames of reference for people's identities than the relatively young nation-state (see van Bruinessen 1992, p. 50).

As Yuval-Davis (2003) notes, nations are often imagined as extensions of kinship and family ties and refer to common myths of the past or future and to essentialist characteristics. Smith (2010) includes in his definition of nationalism the importance of the sentiment or consciousness of belonging to a nation, beyond actual blood ties. Considering also Anderson's reflections on the role of symbols, performances, and actions in the architecture of notions of nationhood, it is plausible that the ideological connotations of belonging to a nation play a more active role in political mobilizing than actual kinship ties. Theorists like Max Weber often concluded the formation of a state—a further social abstraction—as the indicator of successful nation building.

If the nation is a mental concept, is an alternative imaginary not possible? As Butler argues, "The effort to identify the enemy as singular in form is a reverse-discourse that uncritically mimics the strategy of the oppressor instead of offering a different set of terms" (Butler 1999, p. 19). The idea of *democratic nation* disassociates the nation from ethnic implications and aims at forming an identity based on values and principles, consisting of political subjects in a self-managed form of citizenship, rather than objects serving the state (Öcalan 2012, p. 436). Grassroots politics of active and equal participants establishes a sense of belonging to a polity, which is dissociated from abstract yet rigid notions of ethnicity and nationhood but is founded instead on direct action, ethical principles, and social responsibility. Familiarity loses its abstractness when constructed through direct political cooperation. Beyond a mere conceptualization of a referent for belonging and identity, an entire set of tasks for intellectual activity, political and economic organization, and social and cultural transformation are associated with the notion of a *democratic nation*, including self-defense and a critique of positivist social science.

By trying to distill the ethical and aesthetic elements of the Islamic Ummah culture, regional imperial cosmopolitanism, and tribal affiliations, and to radicalize them in favor of libertarian ideals, *democratic nation* is put forward as a more realistic identity concept for the region. "While the state's nation pursues homogenized society, the *democratic nation* mainly consists of different collectivities. It sees diversity as richness. Life itself is only possible through diversity. The nation-state forces citizens to be uniform; in this regard, too, it is contrary to life" (Öcalan 2016, p. 25). Rather than assimilation into a monolithic identity, each component within this ethics-based polity is encouraged to form their autonomous bodies, and express their identity, but also in charge of democratizing their own community from within—hence, "democratic" nation.

While nationalism necessitates women's subordination to make sense of itself, *democratic nation* requires the elimination of the patriarchal concept of honor and a transformation of masculinity: "On the way to building a *democratic nation*, we will have to do the opposite of what has been done to date in the name of honor. I am talking about a transformed Kurdish manhood, and in part I am talking about myself. And it should be done like this: we must abandon any notion of ownership in relation to women. Women should only belong to herself (*xwebûn*)" (Öcalan 2016, p. 40). Against the oppressive implications of the patriarchal family as a microscopic state imposing strict control over women's behavior and bodies, *democratic nation* suggests the "democratic family", founded on the idea of *hevjiyana azad*, translatable as *free joint life*: voluntary, freedom-based modes of togetherness.

## Democratic Nation in Practice

The scope of this chapter cannot adequately describe the practical implementation of the discussed concepts, but a rough sketch of the Rojava Revolution shall at least try to illustrate the ways in which the *democratic nation* model can be manifested in political systems and social institutions.

The people of Rojava-Northern Syria announced a system of Democratic Federalism in 2016, after having initiated their self-governance project since July 2012 in the predominantly Kurdish regions.[13] At the point of writing, the Syrian Democratic Forces, a multi-ethnic military alliance, has nearly fully liberated Raqqa, the self-proclaimed capital of ISIS.

In Rojava, the language of *democratic nation* is widely used in administration, art, and media so that it is increasingly rare to find the word "Kurdistan" anywhere. For instance, the Charter of the Social Contract, which was declared in January 2014, starts as follows: "We, the people of the Democratic Autonomous Regions of Afrin, Jazira and Kobane, a confederation of Kurds, Arabs, Assyrians, Chaldeans, Arameans, Turkmen, Armenians and Chechens, freely and solemnly declare and establish this Charter, which has been drafted according to the principles of Democratic Autonomy."[14]

This is an excerpt from the declaration: "Surely this is the era of the peoples, the nations of the Middle East, who have fought historic battles against the tyranny of the nation-state, the hegemony of power and capital. The people have decided to say NO to all this and have screamed for building a free, democratic and just society and world"[15] The same federalism document elaborates: "[…] finding permanent solutions for issues cannot be possible with the existence of the nation-state. We must switch to the *democratic nation*". The declaration proclaims that "Women's freedom is the essence of the Democratic Federal system".

---

[13] *See* Rodi Said for REUTERS World News, March 16, 2016.
[14] Peace in Kurdistan 2014, Charter of the Social Contract—Self-Rule in Rojava. Available at Peace in Kurdistan Campaign Online.
[15] Document of the Democratic Federal System of Rojava –Northern Syria.

On December 2016, the word Rojava was dropped in the administrative congress to be more inclusive of non-Kurdish communities. Article 2 of the Social Contract for the Democratic Federalism System of Northern Syria states: "The democratic federal system of northern Syria adopts the ecological and democratic system and women's freedom."[16] The same document guarantees that women-related decisions are in the hands of women's justice systems and that women will enjoy equal representation in all elements of life.[17] The preamble encourages women to form their autonomous organizations toward a women's confederalism.[18] An active commitment to the elimination of discrimination, exploitation and objectification of women is enshrined in this constitution-like document.[19]

Immediately in 2012, at the start of the Rojava Revolution, the then operating Kurdish Supreme Council announced a ban on gender-based discrimination, forced marriages, domestic violence, honor killings, polygamy, child marriage, and bride price. Men committing violence against women were to be excluded from administration (see Demir 2015, p. 63). The new educational structures, from primary schools to the people's academies (including education for combatants), are multi-lingual and include gender equality as a central principle. The co-chair system operates from the smallest commune to the federalism level in Rojava.[20] Only women have the right to select the female co-president. Other regulatory mechanisms such as 40% quotas on each gender, along with autonomous structures, are mechanisms to safeguard women's political participation, while a concerted effort is being made to educate the society. Participants of the democratic autonomy structures, the federalism system, and the defense forces undergo education in women's history.

In everyday life, the empowerment of women gains legitimacy more immediately. Mechanisms are established to shape the very character of politics to be a self-defense mechanism against home-grown power. As

---

[16] Social Contract of the Democratic Federalism of Northern Syria.
[17] Ibid. Articles 13, 14, 26, 67, 68, and 69.
[18] Ibid. Articles 12 and 26.
[19] Ibid. Articles 11 and 25.
[20] See Social Contract, Article 12. The co-presidency principle that was introduced by the Kurdish freedom movement shares the chair between one woman and one man. The logic behind this principle is to de-monopolize power and encourage decisions based on consensus.

Üstündağ writes, "Academies, assemblies, and communes are becoming structured spaces where society defends itself not only from the state that is under erasure but also from the one that is always in danger of emerging" (Üstündağ 2016, p. 208). Communes, as self-managed streets and neighborhoods, organize daily self-governance through rotating committees on different issues like peace and justice, economy, safety, education, women, youth, and social services and maintain their respective independence and autonomy while being linked to one another confederally. Several communes together send delegates to people's councils, which are accountable to the communes. The female members of each commune and council form respective autonomous women's communes and councils, which can veto the mixed structures but are not accountable to them (Knapp et al. 2016, p. 64). Women are the authorities in issues concerning women, including the writing and enforcement of legislation, especially in cases of violence. These grassroots structures are led by ordinary people, many of whom had no formal education, leave alone prior political experience. The majority of women I spoke to had entered the public sphere for the first time.

On a direct democracy level, where representation is not delegated to anonymous institutions, the agency of women is directly expressed and impacts society. Seeing women's autonomous productivity in agriculture, food, textile, small businesses, political institutions, social services, education, and defense influences the community more than abstract rights on paper. The direct participation in the increasingly diversified political, social and economic structures functions also as an attempt to break the binary between "private" and "public" sphere, especially as women without professional backgrounds become actors in fields like justice, defense, and economy. Surely, acceptance of women's sudden active role in all spheres of Rojava's society does not happen without challenge, as was pointed out to me by several interview partners, reporting patriarchal backlash (see Demir 2015, p. 65). However, the political atmosphere and organizational mechanisms, established since 2012, created a general climate in which the normalcy of patriarchy is constantly challenged and women's liberation is articulated as the defining factor for social freedom. Undoubtedly, women's role in the fight against ISIS significantly contributed to this.

## Conclusion

With the Kurdish freedom movement's paradigm shift away from the nation-state toward grassroots-democratic mobilization, the radical liberation from patriarchy appeared like an emergency. The reconceptualization of notions of identity was deemed necessary to create democracy-oriented frames of social coherence and relational forms based on political participation and active citizenship. To adequately function as a non-hierarchical, non-oppressive social concept, the *democratic nation* needs to perform non-stateness in its mentality and practice (Üstündağ 2016). Women's autonomous organization from politics to education, economy, and defense is the guarantee against potential backlash and plays a pivotal role in the formation of a new, ethics-based concept of identity. A direct link is made by the protagonists of the revolution between belonging and direct democratic politics.

Leaving out the possibility that identity politics could play an emancipatory role begs the question of constructing democratic politics by overcoming deeply parochial, localist, and essentialist identitarianism and resisting simplifying, one-dimensional narratives of universalism simultaneously. Is it possible to democratize identity and radically localize universality? Future research ought to pay attention to the revolutionary project in Rojava in terms of the viability of its promise to uphold non-nationalistic social coherence and non-statist mode of governance. In the wake of international pressures, war, displacement, and hostilities, the future of the *democratic nation* project remains fragile but could play a critical factor in Middle East politics. And so, on the second year of Kobane's liberation, YPJ General Command member Nesrîn Abdullah condemns the nation-state mind-set as deadly and advocates the democratic nation for a just and free Syria, with women as forerunners: "We will raise our struggle to turn Kobanê into a women's city with all our power and we will lead a democratic Syria. Through Kobanê we will continue to search for truth that has once again been revealed, until we uncover the truth of the women's history reversed by the male mentality."[21]

---

[21] *Nesrîn Ebdullah: We will turn Kobanê into a women's city*, 24.01.2017, Gazete Şûjin.

# References

Açık, Necla. 2014. Redefining the Role of Women in the Kurdish National Movement in Turkey in the 1990s. In *The Kurdish Question in Turkey: New Perspectives on Violence, Representation, and Reconciliation*, ed. Cengiz Güneş and Welat Zeydanlioglu. Oxon: Routledge.
Akkaya, Ahmet Hamdi, and Joost Jongerden. 2012. Reassembling the Political: The PKK and the Project of Radical Democracy. *European Journal of Turkish Studies* 14. http://journals.openedition.org/ejts/4615
Allsopp, Harriett. 2015. *The Kurds in Syria: Political Parties and Identity in the Middle East*. London: I.B. Tauris & Co. Ltd.
Anderson, Benedict. 1983. *Imagined Communities: Reflections on the Origin and Spread of Nationalism*. London: Verso.
Butler, Judith. 1999. *Gender Trouble*. London: Routledge.
Cansız, Sakine. 2015. *Mein ganzes Leben war ein Kampf*, Band 1—Jugendjahre. Neuss: Mezopotamien Verlag.
Cenî—Kurdisches Frauenbüro für Frieden (Editor collective). 2012. *Widerstand und Gelebte Utopien: Frauenguerrilla, Frauenbefreiung und Demokratischer Konföderalismus in Kurdistan*. Neuss: Mesopotamien Verlags- und Vertriebs GmbH.
Demir, Arzu. 2014. *Dagin Kadin Hali*. Istanbul: Ceylan Yayinlari.
———. 2015. *Devrimin Rojava Hali*. Istanbul: Ceylan Yayinlari.
Document of the Democratic Federal System of Rojava—Northern Syria. Personally acquired.
Eisenstein, Zillah. 2007. *Sexual Decoys: Gender, Race and War in Imperial Democracy*. London/New York: Zed Books.
Flach, Anja. 2007. *Frauen in der kurdischen Guerrilla: Motivation, Identität und Geschlechterverhältnis in der Frauenarmee der PKK*. Cologne: PapyRossa.
Flach, Anja, Ercan Ayboğa, and Michael Knapp. 2016. *Revolution in Rojava: Democratic Autonomy and Women's Liberation in Syrian Kurdistan*. London: Pluto Press.
Genç, Yüksel. 2002. *PKK'de Kadının Dönüşüm Anatomisi* (Wesanen Jina Serbilind)
Grayzel, Susan R. 1999. *Women's Identities at War: Gender, Motherhood, and Politics in Britain and France During the First World War*. Chapel Hill: UNC Press Books.
Güneş, Cengiz. 2012. *The Kurdish National Movement in Turkey: From Protest to Resistance*. Oxon: Routledge.

Hall, Stuart. 1995. Fantasy, Identity, Politics. In *Cultural Remix: Theories of Politics and the Popular*, ed. Erica Carter, James Donald, and Judith Squires. London: Lawrence &Wishart.
Hardt, Michael, and Antonio Negri. 2009. *Commonwealth*. Conneticut: Belknap Press of Harvard University Press.
Hipkins, Danielle, and Gill Plain. 2007. *War.Torn Tales: Literature, Film and Gender in the Aftermath of World War II*. Bern: Peter Lang AG.
Knapp, Michael, Anja Flach, and Ercan Ayboğa. 2016. *Revolution in Rojava: Frauenbewegung und Kommunalismus zwischen Krieg und Embargo*. Hamburg: VSA.
Laclau, Ernesto, and Chantal Mouffe. 1985. *Hegemony and Socialist Strategy: Towards a Radical Democratic Politics*. London/New York: Verso.
Lilly, Carol S., and Jill A. Irvine. 2002. Negotiating Interests: Women and Nationalism in Serbia and Croatia, 1990–1997. *East European Politics and Societies 16*: 109.
Marcus, Aliza. 2007. *Blood and Belief: the PKK and the Kurdish Fight for Independence*. New York: New York University Press.
Meyers, Diana Tietjens. 2002. *Gender in the Mirror: Cultural Imagery and Women's Agency: Studies in Feminist Philosophy*. Oxford: Oxford University Press.
Mies, Maria. 1998. *Patriarchy and Accumulation on a World Scale: Women in the International Division of Labour*. London: Palgrave Macmillan.
Mojab, Shahrzad (ed.) 2001. Introduction: The Solitude of the Stateless: Kurdish Women at the Margins of Feminist Knowledge. In *Women of a Non-State Nation: The Kurds*. Costa Mesa: Mazda Publishers.
Morrissey, Belinda. 2003. *When Women Kill: Questions of Agency and Subjectivity*. London: Routledge.
*Nesrîn Ebdullah: We Will Turn Kobanê into a Women's City*, 24.01.2017, Gazete Şûjin https://gazetesujin.com/en/2017/01/nesrin-ebdullah-we-will-turn-kobane-into-a-womens-city/. Accessed 26 Jan 2017.
Öcalan, Abdullah. 1993. *Kürdistan Devriminin Yolu*. Cologne: Agri Verlag.
———. 2009a. *Kapitalist Uygarlik*. Neuss: Mesopotamya Verlag.
———. 2009b. *Özgürlük Sosyolojisi*. Neuss: Mesopotamya Verlag.
———. 2010. *Jenseits von Staat, Macht und Gewalt*. Cologne: Mesopotamien Verlag.
———. 2012. *Kürt Sorunu ve Demokratik Ulus Çözümü*. Neuss: Mesopotamya Verlag.
———. 2013. *Liberating Life: Woman's Revolution*. Cologne: Transmedia Publishing Ltd.
———. 2015. *Manifesto for a Democratic Civilization Volume I: Civilization—The Age of Masked Gods and Disguised Kings*. Porsgrunn: New Compass Press.

———. 2016. *Democratic Nation*. Cologne: Transmedia Publishing.
Papanek, Hannah. 1991. Ideal Woman and Ideal Society: Control and Autonomy in the Construction of Identity. In *Identity Politics and Women: Cultural Reassertions and Feminisms in International Perspective*, ed. V. Moghadem, 46–47. Boulder: Westview.
Peace in Kurdistan. 2014. *Charter of the Social Contract—Self-Rule in Rojava*. Available at: Peace in Kurdistan Campaign Online http://peaceinkurdistancampaign.wordpress.com/resources/rojava/charter-of-the-social-contract/. Accessed 26 Jan 2017.
Romano, David. 2006. *The Kurdish Nationalist Movement: Opportunity, Mobilization and Identity*. Cambridge: Cambridge University Press.
Smith, Anthony D. 2010. *Nationalism: Theory, Ideology, History*. London: Polity Press.
Social Contract of the Democratic Federalism of Northern Syria. Personally acquired.
Solina, Carla. 1997. *Der Weg in die Berge: Eine Frau bei der kurdischen Befreiungsbewegung*. Hamburg: Edition Nautilus.
*Syrian Kurds Set to Announce Federal System in Northern Syria*, Reporting by Rodi Said for REUTERS World News, March 16, 2016. http://www.reuters.com/article/us-mideast-crisis-syria-federalism-idUSKCN0WI0ZT. Accessed 25 Jan 2017.
TATORT Kurdistan. 2013. *Democratic Autonomy in Kurdistan: The Council Movement, Gender Liberation, and Ecology—in Practice*. Porsgrunn: New Compass Press.
*'They came to destroy": ISIS Crimes Against the Yazidis*, Report by Office of the United Nations High Commissioner for Human Rights (OHCHR), published in July 2016. Accessible at http://www.ohchr.org/.
Üstündağ, Nazan. 2016. Self-Defense as a Revolutionary Practice in Rojava, or How to Unmake the State. *South Atlantic Quarterly* 115 (1) (Durham: Duke University Press).
Van Bruinessen, Martin. 1992. *Agha, Shaikh, and State: The Social and Political Structures of Kurdistan*. London: Zed Books Ltd.
Vickers, Jeanne. 1993. *Women and War*. London: Zed Books.
Westrheim, Kariane. 2008. *Education in a Political Context: A Study of Knowledge Processes and Learning Sites in the PKK*. Bergen: University of Bergen.
Yuval-Davis, Nira. 1997. *Gender & Nation*. London: Sage.
———. 2003. Nationalist Projects and Gender Relations. *Narodna Umjetnost* 40 (1): 9–36.

# 9

# Gendering the 'White Backlash': Islam, Patriarchal 'Unfairness', and the Defense of Women's Rights Among Women Supporters of the British National Party

Jon Mulholland

## Introduction

Formed in 1982 out of the overtly fascist National Front, the British National Party (BNP) went on to be the most successful extreme right party[1] in British electoral history, reaching a high point in the 2010 general elections, securing 564,000 votes (though no seats); this on the back of prior successes in securing seats in elections for local government, the Greater London Assembly (GLA), and the European Parliament (Cutts and Goodwin 2014; Ford and Goodwin 2010). However, despite broader socio-economic and political conditions still favorable to the

---

[1] For the purpose of this chapter, I define the British National Party (BNP) as an extreme right party, with important and ongoing fascistic characteristics, but also as a party that while not fully fitting the continental European model of a Populist Radical Right (PRR) party, has nevertheless enlisted important elements of this model.

J. Mulholland (✉)
School of Health and Social Sciences, University of the West of England, Bristol, UK

© The Author(s) 2018
J. Mulholland et al. (eds.), *Gendering Nationalism*,
https://doi.org/10.1007/978-3-319-76699-7_9

BNP's ideological agenda, and largely as an outcome of its own persistent deficiencies, by the time of the 2012 local, GLA, and mayoral elections, the BNP was in terminal decline, suffering huge reductions in its electoral support (Cutts and Goodwin 2014, Goodwin 2014, Goodwin et al. 2012).

Capitalizing on a host of demand-side conditions, including the ever-increasing socio-economic and welfare precarities of the post-industrial working class, and profound social transformations associated with processes of globalization and mass migration, the BNP allied a drive for modernization and professionalization within the party to an effective appeal to important sections of the white 'have-nots' directly on the basis of the latter's sense of resentment at the 'unfairness' of their position in their own 'national home' (Cutts and Goodwin 2014; Ford and Goodwin 2010; Rhodes 2010; Copsey 2008). The nature and effects of such resentment constitutes what has usefully been conceptualized as a white backlash (Rhodes 2010; Hewitt 2005).

As an extreme right, ultra-nationalist party, the BNP belongs to a party family commonly labeled *Männerparteien* (men's parties), on account of the predominance of men in their leadership, membership, and support base. But this rendition may fail to recognize the important role played by women in such organizations. An important research trajectory has illuminated the active role played by women in variable nationalist (see Power and Vickers—this volume Chaps. 7 and 17) and extreme/populist right movements (see Köttig et al. 2017; Spierings et al. 2015; Mudde and Kaltwasser 2015; Akkerman 2015).

Drawing on semi-structured interviews, this chapter explores how resentment and 'unfairness', as key features of the white backlash, become gendered in the hands of women supporters of the BNP, and how the notion of unfairness is deployed as a tool for signifying and pathologizing the Muslim presence in the UK as a direct threat to gender-related justice and equality. The chapter contributes to a broadened, because gendered, understanding of the white backlash thesis and to a richer and more nuanced understanding of how the BNP successfully attracted women supporters via an (albeit Janus-faced) appeal to the latter's interests as 'liberated women' (see Akkerman 2015). The chapter illuminates the ways in which women supporters of the BNP utilize gender and sexuality to fix the nature of, and relationship between, four discursively constructed collective subjectivities and to infuse the respective natures of, and relations between, these subjectivities, as locked into a social drama marked by a gender injustice wrought by the pathology of Muslim patriarchy.

The chapter commences by situating the data within a consideration of the complex and shifting articulations between nationalism, gender, and sexuality, particularly in the context of the extreme and populist radical right (PRR), and calls for a fuller consideration of gender and sexuality within the framework set by the otherwise useful white backlash thesis. It then goes on map out the gendered social and sexual drama constructed by our participants in accounting for the nature and implications of an Islamic/Muslim presence in the West. Specifically, it goes on to delineate the participants' elaboration of four collective subjectivities, or players, within this gendered social drama; namely, the *oppressors* (Muslim men), the *victims* (Muslim women and vulnerable non-Muslim women), the *saved* (liberated non-Muslim women) and the *saviors* (the BNP). The chapter demonstrates how resentful invocations of 'unfairness' inform and lend coherence to women BNP supporters' claims of the wholesale oppression of non-Muslims at the hands of Muslim patriarchy.

## Methodology

This chapter focuses specifically on data drawn from 14 women supporters of the BNP, interviewed as part of a larger project funded by the British Academy/Leverhulme Trust on women supporters of nationalist organizations in the UK. With the exception of one participant born in South Africa, the remaining 13 were born in the UK, and all described themselves as white. Two participants were resident in Wales, four in North West England, three in the Midlands, one in the South East, two in the South West, one in South Africa, and one in Malta. Eight identified themselves as non-practicing Christians, one as Spiritual, two as Agnostic, and three as Atheist. There was a distribution across age cohorts, with one participant under 25, two aged 25–34, four aged 35–44, three aged 45–54, four aged 54–64, and no participants aged over 65. All were heterosexual. In terms of academic qualifications, two participants failed to provide information, one left school at 15, five had secondary school qualifications, four had tertiary level qualifications, and two were graduates. In terms of employment status, five were unemployed, two were home-makers or housewives, four were in part-time employment, one was employed full-time, one self-employed, and one retired.

Reflecting a tendency for extreme right organizations to refuse researcher access (Carter 2005; Sanders-McDonagh 2014), we chose to contact active contributors to the BNP Facebook site to recruit participants and also had some success with snowballing via this route. The interviews were conducted via Skype or telephone. Research suggests that: where participants receive informational support in advance, where interviews take place at a convenient time for the participant, and where care is taken to establish rapport, then telephone/Skype interviews can produce rich data, facilitating open and frank dialogue (Drabble et al. 2015). The lengthy and semi-structured nature of the interviews enabled the generation of a rich and nuanced data set, with some significant degree of saturation. Reflecting the findings of Goodwin (2010), initial uncertainties and even mistrust, on the part of the participants, appeared to quickly give way to some 'de-sensitization', given participants' readiness to articulate views that may readily be deemed racist, Islamophobic, or xenophobic.

## Nationalism, Gender, Sexuality, and Extreme/Populist Radical Right

Gender and sexuality remain enduringly and deeply implicated in the nationalist project. A substantial legacy of scholarly work now attests to the multi-dimensional nature of nationalism's gendering and sexualization, illuminating nationalism's masculinist and patriarchal character, and its accompanying tendency to submit women to a conservative gender order. However, nationalism's ongoing evolution has witnessed important reconfigurations of its relationship to transforming gender and sexual identities and relations, at least in some contexts. An important research trajectory highlights very different positionings for women within (at least some) expressions of nationalism (Vickers, this volume (Chap. 17)). According to Power (this volume (Chap. 7)), research is needed to advance our appreciation of women's own understandings "of their roles, participation in, contributions to, and impact on nationalist movements". Some liberal-democratic nationalisms have deployed representations of gender/sexual liberation, equality, and justice as defining features of their national character and accomplishments. This extends to variants of sexually cosmopolitan homonationalisms (Puar 2013).

Such reconfigurings have become a defining characteristic of an important shift, particularly notable in the context of Europe. This shift concerns the complex, multi-speed, and highly contingent strengthening of a certain Europeanization of national identities and boundaries. This Europeanization is inseparable from an insistent Islamophobic response to both the migration of millions of Muslims to Europe and to global conflicts increasingly framed as expressing a Muslim/non-Muslim polarity (Bunzl 2007). Here the category *Europe* and beyond this, the *West*, emerge as pan-national identities central to the effective framing of relations between the 'Muslim world' and the 'non-Muslim world' as those of a civilizational struggle (Bunzl 2007). Within this 'clash of civilizations' logic, gender and sexuality play a pivotal role. Muslim civilization becomes rendered as archetypically and perpetually patriarchal, with Muslim men constructed as sexual oppressors, and Muslim women as their muted victims. Such renderings draw on longstanding, culturally essentialist constructs of the Orient as despotic, mysterious, inferior, dangerous, and sexual (Ardizzoni 2004).

Reflecting these broader developments, Zúquete (2015, 2008) highlights the manner in which extreme and populist radical right organizations have increasingly deployed a post-national, European, and/or Western framing in their ideological positionings. Europe becomes here a definitely Judeo-Christian geo-political space under threat from an expansionist and invasive Muslim civilization. Muslims have come to replace the Jew as the other to Europe (Bunzl 2007), where cultural fundamentalism renders the Muslim as barbarous and warranting of exclusion from Europe (Fekete 2006).

Extreme and populist radical right organizations have made important strategic usage of gender and sexuality in their anti-Islam/Muslim discourses, but in complex and inconsistent ways (Akkerman 2015). Though it remains the case that the extreme and populist radical right in Europe are characterized by enduring gender conservatism (Akkerman 2015), this conservatism is generally moderated by a prevailing liberal-democratic political and popular culture (Mudde and Kaltwasser 2015). It is also partially displaced by the ways in which such organizations deploy a selective liberal-egalitarian discourse on gender and sexuality as a means to underpinning an account of Islam and Muslim civilization as backward and antithetical to European society (Akkerman 2015; Mayer et al. 2014).

The BNP has sought to strategically position itself as a defender of gender and sexual equality in its opposition to a Muslim and Islamic presence, constructed as a morbid threat to British *and* European civilization, even attacking the media and the political establishment for colluding in the oppression of Muslim women (Zúquete 2008). In so doing, the BNP evidences the Janus-faced nature of extreme and populist radical right positions on gender and sexuality (Akkerman 2015). In line with other extreme and populist right movements across Europe, the BNP has sought to walk a treacherous path between the inherent gender conservativism of its core ideology and the strategic allure of aligning itself to a politics of gender liberation that effectively serves to ground a pathologization of Islam as a faith, and Muslims as a people, on the grounds of their imagined patriarchal violence. In this sense the BNP may serve as a case in point of what Farris and Scrinzi (this volume (Chap. 13)) have referred to as a 'sexualization of racism' and a 'racialization of sexism', whereby the extreme and radical right have strategically deployed a sexualized double standard as a means to effecting the Othering of immigrant and Muslim constituencies.

## Gendering the White Backlash

We have asserted that the appeal of the BNP, along with other extreme and populist radical right organizations, in some measure, lies in their effective self-positioning as the voice of the white backlash. According to

Hewitt (2005), white backlash has tended to articulate resentful accusations of unfairness. These accusations commonly emerge in circumstances: of proximity to migrant and black and minority ethnic (BME) communities; where BME communities are seen to have acquired political power and status; where a legislative framework protects minorities in the name of 'racial' and ethnic equality (Hewitt 2005); and where there exists a perceived lack of commensurate representation for 'white interests' (Rhodes 2010). The majoritarian white population are here invited to construct for themselves a sense being a disadvantaged and betrayed minority in their own national home, performing an 'ethnodemographic inversion' (Cohen, cited in Rhodes 2010). The heartland of the white backlash is in the main those who also make up the support base of the extreme/populist radical right (see Mudde 2004).

According to Rhodes (2010) "it is clear the BNP has become, for many, the champion of 'backlash' sentiments" (90). Rhodes' (2010) study shows how ideas of 'unfairness' were successfully deployed to justify accounts of the white 'have-nots' as the subjects of racism at the hands of multiculturalism's defense of ethnic and religious minorities, and as the cultural and material victims of political neglect and betrayal (Rhodes 2010).

The white backlash thesis has, to date, tended to focus on resentments relating to perceived disadvantages in the field of labor markets, public services and housing, and more generally multiculturalism. This chapter seeks to expand an account of the white backlash thesis by exploring the manner in which ideas of unfairness may speak to, and be utilized by, women supporters of the BNP to construct pathologized accounts of Muslim patriarchy as a morbid threat to an accomplished gender justice in Europe/West.

# Oppressors, Victims, Saviors, and the Saved: The Clash of Civilizations as Gendered Social and Sexual Drama

The chapter now turns to an exploration of the complex ways in which gender and sexuality become deployed, 'on the ground', by women supporters of the BNP. Specifically, it illuminates how gender and sexuality serve to cast and characterize performers in a Clash of Civilizations drama, with the principal players being: The *Oppressor* (The Irredeemable Muslim Patriarch), The *Victim* (Muslim women and vulnerable non-Muslim women and children), the *Saviors* (the BNP) and The *Saved* (liberated non-Muslim women). The chapter will go on to explore how such characterizations are informed by, and go on to inform, resentful accusations of unfairness characteristic of the white backlash (see Rhodes 2010).

## The Oppressor: The Irredeemable Muslim Patriarch

Reflecting Zúquete's (2008) account of the emerging force of a European civilizational logic to the boundary constructing practices of the extreme right, participants routinely articulated a post-nationalist analysis that rendered the relationship between Britain/the British and Islam/Muslims as 'merely' one conflictual manifestation of an enduring civilizational antithesis. Characteristically invoking a modernization thesis, participants also deployed a cultural fundamentalism (Fekete 2006) to account for Muslims as stuck in a religiously fettered 'dark ages', reflecting the commonplace representations of Muslims within Islamophobic tropes as unchanging and, so, dangerous (Zúquete 2008). Serving as both explanation and measure, essentialist accounts of Islamically authorized patriarchy served as the nodal point for our participants' accounts of Muslim civilization more generally.

The central character in this social drama was undoubtedly the irredeemable Muslim patriarch, the primary oppressor, characterized by his unalloyed insistence on the ontological and ethical inferiority of women. Dancing to the compositional tune of the patriarch-oppressor, according to Claire, 'their whole culture is disrespectful, you know, to women. They treat their own like crap…they're disgusting'. Muslim men's rights were constructed as absolute and all-pervasive, and as guaranteeing the rightlessness of Muslim women to the point of the latter's servitude. According to Lucy, Muslim women are rendered 'servants to the men'.

The patriarchal ordering of gender roles and relations within the Muslim population was seen as premised on a foundational double standard in the application of Islamic principles, where Muslim men imposed a systematic and totalitarian application of the most austere Islamic standards on women while simultaneously and hypocritically indulging themselves in evidently un-Islamic behaviors. Jenny refers to the way in which some Muslim men navigate a path between the respectability of their Muslim-facing personas and the code-breaking lives they actually lead beyond the gaze of the moral guardians of Muslim communities.

> Every time my brother did a boxing show, the amount of Muslim men that were there and all over the lap-dancing girls…not just drinking, taking cocaine…I'm thinking, 'Oh my God', and you tell me about this religion and I can see with my own eyes what's going on.

The hegemony of Muslim men was seen, without exception, to spell violence against women and children, both Muslim and non-Muslim. Reflecting many of our participants' claims to self-acquired scriptural expertise, Elizabeth asserts, "if you look at the amount of spousal abuse [in Muslim marriages]… they can beat the hell out of their wives…it's condoned by the Islam views".

Violence, physical and sexual, extended to children. According to Bridget, Muslim fathers "beat their kids, and an eight year old in their [religion], they can marry them. To me that's child abuse".

Reflecting the high profile granted to 'Muslim grooming gangs' within the mainstream media (Tufail 2015) at the time of the project, and the commonplace deployment of the 'Muslim grooming' issue by the extreme right at the same time, 'Muslim grooming gangs' figured significantly in the data. Isabelle, having previously acknowledged herself the ways in which the BNP had exploited the highly mediatized accounts of 'Muslim child sex grooming gangs', nevertheless asserted, in her "unbiased opinion, Muslim men are … a lot more predatory than the white men". While the problem of grooming was generally understood as directed toward vulnerable white children, as an expression of both opportunism and the inferiorization of the non-Muslim other, it was also seen as a further manifestation of a broader normalization of child exploitation in the context of Muslim patriarchy. Elizabeth makes the link, alleging the normalized practice of marriage between adult men and female children, 'with the grooming of young children, taking an eight-year old child and selling an eight-year old child off to a man of fifty-six for arguments sake to be his wife. It's disgusting'.

Our data were here strongly supportive of Farris and Scrinzi's (this volume (Chap. 13)) account of how the extreme and populist right have successfully deployed a 'sexualization of racism' as a means to constructing Muslim men as oppressors. We add to this account by showing how the Muslim man is deployed by women supporters of the BNP as *the* principal referent in supporting a backslash-styled, resentment-fueled, account of the gendered unfairness brought to the UK by an inherently 'out-of-place' Muslim patriarch. In this context, the unfairness brought by the Muslim patriarch appears to rest on the twin elements of their outright oppression of all women and their own willful failure to meet the decrees of their own faith. In this sense, our data also appeared to support accounts of the influence of femo-nationalism among women supporters of the extreme/radical right, where nominally liberal feminist discourses become deployed, however partially and strategically, in support of Islamophobic agendas (see Lim and Fanghanel 2013).

## The Victims

The victims of Muslim men were legion, including at the broadest level the nation as a whole, and there was a very real sense that the nation itself was rendered 'raped' at the hands of the Muslim patriarch. The chapter now turns to a consideration of the two principal victims of Muslim patriarchal injustice, Muslim women and vulnerable non-Muslim women and children.

### Muslim Women

Undoubtedly, the predominant framing of Muslim women within the data was that of victimhood, as a direct outcome of their Islamically authorized inferiorization. Our participants drew on various metaphors in invoking the disrespected status of women in Muslim civilization, including accounts of Muslim women as animals, inanimate material, and even occupying a condition of 'nothingness'. Elizabeth asserts, "within their religion, you know, women are dogs". Anne links the status of women to the realm of the inanimate, "Muslim women are treated like dirt by the Muslim men". For Beatrice, "a woman in a Muslim man's eyes is nothing". The contractual relations of slavery were here commonly invoked.

Muslim women were generally seen to be subjected to a fear-induced passivity, even muteness; "I'm sure they'd love to speak their own mind but they're too scared to, if that makes sense" (Wynona). Constructed as both symbol and mechanism of patriarchal oppression and injustice, and as a device for obstructing social integration, the veil featured heavily within the data. Broadly, Muslim women were assumed to be compelled to wear the veil against their own wishes and interests, at the direct insistence of male patriarchs. According to Beatrice, "they're forced to wear the hijab and they're forced to wear the niqab". Jill makes direct reference to the functionality of veiling for alleviating Muslim men's anxiety about the threat posed by other men's desire: "they're not allowed to show their face, ankles or nothing in case anybody else wants them". While none of our participants explicitly aligned themselves with a feminist position, their standpoint on the veil, as an inherent negation of agency, appeared consistent with the colonialist 'feminist paternalism' of Elizabeth Badinter and Susan Okin, among others (Fekete 2006).

Nevertheless, there was also some important complexity in the data in this respect. There was a recognition from some of our participants that not all Muslim women felt oppressed by their veiling. Nancy remembers, "there was a woman on the television the other day who said it [the burka] gives them more freedom to say what she wants when it's only her eyes that are showing". Furthermore, Muslim women's experiences of oppression, allied to their essential locatedness within a Western national context, was seen to serve as a potential catalyst for circumscribed resistance, even if the inherent unfairness of Muslim patriarchy made genuine liberation unlikely. According to Elizabeth, significant numbers of Muslim women are resisting; 'a lot of [Muslim] women are speaking out and, you know, also taking a stand…against how they are treated'. Claire also suggests the emergence of 'modernized' constituencies of Muslim women who are beginning to find their voice; '…there are the ones that do have a voice that are quite modern, but as a general rule, the majority of them they don't'. Isabelle points to a generational shift, at least in the context of the UK, in opportunities available to, and accessed by, young Muslim women, "I feel that the [Muslim females] who were born here and are British citizens, like the ones in my age group, they go in college, have an active effect on society". Katie was relatively unusual in pointing to sectarian differences as a variable impacting on the position of women in Muslim populations; "there's a lot more leniency within the religion if they're Sunni Muslims as opposed to Shiite Muslims".

This de facto resistance may occasionally come to be witnessed by non-Muslims through occasions of 'leakage', where ethno-religious boundaries are breached and Muslim women find the agency and audience to speak out about their conditions 'behind the wall' of theocratic patriarchy. Muslim/non-Muslim friendship could provide one such opportunity. While none of our participants were prepared to countenance friendship with 'radical Muslims', and some declared themselves unwilling to befriend any Muslim, others acknowledged having friendship-orientated relationships with some Muslim women. Such friendships were often considered to have been formed against the backdrop of a more general tendency for Muslims to not want to befriend non-Muslims as an outcome of their own committed isolationism, and the unfair preferentialism that Muslims were assumed to show toward their 'own kind'. Claire reflects, on being told by a Muslim friend of her experience of violence, that she was "really shocked…[to be told of the violence]… because normally they're quite tight-knit aren't they?". Claire's work provided an institutional context in which to bear witness to such 'leakages', or 'breaches'; "I had a Muslim lady on my books…She was severely abused by her husband…her family actually took her and the children away from him which is very rare".

Despite such recognitions of intersectional complexities and change, it was difficult for the participants, given the relentless patriarchy granted by them to a perpetually hegemonic Muslim masculinity, to envisage Muslim women acquiring game-changing capacities for agency. Isabelle was typical in asserting the over-determining force of the patriarchally framed, and disempowering, 'beaten paths' of Muslim femininity; "I can't imagine them putting their education to work or employment. I know they maybe end up married and then they'll go and swallow up their career dreams and it's quite upsetting really...The lost ones".

## Vulnerable Non-Muslim Women

Patriarchal oppression, at the hands of Muslim men, was not reserved only for Muslim women. In fact, the worst abuses were seen to be metered out to non-Muslim women, and in particular, vulnerable white women, and children. Our participants were unanimous in their view that Islam authorized ethical disregard toward non-Muslims, and in fact, legitimized the abuse of non-Muslim women as the 'corrupted enemy'. Non-Muslim women were seen by Muslim men as 'legitimate targets': "this is where the sex gangs come from, because they see white women, they can do what they like with us...because a woman's wearing a short skirt she deserves to get raped" (Beatrice). Claire is in no doubt, "Muslim men see white women as trash...white women are slags, whores, they're there to be fucked". Invoking a religious authorization of sexual oppression in conditions of civilizational conflict, Isabelle asserts, "it does state in the Koran that they can keep women as sex slaves under issues of war, and we are at war with Muslims at the moment, well Muslim countries anyway".

Invoking a clear sense of white British women as victimized by an unjust Muslim patriarchy, as prevented from exercising their inalienable and fair freedoms in their 'own country', Jill accounts for events in 'some market down London' where in response to white women "wearing what they normally wear...Muslims were just spitting on them because they weren't covered up. The police didn't do anything...[white women]...get attacked, in their own country".

White female vulnerability to Muslim patriarchy was seen to be at its most acute where a predatory Muslim ambition intersected with socio-economic disadvantage and familial dysfunction in the former. Such intersections were seen to offer Muslim men the occasion to express their nature beyond the fettering gaze of their own ethno-religious community. Claire recalls an under-aged girl she knew who was groomed by a Muslim man; "her mum's a serious alcoholic, her dad was a heroin addict, and he's dead…he comes along, shows her all this money, nice lifestyle and she goes for it….I know a lot of girls that have sold themselves out".

Here we have a striking example of the allegations that underpin a gendered white backlash, where white native women become unjustly denied belonging and entitlement in their own 'national home'. Interestingly positioning Christianity as a guardian of gender justice, Katie portends a potentially bleak future for gender justice in the UK, "if Islam is left to spread and override Christianity, all Western women are threatened with oppression".

## The Saved: Liberated Non-Muslim Women

Native British and European women occupied a complex but pivotal role in the narratives of our participants, as authors, beneficiaries, and defenders of gender/sexual liberty, equality, and justice. Pointing to the historical struggles associated with achieving such equality, Jenny insists, "us Europeans have come far too far now to let [Muslim patriarchy] take a hold in our country. We've fought for our freedom…I don't want to be taken back to a barbaric age". This notion of gender equality in the West, as an outcome of hard-fought struggle against indigenous patriarchal resistance, did however exist in complex and uncertain relationship to another rendering, namely, a more teleological account that presents gender equality as an almost pre-determined outcome of civilizational forces inhering within the Western tradition.

Undoubtedly, in the hands of our participants, even in the context of their support for an ultra-conservative party, "Enlightenment values associated with secularism, individualism, gender equality, sexual freedom and freedom of expression…[serve as the]…markers of civilizational superiority" (Kundnani 2012, 155).

The accomplishment of a fully fledged gender equality, and hence fairness in the gendered distribution of rights and opportunities, largely served as a taken for granted fact of European life. According to Jill, "yes, women are more independent now…years ago like men did the work and women stayed at home…But they're more independent now and, you know, they can go do their careers and they can do what they want really". Melissa reflects, "that's why I don't like Muslims. I just think as a free-thinking woman, why would you want to be like that in such a free-standing, free-thinking society?".

Jenny proposes the notion that such freedoms are now in jeopardy, and at the hands of a nexus of interests revolving around Islam/Muslims, multiculturalism, and political correctness. Constructing a constituency of 'we' around the shared interests of non-Muslim women in the West, and a 'they' around the forces of multicultural political correctness and Islam/Muslims, she goes on to say,

> We've been told that women are free in Europe, and we've got free speech. Clearly we haven't, so what happens? Do we submit to everything that they're throwing at us? – 'You're not allowed to say this?' – and go back into the dark ages?

Participants' accounts clearly reflected the ways in which forms of liberal-feminism have been readily deployed by populist and extreme right groups and their supporters, asserting a right for women to be free from compulsion from either the state, or overly protected and gender-conservative religious minorities (Akkerman 2015; Puar 2014). Such accounts also function as an ontological underpinning for a gendered white backlash that asserts indigenous gender fairness as an accomplished fact, and does so in the service of Islamophobic renderings of Muslims and Islam as 'out of place', while 'over here', and specifically on a gendered basis.

## The Saviors: The British National Party

For most of our participants, the BNP represented a pragmatic, if in some ways problematic, means to 'rebalance' the unfairness that has come to characterize the UK in an era of multiculturally sanctioned Muslim privilege (at the hands of an elite rendered 'anti-own people') (Mudde 1996). The BNP are here then accounted for as supporting the interests of 'natives', and their civilizational accomplishments and rights (Rhodes 2010). In the hands of our participants, the BNP warrants support as the only party willing to shine a light on the ways in which white natives have become victimized by the excess of their own virtue and, specifically, their own commitment to a here misguided sense of fairness (see Fekete 2006).

For Harriet,

> I'm not at all racist, I just feel that the balance needs redressing at the moment and I think that's why I'm starting to understand more when I hear certain things from the BNP…I do feel that the natives of this country need to be taken seriously again.

Typically denying their own racism or Islamophobia, participants consistently framed their political standpoint as anti-Islam, with an attested problematization of the Islamic faith (commonly referred to as a cult). Harriet elaborates, and rather paradoxically, "I'm racist against the religion, I'm not racist against people's ethnicity".

The BNPs 'track record' on issues of Muslim grooming, rape gangs, prostitution, and domestic violence was commonly specified as a strength by our participants. According to Katie, "I know they are concerned for the safety of women and children within the Islamic cult due to the rape, beating and child sexual assault at the hands of extremist men".

Participants often referred to the BNP as being pro-women women, in their 'defense' of families and mothers. Anne sees "…the child care policy is a good one. I think they would support working mums better, and I know that they would prefer to make it easier for mums to stay at home". We see here clear testimony of a broader rendering of 'choice' within the gendered narratives of the populist and extreme right, where women are encouraged to choose what is their 'natural' inclination, to be mothers and home builders first, and against the 'ideological' imperative that sees them pressured into the labor market (Mayer et al. 2014). Interestingly, and reflecting the contradiction identified by Mayer et al. (2014), whereas native women's adoption of a reproductive familial role was seen by our participants as a case of 'choice', Muslim women's parallel adoption of this role was taken as evidence of an absence of choice.

Our participants' framing of the BNP in the role of saviors was clearly informed by a sense that the party stood alone in their unalloyed stand against Islam and Muslim 'tyranny'. The BNP was celebrated for the bravery and honesty of its stance, for its unique willingness to say the unsayable, and in ways redolent of Mudde's (2004) account of the populist radical right as profiting "from their role as taboo breakers and fighters against political correctness" (Mudde 2004, 554). Along with organizations of the PRR, the extreme right BNP had clearly secured much traction among our participants with its quasi-populist, anti-elite, anti-pluralist, and 'moralist' positioning (see Mudde and Kaltwasser 2015; Mudde 2004).

However, when participants were asked to talk more specifically about the extent to, and ways in, which the largely male leadership and membership could be expected to ideologically and practically support a politics of female empowerment, far greater levels of ambivalence came into view.

On the one hand, Lucy characterizes the BNP in terms of the fairness of its treatment of women, claiming that "all women members and non-members are treated fairly and with respect". Elizabeth also felt that the greater presence of women within the party could be expected to bring about a corresponding shift in the ideological climate in favor of a fuller support for women's interests; "…a lot of women are actually getting involved, so I would honestly say that the BNP…could sway, and could actually listen to women and listen to their issues and their grievances. Then I would say the BNP would get a lot of support". But the subtext to Elizabeth's hopeful rendition here is clearly an acknowledgment of an underlying truth, namely, that populist and extreme right organizations are rarely programmatic supporters of women's rights, being at best gender blind, and at worst gender conservative (Mudde and Kaltwasser 2015; Mayer et al. 2014).

Against Elizabeth's testimony, Isabelle's account was indicative of a more skeptical standpoint, stressing the enduring nature of BNP members' traditional patriarchal readings of gender roles; "some of the BNP members think that women should be quite subservient…that kind of pissed me off as well…they're just very closed-minded". Isabelle's account did reflect more widely shared misgivings about the political style of the BNP, and in a manner reflective of Harteveld et al.'s (2015) suggestion that the masculinist and adversarial style of populist and extreme right organizations may potentially weaken their appeal to women.

The BNP were in part recognized as a party without a demonstrable and substantive commitment to a holistic politics of gender equality, and it was not even clear that our participants were themselves necessarily overly allied to such a politics. But the BNP *were* seen as only organization that, in standing as a bulwark against the incursions of Muslim civilization, could effectively speak to the understandable resentments of white women's backlash against the threat of Muslim patriarchy.

## Conclusion

Extreme and populist radical right parties have conventionally been understood as *Männerparteien*. However, research suggests that the 'gender gap', seen as so characteristic of the extreme and populist radical right's political appeal, has been overplayed (Mudde and Kaltwasser 2015; Mayer 2013). On this basis, there is a need for further work to explore the context-specific relationship between the gendered and sexed nature of such organization's ideologies, structures, and practices, and the orientations of its women supporters (Spierings and Zaslove 2015).

In addressing this need, this chapter has contributed to an understanding of how women supporters of an extreme right party in the UK signify gender and sexuality in the context of their anti-Islam and anti-Muslim positionings. Specifically, it has illuminated the ways in which gender and sexuality are deployed to pathologize Islam, and Muslim civilization, as irredeemably patriarchal, and Muslim men and Muslim women as, respectively, oppressors and victims. In achieving this end, women supporters of the BNP elaborate a gendered social drama, played out by four principal collective subjects, Muslim men (Oppressors), Muslim and vulnerable non-Muslim women (Victims), the BNP (Saviors), and non-Muslim women in the West (the Saved).

The chapter has sought to apply, and in its application extend, the conceptualization of the white backlash. White backlash politics offered a useful, because flexible and pragmatic, medium for the BNP to enlist support. Central to the white backlash was a constructed sense of 'unfairness' experienced by the 'white have-nots' (Rhodes 2010), in a context of a politics of multicultural recognition of minorities, and the perceived abandonment of a marginalized and disadvantaged white majority-turned-'minority'. Whereas the application of the white backlash thesis within social scientific studies of the extreme/populist radical right has tended to lack a gender framing, and has tended to assume a conventional color-based 'racial' modeling, the application of the concept here specifically illuminates how women supporters of the extreme right may be drawn into a white backlash standpoint through a specifically gendered and ethno-cultural and religious rendering of contemporary 'unfairness' in the UK. Here, women supporters appear to have been drawn to the (inherently gender conservative) BNP precisely because of the latter's positioning of themselves as the only effective defenders of the hard-won gender fairness enjoyed by women of the West in the face of an irredeemably patriarchal Islamic, and Muslim threat in 'our national home'.

This research suggests the value of further exploration of how gender, and sexuality, function as intersectional ingredients informing white backlash politics in a context of multi-ethnic and multi-confessional diversity, and specifically where a 'clash of civilization' politics has re-framed the 'battle-lines' in less obviously 'racial' terms as those between Islam/Muslims and the Rest/West.

# References

Akkerman, Tjitske. 2015. Gender and the Radical Right in Western Europe: A Comparative Analysis of Policy Agendas. *Patterns of Prejudice* 49 (1–2): 37–60.
Ardizzoni, Michela. 2004. Unveiling the Veil: Gendered Discourses and the (In)Visibility of the Female Body in France. *Women's Studies* 33 (5): 629–649.
Bunzl, Matti. 2007. *Anti-semitism and Islamophobia: Hatreds Old and New in Europe*. Chicago: Prickly Paradigm Press.
Carter, Elisabeth. 2005. *The Extreme Right in Western Europe: Success or Failure?* Manchester: Manchester University Press.
Copsey, Nigel. 2008. *Contemporary British Fascism*. Basingstoke: Palgrave Macmillan.

Cutts, David, and Mathew J. Goodwin. 2014. Getting Out the Right Wing Extremist Vote: Extreme Right Party Support and Campaign Effects at a Recent British General Election. *European Political Science Review* 6 (1): 93–114.

Drabble, Laurie, Karen F. Trocki, Brenda Salcedo, Patricia C. Walker, and Rachael A. Korcha. 2015. Conducting Qualitative Interviews by Telephone: Lessons Learned from a Study of Alcohol Use Among Sexual Minority and Heterosexual Women. *Qualitative Social Work: Research and Practice* 15 (1): 118–133.

Fekete, Liz. 2006. Enlightened Fundamentalism? Immigration, Feminism and the Right. *Race and Class* 48 (2): 1–22.

Ford, Robert, and Mathew J. Goodwin. 2010. Angry White Men: Individual and Contextual Predictors of Support for the British National Party. *Political Studies* 58: 1–25.

Goodwin, Mathew J. 2010. Activism in Contemporary Extreme Right Parties: The Case of the British National Party. *Journal of Elections, Public Opinion and Parties* 20 (1): 31–54.

———. 2014. Forever a False Dawn? Explaining the Electoral Collapse of the British National Party (BNP). *Parliamentary Affairs* 67: 887–906.

Goodwin, Mathew J., Robert Ford, and David Cutts. 2012. Extreme Right Foot Soldiers, Legacy Effects and Deprivation: A Contextual Analysis of the Leaked British National Party (BNP) Membership List. *Party Politics* 19 (6): 887–906.

Harteveld, Eelco, Wouter Van Der Brug, Stephan Dahlberg, and Andrej Kokkonen. 2015. The Gender Gap in Populist Radical-Right Voting: Examining the Demand Side in Western and Eastern Europe. *Patterns of Prejudice* 49 (1–2): 103–134.

Hewitt, Roger. 2005. *White Backlash and the Politics of Multiculturalism*. Cambridge: Cambridge University Press.

Köttig, Michaela, Renate Bitzen, and Andrea Petö, eds. 2017. *Gender and Far Right Politics in Europe*. Basingstoke: Palgrave Macmillan.

Kundnani, Arun. 2012. Multiculturalism and Its Discontents: Left, Right and Liberal. *European Journal of Cultural Studies* 15 (2): 155–166.

Lim, Jason, and Alexandra Fanghanel. 2013. 'Hijabs, Hoodies and Hotpants'; Negotiating the 'Slut' in SlutWalk. *Geoforum* 48: 207–215.

Mayer, Nonna. 2013. From Jean-Marie to Marine Le Pen: Electoral Change on the Far Right. *Parliamentary Affairs* 66 (1): 160–178.

Mayer, Stephanie, Edma Ajanovic, and Birgit Sauer. 2014. Intersections and Inconsistencies. Framing Gender in Right-Wing Populist Discourses in

Austria. *NORA—Nordic Journal of Feminist and Gender Research* 22 (4): 250–266.
Mudde, Cas. 1996. The Paradox of the Anti-party Party. *Party Politics* 2 (2): 265–276.
———. 2004. The Populist Zeitgeist. *Government and Opposition* 38 (4): 541–563.
Mudde, Cas, and Cristóbal Rovira Kaltwasser. 2015. Vox Populi or Vox Masculini? Populism and Gender in Northern Europe and South America. *Patterns of Prejudice* 49 (1–2): 16–36.
Puar, Jasbir. 2014. Rethinking Homonationalism. *International Journal of Middle East Studies* 45 (2): 336–339.
Rhodes, James. 2010. White Backlash, 'Unfairness' and Justifications of British National Party (BNP) Support. *Ethnicities* 10 (1): 77–99.
Sanders-McDonagh, Erin. 2014. Conducting 'Dirty Research' with Extreme Groups: Understanding Academia as a Dirty Work Site. *Qualitative Research in Organizations and Management: An International Journal* 9 (3): 241–253.
Spierings, Niels, and Andrej Zaslove. 2015. Conclusion: Dividing the Populist Radical Right Between 'Liberal Nativism' and Traditional Conceptions of Gender. *Patterns of Prejudice* 49 (1–2): 163–173.
Spierings, Niels, Andrej Zaslove, Liza M. Mügge, and Sarah L. de Lange. 2015. Gender and Populist Radical-Right Politics: An Introduction. *Patterns of Prejudice* 49 (1–2): 3–15.
Tufail, Waqas. 2015. Rotherham, Rochdale, and the Racialized Threat of the 'Muslim Grooming Gang'. *International Journal for Crime, Justice and Social Democracy* 4 (3): 30–43.
Zúquete, José Pedro. 2008. The European Extreme-Right and Islam: New Directions? *Journal of Political Ideologies* 13 (3): 321–344.
———. 2015. The New Frontlines of Right-Wing Nationalism. *Journal of Political Ideologies* 20 (1): 69–85.

# 10

# Feminism and Nationalism in Québec

Diane Lamoureux

## Introduction

Feminism and nationalism have intertwined in the Quebec feminist movement since the end of the 1960s. In so doing, this movement situated itself in a long tradition since there was, at the beginning of the century, a feminist organization called la *Fédération nationale Saint-Jean-Baptiste* [The National Saint-Jean-Baptiste Federation]. While Quebec women have been *deboutte*[1] [standing up] since the end of the 1960s, the connection between feminist and nationalist movements in Quebec, but also the definition of the nation elaborated by the feminist movement over the years, are a lot more fluid.

---

[1] *Québécoises deboutte!* [Québécoises stand up!] is the name of the first issue of the journal published by the *Front de libération des femmes du Québec* [Women's Liberation Front of Quebec], a title later taken on by the *Centre des femmes* [Women's Centre]. The slogan was used once again in 2009 by the *Fédération des femmes du Québec* [Quebec Women's Federation] under the guise *Québécoises toujours deboutte* [Quebec women are still standing up].

D. Lamoureux (✉)
Département de science politique, Université Laval, Québec, QC, Canada

© The Author(s) 2018
J. Mulholland et al. (eds.), *Gendering Nationalism*,
https://doi.org/10.1007/978-3-319-76699-7_10

I would like to analyse the links between the two movements from the end of the 1960s to the middle of the 1990s, that is, from the creation of the *Front de Libération des Femmes* to the 1995 referendum. Second, I will examine how the neoliberal turn of the nationalist movement and the social justice turn of the feminist movement opened a space that made audible other voices in the feminist movement, mainly those of immigrant or racialized women and of Aboriginal women. Finally, I will insist on the gendered nature of the nation.

Initially, feminism and nationalism seemed united and Quebec feminists defined themselves as actively involved in the project for *Quebec national liberation*. Later on, the voices of ethnic women of long standing and recent immigration made themselves heard and known to a francophone majority that has had a tendency to ignore their existence. More recently, Aboriginal women have forced a reconfiguration of the nation and have questioned Quebec's national stance towards Aboriginal nations.

These three moments in Quebec feminism echo certain transformations occurring at the same time within Quebec nationalism. If the predominant discourse of the 1960s and 1970s is that of the colonized nation in need of political autonomy, that of the years 1980–1995 is rather that of Quebec Inc., as the movement moves from an ethnic to a civic definition of the nation while dealing with the effects of Bill 101. Since the 1995 referendum, Aboriginal peoples have contested the Indigenizing narrative advanced by the *Québécois de souche* [French Canadians born in Quebec] and have forced (thanks to the threat of partition) people of European background to reconsider their relations with the First Nations whose territory they have appropriated.

## When Women's Liberation Rhymes with Quebec Liberation

Like many social and feminist movements throughout the world, the women's liberation movement which emerged in Quebec at the end of the 1960s defines itself as partaking in the tradition of African, Asian, and Latin American national liberation movements that longed for political sovereignty and attempted to sever their relation of dependence with colonial powers (Fougeyrollas-Schwebel 1997).

The slogan deployed by the Front de libération des femmes [Women's Liberation Front] is very clear on that subject: "No Quebec liberation without women's liberation, no women's liberation without Quebec liberation!".[2] The emergence of this organization is also intricately connected to Quebec's nationalist movement. Following massive protests on the status of the French language (such as French McGill as well as the important mobilization against Bill 63 which aimed to grant parents the right to choose in which language their children could study), the city of Montreal adopted a new regulation which severely limited the right to demonstrate. Radical nationalist groups[3] subsequently decided to organize a protest in reaction to this new measure. This protest took the form of a women's demonstration. These women were subsequently arrested because of the new regulation, and while in prison, they began to discuss their status within the militant groups to which they belonged. "People must know that we fight for women's liberation within the revolutionary movement and that we will no longer tolerate discrimination against us within this movement"[4] (Manifesto 1971: 13). This is where the idea to create a *Front de libération des femmes* [Women's Liberation Front] arose, and the Front emerged a few months later.

The ideas which the *Front de Libération des Femmes* conveyed can be accessed through three main sources: there is a work published retrospectively by two former FLF activists, Véronique O'Leary and Louise Toupin

---

[2] "Pas de Québec libre sans libération des femmes, pas de femmes libres sans libération du Québec!"
[3] The Parti Québécois was founded in 1968 as a result of the fusion between *Option Québec* (a group centred around René Lévesque and which represented the sovereigntist wing of the Liberal Party) and the *Rassemblement national* [National Rally] (a rather ethnic nationalist group). On the same year, the Rassemblement pour l'indépendance nationale [Rally for National Independence] (left-wing nationalist) dissolved and asked its members to join the *Parti Québécois*, a request which did not please its left wing, led by Andrée Ferretti. At that time, the Parti Québécois was far from having homogenized all nationalist forces, and outside this political formation, many nationalist groups were active in the extra-parliamentary arena. Among the most active organizations outside the electoral scene, excluding groups dedicated to the linguistic question as well as the *Société Saint-Jean-Baptiste*, we can mention the *Front de Libération du Québec* [Quebec Liberation Front], which virtually disappeared following the two kidnappings that led to the October Crisis in 1970, and the Front de libération populaire [Popular Liberation Front].
[4] "On doit savoir que nous lutterons pour la libération des femmes au sein du mouvement révolutionnaire et que nous ne tolérerons plus d'être discriminées à l'intérieur même de ce movement"

(1982), which contains a rather lengthy analysis of the emergence of the FLF and reproduces every issue of *Québécoises Deboutte!*; there is the *Manifeste des femmes québécoises* [*Quebec Women's Manifesto*], which was not written by FLF members but contains ideas similar to those the FLF conveyed; and there are academic theses and dissertations on this topic (Lanctôt 1980 and Lamoureux 1986).

What clearly emerges from these sources is that the FLF posited itself as composed of francophone Quebec feminists who, while looking for a way to define their feminism, found the right words to articulate their revolt in the radical nationalism of the time. This implied from the start a decision to take some distance from the group Montreal Women's Liberation, whose members were mostly connected to McGill University and therefore English speaking. However, certain links between the two groups endured because of their common concern for the reference service for abortion. Furthermore, because the Quebec women's movement was intertwined with nationalism, it evolved quite differently from its counterpart in the rest of Canada (ROC).

By defining Quebec as an oppressed and colonized nation, these feminists reclaimed membership in the Quebec nation and adopted the discourse of nationalist decolonization. This narrative pays considerable attention to social dimensions (some even go as far as defining Quebec as a proletarian nation) and borrows the notion of a necessary break from the colonizers from the decolonization movements (mainly Fanon[5] and Memmi) of the 1960s and 1970s:

> Unlike most women in Western feminist movements, early Quebec feminists were more attuned to the Third World than others; we felt very close to women belonging to Third World liberation movements. Feminists of the early seventies were, unlike the international movement, nationalists.[6] (O'Leary and Toupin 1982: 27)

---

[5] Fanon re-emerged later on in postcolonial thought, but only after being reinterpreted by anglophone postcolonial thinkers.

[6] "À l'encontre de la majorité des femmes formant le mouvement féministe des pays occidentaux, les féministes québécoises de la première heure étaient plus tiers-mondistes qu'ailleurs; on se sentait très près des femmes des mouvements de libération du tiers-monde. Les féministes de cette première vague étaient, à l'encontre du mouvement international, nationalistes".

Feminism is therefore perceived by the FLF and the Centre des femmes [Women's Centre] as an inherent part of this decolonization process, as it simultaneously sought the emergence of a new country and a redefinition of women's status within the sovereignty-seeking nation. The importance of the modernizing impulse within Quebec nationalism (i.e. the desire to modernize Quebec by forcing it out of la *grande noirceur* [the Great Darkness]) resulted in a certain convergence between feminism and nationalism that endured, despite its ups and downs, until the 1995 referendum.

At that time, the emphasis was on white francophone women, and they constituted the predominant, if not the only, reference group in the Quebec feminist movement. It is true that some Quebec women, such as Madeleine Parent,[7] supported Aboriginal women's struggle for the recognition of their status, but Parent was long considered to be a Canadian feminist, and her behaviour is far from representative of the dominant stance in Quebec feminism.

In fact, the FLF's main concern was to contest the patriarchal family and the exploitation of women who performed paid or unpaid work. As this passage from *Bulletin de liaison FLFQ* issue 2, August 1971 indicates:

> Because the exploitation specific to women is based on material conditions connected to the division of labour, to the structure of the family, and to class-based society, and that Quebec's women's liberation requires the transformation of the family and the destruction of the current economic and political system.[8] (reproduced in O'Leary and Toupin 1982: 107)

---

[7] Madeleine Parent was a union organizer who became famous after numerous strikes involving mainly women in the textile industry in Quebec during and immediately after World War II. She was a founding member of the National Action Committee on the Status of Women, an organization that sought to federate women's groups in Canada, in 1972, and became Quebec representative on its board from 1972 to 1983. She was also involved in the Fédération des femmes du Québec and participated in the *Marche du pain et des roses* [Bread and Roses March] in 1995 and the World March of Women in 2000.

[8] "Parce que l'exploitation spécifique des femmes est basée sur des conditions matérielles qui sont liées à la division du travail, à la structure de la famille et de la société de classes et que la libération des femmes québécoises nécessite la transformation de la famille et la destruction du système économique et politique actuel".

Feminism has undergone multiple transformations since then, but even though both nationalism and anti-capitalism have faded away, the national referent is not under question. The women that Quebec feminism believes itself to represent and for whom it desires emancipation are still, essentially, the *Québécoises de souche*.

It is only in 1990 that francophone Quebec women will feel a more pressing need to take into consideration their relationship with other Quebec feminists. That year marked the 50th anniversary of women's suffrage[9] in Quebec, an event which was celebrated with great pomp. While seeking a prestigious spokesperson for the event, the organizers chose Lise Payette, a former P.Q. Minister Responsible for the Status of Women, but also the director of a documentary entitled *Disparaître*, a movie which draws attention to the threats to Quebec national survival caused by the combined effects of the low birth-rate among francophone Quebec women and immigration. This choice angered women of immigrant background groups, and forced the Quebec feminist movement to reflect on its practices.

It took some time for this reflection to achieve results, as it is only in 1992 that the *Forum pour un Québec féminin pluriel* was organized. This required a new way to conceive the nation in Quebec, and especially, the role that Quebec women of diverse backgrounds could play in the definition of feminism. This Forum enabled Quebec feminism to take into account the combined effects of Bill 101[10] and Quebec's failure to achieve sovereign status. While the Quebec nation is oppressed in Canada, within its own political sphere, it operates as a majority group that engages in complex relations—relations that have yet to be fully problematized—

---

[9] It would be more appropriate to talk about suffrage for non-Aboriginal women in Quebec. Aboriginal peoples, both men and women, only obtained suffrage in 1960 following an amendment to the Canadian *Indian Act*.

[10] The Charter of the French Language (Bill101) is a law that was passed by the Parti Québécois in 1977 defining French as the official language in Quebec. One of its main provisions was to ensure that the language of instruction, from kindergarten to secondary school, should be French. As a result immigrants, who previously used to attend English-speaking schools and assimilate to the English-speaking group, started to attend French-speaking public schools and became more in contact with the French-speaking majority group and more involved in social movements, including the feminist movement. After Bill 101, Québécois of French descent became more aware of Québec diversity and most of them rally around a civic rather than an ethnic definition of the Québécois nation.

with its anglophone minority, its Aboriginal minority (which were not defined as such during the Forum), and with its diverse cultural minorities of recent immigration background which are politically constituted through the Canadian policy of multiculturalism. Since the adoption of Bill 101 in Quebec, these communities of immigrant background are in more frequent contact with the francophone majority.

The predominant concern which emerged during the *Forum* relates to the desire, on the part of Quebec feminists, to evolve towards a form of civic nationalism in accordance with Quebec intercultural policies. The *Forum* insisted on the need to integrate women from "various backgrounds"[11] within Quebec feminism while maintaining its francophone nature, a process which eventually led to a questioning of the practices of mainstream feminism.

At the same time, many consider these efforts to be too weak and insufficient. For instance, Osmani (2002: 145) insists on the fact that:

> The engagement remains insufficient not because of its modes of actions, but because of the operating practices in these organizations [...] the types of resistance towards "ethnocultural" diversity are strong and reveal the relations of domination between majorities and minorities within the movement.[12]

In the document produced after the *Forum pour un Québec féminin pluriel*, the organizers argued that they had managed

> to gain, for the first time, the participation of groups of women of colour and of ethnic backgrounds, a coming together of prime importance for all, considering the diversity of ethnocultural women's organizations and the tense history of our past alliances.[13] (Beauchamp 1994: 23)

---

[11] Expression used by the FFQ committee concerned with questions of immigration and racism.
[12] "l'engagement reste insuffisant non pas tant en matière de modalités d'action, mais surtout en fait de pratiques au sein des organisations. [...] Les résistances sur la question de la diversité « ethnoculturelle » sont fortes et révèlent une dynamique de domination entre majoritaires et minoritaires au sein du mouvement"
[13] "s'allier, pour la première fois, la participation des groupes de femmes de toutes couleurs et origines ethniques, un rapprochement de première importance pour toutes, vu la diversité des organisations de femmes des communautés ethnoculturelles et l'histoire difficile de nos alliances passées"

One chapter in this volume is dedicated to ethnocultural diversity, dealing with Aboriginal women on the one hand, and ethnocultural communities of more or less recent immigration on the other. Following this meeting, the main feminist organization, the Fédération des femmes du Québec (FFQ), signed a working agreement with Femmes autochtones du Québec (FAQ) [Quebec Native Women (QNW)], and instigated a committee for "women of diverse backgrounds".

As is often the case with Quebec feminism, this question was more effectively addressed in practice than in theory. Not long after the *Forum*, it is possible to notice a certain change in the practices of the feminist movements: since the mid-1970s, the movement was centred on the multiplicity of groups and issues, with a common focus on the question of abortion on demand. As the struggle over abortion was partially won following the Supreme Court decision in the Morgentaler Affair, a gain then confirmed and consolidated in the Tremblay vs. Daigle decision, there no longer was any central mobilizing theme:

Not long after the *Forum*, the preparation for the *Marche du pain et des roses* [Bread and Roses March] began. It enabled the repositioning of feminism in the social field as its dominant theme was that of women's struggle against poverty. This repositioning allowed all women affected by poverty to come together regardless of their ethnic background. The work performed collaboratively during this mobilization created trust and new solidarities beyond the fractures that existed over the question of Quebec's political status.[14]

During these three decades, if the feminist movement developed with a close association to the nationalist movement, it was not a one-sided relationship. If nationalism was a vehicle to mainstream feminism and to obtain major transformations in the status of women in Quebec, the responsiveness of nationalism to feminism and to the LGBTQI rights movement was a guarantee of modernity for Quebec nationalism. It explains why labelling equality between men and women as a core value of Quebec society has been used as a way to oppose the "good" and

---

[14] This fracture however re-emerged when the FFQ, the main organization behind the March, pronounced itself in favour of Quebec sovereignty during the 1992 Bélanger-Campeau Commission, and participated in activities designed by *Partenaires de la souveraineté* [Partners for Sovereignty] during the 1995 referendum.

"modern" Quebec society to the "backward" immigration, mainly the one from the Arab or Muslim worlds.

What united the feminist and the nationalist movements at that time was the project of modernizing Quebec society by the means of a welfare State, although its significance differs in the two movements. For nationalists, the welfare State is a mean of economic prosperity, of sustaining Quebec capitalism, and of developing national cohesion through redistributive policies. For feminists, it means that tasks that were traditionally performed by women, within the family and without pay (like care for young, old, sick, or handicapped persons), will take the form of public services and will provide job opportunities for women.

During this period there exists indeed a "velvet triangle" which allowed major improvements in women's status.[15] The most important is probably civil equality between men and women which resulted from the transformation of family law. There are also major improvements regarding education (from kindergarten to university). The development of a large public service, mainly in the areas of education, health, and social services, provided new job opportunities for women.

In this "velvet triangle", the stimulus came mainly from the feminist movement. Women organized and mobilized to achieve those huge transformations. During this process they forged alliances with other groups (trade unions, community organizations, professional associations, etc.) and accumulated a knowledge that social scientists converted into "expertise". Feminists were heard by professionals in the State administration that transformed them into public policies.

So the association between nationalists and feminists was useful for both. Most feminists support the nationalist project of creating a Quebec nation-State and conferred a progressive varnish to the sovereigntist project. In return feminists obtained major transformations to women's juridical, social, and political status. But things started to change after the 1995 referendum: while nationalism converted to neoliberalism, feminism engaged more deeply in a social justice agenda.

---

[15] During this period most governments were formed by the Liberal Party although the Parti Québécois was in power from 1976 to 1985 and from 1994 to 2003. But at that time the Liberal Party although it strongly rejected Quebec sovereignty was nationalist and contributed to the development of Quebec welfare State.

## 1995 as a Turning Point

This reorientation of feminist concerns led to a better integration of women of immigrant background "The modes of action adopted by these movements [Bread and Roses March in 1995 and the World March of Women (WMW) in 2000] were more inclusive and integrated the concerns of immigrant women who, it should be noted, did not boycott these mobilizations"[16] (Osmani 2002: 144).

This new sensitivity towards ethnic diversity within Quebec society was amplified once the FFQ decided to participate in the WMW's process and developed links with women's groups around the world. The WMW also led to participation in the first World Social Forum in Porto Alegre in 2001, a forum which advocated, among other things, engagements towards antiracism and maintained a certain level of interest in Aboriginal issues, due in part to the political progression of Indigenous movements in many Latin American countries.

In any case, this new sensitivity was developed more on the basis of international solidarity than on that of antiracism within Quebec feminism. However, it is only during the *États généraux du féminisme* in 2012–2013 that the concerns of Aboriginal women were clearly addressed, and intersectionality became more widespread within Quebec feminism.

The relations between feminists of European background and Aboriginal women are older than the process which led to the 2012–2013 *États généraux du féminisme*. For instance, as I mentioned previously, Madeleine Parent played a ground-breaking role in developing those relations, and so did the 2004 agreement between the FFQ and Quebec Native Women. Furthermore, it should be noted that the World March of Women[17] played a crucial part in furthering these relations and that

---

[16] "Les modalités d'action de ces mouvements [*du Pain et des roses en 1995* et la Marche mondiale des femmes (MMF) en 2000] ont alors été plus inclusives et ont intégré les préoccupations des immigrantes qui n'ont d'ailleurs pas boudé ces mobilisations".

[17] The World March of Women is an international movement connecting grassroots groups and organizations working to eliminate poverty and violence against women. The movement developed after the Fédération des femmes du Québec, in the aftermath of the Marche du Pain et des Roses, and launched an appeal to international action and solidarity. The first World March took place in

anti-globalization movements have generated accrued sensitivity to Aboriginal issues.

The most striking element of the *États généraux* was however the place given to Aboriginal women. Not only did they co-organize the event (the organization committee was led by the president of the FFQ, Alexa Conradi; a representative from the women of cultural communities, Délice Mugabo; and a representative from Quebec Native Women, Isabelle Picard), but one of the convention's main concern was also the issue of solidarity with Aboriginal women.

This concern for Aboriginal women can be viewed as an indirect result of the *Idle No More* movement. Composed of Aboriginal women, this movement functions outside the usual frameworks of Aboriginal organizations and operates as a crossroad between Aboriginal land claims, environmental concerns, and feminist activism.

It is nonetheless important to note that the theme of the États généraux's attention to Aboriginal issues, entitled "Autodétermination et solidarité avec les femmes autochtones" [Self-Determination and Solidarity with Aboriginal Women], recognized the right of Aboriginal women (and Aboriginal communities) to self-determination. It also stresses the autonomy of their movement in relation to mainstream feminism in Quebec, as the links between the two movements were defined through the notion of solidarity.

Despite the remarkable advance represented by the attention mainstream feminism in Quebec paid to the concerns of Aboriginal women, the *États généraux* barely addressed the fraught subject, that is, the colonial relations of power between Canadian and Quebec elites on the one hand and Aboriginal peoples on the other. For that reason, the issue of white solipsism[18] and its impact on the self-constructions of Aboriginal women and "white"[19] feminists was largely pushed aside.

---

2000. Since then the WMW has organized international actions every five years. The WMW also attended the first Social Forum in Porto Alegre in 2001.

[18] I am borrowing this concept from Adrienne Rich (1979, 306), who uses it to describe "not the consciously held *belief* that one race is inherently Superior to all others, but a tunnel-vision which simply does not see nonwhite experience or existence as precious or significant".

[19] I place this term between quotation marks because there is no proof that racialized feminists possess a different attitude towards Aboriginal peoples than their counterparts of European descent.

More specifically, postcolonial feminist theories can demonstrate how social subjects are constructed and contribute to the construction of the social relations in which they are located. They thereby prevent the victimization of some women and enable a real understanding of their experiences within the elaboration of a truly inclusive feminist discourse. Postcolonial theories also enable a thorough understanding of the construction of a historical narrative which not only erased women but also all subaltern subjects. In the complex relationship Quebec maintains with the colonization/decolonization process, as a "conquered nation, but also as a nation complicit with the triumphant West, which adheres to the narrative of the two founding nations, from which the notions of conquest, genocide, and slavery have been erased"[20] (Maillé 2007: 98) such theories might be helpful. However, if we want to reinsert all women within history and not only those who might benefit from neoliberal policies of "elite diversification", it is necessary to bring all those experiences to light and demonstrate that women's liberation can never occur through a racist framework that allows some to be more equal than others.

This implies, as Maillé mentions, a rethinking of the relationships between mainstream feminists and other Quebec feminists in terms of co-subjectivity. While discussing the paradoxes inherent to mainstream feminism in Quebec, she mentions that:

> If Quebec feminism has recently demonstrated an interest in notions of difference, without however allowing subaltern women to fully occupy the status of subjects within that feminism, it is because this interest occurred without any real understanding of the power relations which continue to operate in the definition of the essentialist female subject at the heart of feminist activism in Quebec.[21] (Maillé 2007: 96)

---

[20] "nation conquise, mais également nation complice d'un Occident triomphant, adhérant au récit des deux peuples fondateurs, duquel est occulté toute référence à l'idée de conquête, de génocide ou d'esclavage".

[21] "[s]i le féminisme québécois a montré récemment des signes d'ouverture aux questions de différences, sans toutefois que les femmes subalternes accèdent pleinement au statut de sujets de ce féminisme, c'est que cette ouverture s'est faite sans véritable réflexion sur les dynamiques de pouvoir qui continuent d'opérer dans la définition du sujet-femme universel au centre des revendications des féministes québécoises".

Unfortunately, the *États généraux* represent a partially failed endeavour in this respect.

## Gendering the Nation

We can think about the gendered nature of the nation at least from two perspectives. The first one consists in the manner in which nationalists (of any gender) apprehend the gender of the nation. When the emphasis is put on oppression, it is either gendered as female or as an emasculated male. During the referendum campaign of 1995, nationalists compared the political situation of Quebec with that of a battered wife, or a younger sister that is pushed aside by her older brother (ROC). Many poets used the metaphor of a man standing on his knees to describe the political situation of Quebec, others described the incapacity of having a sovereign State as an emasculation. When described as a male, Quebec society is always a son who will never reach adulthood. In the past, the "son" was under the domination the Catholic Church, a kind of phallic mother. Nowadays, it is governed by the federal government, a kind of absent father, that deprives the "son" of his natural development.

When the emphasis is put on affirmation and self-definition, suddenly Quebec society is defined as a modern man, featuring such masculine traits as audacity, ambition, and performance. No longer a "son", this man is able to become the founding father of the future State, the hero of his own liberation.

When discussing the reproduction of the nation, this reproduction can be conceptualized from the perspective of gendered social roles that allow it to operate biologically (such as the role women played in the *revanche des berceaux* [the revenge of the cradles] or in the production of "white babies") or culturally (such as the father's role in the transmission of culture) within a heteronormative framework. When the culture is transmitted in the privacy of the family, it is the responsibility of the mother to ensure this reproduction, by teaching the "langue maternelle", but when it is transmitted through State institutions such as schools, even if most of the teachers in elementary and secondary schools are women, it becomes la "culture de nos pères" [the culture of our fathers].[22]

The second perspective consists in the manner in which feminists problematize their relation to the nation. As we can see, this problematization has fluctuated over time. At first, Quebec feminism situated itself within a politically charged ethnic nationalism. However, it was not perceived as ethnic by the feminists since it was associated with a national liberation project that can be compared with the accession to independence of Third World countries that were previously colonized by European powers.

The critiques articulated by ethnicized or racialized women's groups, as well as its engagement in mobilizations against violence and poverty, or in international solidarity through the WMW, eventually led the movement to endorse a form of civic nationalism. In this view, women of the majority group (French-speaking white Quebeckers) have either to open up to "others'" realities, trying to understand their experiences and make space for them in order to include them in the Québécois society or to assimilate them to the majority/dominant group. If they professed the first solution, most of Quebec feminists have in reality adopted the second. It is exemplified by the fact that the FFQ, the main feminist organization of this period, had a committee dealing with the issues of immigration and racism that was labelled "femmes de diverses origines".

It is only recently that mainstream feminism in Quebec has opened itself up to intersectionality. It is possible to argue that the recent attention to intersectionality enabled the development of practices that take into account the interactions between different systems of power and develop modes of solidarity that take women's diverse localizations within social relations into consideration. However, if, at a pragmatic level, intersectionality appears to be a relevant compass, it is clearly insufficient to understand the complex social relations within feminist activism or to enable subaltern voices to emerge, even within feminist movements. It is true that it has prevented many from adopting the deceitful discourse of "benevolent racism" that understands Third World women—particularly Muslim women—as the new terrain to be liberated and modernized,

---

[22] I have already addressed this issue in more detail in Lamoureux 2001.

especially since September 11, 2001. Nevertheless, a feminist critique of past and present modes of globalization still needs to be elaborated, and then translated into feminist activism.

## Conclusion

Inasmuch as the defeat of the 1995 referendum coincides with a new strand of feminist activism dedicated to end violence and poverty, nationalist and feminist concerns have become increasingly divergent; yet, some points of convergence remain. Thus, the equality between the sexes has become a "*valeur fondamentale de la société québécoise* [fundamental value in Quebec society]" and has even been instrumentalized through a form of "benevolent racism" by ethnonationalists who want to differentiate themselves from the "barbarians" of immigrant background who veil "their" women.

Moreover, some feminists did believe that the modernization of the Quebec state had succeeded in creating a secular society, which must now be defended because the rise of religious fundamentalism threatens the equality between the sexes (Guilbault 2008). There were harsh debates when the Parti Québécois decided to promote a Charter that linked equality between men and women, secularism, and employment in the public services. While some feminists agree with the PQ's project (those who were convinced of the link between secularism and the equality between women and men), which is a new variation of the trope of the white man saving the women of colour from the men of colour that was denounced in Spivak's famous essay, most feminists, including the main organization, the FFQ, developed another kind of argument: how can we equate feminism with the exclusion of women from public schools and employment in public services? Since the main purpose of the Charter was to ban "ostensible religious signs" from public organizations, and the debate mainly focused on Muslim women headscarves, they argued that the right of Muslim women to enrol in public schools and eventually get a job in the public services was more important than the way they dressed. In that respect there was a gap between feminists and nationalists regarding the very definition of the nation.

Furthermore, the fact that the *Parti Québécois* adopted an increasingly neoliberal agenda after its defeat in the 1995 referendum and that the feminist movement promoted a social justice agenda added to the gap between feminists and nationalists. If, in the 1960s and the 1970s, nationalism was perceived by most social movements, including the feminist movement, as a means to develop a welfare State that promoted the economic and social development of Québec, it is not the case anymore. This neoliberal agenda explains why the *Parti Québécois* moved back to an ethnic vision of the nation while the majority of feminists, including those who still promote Quebec independence, still adhere to a civic vision of the nation and are increasingly adopting an intersectional version of feminism.

# References

Beauchamp, Colette, ed. 1994. *Pour Changer le Monde. Le Forum Pour un Québec Féminin Pluriel*. Montréal: Écosociété.
Fougeyrollas-Schwebel, Dominique. 1997. Le Féminisme des Années 1970. In *Encyclopédie Politique et Historique du Féminisme*, ed. Christine Fauré, 729–770. Paris: Presses Universitaires de France.
Guilbault, Diane. 2008. *Démocratie et Égalité des Sexes*. Montréal: Sisyphe.
Lamoureux, Diane. 1986. *Fragments et Collages. Essai sur le Féminisme Québécois des Années 70*. Montréal: Remue-ménage.
———. 2001. *L'Amère Patrie*. Montréal: Remue-ménage.
Lanctôt, Martine. 1980. *Genèse et Evolution du Mouvement Féministe à Montréal*. M.A. Dissertation, UQAM.
Maillé, Chantal. 2007. Réception de la Théorie Postcoloniale dans le Féminisme Québécois. *Recherches Féministes* 20 (2): 91–111.
*Manifeste des Femmes Québécoises*. 1971. Montréal: L'Étincelle.
O'Leary, Véronique, and Louise Toupin. 1982. *Québécoises Deboutte!* Tome 1. Montréal: Remue-Ménage.
Osmani, Farida. 2002. L'égalité pour Toutes? L'Engagement Féministe et les Droits des Immigrantes au Québec. *Recherches Féministes* 15 (2): 124–145.
Rich, Adrienne. 1979. *Disloyal to Civilization: Feminism, Racism, Gynephobia (1978)*, On Lies, Secret and Silence, 275–310. New York: Norton.

# 11

# Women's Support for UKIP: Exploring Gender, Nativism, and the Populist Radical Right (PRR)

Erin Sanders-McDonagh

## Introduction

In May of 2015, the UK Independence Party (UKIP), led by Nigel Farage, garnered 3,881,099 votes from the UK public in the national general elections. While this resulted in only one parliamentary seat, the vote share for UKIP was 12.6% making them the third most popular party among UK voters (behind the Conservatives who held 36.9% and Labour with 30.4%). In the 2016 local elections, UKIP were able to increase their share of seats across Local Councils by 26, giving them a total of 58 seats across England. UKIP Wales also gained seven regional seats in the Welsh Assembly, and two seats in the London Assembly. UKIP's 2014 manifesto makes clear their anti-EU stance, and at the same time focuses on the 'real alternative' they provide to other UK political parties that, they claim, fail to tell the truth about issues such as immigration, jobs, and housing (UKIP 2014). While UKIP's vote share was

E. Sanders-McDonagh (✉)
School of Social Policy, Sociology and Social Research, University of Kent, Canterbury, UK

greatly diminished in the 2017 General Election, an exploration of UKIP as a populist radical right (PRR) party is still worthy of academic attention in the context of wider discussions about the nature of PRR parties in Europe (c.f. Mudde 2007; Akkerman 2015).

Populist radical right parties emerged in Europe in the 1990s and have become an important feature of Western democracies (Akkerman 2015), achieving electoral success in the past decade in many European countries (Spierings and Zaslove 2015). PRR parties have also been successful to the extent that some populist ideas have been incorporated into mainstream political parties (Mudde 2004). While some have argued that populism exists as a political style (Moffitt and Toomey 2014) or a political strategy (Wetland 2001), Mudde (2004) and Spierings et al. (2015) consider populism to be a 'thin centered-ideology'. PRR parties often self-define as anti-establishment and anti-ideological and suggest their policies and approaches are 'common sense' (Mayer 2013). They claim to express the will of the people, and as such do not seek to change 'the people' (their way of life, value-systems, etc.), but rather seek to emancipate them from the oppression they currently experience under the rule of the political elites (Mudde 2014). Mudde (2014) argues that populism in this sense is reactive, rather than original or generative, and PRR parties often emerge in times of upheaval or crisis and capitalize on feelings of discontent and sometimes fear in order to present themselves as viable alternatives to mainstream politics. There have been a number of recent European studies that suggest there has been an increase in people supporting and voting for PRR parties, with some researchers suggesting this surge is the result of a shift in voters' concerns about social and cultural changes, as opposed to concerns about the economy or fiscal issues (Webb and Bale 2014; Van der Brug and Van Spanje 2009; Mudde 2009).

This chapter adds to existing literature on the nature of PRR parties by looking at the particular context of the UK, offering empirical evidence from supporters of England's leading PRR party: UKIP. Data drawn from in-depth qualitative interviews are presented here, collected as part of a wider study on women and nationalist movements in the UK (see Mulholland, this collection). This chapter will explore issues related to women's support for UKIP as a PRR party, and will focus on a key characteristic associated with PRR support as outlined by Mudde (2007): nativism. Mudde (2007) provides an in-depth overview of nativism, suggesting that nativist sentiments draw both in nationalist/patriotic ideas about a given country and, consonantly, a fear of immigrants and Others (often non-white Others). Nativism can thus be understood as a preference for people/ideas that are seen as 'native' to one's own country and, at the same time, 'a fear/hatred of everything that is non-native' (Immerzeel et al. 2015: 266). Harteveld et al. (2015) suggest that within Europe, nativism is a strong predictor of PRR voting, and as such warrants attention—particularly in relation to women's support for PRR parties. Understanding the relationship between nativism and gender, however, is rather complicated; Mudde (2007, 113) argues, for example, that there is little variation by gender in relation to expressions of nativism: 'the difference between men and women in terms of nativist attitudes is far from striking, if at all present', while Coenders et al. (2004) argue that in some cases women are more likely than men to express nativist opinions. In their comparative study of PRR parties in Europe, Harteveld et al. (2015) suggest that while men and women express similar levels of nativist sentiments, they maintain that women are less likely to vote for PRR parties. Immerzeel et al. (2015), on the other hand, suggest that men are more likely to be attracted by nativism than women. This chapter seeks to provide further insights into this debate by presenting data from female PRR supporters, specifically UKIP supporters; I argue that nativism is interpolated by our female interviewees in highly gendered ways and is an important part of our participants' motivations for supporting UKIP. This chapter maintains that for these women, expressions of nativism focus largely on the threat of Islam on British culture and values. In particular the threat of Islam in relation to women's rights is highlighted as a key issue, and interviews suggest that participants see 'indigenous', British women as fully fledged citizens in a gender-equal nation, while Muslim women are seen as subjugated by their culture. This chapter adds to extant research on women's support for PRR parties by demonstrating the importance of this dyadic trope in the narratives of these interviewees.

## Methodology

This chapter draws on data gathered as part of a British Academy/Leverhulme-funded qualitative study of women supporters of nationalist organizations in the UK, specifically UKIP, the English Defence League, and the British National Party. The data informing this chapter are drawn from 11 in-depth semi-structured interviews with UKIP supporters. Having failed to secure access to UKIP members via UKIP themselves, participants were recruited via their participation on UKIP Facebook pages, and specifically by private messaging those who were actively posting, or contributing to existing posts, on such pages. The effect of Facebook privacy settings was such that up to 90% of all messages were directed to the 'other folder', meaning it is highly likely that the bulk of those approached would have been unaware of our communication unless they happened to check the content of this folder. With only a 10% response rate, allied to those recipients who refused to participate in the project, the population sample was very small, entirely self-selected, and lacking in any capacity for substantive representativeness, or even purposive sampling. In the main, and in the interests of viability, the interviews were conducted via Skype or telephone. Research suggests that: where participants receive informational support in advance, where interviews take place at a convenient time for the participant, and where care is taken to establish rapport, then telephone/Skype interviews can produce rich data, and may even prove preferable to face-to-face interviews in facilitating open and frank dialogue (Drabble et al. 2016). Certainly, the lengthy and semi-structured nature of the interviews enables the generation of a rich and nuanced dataset, with some significant degree of saturation. We present data from 11 participants here, all of whom consider themselves to be UKIP supporters. Participants had an older profile, with two aged 40–59, three aged 50–59, and six over 60. Four reported themselves as married, five as single, one widowed, and one as dating. Nine described themselves as straight, and two as lesbian. Four participants were educated to graduate level, two to tertiary level, three to secondary level, and two declined to comment. Six were retired, three were self-employed, and two were employed in semi-skilled or unskilled capacity. All identified their country of birth as English and their ethnicity as white. Three identified themselves as practicing Christians, three as non-practicing believers, one as agnostic, and four as atheists. Four confirmed themselves as UKIP members, and seven as voters/supporters.

## Gender and PRR Parties: The Case of UKIP

Many have argued that UKIP is best understood as a PRR party (Abedi and Lundberg 2009; Ford and Goodwin 2014; Clarke et al. 2016; Evans and Mellon 2016; Hayton 2016). Lynch and Whitaker (2013) suggest that immigration, concerns about Islam, and euro-skepticism are all key issues of concern for this group of voters, and maintain UKIP voters tend to have lower levels of trust in mainstream parties/politicians. In a similar vein, Ford et al. (2012) argue that while euro-skepticism is a main driver for many UKIP supporters—indeed, 99% of UKIP supporters voted to leave the EU in the 2016 referendum (IPSOS Mori 2016)—other attitudinal drives such as xenophobia and dissatisfaction with mainstream political parties are also important. Their quantitative study of 6000 UKIP supporters suggests that there are two types of UKIP voters—strategic voters and core supporters. Strategic voters, they argue, are more likely to be older, middle-class men who are financially secure and share similar attitudes with Conservative Party voters. While strategic voters express relatively high levels of racism and xenophobia, these are much lower than for the core supporters. Core supporters, they argue, share many of demographic features of those who support the far-right British National Party (BNP)—they are likely to be working class, have familial political histories associated with the Labour Party, and report struggling to live on their current incomes. UKIP supporters are generally older than BNP supporters, however, and while they share a sense of dissatisfaction with the mainstream parties, they are more moderate than those who support the BNP. The fact that UKIP's core support base has similar attitudinal features to far-right supporters is concerning, and their ability to engage women and older populations (who tend not to support the BNP) suggests that UKIP is a polite alternative to the BNP (Ford et al. 2012).

Others have outlined hypotheses that point to feelings of nostalgia and cultural nationalism as explanatory factors (Hayton 2016; Thorleifsson 2016). Thorleifsson (2016) in her study of former mining communities in the north of England (Doncaster specifically) suggests that this nostalgia, and the attendant support for UKIP, must be understood within the context of a post-Fordist, hyper-capitalist society that has left many areas like Doncaster in precarious positions. 'Contrary to only framing migrants and minorities as dangerous and polluting others, the Ukip [sic] supporters I interviewed framed newcomers as competitors in a precarious labor market, a factor driving anti-immigrant sentiment' (2016, 563). Thorleifsson suggests that in her study, white as well as non-white residents expressed these anxious sentiments. In a similar vein, Hayton (2016) argues that the politics of national identity are key to understanding UKIP's electoral base, and suggests that UKIP supporters are typically concerned with immigration. He cites research from Lord Ashcroft on UKIP support that maintains these concerns are 'emblematic of a deeper "dissatisfaction with the way they see things going in Britain" particularly in cultural terms' (Hayton 2016, 401). UKIP, Hayton argues, taps into pride about Britishness and its members are doubly compelled, both by UKIP's anti-immigration stance and by its focus on preserving traditional 'Britishness'. Hayton cites the 2015 UKIP Manifesto, which pledged specifically to celebrate 'Britishness' by taking pride in 'our country' and to 'promote a unifying British culture' (UKIP Manifesto 2015, in Hayton 2016, 403).

Akkerman (2015, 38) argues that 'gender issues have traditionally been important to the ideological profile of populist radical-right parties'. Gender in the PRR, she maintains, has often been characterized by the same conservative ideas about the valorization of the heteronormative family and the enshrining of normative gender roles. However, many studies on PRR parties (Kitschelt 1995; Norris 2005; Mudde 2007; Akkerman 2015) suggest that a shift within some European PRR parties has altered the political terrain. Rather than emphasizing traditional gender roles, many PRR parties have strategically employed ideas that seek to embrace gender equality and same-sex partnerships as a way to more clearly highlight the problems associated with immigrant Others. Akkerman (2015) suggests the PRR's renewed interest in gender issues is predicated on two key developments: the first is the heightened threat of Islam since 9/11, which resulted in an increased concern about immigration and integration and focuses on Islam as a particular threat to Western democracy. The second is related to the issue of family migration, which has gained political prominence in many European countries and replaces concerns about work and refugee immigration. As such, she maintains that 'debates about immigration and integration therefore increasingly focus on the family and the status of women' (Akkerman 2015, 40).

While UKIP has long been concerned with issues related to EU membership and relatedly immigration (Ford and Goodwin 2014; Clarke et al. 2016), they have only recently started to concern themselves with issues related to gender inequality. The 2014 Manifesto, for example, largely focuses on wresting national control from the European Union—neither gender nor issues related to women's rights are mentioned at all. The 2015 Manifesto is a more developed document and goes into more detail about concerns related to Muslim extremism and immigration. Concerns about gender and sex are highlighted in relation to education, including allowing parents to opt their children out of sex-education classes and addressing gender imbalances in the sciences; pushing for the increase of 'father's rights' in relation to custody splits and one mention of female genital mutilation (FGM) is included in the section on 'British Culture' (UKIP 2015, 61), making clear that FGM is a cultural issue that needs to be addressed in order to unify and 'reinvigorate' British culture.

By 2017, however, the Manifesto is much more obviously concerned with gender equality. Margot Parker, a UKIP MEP, is included in the Manifesto as the Women and Equalities spokesperson, and there are a number of pledges related to women's rights. Parker is quoted in the Manifesto in relation to the expansion of affordable childcare as saying: 'Affordable, safe childcare is vital if we are to help women obtain or return to work. We simply cannot afford to have highly skilled, highly trained women leaving the workplace, especially not if they are working in public service industries such as nursing and teaching' (UKIP 2015, 27). The specific mention of nursing and teaching, industries that are highly feminized and traditionally associated with women, is an important caveat here in their attention to women's rights. Equally problematic is their discussion of gender equality in the section entitled 'Britain United

Under One Law For All', where concerns about gender are very much framed as part of a wider discussion on British culture and values. The first paragraph speaks volumes about women's rights and clearly frames the political message (and is worth noting in its full form):

> If we compare the rights of women in the UK to those of the majority of women overseas, the contrast is striking. Acceptance of the concept of sexual equality is largely confined to a handful of economically advanced nations. Mass uncontrolled immigration has opened the door to a host of people from cultures with little or no respect for women, yet when their views have been challenged, some on the 'Left' of politics, in particular, have encouraged them to claim a 'victim' status they do not deserve. UKIP will challenge those who do not uphold the rights of women, or who set themselves on a deliberate collision course with core British values of equality, free speech and democracy. We will protect all women, regardless of their race, ethnicity or religion. Culture is not an excuse for crime, nor is ignorance of the law. (UKIP 2017, 36)

Honor-based violence, polygamy and child marriage, and FGM are highlighted in this section as the most critical issues that demand immediate attention; there is no mention of how UKIP would address issues like the gender wage gap, increasing the number of women in politics, or addressing domestic or sexual violence for other groups of women. The clear progression in a relatively short space of time is important here for understanding UKIP's position as a PRR party, recognizing issues relevant to many women, for example, providing childcare to allow women to continue working, could be seen as relatively progressive for a PRR party, if not for the specific mention of 'appropriate', feminized roles for women in the labor force (i.e. nurses or teachers). Equally, devoting large sections of the manifesto to women's rights would also be a progressive move forward if these issues were not framed almost exclusively as problems of 'culture'. While immigration is clearly an underlying concern for UKIP, so is the maintenance of what they see as 'British' values. Women's rights only become priorities when they are understood as under threat from an 'uncivilized' Other.

## Interview Data

Concerns about Islam and its impact on women's equality were something that clearly emerged from interviews with female UKIP supporters. This was often framed in a way that suggested that 'indigenous' women had already obtained gender equality, and highlighted the threat that Muslim Others posed in taking away these freedoms.

Anna, a retired woman living in the north of England, speaks at length about the ways in which women's role in society has changed, noting both their inclusion in politics, but also highlights other ways in which women have become more emancipated:

**Anna:** I think women are now more open to politics and because more women are out being breadwinners, as opposed to mothers or just to help the family income. I mean women have careers now, which wasn't heard of when I left school.

Like many other participants, Anna expressed feelings of fear about being, as she says, 'overrun' with immigrants who refused to integrate and live the 'British' way of life. Carole, a 55-year-old woman living in near the Scottish borders, echoes this and notes that she is afraid about losing her identity. The threat of Islam in particular is threatening not just her sense of Englishness but the country's more widely:

Everybody is losing their identity, every country is losing its identity: It's alright if [immigrants] want to become English and live like the English but there are certain races and religions that do not – in fact they hate the English... if it goes on like this one day there will be no individual countries anymore, it'll all be one big middle-eastern mishmash and it's a shame to lost all this beautiful country and heritage.

The threat of Islam looms large here—the 'beautiful country and heritage' are at risk from immigration, and the specific fear about England becoming a 'middle-eastern mishmash' makes clear that some immigrants are more dangerous than others. While nativism can be seen here in both the expression of patriotism and the fear of the foreign Other, it is clear that Muslim migrants present to most challenging obstacle. Karen, a pensioner living in the midlands, expresses similar concerns. She notes that in her local shopping area there is 'hardly a British shop left', and notes that Polish and Romanian shops have taken over, making her feel like a 'stranger' in her own country. While Karen is concerned about the rise of immigration at a general level, she expressed specific reservations about the threat to Britishness vis-à-vis the threat of Sharia Law.

**Karen:** You know, if you want to live under Sharia Law, live in a Muslim country. I really don't understand why people come here to live in Britain, the British way of life. Well, they don't want to live the British way of life. They come here with the intent to change it and I certainly wouldn't want it changed, not for Sharia Law anyway.

While Karen worries about the lack of British shops and the threat that Eastern European immigrants pose, the threat to Britishness really comes to fore when considering Muslim migrants. Here, nativism is expressed in both the ways that she imagines 'the British way of life' and the fear and anxiety that she displays in relation to the Muslim Other. Karen's support for UKIP is very much predicated on the UKIP defending English values. She notes:

> I'm very proud of British people, our English people, because they do accept everyone as long as they're getting on with it and leaving well enough alone. But the trouble with immigrants, especially Pakistani immigrants… is they're manipulative, they've very devious…they want to change everything so it's their way and they're actually crushing our way of life.

The valorization of the British people and the English way of life is held up here rather ironically as being great because it is tolerant and open. The patriotic sentiments expressed here—a central tenant of nativism—must be understood contra the threat posed by the Other trying to destroy this way of life. Karen supports UKIP because they seek to both defend the English values that she holds sacred and to rid the country of the Others who would attempt to derail this nationalist vision.

Similar to Karen, most of our participants spoke at length about the threat that Muslim immigrants posed not just in relation to immigration but also related to the fear that Islam would undermine British values. While these women understood Britishness in a variety of ways, they all agreed that one of the fundamental foundations of Great Britain was its attention to gender equality. Like the discourse laid out in the UKIP Manifesto, there was little concern about issues like the gender pay gap, rates of domestic and sexual violence, or women's representation in Parliament. Rather, the focus was squarely on Islam. In the main, our participants suggested that Muslim women were victims of misogyny posed by the Islamic faith. UKIP was seen as a party that would work to dismantle Islam and critically weren't afraid of being politically incorrect. Most of our interviewees noted 'political correctness' was a key factor that prevented mainstream political parties from standing up for British values, which for our participants, includes the prioritization of gender equality. Paula, a retiree living in the northeast of England, expresses concerns about the subjugation of Muslim women, and suggests that both the burka and Muslim women's lack of access to education are particularly problematic:

**Paula:** It's like subjugation of [Muslim] women, they're subjugated; they're below the man. I don't believe in wearing the burka. I think that's wrong. Some of them don't like them being educated. Well to me, that's akin to apartheid. Don't educate them because if you educate someone, they start thinking and standing up for themselves. And that's wrong. I just don't think that lifestyle's right. To me, it's unfair, it's unfair and it's wrong. But if that's the way they want to live, that's the way they want to live but I don't think we need it in Great Britain. I don't like to see them problems here. It's been and gone in the past in history. We had the crusades and we don't want it anymore, you know.

Paula demonstrates the importance of history here, suggesting that Britain had been fighting against the oppression of Islam since the crusades. The focus on British history and the crusades in particular highlights the importance of Enlightenment values. Paula is not simply worried that Muslim women are not being educated, but that they do not *want* to be educated. The assumption made here about Other women is that they cannot stand up for themselves, while British women can; that they cannot think for themselves but British women can. Emily, a 59-year-old woman living in the south of England, echoes Paula's comments and pinpoints the burka as a source of oppression for Muslim women.

**Emily:** Well I don't like women wearing burkas for a start. I find them very intimidating and I think it should be like France where they banned the burka because that doesn't reflect very well on women. I don't care if the person thinks that wearing the burka thinks that that is liberating her from the eyes of men. I find that complete and utter rubbish. I think that, according to…if you want to live in England or the UK or western British country, if you want to wear a burka, then you should go to a country where it's the norm to wear a burka because it's very off-putting for ordinary British women to come across women clothed like that. To us it looks like repression and we don't want to see any of our women in this country looking like they're repressed.

Emily looks to France as providing an alternative political approach to managing the problems that Islam present for women. By banning the burka, France has taken proactive steps to ensure that women are 'liberated' from this symbolically problematic piece of clothing. Her assertion the burka 'looks like oppression' and that there is a national reluctance to see women experiencing repression suggests that 'indigenous' women don't experience repression. This discourse can be seen in the following excerpt from Alison's interview:

**Alison:** the fundamental Muslims—that was a shock for me. I'd never heard people talk like that about women but generally even the men from Albania and Eastern Europe. They're more chauvinist. Lots of the wives do not work. You know, you say to them

'What does your wife do' 'Oh, she's at home' 'Did she go to university?' 'Yes' 'Doesn't she go to work?' 'No, she's at home with the children'. They are, as you get further and further into Eastern bloc countries, yes I see more traditional views about keeping women down. Yes, they're not emancipated like we are.

Interestingly, for Alison, who lives in the southeast of England, the threat of oppression, while related to Islam in some instances, can also be seen from Eastern European immigrants. Here, the discourse that places concerns about gender equality at the heart of 'British values' is also being undermined by chauvinistic ideologies from other groups of migrants. While Islam and its attendant underlying misogyny is overwhelmingly highlighted by the participants as being an impediment to the free flow of seemingly feminist values that are apparently championed in the UK, it was theoretically possible that any Others who came to the UK could undermine these ideals.

All of the participants in our study expressed a great deal of concern about the impacts of immigration on Britishness and British values. While some women spoke about the glorious history of Britain, some about the open and tolerant nature of British people, some of the beauty and heritage of England—almost all of them spoke specifically about gender equality as a key feature of the UK. Little attention was paid to inequalities that have persevered for decades, in spite of feminist efforts to address them—rather the focus was squarely focused in Islam as a misogynistic religion, and the threat this apparently sexist culture presented to the already-equal women in England. Nativism here needs to be understood as both the valorization of the UK as a tolerant, equality-minded country by these self-professed patriots, but it is clear that the participants in this study are worried that Islam will undermine these essentially English values. The threat to English culture is very much gendered here—Muslim women, *imagined* here as uneducated and forced to wear burkas, are subjugated by Islam, while British women are seen as fully fledged citizens who possess the same rights and privileges as their British male counterparts. The fact that women make up only 32% of the Members of Parliament seems somewhat at odds with this glowing assessment of the UK, as does the fact that one in four women will experience domestic violence in her lifetime, more than 80% of company board positions are held by men, or that women in the UK still earn 15% less than men, despite having legislation in place that makes this illegal. As Mudde (2007) has argued, nativism is an *imagined* idea—there is little basis in reality here to suggest that gender equality is a defining characteristic of Britishness. However, it is clear that for our participants, their support for UKIP is often predicated in this very assumption, and the attendant xenophobia that allows them to make Islam the scapegoat.

## Conclusions

In conclusion, this chapter has presented evidence from female supporters of UKIP to suggest that gendered expressions of nativism are essential to their support for the UK's most influential PRR party. Akkerman (2015) argues that PRR parties in many European contexts have shifted from safeguarding traditional family values and normative gender roles to framing gender as an issue intrinsically related broadly to mass immigration, and to Islam in particular. This gendered narrative about Islam as a threat to women's equality has been put forward by UKIP in their most recent manifesto, and echoes the concerns from our participants who express anxieties about the influx of immigrants, particularly Muslim migrants. UKIP have incorporated such discourses in a relatively short timeframe, moving from a 2014 Manifesto that does not mention gender equality or Islam at all to a 2016 Manifesto that is replete with references to concerns about the impact of Other cultures on the rights of women, and British women specifically. This movement allows PRR parties to demonstrate their commitment to liberal values and the European Enlightenment project (Akkerman 2015), and links directly to concerns expressed by our female participants about the threat of Islam to British values.

By framing these concerns about Islam as apprehensiveness about gender equality, this allows for a patriotic vision of the UK as a gender-equal country to emerge. Muslim women in particular are held up as being victims of a type of misogyny that 'native' women have completely outgrown. It is clear that for female supporters of UKIP in this study, there is little suggestion that they adhere to the traditional, heteronormative discourses that might have previously defined backing for PRR parties. Rather, there is a shift here to focusing on immigration and Islam as threats to Britishness, and in particular as a potential threat to gender equality. As such, it behooves us to pay attention to both the ways in which parties like UKIP deploy these narratives, and how female supporters of PRR parties take up these discourses if we are to understand the gendered dynamics of PRR support in the UK. Understanding the ways in which nativism underpins gendered support for UKIP in this particular instance may help understand women's political affiliations to right-wing parties in other contexts, particularly in light of the shifting political discourse being employed by UKIP in relation to Islam and its place in 'Western' society (which is in line with many other PRR parties in Europe); studying expressions and affinities to nativist sentiments may shed light on the motivations for women supporting PRR parties in other European nations.

# References

Abedi, Amir, and Thomas Carl Lundberg. 2009. Doomed to Failure? UKIP and the Organisational Challenges Facing Right-Wing Populist Anti-Political Establishment Parties. *Parliamentary Affairs* 61 (1): 72–87.

Akkerman, Tjitske. 2015. Gender and the Radical Right in Western Europe: A Comparative Analysis of Policy Agendas. *Patterns of Prejudice* 49 (1–2): 37–60.

Clarke, Harold, Paul Whiteley, Walter Borges, David Sanders, and Marianne Stewart. 2016. Modelling the Dynamics Of Support for a Right-wing Populist Party: The Case of UKIP. *Journal of Elections, Public Opinion and Parties* 26 (2): 135–154.

Coenders, Marcel, Merove Gijsberts, and Peer Scheepers. 2004. Resistance to the Presence of Immigrants and Refugees in 22 Countries. In *Nationalism and Exclusion Of Migrants: Cross-National Comparisons*, ed. Mérove Gijsberts, Louk Hagendoorn, and Peer Scheepers, 97–120. Aldershot: Ashgate.

Drabble, Laurie, Karen Trocki, Brenda Salcedo, Patricia Walker, and Rachael Korcha. 2016. Conducting Qualitative Interviews by Telephone: Lessons Learned from a Study of Alcohol Use Among Sexual Minority and Heterosexual Women. *Qualitative Social Work* 15 (1): 118–133.

Evans, Geoffrey, and Jon Mellon. 2016. Working Class Votes and Conservative Losses: Solving the UKIP Puzzle. *Parliamentary Affairs* 69 (2): 464–479.

Ford, Robert, and Matthew Goodwin. 2014. Understanding UKIP: Identity, Social Change and the Left Behind. *The Political Quarterly* 85 (3): 277–284.

Ford, Robert, David Cutts, and Matthew Goodwin. 2012. Strategic Eurosceptics and Polite Xenophobes: Support for the United Kingdom Independence Party (UKIP) in the 2009 European Parliament Elections. *European Journal of Political Research* 51 (2): 204–234.

Harteveld, Eelco, Wouter Van der Brug, Stefan Dahlberg, and Andrej Kokkonen. 2015. The Gender Gap in Populist Radical-right Voting: Examining the Demand Side in Western and Eastern Europe. *Patterns of Prejudice* 49 (1–2): 103–134.

Hayton, Richard. 2016. The UK Independence Party and the Politics of Englishness. *Political Studies Review* 14 (3): 400–410.

Immerzeel, Tim, Hilde Coffé, and T. Tanja van der Lippe. 2015. Explaining the Gender Gap in Radical Right Voting: A Cross-National Investigation in Western European Countries. *Comparative European Politics* 13 (2): 263–286.

IPSOS-Mori. 2016. *How Britain voted in 2015*. [Online]: IPSOS-Mori. Available at: https://www.ipsos.com/ipsos-mori/en-uk/how-britain-voted-2015. Accessed 1 Sept 2016.

Kitschelt, Herbert. 1995. *The Radical Right in Western Europe*. Ann Arbor: University of Michigan Press.

Lynch, Philip, and Richard Whitaker. 2013. Rivalry on the Right: The Conservatives, the UK Independence Party (UKIP) and the EU Issue. *British Politics* 8 (3): 285–312.

Mayer, Nonna. 2013. From Jean-Marie to Marine Le Pen: Electoral Change on the Far Right. *Parliamentary Affairs* 66: 160–178.

Moffitt, Benjamin, and Simon Toomey. 2014. Rethinking Populism: Politics, Mediatisation and Political Style. *Political Studies* 62 (2): 381–397.

Mudde, Cas. 2004. 'The Popular Zeitgeist'. *Government and opposition* 39 (4): 541–563.

———. 2007. *Populist Radical Right Parties in Europe*. Cambridge: Cambridge University Press.

———. 2009. Populist Radical Right Parties in Europe Redux. *Political Studies Review* 7 (3): 330–337.

———. 2014. Fighting the System? Populist Radical Right Parties and Party System Change. *Party Politics* 20 (2): 217–226.

Norris, Pippa. 2005. *Radical Right: Voters and Parties in the Electoral Market*. Cambridge: Cambridge University Press.

Spierings, Niels, and Andrej Zaslove. 2015. Gendering the Vote for Populist Radical-right Parties. *Patterns of Prejudice* 49 (1–2): 135–162.

Spierings, Niels, Andrej Zaslove, Liza M. Mügge, and Sarah L. de Lange. 2015. Gender and Populist Radical-right Politics: An Introduction. *Patterns of Prejudice* 49 (1–2): 3–15.

Thorleifsson, Cathrine. 2016. From Coal to ukip: The Struggle Over Identity in Post-industrial Doncaster. *History and Anthropology* 27 (5): 555–568.

UKIP. 2014. *UKIP Manifesto: Creating and Earthquake.* [online]: UK independence party. Available at: https://d3n8a8pro7vhmx.cloudfront.net/themes/5308a93901925b5b09000002/attachments/original/1398869254/EuroManifestoLaunch.pdf?1398869254

———. 2015 *UKIP Manifesto: Believe in Britain.* [online]: UK Independence Party. Available at: https://d3n8a8pro7vhmx.cloudfront.net/ukipdev/pages/1103/attachments/original/1429295050/UKIPManifesto2015.pdf?1429295050

———. 2017. *UKIP Manifesto: Britain Together.* [online] UK Independence Party. Available at: https://d3n8a8pro7vhmx.cloudfront.net/ukipdev/pages/3944/attachments/original/1495695469/UKIP_Manifesto_June2017opt.pdf?1495695469

Van Der Brug, Wouter, and Joost Van Spanje. 2009. Immigration, Europe and the 'New' Cultural Dimension. *European Journal of Political Research* 48: 309–334.

Webb, Paul, and Tim Bale. 2014. Why Do Tories Defect to UKIP? Conservative Party Members and the Temptations of the Populist Radical Right. *Political Studies* 62 (4): 961–970.

Wetland, Kurt. 2001. Clarifying a Contested Concept: Populism in the Study of Latin American Politics. *Comparative Politics* 34 (1): 1–22.

# Part III

Nations, Borders, and the Gendered Signification of Migration

# 12

# Policing the Intimate Borders of the Nation: A Review of Recent Trends in Family-Related Forms of Immigration Control

Paola Bonizzoni

## Introduction

The chapter identifies and critically reviews some main themes arising from different streams of literature having tackled, in recent years, states' efforts to reproduce their national boundaries regulating the intimate lives of their (aspiring) citizens and residents. It recalls to the broader scope of the book showing how reproductive practices and family ties are critical for both questioning and controlling the kinds and size of the immigrant population, as well as for the articulation and reaffirmation of particular visions of nationhood.

While family ties have historically played a central role in regulating access to membership entitlements (Turner 2008) and the symbolic relevance of "proper" forms of kinship, sexuality and reproduction for nation-building projects is by no means new, the mutually constitutive

---

P. Bonizzoni (✉)
Dipartimento di Scienze Sociali e Politiche, Università degli Studi di Milano, Milan, Italy

© The Author(s) 2018
J. Mulholland et al. (eds.), *Gendering Nationalism*,
https://doi.org/10.1007/978-3-319-76699-7_12

relationship between the nation-state, gender, sexuality and race/ethnicity is undergoing deep reconfigurations at the light of the challenges brought by contemporary migration flows and the re-nationalizing outbursts that followed (Luibhéid 2006). Understanding the implications of contemporary migration management for intimate, reproductive and sexual citizenship issues has become, in this respect, timely.

The chapter addresses this issue exploring how different aspects of social reproduction—love and marriage; parenthood, fertility and childbearing; care and dependency among adult relatives—are implicated in issues of migration control. It shows how matters of legitimacy (regarding the value and worthiness of selected reproductive ties) and veracity (issues surrounding the verifiability and potential misuse of family-related claims) have triggered an emerging set of controls centred on the intimate and bodily life of both native citizens and migrants. As immigration policy-making conveys meanings and assumptions regarding more or less good, desired and suitable future subjects, these regulatory efforts reflect the "double helix" of a neo-liberal/neo-communitarian (Schinkel and Van Houdt 2010) governance, in which citizens' reproductive contributions to the nation are contested and subjected to gendered, ethno-racialized and classed assessments, rather than valued as legitimate grounds for claiming belonging (Lee 2013).

## Reproducing Nations: Families and Border-Drawing

Nations are commonly conceived as felt and lived communities whose members share a homeland and ideas about "who we are", a common history and fate, as well as forms of solidarity accompanying membership (Anderson 2006; Smith 2010). They not merely represent but actively construct "the people", through a variety of policy interventions and forms of population governance addressing insiders but also outsiders as potential and prospective, more or less desirable, future members.

In this respect, immigration and naturalization policies provide an especially interesting locus to explore how the boundaries of nations are drawn and reworked in an era of increased population movement. They convey contested meanings and assumptions regarding more or less good and suitable future citizens (Anderson 2013) reflecting governments' desires to engineer their populations according to certain principles and values. Some have argued, in this vein, that borders operate as filters or membranes, sorting out and distinguishing the useful from the dangerous, the genuine from the bogus, the deserving from the undeserving (Chauvin and Garcés-Mascareñas 2014). While these categorizing efforts greatly affect migrants' rights, opportunities and lives, they also reveal how receiving nation-states reassert themselves as communities of value through border control. Immigration policy-making (from legalization to foreign labour recruitment, to the management of family and humanitarian migration, to naturalization and permanent settlement) is therefore a powerful mechanism through which citizens and non-citizens define each other (Bonjour and de Hart 2013).

The relevance of the "intimate" for nation-building processes is not new, as practices such as marriage, sexual intimacy, abortion, assisted conception and adoption have often been regulated in the name of a national need for cultural distinction. Family, ethnicity/race and nation all constitute categories of relatedness that define appropriate behaviours and access to resources through connections and substance (Lee 2013). As such, the implications of (and tensions among) these intersecting memberships and belongings become an especially relevant matter in an era of intensified transnational population movement, making social reproductive issues a key site for contemporary forms of migration control (Kofman and Raghuram 2015; Yuval-Davis and Anthias 1989). Several aspects of social reproduction—marriage and childbirth, parenthood and children's socialization, intergenerational care along the lifecourse—are in fact increasingly questioned as (il)legitimate gateways for claiming or contesting outsiders' membership. Families, rather than sources of integration (Bonjour and Kraler 2014), turn into threats: for the nation-state solidarity embedded in welfare state regimes (Eggebø 2010), for key national values such as individual freedom and gender equality, for the effectiveness of border control.

As the "ideal migrant" increasingly turns out to be either highly skilled or (at best) temporary/circular, self-sufficient and productive, also posing few risks in terms of both economic integration and social cohesion, all those intimate ties which could provide grounds for claiming membership and long-term settlement become the source of scrutiny and suspect. In this respect, the ambivalences and dilemmas raised by the governance of transnational intimacies should firstly be cast in the light of increased demographic anxieties (such as low birth rates, shrinking workforce and demographic ageing) spreading in several receiving states and, secondly, in pervasive neo-liberal/neo-communal trends towards usefulness, self-sufficiency and loyalty as foundational categories for good membership (Schinkel and Van Houdt 2010). Defining and contesting what the good family is (Strasser et al. 2009), immigration stakeholders engage in gendered and ethno-racialized constructions distinguishing true and acceptable families from the sham and inacceptable ones, showing how the family provides a malleable and powerful ideological construct (Lee 2013) for nation-building processes.

## Proper Lovers: Investigating Migrants' Sexuality and Marriage

How ideals, meanings and practices around love, sexuality and marriage permeate immigration control has become a widely debated topic (Charsley 2013), as the growth of international marriages and geographically dispersed families due to transnational mobility complicates the historical pattern between the state and reproductive citizenship (Richardson and Turner 2001).

Couples are subject to scrutiny by State authorities as their relations should dispel any doubts of fraud and deception (Eggebø 2013; Lan 2008; Pellander 2015). "True" marriages are assessed according to idealized notions of "modern" love and pure relationships and/or culturalized assumptions regarding how marriage is supposedly performed in other countries (Wray 2011), through surveillance practices (from interviews to the request of ostensible proofs in terms of extended cohabitation, photographs, love letters, etc.) which D'Aoust (2013) calls "technologies of love". Issues such as wide age gap, disability, a previous history of separation or divorce, lack of a long-standing cohabitation, while part of the increasingly varied scenario of receiving states' marriage arrangements, can instead cast doubts on foreigners, as any other element (such as a failed asylum claim or previous breach of immigration law) might raise gatekeepers' suspect that true love is not the ultimate and only reason for their marriage.

Couple relationships should also be culturally and morally acceptable. European debates around marriage migration are, in this respect, especially imbued with "sexual democracy" (Fassin 2010) concerns raised by Islamic alterity and troubling family practices, including polygamy and cousin and arranged transnational marriage (Charsley and Liversage 2013). Especially troubling is the intergenerational reproduction of transnational marriage practices by second-generation youth (Bonjour and Kraler 2014): these "wrong" marriages are read not only (as much of the debate on the so-called mail order brides suggests) as a matter of gender (in)equality and female victimization but as an issue of loyalty and lack of cultural integration. To address this issue, states have introduced specific measures, such as raising the minimum age of spouses, banning cousin marriages (Rytter 2010) or raising the minimum income required to sponsor one's spouse (Fair 2010). While these policy interventions had been generally targeted at selected immigrant communities (such as North Africans and South Asians) and justified as means to protect ethnic youth from forced marriages, they ended up affecting a much wider population segment, including native whites (Fernandez and Jensen 2014).

Sexual democracy and cultural issues are not, however, the only factor driving the complex boundary-making work aiming at constructing, distinguishing and selecting proper and deserving couples. Even where the governance of family migration is less strongly marked by worries around "culturally incompatible" marriage practices (such as in the Americas or in Asia),[1] States are, in fact, often engaged in securing borders against uncontrolled inflows of "low-quality" marriage migrants. As Bragg and Wong (2015) have shown in the Canadian case, the enjoyment of family migration rights is tied to increasingly demanding economic-related integration requirements (see also Sirriyeh 2015; Staver 2015 for a

---

[1] For the USA, see Enchautegui and Menjívar (2015); for Canada, Bragg and Wong (2015); for Asia, Constable (2013), Friedman (2010), Lan (2008) and So (2003).

European perspective). Moreover, family migration rights can be used as tools to attract and favour the long-term settlement of a (supposedly) highly mobile qualified workforce (Khoo 2003).[2] In this respect, economic and integration-related requirements not only reassure receiving States against a flow of supposedly inactive, unskilled and welfare-dependent population but also contain and indirectly select family migrants according to their education and skills (Gutekunst 2015). Shifts towards low-skilled labour migration management through temporary migration schemes can be understood, in this sense, as a form of reproductive governance (Askola 2016b) allowing states to deflecting social reproductive costs while creating an insecure underclass of cheap, flexible and compliant workers which can be discarded when no longer required.

Because of these processes, a complex, stratified geometry of family migration regimes is taking shape, with different degrees of rights and controls assigned to national, gendered and classed citizens, skilled/unskilled workers, students, temporary/long-term migrants and so on. Family migration rights are, in turn, not only unevenly bestowed but also unequally accessed by different categories of (non)citizens, according to their gender, sexual orientation, education/skills and economic resources.

As regards gender, uneven forms of participation to productive and reproductive activities heavily shape both men's and women's experiences of marriage migration. Women are well known to represent a relevant proportion of marriage migrants across the globe. Female marriage migrants, while often targeted as privileged recipients of integration measures (Kofman et al. 2013) aimed at fostering their autonomy and employability, are caught in a sponsorship system reproducing prolonged intra-family dependencies exposing them to gendered-specific risks in the case of divorce (Liversage 2013; Salcido and Menjívar 2012). On the contrary, when sponsoring their relatives, female migrant workers have to overcome the challenges posed by performing the role of breadwinners in segregated labour markets (Bonizzoni 2015), also facing work and family reconciliation in unfavourable and often discriminatory care regimes

---

[2] Evidence from Norway and the UK shows that women's unfavourable position in the labour market can lead to (female) citizen's de facto discrimination, compared to (male) foreign skilled workers' more favourable condition.

(Bonizzoni 2014). However, gendered social expectations and inequalities in the sphere of work and care do not shape only women's experiences, as men can face serious difficulties in taking advantage of family migration routes due to their female spouses' breadwinning jeopardies and their socially expected role of primary wage earners can raise suspect and weaken claims made on grounds of spousal dependency (de Hart 2015; Wray 2015).

## Parents and Their Children: Contested Fertilities and Age-Related Thresholds

As transnational love and marriage, also migrants' parenting and reproductive life has relevant implications for nation-building processes, as the birth (and presence) of children implies the reproduction of national, racial-ethnicized and classed identities and the perpetuation of social hierarchies and inequalities across generations.

An emerging body of literature has shown a global array of figures that, in contexts shaped by profoundly different regulatory regimes, uncover similar tensions brought by cross-border parenting and childbearing. These include black pregnant women seeking asylum at the Irish border (Luibhéid 2004); the over-fertile bodies of undocumented Latina mothers (Chavez 2004) and their wealthy Chinese counterparts delivering citizen children at Californian maternity clinics (Wang 2016); Nicaraguan labour migrants accused of scrounging Costa Rican maternity services (Dos Santos and Spesny 2015); imprisoned and deported pregnant domestic workers in the Middle East and Asia (Lan 2008); migrant mothers charged of providing falsified German paternity claims (Castañeda 2008); or undocumented fathers of British children challenging deportation orders (Wray 2015). What all these subjects speak about is how reproductive issues concerning parenting and childbearing represent a crucial matter for the regulation of membership and belonging in the face of increased global mobility and demographic anxieties.

In several immigrant-receiving societies population replacement is increasingly perceived as at odds with the reproduction of societies as cohesive and homogeneous ethno-racial bodies (Askola 2016b; Constable 2013; Krause and Marchesi 2007). Fears of hyper-fertile baby machines (Chavez 2004) among (racial/ethnic, classed, religious) "others" are linked to fears of challenges to the existing demographic (and geopolitical) order, as clearly shown by concerns around an alleged Muslim plot to take over Europe through excessive reproduction resonating in right-wing nationalist parties (Dumbrava 2016).

The problematization of migrants' reproduction is especially felt in those countries (such as in the Americas or, until recently, Ireland) where jus soli provisions make migrants and their children especially exposed to moral allegations of unauthorized intrusions into a country's citizenship regime. This even despite the very limited chances that immigrant-born citizen children often have of sponsoring their relatives, leading Bhabha (2004) to question the very idea of citizenship for minors forced to choose between family separation and deportation. The issue of mixed-status families has voiced increasing concern in the US and has become the focus of much scholarly debate and political activism (Pallares 2014). Claims on the right of the citizen child to have a family has become a powerful (while contested) basis for asking legalization measure, based on the valuable contribution parenting future citizens represents for the nation (Sullivan 2014).

As long as parent-child relationships can open membership pathways (either from children through their parents or the other way round, Bledsoe 2004), they also become subject to state scrutiny and suspect. The search for authenticity in intergenerational relationships has, for instance, led to increased use of DNA-testing (Heinemann and Lemke 2013), revealing a process of geneticization of the family devaluing those same social and caregiving ties which have gained increased relevance and recognition in most receiving countries' legal and socio-cultural understandings of family life.

The governance of immigrants' parenting and childbearing bears gendered implications due to the bodily implications of pregnancy but also to gendered social expectations revolving around parenting and (child) care. While women might face greater blaming and opposition—but also privileged grounds for claiming belonging—as biological and socio-cultural reproducers of national collectivities (Yuval-Davis and Anthias

1989), men's claims can face greater opposition and suspect, due to their ethno-racialized construction as dangerous sexualized subjects and their weaker association with caregiving roles and responsibilities (Wray 2015).

Socio-legal constructions of legitimate intergenerational bonds of dependency centred on the child-adult distinction reveal how age, as much as gender, is a powerful categorization mechanism influencing chances to claiming memberships and belonging (Horsti and Pellander 2015). While drawing a line between adolescence and adulthood is in itself an arbitrary exercise (especially at the light of diffused societal changes that have relevantly postponed adolescence well beyond the usual 18-year-old threshold, Askola 2016b), this can instead represent an abrupt transition for non-citizen migrant children (Gonzales and Chavez 2012). Children's family reunification[3] rights are usually limited after the age of majority but sometimes even earlier: according to the European Directive on Family Reunification, for instance, children aged over 12 years may be requested to provide proofs of integration before entry, and member states can require families to apply for entry and residence for their children before the latter reach the age of 15 (Drywood 2010). Moreover, married minor children are often considered as adults and ipso facto excluded from their families of origin (Mustasaari 2015).

The minor-adult nexus and "troublesome" adulthood transitions have also become a matter for increased state scrutiny and intervention. On the one hand, the problematization of migrant youth (in terms of lower school achievement and labour market performance, as well as "deviant" identities and marriage practices) has justified restrictive turns in immigration policies. On the other hand, unaccompanied minors are increasingly framed as disguised economic migrants that, after having received state protection, can act as "anchor babies" starting chain migration towards their families back home leading, in turn, to an expansion of forensic age assessment. The minor child is therefore placed in an ambiguous position: while to prove deservingness she has to lack agency and capacity (Mustasaari 2015), her family belonging is denied full-length recognition, as states do not usually acknowledge either the socio-cultural

---

[3] Also, for instance, changes to derive citizenship from naturalizing parents, or permanent residency.

complexities of intergenerational dependencies, nor the active role that children can play in families involved in international migration, as both potential earners and care providers.

## Dangerous Dependencies: Regulating Membership Beyond the "Nuclear Family"

The widespread restrictions faced not only by adult children but also by elderly parents (let alone siblings and other members of the extended family) in being considered as "legitimate" family members for immigration purposes show that family migration regimes severely narrow the range of intra-family legitimate dependencies to the nuclear family.

The few studies exploring the logics and the consequences of this process (Askola 2016a, b; Bragg and Wong 2015; Horsti and Pellander 2015; Leinonen and Pellander 2014) show that states' will to protect endangered welfare state and labour markets by a flow of unskilled workers or inactive "unproductive burdens" plays a key role. What seems to be at stake here is not as much a form of cultural problematization of migrants' family relationships but the consequence of constructing them as useless for the states' economy and unworthy to participate to welfare state solidarity (Eggebø 2010). Restrictive policies targeting elderly parents of citizens and foreign residents[4] are aimed at deflecting care responsibilities and preventing these "dangerous dependencies" to cross the border, while turning them into a private, transnational, family matter. While vulnerability and "extreme hardship" can sometimes pave the way for "compassionate inclusion" (Ambrosini 2016), they also represent a threat to national resources (Horsti and Pellander 2015), leading to highly ambivalent incorporation processes.

If the impact of state-enforced separation on immigrant family life has risen considerable concerns in respect to the well-being and integration

---

[4] These restrictions include the affidavit system in the USA (Enchautegui and Menjívar 2015), those attached to the Canadian Parent and Grandparent Super Visa (Bragg and Wong 2015) and the multi-layered policies experimented in Europe (based on—often combined—age-related requirements, exclusive dependency and/or health-related proofs, private medical insurance request, etc.).

prospects of both spouses and children (being they reunited and/or "left behind"), what forced transnationality might mean for elderly and their families has still to be fully understood by research and raises relevant concerns regarding the missed recognition of the value of care and reproductive unpaid work in immigration management. Immigration policies are acknowledged to play a critical role in jeopardizing the circulation of care across borders, especially when relatives are "too sick to move" (Baldassar 2014; Kilkey and Merla 2014). Studies have shown, moreover, that in contexts shaped by increasingly privatized and/or (re)familiarized childcare, the role played by grandparents is often strategic to allow working-class migrant women to successfully match work and family responsibilities, with relevant implications in terms of female autonomy and poverty reduction. The same long-standing lack of recognition of the value of unpaid work in the family recognized by feminist analyses of the welfare state (Lewis 1992) can, therefore, be also found at play in immigration policies, despite the inherent value often placed in these policies on promoting female migrants' emancipation through paid employment. Again, women, as primarily responsible for managing the consequences of human dependency risk being especially hit by these policies, as recently shown by the widely debated case of a British long-term resident, married to a UK citizen who had lost right to remain in the UK due to prolonged, transnational, elderly care responsibilities.[5]

## Concluding Remarks

The academic debates reviewed in this chapter show the key role played by families as core organizing institutions for the exercise of contemporary forms of migration control.

Family migration management reflects the tensions brought by the dangers of culturally problematized immigrant social reproduction: *excessive* fertilities, *backward* marriages and gender relationships, *low-quality* human capital and welfare dependency. Nation-states reproduce themselves redrawing borders through an intensified scrutiny of cross-border

---

[5] "Woman sent back to Singapore despite 27-year marriage" on www.bbc.com.

intimate relationships centred on the distinction between those ties recognized as real, useful and legitimate from the instrumentalized, useless and dangerous ones. These efforts require the deployment of an expanding documentary regime centred on the collection of ostensible "proofs" of ones' intimate life as well as checks and controls over the reliability of migrants' bodies, conveying an idealized (nuclear, biological) family model which hardly matches with both natives' and immigrants' experiences and current societal definitions of relatedness.

As racial-culturalized and classed social reproduction challenge the imagined homogeneity of nations crossing state borders, the rewards of membership are unevenly granted only to those capable to perform increasingly selective societal expectations. In this newly emerging reproductive regime, nationality/status, ethnicity, gender, age, class and sexuality unevenly affect and concretely stratify the chances to practise one's intimate life in and across borders, as these ties provide uneven grounds for claiming belonging to the state and the nation.

These studies also show that families are powerful socio-cultural constructs that are constantly reworked and contested. As the intimate delineates a porous zone of experience and relationships between insiders and outsiders, defining the family proves critical for both formulating immigration policy and for a better understanding of what immigration means for the nation, calling for a deeper exploration of the nexus between the governance of national reproduction, citizenship and mobility.

# References

Ambrosini, Maurizio. 2016. From 'Illegality' to Tolerance and Beyond: Irregular Immigration as a Selective and Dynamic Process. *International Migration* 54 (2): 144–159.

Anderson, Benedict. 2006. *Imagined Communities: Reflections on the Origin and Spread of Nationalism*. New York: Verso Books.

Anderson, Bridget. 2013. *Us and them? The Dangerous Politics of Immigration Control*. Oxford: Oxford University Press.

Askola, Heli. 2016a. (No) Migrating for Family Care in Later Life: Senchishak v Finland, Older Parents and Family Reunification. *European Journal of Migration and Law* 18 (3): 351–372.

———. 2016b. *The Demographic Transformations of Citizenship*. Cambridge: Cambridge University Press.

Baldassar, Loretta. 2014. Too Sick to Move: Distant 'Crisis' Care in Transnational Families. *International Review of Sociology: Revue Internationale de Sociologie* 24 (3): 391–405.

Bhabha, Jacqueline. 2004. The "Mere Fortuity" of Birth? Are Children Citizens? *Differences: A Journal of Feminist Cultural Studies* 15 (2): 91–117.

Bledsoe, Caroline H. 2004. Reproduction at the Margins: Migration and Legitimacy in the New Europe. *Demographic Research* 3 (4): 85–116.

Bonizzoni, Paola. 2014. Immigrant Working Mothers Reconciling Work and Childcare: The Experience of Latin American and Eastern European Women in Milan. *Social Politics: International Studies in Gender, State and Society* 21 (2): 194–217.

———. 2015. Uneven Paths: Latin American Women Facing Italian Family Reunification Policies. *Journal of Ethnic and Migration Studies* 41 (12): 2001–2020.

Bonjour, Saskia, and Betty de Hart. 2013. A Proper Wife, a Proper Marriage: Constructions of 'Us' and 'Them' in Dutch Family Migration Policy. *European Journal of Women's Studies* 20 (1): 61–76.

Bonjour, Saskia, and Albert Kraler. 2014. Introduction. Family Migration as an Integration Issue? Policy Perspectives and Academic Insights. *Journal of Family Issues* 36 (11): 1407–1432.

Bragg, Bronwyn, and Lee L. Wong. 2015. "'Cancelled Dreams'": Family Reunification and Shifting Canadian Immigration Policy. *Journal of Immigrant and Refugee Studies* 14 (1): 46–65.

Castañeda, Heide. 2008. Paternity for Sale. *Medical Anthropology Quarterly* 22 (4): 340–359.

Charsley, Katharine, ed. 2013. *Transnational Marriage: New Perspectives from Europe and Beyond*. Abingdon: Routledge.

Charsley, Katharine, and Anika Liversage. 2013. Transforming Polygamy: Migration, Transnationalism and Multiple Marriages among Muslim Minorities. *Global Networks* 13 (1): 60–78.

Chauvin, Sébastien, and Bianca Garcés-Mascareñas. 2014. Becoming Less Illegal: Deservingness Frames and Undocumented Migrant Incorporation. *Sociology Compass* 8 (4): 422–432.

Chavez, Leo R. 2004. A Glass Half Empty: Latina Reproduction and Public Discourse. *Human Organization* 63 (2): 173–188.

Constable, Nicole. 2013. Migrant Workers, Legal Tactics, and Fragile Family Formation in Hong Kong. *Oñati Socio-Legal Series* 3 (6): 1004–1022.

D'Aoust, Anne-Marie. 2013. In the Name of Love: Marriage Migration, Governmentality, and Technologies of Love. *International Political Sociology* 7 (3): 258–274.

de Hart, Betty. 2015. Superdads Migrant Fathers' Right to Family Life Before the European Court of Human Rights. *Men and Masculinities* 18 (4): 448–467.

Dos Santos, Sara Leon Spesny. 2015. Undeserving Mothers? Shifting Rationalities in the Maternal Healthcare of Undocumented Nicaraguan Migrants in Costa Rica. *Anthropology and Medicine* 22 (2): 191–201.

Drywood, Eleonor. 2010. Challenging Concepts of the 'Child' in Asylum and Immigration Law: The Example of the EU. *Journal of Social Welfare and Family Law* 32 (3): 309–323.

Dumbrava, Costica. 2016. Reproducing the Nation: Reproduction, Citizenship and Ethno-Demographic Survival in Post-Communist Romania. *Journal of Ethnic and Migration Studies* 43 (9): 1490–1507.

Eggebø, Helga. 2010. The Problem of Dependency: Immigration, Gender, and the Welfare State. *Social Politics: International Studies in Gender, State and Society* 17 (3): 295–322.

———. 2013. A Real Marriage? Applying for Marriage Migration to Norway. *Journal of Ethnic and Migration Studies* 39 (5): 773–789.

Enchautegui, Maria E., and Cecilia Menjívar. 2015. Paradoxes of Family Immigration Policy: Separation, Reorganization, and Reunification of Families Under Current Immigration Laws. *Law and Policy* 37 (1–2): 32–60.

Fair, Linda S. 2010. 'Why Can't I get married?'—Denmark and the 'Twenty-four Year Law'. *Social and Cultural Geography* 11 (2): 139–153.

Fassin, Éric. 2010. National Identities and Transnational Intimacies: Sexual Democracy and the Politics of Immigration in Europe. *Public Culture* 22 (3): 507–529.

Fernandez, Nadine T., and Tina Jensen. 2014. Intimate Contradictions: Comparing the Impact of Danish Family Unification Laws on Pakistani and Cuban Marriage Migrants. *Journal of Ethnic and Migration Studies* 40 (7): 1136–1153.

Friedman, Sara L. 2010. Determining 'Truth' at the Border: Immigration Interviews, Chinese Marital Migrants, and Taiwan's Sovereignty Dilemmas. *Citizenship Studies* 14 (2): 167–183.

Gonzales, Roberto G., and Leo R. Chavez. 2012. 'Awakening to a Nightmare'. Abjectivity and Illegality in the Lives of Undocumented 1.5-Generation Latino Immigrants in the United States. *Current Anthropology* 53 (3): 255–281.

Gutekunst, Miriam. 2015. Language as a New Instrument of Border Control: The Regulation of Marriage Migration from Morocco to Germany. *The Journal of North African Studies* 20 (4): 540–552.

Heinemann, Torsten, and Thomas Lemke. 2013. Suspect Families: DNA Kinship Testing in German Immigration Policy. *Sociology* 47 (4): 810–826.

Horsti, Karina, and Saara Pellander. 2015. Conditions of Cultural Citizenship: Intersections of Gender, Race and Age in Public Debates on Family Migration. *Citizenship Studies* 19 (6–7): 751–767.

Khoo, Siew-Ean. 2003. Sponsorship of Relatives for Migration and Immigrant Settlement Intention. *International Migration* 41 (5): 177–199.

Kilkey, Majella, and Laura Merla. 2014. Situating Transnational Families' Care-Giving Arrangements: The Role of Institutional Contexts. *Global Networks* 14 (2): 210–229.

Kofman, Eleonore, and Parvati Raghuram. 2015. *Gendered Migrations and Global Social Reproduction*. Berlin: Springer.

Kofman, Eleonore, Sawitri Saharso, and Elena Vacchelli. 2013. Gendered Perspectives on Integration Discourses and Measures. *International Migration* 53 (4): 77–89.

Krause, Elizabeth L., and Milena Marchesi. 2007. Fertility Politics as 'Social Viagra': Reproducing Boundaries, Social Cohesion, and Modernity in Italy. *American Anthropologist* 109 (2): 350–362.

Lan, Pei-Chia. 2008. Migrant Women's Bodies as Boundary Markers: Reproductive Crisis and Sexual Control in the Ethnic Frontiers of Taiwan. *Signs* 33 (4): 833–861.

Lee, Catherine. 2013. *Fictive Kinship: Family Reunification and the Meaning of Race and Nation in American Migration*. New York: Russell Sage Foundation.

Leinonen, Johanna, and Saara Pellander. 2014. Court Decisions over Marriage Migration in Finland: A Problem with Transnational Family Ties. *Journal of Ethnic and Migration Studies* 40 (9): 1488–1506.

Lewis, Jane. 1992. Gender and the Development of Welfare Regimes. *Journal of European Social Policy* 2 (3): 159–173.

Liversage, Anika. 2013. Gendered Struggles over Residency Rights When Turkish Immigrant Marriages Break Up. *Oñati Socio-Legal Series* 3 (6): 1070–1090.

Luibhéid, Eithne. 2004. Childbearing Against the State? Asylum Seeker Women in the Irish Republic. *Women's Studies International Forum* 7 (4): 335–349.

———. 2006. Sexual Regimes and Migration Controls: Reproducing the Irish Nation-State in Transnational Contexts. *Feminist Review* 83 (1): 60–78.

Mustasaari, Sanna. 2015. The 'Nuclear Family Paradigm' as a Marker of Rights and Belonging in Transnational Families. *Social Identities* 21 (4): 359–372.

Pallares, Amalia. 2014. *Family Activism: Immigrant Struggles and the Politics of Noncitizenship*. New Brunswick: Rutgers University Press.

Pellander, Saara. 2015. 'An Acceptable Marriage'. Marriage Migration and Moral Gatekeeping in Finland. *Journal of Family Issues* 36 (11): 1472–1489.

Richardson, Eileen H., and Bryan Stephen Turner. 2001. Sexual, Intimate or Reproductive Citizenship? *Citizenship Studies* 5 (3): 329–338.

Rytter, Mikkel. 2010. 'The Family of Denmark' and 'the Aliens': Kinship Images in Danish Integration Politics. *Ethnos* 75 (3): 301–322.

Salcido, Olivia, and Cecilia Menjívar. 2012. Gendered Paths to Legal Citizenship: The Case of Latin-American Immigrants in Phoenix, Arizona. *Law and Society Review* 46 (2): 335–368.

Schinkel, Willem, and Friso Van Houdt. 2010. The Double Helix of Cultural Assimilationism and Neo-liberalism: Citizenship in Contemporary Governmentality. *The British Journal of Sociology* 61 (4): 696–715.

Sirriyeh, Ala. 2015. 'All You Need Is Love and £18,600': Class and the New UK Family Migration Rules. *Critical Social Policy* 35 (2): 228–247.

Smith, Anthony. 2010. *Nationalism: Theory, Ideology, History*. Cambridge: Polity.

So, Alvin. 2003. Cross-border families in Hong Kong: The Role of Social Class and Politics. *Critical Asian Studies* 35 (4): 515–0534.

Staver, Anne. 2015. Hard Work for Love. The Economic Drift in Norwegian Family Immigration and Integration Policies. *Journal of Family Issues* 36 (11): 1453–1471.

Strasser, Elisabeth, Albert Kraler, Saskia Bonjour, and Veronika Bilger. 2009. Doing Family Responses to the Constructions of 'the Migrant Family' Across Europe. *The History of the Family* 14 (2): 165–176.

Sullivan, Michael J. 2014. Legalizing Parents and Other Caregivers: A Family Immigration Policy Guided by a Public Ethic of Care. *Social Politics: International Studies in Gender, State and Society* 23 (2): 263–283.

Turner, Bryan S. 2008. Citizenship, Reproduction and the State: International Marriage and Human Rights. *Citizenship Studies* 12 (1): 45–54.
Wang, Sean H. 2016. Fetal citizens? Birthright Citizenship, Reproductive Futurism, and the 'Panic' over Chinese Birth Tourism in Southern California. *Environment and Planning D: Society and Space* 35 (2): 263–280.
Wray, Helena. 2011. *Regulating Marriage Migration into the UK: A Stranger in the Home*. Farnham: Ashgate Publishing.
———. 2015. 'A Thing Apart' Controlling Male Family Migration to the United Kingdom. *Men and Masculinities* 18 (4): 424–447.
Yuval-Davis, Nira, and Floya Anthias, eds. 1989. *Woman, Nation, State*. Basingstoke: Palgrave Macmillan.

# 13

# 'Subaltern Victims' or 'Useful Resources'? Migrant Women in the *Lega Nord* Ideology and Politics

Sara R. Farris and Francesca Scrinzi

Since the mid-2000s we have witnessed the emergence of a new phenomenon in several European countries: the mobilization of issues of women's rights and gender equality by populist radical right parties (PRR)[1] in anti-immigration campaigns. For instance, the National Front (*Front National*) in France, the Party for Freedom (*Partij voor de Vrijheid*) in the Netherlands and the Northern League (*Lega Nord*, hereafter LN) in Italy have all begun to adopt pseudo-feminist arguments to stigmatize migrant—especially Muslim—communities for their alleged intrinsic misogyny and patriarchy. These developments appear as a strategy of 'agenda-grabbing' by the PRR (Akkerman and Hagelund 2007: 213)

---

[1] Cas Mudde (2007) defines the PRR on the basis of its nativist, populist and authoritarian ideology (Mudde 2007). There is no consensus among scholars on the definition of this party family, and several other categories are used such as far right, extreme right and nationalist right (Farris 2017).

S. R. Farris (✉)
Department of Sociology, Goldsmiths, University of London, London, UK

F. Scrinzi
Sociology, School of Social & Political Sciences, University of Glasgow, Glasgow, UK

seeking to normalize their public image and legitimize their anti-immigration arguments. In the PRR propaganda, the issue of women's rights is appropriated to re-frame the anti-immigration agenda. PRR parties treat gender equality as a standard against which a superior national self can be measured in comparison with inferior foreign others (Towns et al. 2014). Within this discourse gender equality is considered a trait, which is specific to the culture of European nations as opposed to the culture of non-European racialized Others. PRR parties' pseudo-feminist arguments are in sharp contradiction with their anti-feminist politics and policies. While advocating women's emancipation as the capital value of the European (Christian) social fabric, which migrants allegedly lack, these parties also promote policies that encourage the maintenance of traditional roles for women. Thus a tension lies at the heart of current gendered developments in the PRR ideology and politics, between the traditional gender models promoted by nationalist movements where women are cast as biological and social reproducers of the nation (Yuval-Davis 1997) and this pseudo-feminist discourse.

Recent contributions have illustrated some aspects and contradictions of these phenomena, for instance in relation to the PRR parties' embrace not only of women's but also gay rights (Bracke 2011). Others have described the double standard applied to migrant men and women in the context of raising hostility towards the Muslim population, not only by PRR parties, but within the mainstream more generally; whereas Muslim men have been mostly described as representing a social and cultural danger to European societies as well as being inherently misogynist, Muslim women have been portrayed prevalently as victims to be rescued (Abu-Lughod 2013). Little however has been written on the gendered ideology and strategies of these parties, particularly when it comes to addressing the issue of migrant women. If the gendered narratives used by the PRR create gender-specific roles for men (breadwinners and defenders of the nation) and women (caring mothers), what are the gender-specific roles assigned to migrant men and to migrant women?

Further, little is known about how gender impacts on activism in these parties (Blee and Linden 2012; Mulinari and Neergard 2013; Scrinzi 2014a, b, c; Scrinzi 2017a). Yet, women are actively engaged in conservative and right-wing organizations across the world and may feel empowered 'as women' by their activism (Bacchetta and Power 2002). Finally, in spite of its importance in the context of the development of PRR politics across Europe, little has been written on these issues in the case of the LN in Italy.[2]

This chapter aims to address these gaps in the scholarly literature by focusing on the gendered dimensions of anti-immigration ideology, policy and politics in the case of the LN. In particular, we draw on the empirical findings of two research projects to analyse the instrumental mobilization of women's rights by the LN to stigmatize migrant, particularly Muslim, communities.[3] By combining ethnographic and documentary data, we shed light on what we call the 'sexualization of racism' (Farris 2017) and the 'racialization of sexism' (Scrinzi 2014a; b) in the LN discourse. These concepts refer to the application of a sexualized double standard to migrant men and women as the former are treated as 'oppressors' and the latter as 'victims'. The former means that different racist registers are applied to construct migrant men and women. The latter refers to the processes through which sexism is treated as a problem affecting only migrant communities within allegedly liberated European societies.

The chapter is organized as follows. Firstly, by drawing upon discourse analysis of the party's programme, propaganda materials and political speeches, we reconstruct both the ways in which the LN has publicly presented the issue of gender equality among migrants and the party's depictions of migrant women—Muslim and non-Muslim alike.[4]

---

[2] Excluding our own research (Farris 2012; Farris 2017; Scrinzi 2014a, Scrinzi 2014b; Scrinzi 2017), so far only two other authors have addressed these issues in the case of the LN (Avanza 2008; Huysseune 2000).

[3] Francesca Scrinzi, 'Gendering activism in populist radical right parties. A comparative study of women's and men's participation in the Northern League (Italy) and the National Front (France)', funded by the European Research Council (2012–2014), and Sara R. Farris, 'The Political Economy of Femonationalism. On the instrumentalisation of gender equality in anti-immigration campaigns in France, Italy and the Netherlands', funded by the Institute for Advanced Study, Princeton (2012–2013).

[4] This section of the chapter draws mainly on an analysis of the official LN positions that were found on the LN's official website between 2009 and 2013. The analysis was conducted by means of 'critical discourse analysis' methodology—CDA (Fairclough and Wodak 1997). Documents analysed also included political posters, relevant parliamentary discussions and interviews with

Secondly, based on official party documents and existing studies, we analyse the LN agenda on gender and the family as well as its seemingly 'contradictory' policy with regard to female migrants. Thirdly, through the analysis of interviews, we illustrate how LN activists negotiate the party's treatment of migrant care-givers.[5]

In the conclusion, we argue that the mobilization of women's rights by the LN is not simply the paternalistic facet of anti-immigration politics, nor a mere electoral strategy—as it has been commonly held to be in most literature on the sudden 'treacherous sympathy' of right-wing parties for migrant women, to borrow Ahmed's (2011) definition. Rather, it is also linked to the familistic culture and traditional arrangements of the gendered division of work dominant in Italy that the party supports, and in which migrant women, Muslim and non-Muslim alike, play a key role as providers of paid care.

## Migrant Women as Subaltern Victims

Upon its foundation in 1991 the LN presented itself as the party of a new era in Italian politics, denouncing the corrupt political élite and the theft of the northern regions' resources and autonomy by the central government. In the 1990s, the LN was still bound to an ethno-regionalist ideology demanding the independence of Padania (roughly corresponding to the Italian regions north of the Po river) based on the idea of it being a homogenous nation with a common history and ethnic identity. The

---

party leaders that appeared in national newspapers. The concept of 'discourse' within CDA refers to a 'social practice' that produces meanings by linking the linguistic and the societal level (institutions and social structures) (Fairclough and Wodak 1997, 258). In particular, critical discourse analysis is interested in identifying the linkages between (political) discourse and the ways in which such discourse produces and reproduces power hierarchies, ideologies and forms of domination.

[5] This section of the chapter draws on biographical interviews with 12 male and 12 female LN activists based in Lombardy: most of these belonged to the middle classes, reflecting the class composition of the LN electorate. Traditionally, LN voters are business owners and artisans, but there has been a recent increase in working-class manual workers among them (Passarelli and Tuorto 2012). The biographical approach is often used in ethnographic studies of rightist activism to overcome attitudes of suspicion vis-à-vis the researcher: in life histories, which focus on the respondent's own individual trajectory rather than on issues of belief or political commitment, informants will be less likely to present their organization's ideology as personal sentiment (Blee 1996).

LN's regional nationalism at this time led to an identification of southern Italians as the racialized Other. At the end of the 1990s and in the 2000s, particularly after its participation in the Berlusconi government and therefore its co-optation into national politics, the LN moved from demanding secession to fiscal federalism, and the Other was increasingly identified in non-Italian, non-Western migrants. From its entrance into the government in 2001 onwards, the LN has distinguished itself with its harsh anti-immigration and increasingly anti-Islam propaganda. Migrants in general are depicted as a threat to national security, and Muslims in particular are indicted as a danger to the Christian roots of Italian culture but also on account of their allegedly violent treatment of women.

The mobilization of the issue of gender equality by the LN in anti-immigration campaigns begins—at least in a discernible way—with its campaign against Turkey's entry into the EU in 2005. In line with the vitriolic style of the party, the LN encapsulated its opposition in a poster, which remained on the walls of the peninsula for many months.[6] The poster portrays three women. On the left is a veiled woman behind prison bars: she is surrounded by darkness but her state of suffering is clearly discernible; on the right-hand side are two women with short hair and Western clothes sitting at an office desk and seemingly discussing work issues in an illuminated environment. The caption on the left states 'them…', while that on the right states 'us…'. Beneath the image is an almost rhetorical question: 'Are you willing to take the risk? No to Turkey in Europe'. The message is very clear: admitting Turkey to the European Union would allow the entrance of a country with an Islamic majoritarian culture into a traditionally Christian area and therefore run the risk of exposing European women to a religion which subjugates the female sex.

From 2006 onwards in particular, the LN has continued to use gender equality against Islam in obvious instrumental ways. In February 2006 the city councillor for the LN in Milan, Matteo Salvini (now the president of the party), proposed a 'Decalogue of freedoms' to be presented to immigrants applying for Italian citizenship. Five out of ten questions focus on women's issues and are motivated by the idea that migrants—particularly Muslims—do not respect women's rights. One can read:

---

[6] The image can be seen by searching images on the internet using the following search criteria—'Siete disposti a rischiare? No alla Turchia in Europe'.

Would you forbid your wife or daughter to dress like Italian women? What do you think of the statement according to which a woman must obey her husband, and that he can beat her in the case she does not obey him? Do you think it is acceptable that a man locks his wife or daughter at home to avoid that she dishonors the family in public? What would you do if your daughter or son wanted to marry a person from another religion? Would you allow a male doctor to visit you (if you are a woman) or a female doctor to visit you (if you are a man)?

In October 2009 the LN presented a law proposal for banning the burqa and niqab in public spaces. The proposal aimed to modify a previous law from 1975 allowing some categories of people to keep their faces covered if there was a 'justified motive'. It was officially motivated by security reasons but was largely presented in the media as seeking to enable Muslim women who were victims of violence and obliged to use the integral veil to free themselves from the imposition.[7] This recalls what happened in France, where the 2010 law banning full veils in public spaces was officially presented as a measure seeking to enhance public security but was conveyed in the media as a women-friendly law (Tissot 2011). In 2013, the vice-president of the LN group in the Chamber of Deputies, Gianluca Buonanno, addressed the Imam of Florence Elzir, who dismissed the LN's anti-Islam propaganda as 'uncivilized', with the following words: 'it is laughable even only the idea that he [the Imam] thinks he can teach us civilized manners. We do not treat women like beasts'.[8] The campaign against Muslim communities as 'uncivilized', and Muslim men as oppressors of women, thus represents the main way in which the issue of gender inequality and violence as the exclusive domain of the (Muslim) Other has dominated the LN's anti-Islam propaganda. The idea that the LN belongs to a nation and civilization that protects women's rights, in contrast to Islam, is increasingly mobilized in different instances, at both national and local levels.

---

[7] http://www.leganord.org/index.php/notizie2/7743-Pdl_leghista_per_rendere_illegale_il_velo_islamico_integrale_
[8] http://www.leganord.org/index.php/notizie2/11015-chaouki-buonanno-a-elzir-nessuna-lezione-da-islam-noi-non-trattiamo-le-donne-come-bestie

However, it is important to highlight that it is not only Muslim men who are singled out as women's main enemies; nor is it only Muslim women who are foregrounded as victims. In the xenophobic campaign in which the issues of sexism and gender violence are strongly racialized, and where racism itself takes the form of a distinction between migrant men as 'bad' and migrant women as 'victims', the LN openly identifies all men from Eastern Europe and the Global South more generally as misogynists and especially as 'rapists', and all women from these regions as passive 'victims'. For instance, in April 2013, Salvini promoted on Twitter a new website called 'All the immigrants' crimes'. The site exclusively hosts journal articles reporting cases of violence in which an immigrant is the perpetrator, with cases of rape emerging as the most common crime among non-Italian, non-Western citizens. Migrant men in general are thus identified by the LN as a social threat that puts the female sex in danger. The racist register employed by the LN in order to express concern for Italian as well as non-Italian women mainly takes the form of a warning of the risks faced by women if immigrants are allowed to continue entering the country. The closure of Italian borders and the call for a 'law and order' agenda against the 'crimes' of migrant males in particular are thus the corollary of the contemporary 'sexualization of racism' and 'racialization of sexism' deployed by the LN, with deportation and harsher penalties being increasingly proposed as a panacea for the failures of multiculturalism.

But what is the position of the LN on gender equality in general? And how does the party concretely address the contradiction between campaigning against immigration and considering migrant women as victims to be rescued?

## Migrant Women as 'Useful Resources'

Despite the LN's embrace of women's rights, the party has been strongly associated with a masculinist rhetoric. The latter is not only played out at the level of political discourse but is organic to its anti-feminist and conservative positions on gender.

Women are assigned the role of biologically reproducing and caring for the nation/domestic community, and demographic issues are raised as arguments against immigration, as migrant/racialized women are associated with high rates of pregnancies and depicted as a threat to the nation (Avanza 2009; Huysseune 2000; Scrinzi 2014b). The LN thus presents all features of 'nationalist' gender politics whereby women are considered mainly as the reproducers of the nation. Further, not just women but also elderly people are presented as those who should transmit the Padanian cultural heritage to the younger generations, especially within the context of the family. The party proposes an idealized view of how elderly care should be arranged in society, stating that elderly people should be cared for at home.[9] It celebrates the role of the family, and within it of women, in the provision of unpaid care work for the elderly. At the same time, however, the LN, unlike other populist radical right parties, does not claim that women should be confined to the domestic roles: instead, it is acknowledged that women have to work. The LN thus exhibits an ambivalent position on the issue of women's work. While maternity is celebrated as the 'natural' role of women, and it is assumed that women should be the main unpaid carers for the elderly in the family, the LN does not fully condemn their desire to be professionally active. Women's paid work is explicitly supported as long as this does not jeopardize their domestic responsibilities. This is linked to the traditional predominance of owners of family-run businesses among the LN constituency: women are celebrated as 'honorary men' partaking of the 'masculine' qualities of hard-working members of the nation and contributing to the economic well-being of Padania (Huysseune 2000). The LN has promoted some measures to support work/family balance, such as the creation of nurseries in the workplace. The trade union linked to the LN claims part-time work arrangements for women to enable them to combine their domestic responsibilities with their jobs (Avanza 2009).

The centrality of the family to the LN's ideology, the conception of elderly care as a women's duty but also the pragmatic recognition of women's need to work have contributed to give rise to a peculiar contradiction within the LN's anti-immigration agenda.

---

[9] http://www.leganord.org/i-documenti/161-welfare-e-salute.html

The growing demand for social care in Italian families in the last 20 years in particular is the reason for the mounting numbers of migrant women employed by families as housekeepers and especially care-givers. The demand for migrant care labour is located in the context of the ageing of the Italian population, the resilient unequal division of care work and the paucity of publicly-funded care services in Italy, where the 'familistic' welfare state model rests on the role attributed to the family and to women in the delivery of unpaid and unrecognized personal care services. This situation has not only received wide media attention but has also prompted sociologists, migration scholars and feminists to speak of a fundamental transition occurring in Italian society from a 'family model of care' to a *migrant in the family* model of care' (Bettio et al. 2006). In 2010 the National Institute for Social Insurance (INPS) counted 871,834 contracts for care-givers and domestic workers, whereas estimates speak of more than one million workers being employed in this sector, often informally, a large number of whom are migrant women (Pasquinelli 2012). Thanks to generous cash-for-care allowances and due to the paucity of long-term care services, the practice of recruiting migrant care workers extends beyond the middle-class to lower-middle-class and working-class families (Gallo and Scrinzi 2016).

In this context, on the one hand, migrant women, especially Muslims, are portrayed as the 'victims' of non-Western male gender violence and thus are 'offered' opportunities to emancipate and integrate into their 'hosting' societies, more often through assimilationist measures as in the case of the veil bans. On the other hand, migrant women in general are identified not only as potential victims of foreign masculine violence but also as 'useful resources' in a context in which the demand for care and domestic work is on the rise. Whereas the identification of migrant women as victims of gender violence and patriarchy leads the LN to endorse law proposals demanding both stricter penalties and deportation for migrants and the assimilation of Muslim women to Western models of womanhood, the identification of migrant women as carers has led the LN to advocate a number of measures that are perceived as being in contradiction with its strong anti-immigration agenda.

In Italy, working permit quotas for care-givers have been regularly established since 2005, and special regularization schemes were issued for care workers in 2002 and 2009. Furthermore, since January 2012, citizens from Romania and Bulgaria have not needed a permit to work in Italy, thereby allowing a significant pool of care-givers already present in the country to establish themselves more easily in this niche of the labour market. In Italy immigration policies for care and domestic workers have been very expansive, mostly in the attempt to cope with the massive presence of migrants informally employed in private households but also in order to meet the growing demand for these workers by Italian families. In 2002 a new immigration law, the so-called Bossi-Fini Act, taking its name from the then leaders of the harshest anti-immigration parties in the Berlusconi government, the LN and National Alliance (*Alleanza Nazionale*), respectively, was soon followed by a regularization of care/domestic workers. Between 2001 and 2002, under the pressure of demonstrations across the country with elderly people and their care-givers taking to the streets of Italian major cities, Roberto Maroni (LN) declared the support of his party for the regularization of 'all these extra-communitarians, the majority of whom are women, who carry out activities of high social importance for families' (cited in van Hooren 2011, 67). In 2005, again under Berlusconi's government, specific immigration quotas for domestic and care workers were issued for the first time, allowing 15,000 domestic and care workers to enter the country—the same number established for other occupations altogether. In 2006, the same government 'allowed the entrance of another 45,000 domestic and care workers, which was even more than the total (33,500) set for other occupations' (van Hooren 2011, 68). The tougher anti-immigration agenda of the new Berlusconi government in 2008 resulted in a moratorium on quotas for immigration. This was presented as a response to the global economic crisis that had seemingly made the recourse to migrant workers unnecessary. Tellingly, the only exception was made for domestic and care workers, for which instead the record quota of 105,400 was established. On this occasion, Roberto Maroni (then Minister of the Interior) again declared: 'There cannot be an amnesty for those who entered the country illegally, for those who rape women or rob a villa; but we will certainly take into account all those situations that have a strong social impact, as in the case of female migrant care-givers'.[10] In 2009 the government granted an amnesty only for illegal migrants working as care-givers and domestic workers since that was considered the only sector where the national supply could not meet the demand for labour.

Despite campaigning against immigrants' entrance into the country, the LN has thus not only closed an eye towards the general practice of hiring 'illegal' migrant women as carers and domestic workers in private households, but has even implemented concrete policies for their regularization and recruitment. In so doing the LN has pragmatically accommodated the current Italian crisis of social reproduction (Caffentzis 2002).

## The 'Good Migrants': LN Activists Employing Migrant Care-Givers

The pragmatism of the LN's politics vis-à-vis migrant care workers is reflected by the activists' practices. Most informants—men and women alike belonging to both the middle and working classes—tended to agree, at least in principle, with the prescriptive view of family-based elderly care. Some older female activists however blamed the younger generations of Italian women who delegate elderly care tasks wholly to migrant care workers, who are foreigners to both the ethnic and domestic community: they themselves had not done this to their own parents. Nonetheless many female informants, while they said that ideally elderly people should be cared for at home, saw this as an unrealistic option, due to the lack of state-funded home-based care services and to the competing demands faced by women arising from their jobs, other domestic responsibilities as well as their political engagements. Most informants tended also to take for granted the regularizations of care-givers as a 'lesser evil', emphasizing that the latter are hard-working migrants whose contribution is needed by Italian society. While they said that immigration policies should be selective and that illegal migrant workers constitute a

---

[10] http://www.repubblica.it/2008/05/sezioni/cronaca/sicurezza-politica4/bossi-spagna/bossi-spagna.html

threat because they steal jobs and lower the pay of the Italian workers, activists also stated that they would allow for care-givers to be 'imported' because there is a real need for them. The interviews below are representative of this pragmatism:

> If these care workers were already here with a job and a place to live, anyway they are already established, they might as well be regularized, so that they pay taxes on their work and fully respect the Italian law (middle-class male activist, 30 years old).
>
> If someone is legal and respects our laws and is here to work then we are not against them, but they must be aware that they are in a country which has rules (middle-class female activist, 66 years old).

Several activists declared that they hired migrant care-givers themselves. Some of them displayed a rather disinhibited attitude, stating that they hired illegal workers; however, quite a few among them had subsequently regularized the workers' juridical position. Some of these employers seemed quite happy with this arrangement and told ordinary stories of acquaintance and collaboration between the family members and the employee. They considered the migrant care-givers to be a necessity in Italian society:

> I think that we need the migrant care-givers because we [Italians] have become spoiled, it is not easy to work full-time with someone who has Alzheimer's disease and we would not do this job any longer (…). The birth rate decreases, the people get old and we have this problem (…) The residential care homes for the elderly are expensive so I think the migrant care-givers are a resource (working-class male activist, 36 years old).
>
> We have had some problems with my grand-father who was ill with Alzheimer's disease so we hired a male care-giver, an Indian boy whose juridical position we regularized. My aunt took care of my grand-father together with this boy (…). We did not want to hire him illegally because if a migrant works here, he or she must have both the rights and the duties of an Italian citizen. We need migrants who are willing to take on these jobs which the Italians no longer want to do but if they come here to work then they have to be legal, lead a regular life, health services, pay taxes, not

living here as illegal migrants. We can't accept everybody here (middle-class female activist, 40 years old).

Other activists described their experiences with migrant care-givers as negative. According to them, these workers tended to take advantage of the generosity of their employers and were either lazy or thieves:

> These people lived in houses which do not even have a tiled floor, they have soil in their houses. (…) Then they come here and find that we have floors to be polished, furniture to be cleaned, windows to be cleaned. They get lost and little by little they learn thanks to us, at our expenses, because when they are not able to do the work they are a calamity (middle-class female activist, 80 years old).

These narratives do not greatly differ from those which have been observed in the case of employers of migrant domestic and care workers who are not anti-immigration activists: it has been shown (Anderson 2000) that middle-class female employers tend to describe domestic service as an opportunity for integration into Italian society and for the moral improvement of migrant care and domestic workers, as these are described as women who come from pre-modern cultures. In these narratives, the work relationship and class hierarchy between the employers and their employees are obscured while alleged cultural differences are put to the fore.

Thus, on the one hand, in spite of the official party positions on care as something that should be carried out by (female) family members, the presence of migrant care-givers was overtly tolerated, if not appreciated, by LN activists, who, in many cases, acted as their employers. This was especially true in the case of women, who were assigned the task of supervising migrant care workers. On the other hand, these workers were seen with suspicion. All the informants distinguished between 'good' and 'bad' migrants while talking about the care-givers: between those migrants who are tolerated as long as they 'integrate' themselves being inserted into labour market niches such as care work in the private sphere and those who are perceived as deviant and behaving aggressively in the public space and between those migrants whose integration are deemed possible and those who are constructed as belonging to radically different cultures, such as Muslims. Migrant care-givers fall into the first category but are always at risk of shifting into the second one.

## Conclusion

The analysis has shown a contradictory picture. First, migrant women, particularly in the case of Muslims, are portrayed as 'victims' of male violence, whereby gender violence is treated as something inherent to their culture. At the same time, qua victims, these women are also subtracted from the category of the 'dangerous' migrant, which the LN applies to most foreigners. The LN thus fully participates in what we have called the 'sexualization of racism' and the 'racialization of sexism'. Migrant women are ambiguously indicted as different from Italian standards of womanhood but also given a chance to meet such standards. As care-givers who help Italian families to cope with the demands of everyday life, migrant women are pragmatically portrayed as a 'lesser evil'.

Second, though the LN advocates a traditional role for women in society as mothers, wives and care providers, which is—in principle—shared by most female activists, its 'ambivalent familism' recognizes that migrant care and domestic workers are needed to support women's paid work. Thus the party acknowledges the need for women to have a 'gender'-acceptable replacement for them at home. That is, the LN does not oppose the employment of migrant women in private households because they are 'women'. Similarly, LN activists are willing to accept the 'exception' constituted by the regularization of migrant women who work as care-givers to an otherwise aggressive and overt anti-immigration rhetoric.

To interpret the attitude of anti-immigration parties like the LN in constructing migrant women as both victims and 'useful resources', thereby excluding them (albeit not without ambiguities) from the category of undesirable migrants (in which migrant men tend to be confined), we propose the following framework.

To begin with, by singling out Muslim migrant women in particular as fragile subjects in need of rescue, the LN participates in a trope which is common to nationalist politics: namely, the identification of women as lacking agency and as cultural and social reproducers of the nation. Accordingly, migrant women can be presented with offers of salvation and invited to adopt Western lifestyles: it is assumed they can be moulded to absorb the culture of the 'host' nation and thus become its cultural reproducers. Further, while conservative gender positions are attributed to the racialized Other, the unequal relations of gender which are dominant in the immigration society are reproduced through outsourcing care work to the racialized Other. Through the rhetoric of the 'sexualization of racism' and the 'racialization of sexism', different figures of femininity are thus constructed: Italian/Padanian women, whose emancipation is predicated, among other things, upon their participation in paid work; stigmatized Muslim subaltern women; and migrant (often Christian) docile and idealized care-givers. The migrant care-giver embodies the sexist stereotypes and feminine caring figure on which LN ideology is centrally based.

This notwithstanding, we should note that by admitting an exception for the regularization of those migrant women who work as domestic workers and care-givers, the LN adopts a contradictory attitude in terms of its immigration politics, but a coherent attitude in terms of its gender and class politics. In other words, the LN's pragmatic participation in the regularization of migrant women care-givers is coherent with its gender politics because it is in line with the party's familism: namely, it is in line with the party's focus on the defence of the family and the promotion of the family as the main site where care is provided. At the same time, we have shown that the LN tolerates women's work outside the family. This element adds to the continuity between the LN's policies on migrant care-givers and its gender politics and ideology: as migrant women help Italian women to combine their paid work with their domestic responsibilities, the party can tolerate their presence. In so doing, the LN widely shares the familistic culture of the country.

The LN position is also coherent with its class politics: its electorate mostly belongs to the lower-middle classes and middle classes in Northern Italy. These families are likely to hire a migrant care worker and therefore to benefit from liberal policies towards these migrants. Female activists reproduce their middle-class femininity through hiring migrant care workers and delegating the 'dirty work' to them. Through domestic service, LN female activists can thus combine their domestic responsibilities with their jobs as well as with their political engagement; they reproduce their femininity as 'modern' Italian women, as opposed to the stigmatizing representation of Muslim and migrant women constructed as victims.

# References

Abu-Lughod, Lila. 2013. *Do Muslim Women Need Saving?* Cambridge, MA: Harvard University Press.
Ahmed, Leila. 2011. Feminism, Colonialism and Islamophobia. Treacherous Sympathy with Muslim Women. *Qantara.de*. August 18.
Akkerman, Tjitske, and Anniken Hagelund. 2007. Women and Children First! *Patterns of Prejudice* 41 (2): 197–214.
Anderson, Bridget. 2000. *Doing the Dirty Work?* London: Zed Books.
Avanza, Martina. 2009. Un Parti qui 'l'a Dure'. Les 'Femmes Padanes' dans la Ligue du Nord. In *Le Sexe du Militantisme*, ed. Olivier Fillieule and Patricia Roux, 143–166. Paris: Presses de Sciences Po.
Bacchetta, Paola. 2002. In *Right-Wing Women*, ed. Margaret Power. New York: Routledge.
Bettio, Francesca, Annamaria Simonazzi, and Paola Villa. 2006. Change in Care Regimes and Female Migration. *Journal of European Social Policy* 16 (3): 271–285.
Blee, Kathleen M. 1996. Becoming a Racist. *Gender and Society* 10 (6): 680–702.
Blee, Kathleen M., and Annette Linden. 2012. Women in Extreme Right Parties and Movements. In *Women of the Right*, ed. Kathleen M. Blee and Sandra McGee Deutsch. University Park: Pennsylvania State University Press.
Bracke, Sara. 2011. Subjects of Debate. *Feminist Review* 98: 28–46.
Caffentzis, George. 2002. "On the Notion of a Crisis of Social Reproduction." *The Commoner*.
Fairclough, Norman, and Ruth Wodak. 1997. Critical Discourse Analysis. In *In Discourse as Social Interaction*, ed. Teun van Dijk. London: Sage.
Farris, Sara R. 2012. Femonationalism and the Regular Army of Labour Called Migrant Women. *History of the Present* 2 (2): 184–199.
———. 2017. *In the Name of Women's Rights. The Rise of Femonationalism*. Durham: Duke University Press.
Gallo, Ester, and Francesca Scrinzi. 2016. Outsourcing Elderly Care to Migrant Workers. *Sociology* 50 (2): 366–382.

Huysseune, Michel. 2000. Masculinity and Secessionism in Italy. *Nations and Nationalism* 6 (4): 591–610.
Mudde, Cas. 2007. *Populist Radical Right Parties in Europe*. Cambridge: Cambridge University Press.
Mulinari, Diana, and Anders Neergard. 2013. We Are Sweden Democrats Because We Care for Others. *European Journal of Women's Studies* 21 (1): 43–56.
Pasquinelli, Sergio. 2012. "Badanti: Dilaga il Lavoro Nero." *Qualificare*, January, http://www.qualificare.info/home.php?id=585. Accessed on 11 Nov 2014.
Passarelli, Gianluca, and Dario Tuorto. 2012. *Lega e Padania*. Bologna: Il Mulino.
Scrinzi, Francesca. 2014a. *Gendering Activism in Populist Radical Right Parties. In-Progress Preliminary Report*, ERC Starting Grant. http://www.gla.ac.uk/schools/socialpolitical/research/sociology/projects/genderingactivisminpopulistradicalrightparties/publications/preliminary%20report/. Accessed on 11 Nov 2014.
———. 2014b. Rapporti di Genere e Militanza nella Lega Nord. In *Attraverso la Lega*, ed. Anna Curcio and Lorenza Perini, 163–184. Bologna: Il Mulino.
———. 2014c. *Caring for the Nation. Men and Women Activists in Radical Right Populist Parties. Final Research Report*, ERC Starting Grant, http://www.gla.ac.uk/media/media_383799_en.pdf. Accessed on 11 Nov 2014.
———. 2017a. Caring for the Elderly in the Family or in the Nation? Women Activists and Migrant Care Labour in the Lega Nord (Italy). *West European Politics* 40 (4): 869–886.
———. 2017b. A 'New' National Front? Gender, Religion, Secularism and the French Populist Radical Right. In *Gender and Far Right Politics in Europe*, ed. M. Köttig, R. Bitzan, and A. Petö, 127–140. Aldershot: Ashgate.
Tissot, Sylvie. 2011. Excluding Muslim Women. *Public Culture* 23 (1): 39–46.
Towns, Ann, Erika Karlsson, and Joshua Eyre. 2014. The Equality Conundrum. *Party Politics* 20 (2): 237–247.
Van Hooren, Franca. 2011. *Caring Migrants in European Welfare Regimes*. PhD diss., Department of Political and Social Sciences, European University Institute.
Yuval-Davis, Nira. 1997. *Gender and Nation*. London: Sage.

# 14

# The Media Framing of Migration in Sending and Receiving Countries: The Case of Romanians Migrating to the UK

Bianca-Florentina Cheregi

## Introduction

In March 2016, the British newspaper *The Guardian* published an article entitled "Romania: hellhole or country of romance and mystery?", debating a survey that indicated that Romania was the very last place that British people would like to live. The explanation lies in the fact that most Britons believe that Romanians come to Britain to "steal their jobs and get their teeth fixed on the NHS" (Cadwalladr 2016). However, the article cites Michael Bird, an English journalist who runs an investigative website based in Bucharest. According to Bird, Romania tends to inspire two extreme reactions in the British press. Either it's a hellhole for the right-wing press or it has this mysterious romanticism. "It's where the middle ages meets totalitarianism" (Cadwalladr 2016).

---

B.-F. Cheregi (✉)
National University of Political Science and Public Administration, Bucharest, Romania

© The Author(s) 2018
J. Mulholland et al. (eds.), *Gendering Nationalism*,
https://doi.org/10.1007/978-3-319-76699-7_14

In the contemporary "age of migration" (Castles and Miller 2003), people develop transnational identities by traveling between different locations. This phenomenon raises the issue of a *politics of belonging* (Yuval-Davis 2011), affected by neoliberal ideology and the mobility of the globalized economy. Constructions of self and identity are commonly constructed through medium of boundaries that "sometimes physically, but always symbolically, separate the world population into 'Us' and 'Them'" (Yuval-Davis 2011: 20). In this regard, "identity versus alterity" is a common strategy used by the media when portraying Romanian migrants.

The topic of labor migration to the EU (the new diaspora) is a near constant theme of the media, sometimes involving intense *mediatization*, depending on social and political contexts. The 2010 crisis associated with Romani expulsions from France, the broader economic crisis, the implications of Romania's accession to the Schengen Area and subsequent freedom of movement to work in the EU, and, more recently, the EU referendum in the UK, have all served as important contexts for media engagements with Romanian migration. This chapter explores how the media—particularly the British and Romanian media—frame the issue of Romanian immigration to Great Britain. Furthermore, it reveals the stereotypes about Romanian people employed in the British and Romanian press and how they affect Romania's national image overseas. A further dimension investigated here is that of gender, specifically, the deployment of gender stereotyping in the portrayal of Romanian migrants in the British and Romanian press, comparatively.

On January 1, 2014, the restrictions for Romanians and Bulgarians to work in the EU and, therefore, the UK were lifted. Victor Spirescu was one of the Romanians to arrive in the UK on the first day of unrestricted access. After introducing him as a Romanian who came to Britain to work, the British tabloid press quickly moved on to a framing of the discussion in terms of health benefits, migration, employment, his personal life, and his plans to move his girlfriend over to London ("Romanian migrant No. 1 exposed as brute. Vaz[1] shake (sic) newcomer is crook", *The Sun*, January 1, 2014; "Washing car in Biggleswade, the Romanian welcomed to UK on New Year's Day by Keith Vaz…meanwhile, his fiancée

---

[1] Vaz stands for Keith Vaz, Labour MP and chairman of the Home Affairs Committee from July 2007 to September 2016.

is left chopping wood in Transylvania", *Daily Mail*, January 3, 2014; "Romanian migrant treated to Costa Coffee by Keith Vaz is accused of being a drug user who beat up his girlfriend and threatened to drown her", *Daily Mail*, January 8, 2014; "Now Romanian migrant treated to Costa Coffee by Keith Vaz lands a 60 pounds-a-day building job in London after quitting car wash following just one shift", *Daily Mail*, January 18, 2014).

Furthermore, the press pictured him with politicians such as the Labour MP Keith Vaz, who greeted him at Luton airport on his day of arrival in the UK. Victor Spirescu, a 30-year-old man living in a small village in Transylvania, quickly became the symbol of public and media debates around Romanian migration. Following months of stories regarding "the wave" of Romanians and Bulgarians expected to "invade" Great Britain from January 1, 2014, when the working restrictions were lifted, Victor Spirescu was immediately portrayed as a potential threat to the UK by the tabloid press (*Daily Mail, Daily Express*, and *The Sun*): he quit his job after the first day, he is a drug user, and he was guilty of assaulting his former girlfriend.

Media accounts of the Romanian migrant heading to Britain were quickly linked to the immigration debate. At the beginning of 2013, the British Government launched the "Don't Come to Britain" campaign, to discourage potential migrants from Romania and Bulgaria coming to Britain. After a short time, the Romanian newspaper *Gândul* responded with the "Why don't you come over?" campaign, hitting back at Britain's negative portrayal of Romanian immigrants. The debate about migration intensified during 2013 in the British press, especially in the tabloids (*Daily Mail, Daily Express*). The ways in which Victor Spirescu was portrayed in the British media were understandable as cases of broader framings employed by different newspapers and television channels when debating the theme of Romanian migrants in the UK. The tabloid press focused on the human interest aspect, while the quality press addressed political and economic issues.

However, the theme of Romanian emigration as a *public problem* (Jean et al. 2001), discussed in the Romanian media, related strongly to the impact of migrants' actions on Romania's image abroad—a key element of the "symbolic capital" of the nation (Beciu 2012). Frames of migration directly address the question of national image building. As a public issue, migration is "a factor of modernization independent from the state" (Schifirneţ 2012: 46).

In order to explore British and Romanian journalists' framing of the social issue of Romanian migration to the UK, comparatively, this chapter is structured in three main parts: (1) media frames on migration employed in the British and Romanian media, (2) stereotypes about Romanian people in the British media, and (3) the visual framing of Romanian migrants in the national press. Each section in turn addresses findings associated with the media analysis of Romanian migration both in the context of sending and receiving countries.

The corpus contains a total of 562 news articles from the British and Romanian press: 271 news items from the British quality press (*The Guardian*, *The Independent*) and from the tabloids (*Daily Mail*) discussing the topic of Romanian migrants in the UK, published between January 1, 2013 and March 31, 2014, together with 291 news articles from the Romanian press, discussing the topic of Romanians migrating to the UK, published in the online editions of three national newspapers—*Gândul*, *Adevărul*, and *Jurnalul Naţional*.

When discussing Romanian migrants in the UK, British and Romanian journalists shape media discourses through the frames they use. The framing analysis employed in this article is based on Entman's (1993) approach.

The chapter will now address the question of migration as a public issue in the context of the free movement of labor in the EU, and as such the UK. The British and Romanian media are investigated comparatively, in terms of the media frames employed, and in relation to the impact of gender.

## Migration as a Public Problem

The neoliberal ideology and the mobility of the globalized economy have affected nationalist political projects of belonging. Thus, constructions of self and identity can be forced on people, constituting a field of contestation. In this case, the boundaries of the politics of belonging are the boundaries which "sometimes physically, but always symbolically, separate the world population into "Us" and "Them" (Yuval-Davis 2011: 20). Nowadays, people develop transnational identities by traveling between different locations for professional and other purposes. This is also the case with the Romanian people who migrated in the UK after January 1, 2014.

Research in the area of migration studies raises the issue of the *politics of belonging* (Yuval-Davis 2011: 17), describing "not only the construction of boundaries but also the inclusion or exclusion of particular people, social categories and groupings within these boundaries by those who have the power to do this". Some of the studies concentrate on the role played by mediation in the construction of immigration as a "public problem" (Mawby and Gisby 2009; Pijpers 2006), while others rely on media framings of intra-EU migration (Balabanova and Balch 2010, 2016). Balabanova and Balch (2016) show in their most recent study that communitarian, rather than cosmopolitan, frames dominate discussions of Romanian and Bulgarian migrants. Their study is comparative, analyzing UK newspapers in two different periods: 2006 and 2013.

Compared to other research relying on the media framing of intra-EU migration, this chapter insists both on textual and visual framing of Romanian migrants, leading to multiple understandings of the ways in which migration is constructed as a public problem. The theme of Romanian people migrating to other countries has launched an intense debate in the media about migration and the national image building problem. In Romania, "migration to other countries is a factor of modernization independent from the state" (Schifirneț 2012: 46). Freedom to travel, since 1989, has revolutionized a Romanians' daily mobility thinking and behavior.

Following the Revolution of 1989, the image of Romania has emerged as an important theme in public discourse. This discourse related to positive and negative evaluations found in the international press but also on the ways in which Romanians were perceived overseas. In this context, the diaspora was seen as "the result of massive migration occurring after the fall of communism, be it the migration of the unskilled labor force, benefiting preeminence both in media and public debates, or the migration of highly-skilled professionals" (Ciocea and Cârlan 2012: 184).

Romanian migration to the UK has become a more salient issue, both in the Romanian and British media, especially after January 1, 2014, when the restrictions for Romanians and Bulgarians to work in the EU and, therefore, the UK as well were lifted. Identity versus alterity is a common strategy used by the media when portraying Romanian migrants, as demonstrated in the following sections.

## Frames and Framing Migration

The concept of "frames" was introduced by Erving Goffman (1987) and was related to the organization and interpretation of life experiences for the purpose of sense-making. Frames, also defined as the "schemata of interpretation", enable individuals "to locate, perceive, identify and label" (Goffman 1987: 21) occurrences of information. In the light of Goffman's contribution, research has come to define frames as patterns of interpretation rooted in culture and articulated by the individual (Entman 1993; Gamson et al. 1992: 384; Pan and Kosicki 1993; Reese 2001; Van Gorp 2007).

From a sociological perspective, frames represent cognitive structures and form an important element of public discourse. The framing process is also a central dynamic in understanding the character and course of social movements (Benford and Snow 2000: 611). Collective action frames are "intended to mobilize potential adherents and constituents, to garner bystander support, and to demobilize antagonists" (Snow and Benford 1988: 198). Put simply, movements are related to the production and maintenance of meaning for protagonists, antagonists, and bystanders. Thus, the constructed meanings are subject to change, as the social context changes.

Brexit and the broader the rise of the right-wing nationalist parties in the UK and Europe (such as the UK Independence Party—UKIP—and the National Front in France) force us to rethink the basis of transnational migration, at both the individual and societal levels. Migration has become a more salient issue in public debates, so it is important to investigate the media discourses and counter-discourses around Romanians migrating to the UK.

According to Entman (1993: 52), framing is the process of selecting "some aspects of a perceived reality and make them more salient in a communicating text, in such a way as to promote a particular problem definition, causal interpretation, moral evaluation, and/or treatment recommendation". Moreover, Van Gorp (2005) claims that frames are part of a culture and that they can be localized quite independently of individuals. In fact, "journalists can construct a news report *deliberately* starting from a certain frame, but not incorporating the frame *itself* in the text" (Van Gorp 2005: 487). Frames are not mere heuristic tools, and the connection between the frame and its cultural motive is made by the reader in his perception of the news text.

Thus, a frame is an abstract variable that is hard to identify. There are many different approaches to derive a set of frames in the context of any particular issue (Gamson and Modigliani 1989; Hertog and McLeod 2001; Scheufele 1999; Tankard 2001; Van Gorp 2005), and most of them are inductive. Content analysis of media frames range from completely qualitative interpretive or hermeneutic-qualitative approaches to automated device-oriented methods, such as semantic network analyses (Scheufele and Scheufele 2010). Framing can also be studied from a visual perspective, considering the metaphor of cropping a frame around a picture. The perspective of the image allows the interference of subjectivity, or what Panofsky (1957: 30) calls seeing pictures as "windows of the world". Visual and verbal elements work together to frame topics, but sometimes images appear more closely linked to reality than words, even if images are "human-made artificial constructions" (Messaris and Abraham 2010: 215). The media presents both visual and verbal elements, while journalists construct additional layers of interpretation in the form of a news story.

Furthermore, attention needs to be paid to the deeper framing which operates in the context of labor migration and to the ways in which migrants are portrayed. Belonging is constructed in relation to particular collectivities, such as Romanian migrants. Balabanova and Balch (2010, 2011, 2016) analyze communitarian and cosmopolitan frames over the topic of intra-EU migration. Their results show that communitarian frames dominate discussions of Romanian and Bulgarian migrants. Their research shows that "welfare chauvinist ideas became more prevalent in the public debate when times were harder economically" (Balabanova and Balch 2016: 32). Moreover, the media generally frame intra-EU migration using nationalist and communitarian arguments.

Many studies have focused on media frames in the context of migration. Some of these employ quantitative research (Fryberg et al. 2012; Van Gorp 2005; Vliegenthart and Roggeband 2007) in order to determine frames, while others use qualitative research (Durham and Carpenter 2014; Polson and Kahle 2010) or some combination of both (Balabanova and Balch 2010). Other works on media framing of immigration insist on political aspects, considering the dominance of 'conservative' and 'progressive' frames (Lakoff and Ferguson 2006). Compared to previous research on framing migration, this chapter brings a new way of understanding public debates on migration by drawing on Entman's four function frames in order to explore how British and Romanian journalists frame the issue of Romanians migrating to the UK, both textually and visually. In his opinion, frames diagnose, evaluate, and prescribe issues discussed in the media:

> *define problems* – determine what a causal agent is doing with what costs and benefits, usually measured in terms of common cultural values; *diagnose causes* – identify the forces creating the problem; *make moral judgments* – evaluate causal agents and their effect; and *suggest remedies* – offer and justify treatments for the problems and predict their likely effects. (Entman 1993: 52)

According to Entman's model, a single sentence may perform more than one of the four framing functions and a frame in any particular text may not necessarily include all four functions. Next, the focus will be on the patterns used by the journalists in the coverage of Romanian migration by the British and Romanian media, immediately following the lifting of restrictions for Romanians and Bulgarians to work in the EU.

# The Framing of Migration in the British and Romanian Media: A Comparative Analysis

The results of the framing analysis performed on 562 news articles show that there are 7 media frames present in the British and Romanian media. The frames were identified from a close reading of a 20% sample of texts. Each frame was coded using Entman's framing functions. The dependent variables employed in the content analysis were: define problems, diagnose causes, make moral judgments, and suggest remedies. In fact, the coded variables were systematically grouped together, leading to seven dominant frames. A frame is, therefore, the sum of frame elements (define problems, diagnose causes, make moral judgments, and suggest remedies).

First of all, the *economic* frame insists on the migration costs and economic consequences of migration. The *educational* frame is based on the impact of Romanian students who study in the UK, considering the maintenance they receive from the state. The *political* frame is linked with the political voices present in the debate over Romanian migration. The *social benefits* frame refers to the Romanian migrants abusing the social benefits system in Great Britain (NHS, housing, benefits for families, child, etc.). The *employment* frame focuses on the working practices of Romanians in the UK. The *public security* frame emphasizes the fact that Romanians are a threat to the security of the UK citizens, often focusing on crimes such as begging and pickpocketing. Finally, the *EU policy* frame concerns the question of freedom of movement in relation with migration.

When comparing the frames used by the British and Romanian journalists in the 562 news articles analyzed (Fig. 14.1), one notices that all seven frames are employed more frequently in the British press. The use of economic, political, and employment frames are predominant in the case of British newspapers, whereas EU policy and political frames feature most in the case of Romanian newspapers. Significant differences are to be seen when using the economic, employment, or public security frames. The British press tend to place an emphasis on migration costs and the impact on the economy of the receiving country, tending to

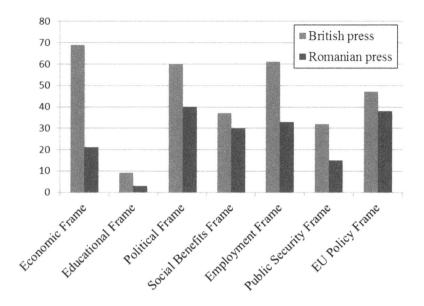

Fig. 14.1 Frame frequencies in the British and Romanian press

make reference to the poverty characterizing Romanian society. The Romanian press reinforces this frame too, by quoting many articles published in the *Daily Mail* or *Daily Express*. As for the employment frame, the British newspapers commonly focus on the status of jobs offered to the migrants, implicitly or explicitly asserting that these jobs are stolen from British people. Conversely, the Romanian newspapers tend to use this frame to present successful cases of Romanians working in the UK.

The public security frame constructs Romanian men and women as a threat to the security of UK citizens, highlighting crimes associated, among other things, with begging, and pickpocketing. This frame is employed both in the sending and receiving countries, but with intense coverage in the British media. In both cases, images of Roma people are directly associated with a framing of threat. Both the British and Romanian press present images of both men and women in this context, but with a slight predominance of men. Even though men are slightly more frequently represented than women, both at a textual and visual level, there is no gender difference in terms of the stereotypical portrayal of Romanian migrants. Romania is metonymically represented by Romanian Roma people. In its use of the public security frame, the Romanian press reinforces anti-Roma discourses, blaming Romas for the negative portrayal of the Romanians, as a whole, in the British press.

Furthermore, the rhetorical structures used by the Romanian journalists in framing the theme of migration reveal a critical position regarding the anti-immigration discourses of the British tabloid press: "the rhetoric against immigration which dominated the political British discourse" (*Adevarul*, January 13, 2014), "anti-immigration British rhetoric" (*Adevarul*, March 14, 2013), "Romanian people invasion" (*Adevarul*, March 20, 2014), and "myth of the Romanian invader" (*Adevarul*, March 21, 2014). The word "anti-immigration" is mentioned in the news headlines as well, being a frame device, and appealing to intertextuality. In fact, the journalists create a story within a story by using counter-discourses to fight against negative stereotypes found in the British press.

News headlines such as "The anti-Romanians campaign in Great Britain intensifies. From the invasion of 29 millions of "bulgoromanians" to aliens who look like Victor Ciorbea" (Andrei Luca Popescu, *Gândul*, December 6, 2013); "The anti-immigration campaign from Great Britain challenges a new issue: interdicted areas for Roma people" (Diana Rusu, *Adevarul*, December 22, 2013); "London plans an anti-immigration campaign for Romanians: "Please, do not come to Great Britain!" (Veronica Micu, *Jurnalul Național*, January 28, 2013); "Stinging attack to the Romanians, launched by an anti-immigration British leader" (*Jurnalul Național*, September 20, 2013); "The British publication Daily Express affirms that the petition against immigration is now signed by 150,000 people" (*Adevarul*, November 25, 2013); "*Bloomberg*: R is for Romania, Roma people and Racism in the European Debate on Immigration" (Alina Vasile, *Adevarul*, March 14, 2013); or "Romanians do no hurry to emigrate in a "racist" Great Britain" (Diana Rusu, *Adevarul*, January 13, 2014) suggest that the subject of Romanian immigrants in Great Britain is controversial. Furthermore, there are no gender differences in portraying the Romanian migrants; both men and women are referred through the term "migrants". Thus, the Romanian press emphasizes positive stories of well-integrated Romanians, compared to the British tabloid press, who insists on negative examples of Romanians living in the UK.

The official sources quoted in the Romanian newspapers were the Romanian Prime Minister Victor Ponta, Ion Jinga, the Ambassador of Romania in Great Britain, the Ministry of Foreign Affairs, Titus Corlățean, the UK Prime Minister David Cameron, UKIP, and Nigel Farage. In this way, the journalists position themselves by citing credible sources which have a contribution in shaping the discourses about Romanian migrants. Conversely, the most quoted official sources in the British quality and tabloid press were the British Prime Minister, David Cameron; the UK Immigration Minister, Mark Harper; the Labour Government; the Home Secretary, Theresa May; the Bulgarian President, Rosen Plevneliev; the Romanian Prime Minister, Victor Ponta; the Romanian Ambassador to the UK, Ion Jinga; UKIP, Nigel Farage; and the pressure group arguing for tighter immigration controls, Migration Watch.[2] Quoting political actors may also function as an argument to sustain a certain position about migration. Therefore, when the press quotes chiefly expert or elite, recognized sources, it is liable to overlook lay knowledge and hence construct groups—such as migrants—from a distance, without exploring their beliefs, identities, and lives in host societies (Beciu 2011: 166). This way, the tabloid press may employ expert or elite knowledge to gain a false legitimacy through the use of fallacies (such as hasty generalization).

Another frame covered by both Romanian and British press is EU policy, mentioning the effects of the freedom of movement on the migration issue. In fact, the British press employs this frame more frequently, discussing the implications of EU policies in terms of advantages and disadvantages for the UK (social benefits, labor market, economic growth).

---

[2] Migration Watch is an immigration and asylum research organization and think-thank that concentrates on migration as a public issue. They describe themselves as independent and nonpolitical, even though they have argued that very large-scale immigration is of little benefit to the indigenous population. Migration Watch is a controversial organization, especially because under the claim to support political asylum, they believe that many asylum seekers are using the system to gain entry to the UK for economic reasons.

## Portraying Romanian People in the British Media: Representations and Stereotypes

In portraying Romanian migrants, British journalists from the tabloid press drew on metaphors suggesting natural disasters, such as "flood" ("a flood of Romanians coming to the UK), "tsunami", the expression "invader", and a lot of arguments about the huge number of Romanians coming to the UK ("hordes of Romanians and Bulgarians"). Conversely, the Romanian journalists used a military-infused discourse ("British crusade against Romanians", "Romanians are used as ammunition in the crusade") in order to challenge the anti-immigration discourses of the British tabloid press. In this regard, Romanian migrants were presented as victims. In the British quality and tabloid press, Romanians and Bulgarians were often referred to as "EU migrants", "A2 nationals", or "EU nationals", raising the question of the number of people that are likely to come to Britain on January 1, 2014, when EU restrictions will be lifted. By framing Romanian people as "EU migrants", the British journalists (especially from tabloid newspapers such as *Daily Mail*) construct a negative stereotype, linking this to the idea that migrants are a threat to the welfare state. They also mention the fear of invasion, comparing this phenomenon with the invasion of Poles in 2004.

In terms of gender, there are some differences when portraying Romanian migrants. For instance, the British press focuses predominantly on males, mainly professionally unsuccessful (such as Victor Spirescu), while the Romanian press gives examples of both professionally successful men and women living and working in Great Britain. Here, the British media offers a one-dimensional view of Romanian migrants in the UK. Conversely, the Romanian media offers positive narratives of well-integrated Romanians (both men and women), in order to provide a more balanced view on Romanian migration to the UK. Overall, Romanians are portrayed as being fraudsters, criminals, beggars, pickpockets, and poor. There is a slight predominance of male references, in terms of gender, but the focus is not on emphasizing differences between men and women from the Romanian community. In fact, the British journalists offer a biased view of Romanian migrants, insisting on over-generalization from a minority (Romanian Roma people). For example, one headline from *Daily Mail* stated: "Romanians arrested at seven times rate of Britons: 800 held in London last month" (Chris Greenwood, 13 December 2013). In the article, the British journalist also cited statistics to strengthen the case: "for every 1,000 Romanians in London 183 are arrested". This discursive strategy is based on differentiation, as the journalist from the *Daily Mail* compares the delinquency rate of Britons with the number of Romanian people arrested in London.

## The Visual Framing of Romanian Migrants in the National Press

Now that we have seen how the British and Romanian journalists frame the issue of Romanians migrating to the UK, special attention is given to the visual framing of Romanian migrants in the national press. In fact, "visual and verbal messages occur simultaneously in the media, and audiences process them simultaneously" (Coleman 2010: 235). Thus, even if verbal and visual elements work together to frame topics, sometimes "visual elements frame stories independently of the verbal elements" (Coleman 2010: 236). Therefore, framing refers to the selection of one view, scene, or angle, when making the image, cropping, editing, or selecting it. In this section, the focus is on the role 101 news photographs from three Romanian newspapers (*Adevărul, Gândul, Jurnalul Național*) play in framing the issue of Romanian migration to the UK, considering images as "largely analogical system of communication" (Messaris and Abraham 2010: 216). The unit of analysis was still photographs from newspapers, along with their associated captions. This period in particular is linked with the intensification of the migration issue in the Romanian and foreign media, hence providing not only more material for study but also capturing the debate at its highest intensity. The data was collected from the online editions of the newspapers, searching for key terms such as "Romanian migrants", "anti-immigration discourses", "Romanians migrating to the UK", or "'January 1 2014". In the early stage, 271 news articles were found about Romanian migration to Great Britain, containing 290 photographs. Duplicate photos were removed from the analysis, along with photos illustrating political leaders, landscapes, or flags. By focusing on the depiction of Romanian migrants, only 101 were relevant for the analysis.

The main objective was to reveal how journalists construct the social issue of migration through images. As "mirrors of the events" (Zelizer 2010), press photographs are valued by the journalists for their "eyewitness" authority and the act of "having been there" that they imply (Zelizer 2010: 16–17). By reducing complex issues such as migration to memorable visual frames, news images draw public attention. The results show that the Romanian media reinforce especially the categorization of Roma people, ostracizing one of Romania's many ethnic groups. A total of 67 out of 101 news photographs are representing Roma people. Some images show big families, other show portraits of Roma children, while others reveal people rough sleeping. A total of 13 news photographs are representing Roma women in different situations: holding their child, sitting next to men or next to other women, dressed in traditional or poor clothes. Although there is no gender difference, one can notice the predominance of men in the photographs. The focus is on the over-generalization of a minority, leading to a metonymical image of Romania, specifically represented by the Romanian Roma people. The majority of the press photographs were imported from the British tabloid press, especially from newspapers such as *Daily Mail*, *Daily Express*, or *The Sun*, the tabloids that fueled in part the British anti-immigration frenzy.

Three dominant visual frames also emerge: the public security (images of homeless Romanians rough sleeping), economic (images of pauper Romanian villages) and employment (images of job seekers and unemployed) frames. The photographs represent both men and women, with a predominance of male images. A total of 70 out of 101 news photographs are representing Roma men, but there is no gender difference in terms of stereotyping. The negative portrayal is present both in images with males and females, focusing on pauperization, unemployment, and homelessness. The frames are also semiotic resources, because they insist on signifiers, observable actions, and objects that have been drawn into the domain of social communication. The main semiotic resources employed by the Romanian journalist are the three dominant visual frames. As one can see in Fig. 14.2, the public security frame is most

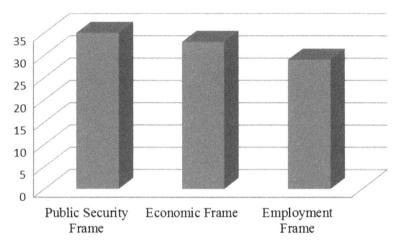

Fig. 14.2 The visual framing of Romanian migrants in three Romanian national newspapers

employed by the Romanian journalists, presenting images with homeless Romanians and beggars threatening the British citizens' security:

*Adevărul* newspaper mostly uses the economic frame to depict Romanian migrants (32 news images out of 74); *Gândul* concentrates on the employment frame (seven news images out of 13) and *Jurnalul Național* on the public security frame (nine news images out of 14).

Firstly, the public security frame presents images of homeless Romanians rough sleeping on London streets (*Adevărul*, December 29, 2013, January 7, *Jurnalul Național*, January 14, 2014), implying that Romanians are a threat to the security of the UK citizens. The photograph representing a family of Roma people walking down the streets with luggage is used three times after the headlines about Romanian migration ("Daily Mail: The economy of Great Britain will suffer because of Romanian and Bulgarian immigrants", *Adevărul*, December 29, 2013, "Be careful, in only six days: the Romanians are coming! The ugly face of Great Britain, Romanian immigrants and the myth of the Polish plummer", *Adevărul*, December 26, 2013, "The Daily Mail: Romanians and Bulgarians snapped up 175.000 jobs in Great Britain until 2012", *Adevărul*, March 3, 2013). Another photograph from the public security frame is representing a homeless Romanian Roma man, rough sleeping in a park, with clothes and luggage around him (*Adevărul*, January 7, 2013). Last, but not least, another image portrays a Romanian Roma woman walking down the streets with luggage, followed by a group of British police officers (*Jurnalul Național*, January 14, 2014).

The economic frame highlights pauper Romanian villages, implying that for migrants from poor countries such as Romania, it is the economic prosperity of more developed countries (such as the UK) that presents the attraction (*Adevărul*, November 11, November 25, December 2, 2013). To emphasize the differences between the respective development and underdevelopment of the UK and Romania, the visual representations portray Roma villages and piles of junk. One of the news photographs shows a deserted blue house, surrounded by detritus, while another image portrays Romanian Roma children playing near a landfill. A third image represents a Roma family sitting in front of a blue clay house, in pauper conditions (Franț & Silaghi 2013).

Another frame regularly employed by Romanian journalists is the employment frame, presenting images of job seekers, the unemployed, or Romanians that work in the UK (*Gândul*, January 3, 2014, January 15, 2014, February 7, 2014). The majority of visual images represent unemployed migrants searching for a job, both men and women, with a predominance of men. There is no gender difference in terms of stereotyping, both images with men and women serve to reinforce underlying negative representations of unemployment. Conversely, there are some images presenting Romanian men and women who are successful professionally. With a focus on the lower class (only nine pictures portraying Romanians from middle- and upper-class backgrounds), the images are emphasizing a similar negative frame of economic underdevelopment.

Romanian journalists have commonly imported pictures from the British tabloid press, misleading the reader unfamiliar with the context to believe that the portrayals of Romania and Romanians were overly negative, with an emphasis on poverty, otherness, risk, and threat. Some visuals were more salient than others, and some images were used several times in different articles (such as the photograph representing a family of Roma people walking down the streets with luggage, used three times in articles from *Adevărul* newspaper). The majority of the news photographs specifically represent Roma people, reinforcing anti-Roma discourses, in a manner common to the textual narratives of the news articles. The deployment of images and narratives of the Roma serve to locate the causes and culprits responsible for Romania's tainted image abroad.

## Conclusion

One of the main questions addressed in this chapter is how the British and Romanian journalists textually and visually frame the public issue of migration, considering that this issue impacts both the individual and society. Seven frames have emerged from analyzing the British and Romanian media: the *economic, educational, political, social benefits, employment, public security*, and *EU policy* frames.

The Romanian press mainly reinforce the frames used by the British journalists. The use of economic, political, and employment frames in the case of British newspapers contrasts with the use of political, EU policy and employment frames in the case of Romanian newspapers. The Romanian journalists quote many articles published in *Daily Mail* or *Daily Express*, on the topic of Romanian migration. An interesting case is to be found when employing the public security frame both in the sending and receiving countries, with an intense coverage in the British media. In both cases, images with Roma people are used to present them as a potential threat. By using the public security frame, the Romanian press reinforces anti-Roma discourses, blaming Romas for the negative portrayal of the Romanians in the British press. There are some differences in terms of gender when portraying Romanian migrants in the British and Romanian press, comparatively. For instance, the British press focuses on professionally unsuccessful males, while the Romanian press offers positive narratives of well-integrated Romanians (both men and women). This leads to the fact that the British media offers a unilateral view of Romanian migrants in the UK, while the Romanian media provides a more balanced view on the public issue of migration to Great Britain.

The stereotypes about Romanian people circulated in British newspapers such as *The Guardian*, *The Independent*, or *Daily Mail* ("beggars", "murderers", "criminals", "fraudsters", "corrupt") are linked to Romania's image overseas. As a matter of fact, the British journalist legitimates his position by framing the Romanian migrants in terms of economy, politics, social benefits, employment, national security, and EU policy.

As for the visual framing of Romanian migrants in the national newspapers, journalists have imported many pictures from the British tabloid press, misleading the reader unfamiliar with the context to believe that the portrayals of Romania and Romanians were overly negative, with an emphasis on poverty, otherness, risk and threat. Some news images are more powerful than others and one possible explanation is the ideological weight carried by photographs. In terms of gender, the news photographs represent both men and women, with a predominance of images of men. A total of 70 out of 101 news photographs are representing Roma men, but there is no gender difference in terms of stereotyping. The negative portrayal is present both in images with males and females, focusing on pauperization, unemployment, and homelessness.

This chapter also shows that there are three dominant visual frames of migrants emerging in the Romanian national press: the *public security* (images of homeless Romanians rough sleeping), *economic* (images of pauper Romanian villages), and *employment* (images of job seekers and unemployed) frames. The majority of the news photographs represent Roma people. This confirms Boia's (2001) claim that Romas continue to be blamed for many of the ills of Romanian society. While reinforcing the anti-Roma discourses found in the Romanian society, the images tell a more complex story about legitimization and validation of national values and about definitions of national image. To a degree, these images highlight an unspoken effort to identify causes and culprits contributing to Romania's tainted image abroad. In so doing, they exonerate those not fitting the stereotypes portrayed. In demonstrating the prevalence of negative, threatening, and demeaning framings of Romanians and Romas, through the analysis of both textual and visual representations, of Romanian migration and immigration, this chapter draws attention to the important role news plays in portraying current events. Seen as "mirrors of the event" (Zelizer, 2010), images capture media discourses that attempt either to define, explain, or judge the context of news and of reality. In this respect, images should be further explored in relation to the function they play within the story and function frame they serve.

In the context of the increasing importance of journalism mediated by technology, observing the dynamics and interactions between various communicative actors is important. What this analysis shows is that although Europe is legislatively and rhetorically open to Romanians, visual and media discourses from home and abroad are seeking, contesting, and constantly reshaping what in fact is at the heart of Romania's identity and its contribution to Europe.

## References

Balabanova, Ekaterina, and Alex Balch. 2010. Sending and Receiving: The Ethical Framing of Intra-EU Migration in the European Press. *European Journal of Communication* 25: 382–397.
Balch, Alex, and Ekaterina Balabanova. 2011. A System in Chaos? Knowledge and Sense-Making on Immigration Policy in Public Debates. *Media, Culture & Society* 33 (6): 885–904.
———. 2016. Ethics, Politics and Migration: Public Debates on the Free Movement of Romanian and Bulgarians in the UK, 2006–2013. *Politics* 36 (1): 19–35.
Beciu, Camelia. 2011. *Sociologia Comunicării Și a Spațiului Public [Sociology of Communication and Public Space]*. Iasi: Polirom.
———. 2012. Diaspora Și Experiența Transnațională, Practici de Mediatizare În Presa Românească [Diaspora and the Transnational Experience, Mediating Practices in the Romanian Press]. *Romanian Journal of Sociology* 1–2: 49–66.
Benford, Robert, and David A. Snow. 2000. Framing Processes and Social Movements: An Overview and Assessment. *Annual Review of Sociology* 26: 611–639.
Cadwalladr, Carole. 2016. Romania: Hellhole or Country of Romance and Mystery? *The Guardian*, March 20 2016. https://www.theguardian.com/world/2016/mar/20/romania-hellhole-or-mysterious-romanticism-europe-uncovered
Castles, Stephen, and Mark J. Miller. 2003. *The Age of Migration*. New York: Guilford Press.
Ciocea, Madalina, and Alexandru Cârlan. 2012. Debating Migration as a Public Problem: Diasporic Stances in Media Discourse. *Romanian Journal of Communication and Public Relations* 27: 181–201.
Coleman, Renita. 2010. Framing the Pictures in Our Heads: Exploring the Framing and Agenda Setting Effects on Visual Images. In *Doing News*

*Framing Analysis: Empirical and Theoretical Perspectives*, ed. Paul D'Angelo and Jim A. Kuypers, 233–255. New York: Routledge.

Durham, Frank D., and John Carpenter. 2014. The Face of Multiculturalism in Korea: Media Ritual as Framing in News Coverage of Jasmine Lee. *Journalism*: 1–18.

Entman, Robert. 1993. Framing: Towards Clarification of a Fractured Paradigm. *Journal of Communication* 43 (4): 51–58.

Franț, Cristian, and Silaghi, Vali. 2013. Exclusiv video Cum scornește "Daily Mail" știri cu invazia românilor. Jurnaliștii britanici au fabricat o poveste cu romi, sărăcie și "caprele vecinilor" *Adevărul*, November 11 2013. http://adevarul.ro/locale/timisoara/daily-mail-1_52812d88c7b855ff56e432be/index.html

Fryberg, Stephanie A., Nicole M. Stephens, Rebecca Covarrubias, Hazel Rose Markus, Erin D. Carter, Giselle A. Laiduc, and Ana J. Salido. 2012. How the Media Frames the Immigration Debate: The Critical Role of Location and Politics. *Analyses of Social Issues and Public Policy* 12 (1): 96–112.

Gadrey, Jean, Armand Hatchuel, Luc Boltanski, and Eve Chiapello. 2001. SYMPOSIUM sur : Le nouvel esprit du capitalisme, de Luc Boltanski et Eve Chiapello. *Sociologie du Travail* 43 (3): 389–421.

Gamson, William A., and Andre Modigliani. 1989. Media Discourse and Public Opinion on Nuclear Power: A Constructionist Approach. *American Journal of Sociology* 95 (1): 1–37.

Gamson, William A., David Croteau, William Hoynes, and Theodore Sasson. 1992. Media Images and the Social Construction of Reality. *Annual Review of Sociology* 18 (1): 373–393.

Goffman, Erving. 1987. *Frame Analysis*. New York: Harper & Row.

Hertog, James, and Douglas McLeod. 2001. A Multiperspectival Approach to Framing Analysis: A Field Guide. In *Framing Public Life: Perspectives on Media and Our Understanding of the Social World*, ed. Stephen D. Reese, Oscar Gandy, and August Grant, 136–161. Mahwah: Lawrence Erlbaum Associates.

Lakoff, George, and Sam Ferguson. 2006. *The Framing of Immigration*. Berkeley: The Rockridge Institute.

Mawby, Rob C., and William Gisby. 2009. Crime, Media and Moral Panic in an Expanding European Union. *The Howard Journal of Criminal Justice* 48 (1): 37–51.

Messaris, Paul, and Linus Abraham. 2010. The Role of Images in Framing News Stories. In *Framing Public Life: Perspectives on Media and Our Understanding of the Social World*, ed. Reese Stephen, Gandy Oscar, and Grant August, 215–225. Mahwah: Lawrence Erlbaum Associates.

Pan, Zhongdang, and Gerald Kosicki. 1993. Framing Analysis: An Approach to News Discourse. *Political Communication* 10 (1): 55–75.

Panofsky, Erwin. 1957. *Meaning in the Visual Arts*. Garden City: Doubleday Anchor Books.

Pijpers, R. 2006. Help! The Poles Are Coming' Narrating a Contemporary Moral Panic. *Geografiska Annaler: Series B. Human Geography* 88 (1): 91–103.

Polson, Erika, and Shannon Kahle. 2010. Limits of National Discourse on a Transnational Phenomenon. *International Communication Gazette* 72 (3): 251–268.

Reese, Stephen D. 2001. Framing Public Life. A Bridging Model for Media Research. In *Framing Public Life: Perspectives on Media and Our Understanding of the Social World*, ed. Stephen D. Reese, Gandy Oscar, and Grant August, 7–31. Mahwah: Lawrence Erlbaum Associates.

Scheufele, Dietram A. 1999. Framing as a Theory of Media Effects. *Journal of Communication* 49 (1): 103–122.

Scheufele, Bertram, and Dietram A. Scheufele. 2010. Of Spreading Activation, Applicability, and Schemas Conceptual Distinctions and Their Operational Implications. In *Doing News Framing Analysis: Empirical and Theoretical Perspectives*, ed. Paul D'Angelo and Jim A. Kuypers. New York: Routledge.

Schifirneţ, Constantin. 2012. Tendential Modernity. *Social Science Information* 51 (1): 22–51.

Snow, David A., and Robert Benford. 1988. Ideology, Frame Resonance and Participant Mobilization. *International Social Movements Res.* 1: 197–218.

Tankard, James. 2001. The Empirical Approach to the Study of Media Framing. In *Framing Public Life: Perspectives on Media and Our Understanding of the Social World*, ed. Stephen D. Reese, Oscar Gandy, and August Grant, 95–106. Mahwah: Lawrence Erlbaum Associates.

Van Gorp, Baldwin. 2005. Where Is the Frame? Victims and Intruders in the Belgian Press Coverage of the Asylum Issue. *European Journal of Communication* 20 (4): 484–507.

———. 2007. The Constructionist Approach to Framing: Bringing Culture Back In. *Journal of Communication* 57: 60–78.

Vliegenthart, Rens, and Conny Roggeband. 2007. Framing Immigration and Integration. Relationships Between Press and Parliament in the Netherlands. *Discourse & Society* 69 (3): 295–319.

Yuval-Davis, Nira. 2011. *The Politics of Belonging: Intersectional Contestations*. London: Sage Publications.

Zelizer, Barbie. 2010. *About to Die: How News Images Move the Public*. New York: Oxford University Press.

# 15

# The British Nationalist Right and the Gendering of Anti-migration Politics

Nicola Montagna

## Introduction

Migration has increasingly become a major political cleavage and a divisive issue in the UK. In particular, since the second half of the 2000s, it is one of the most important themes for voters and a mobilizing factor of electoral campaigns, including the Brexit referendum. This phenomenon is not new. Political concerns and electoral calculations have influenced several migration acts,[1] and there have been movements that exploited fears about immigration in the past.[2] What *is* new is the coincidence of a number of contextual processes. First, several years of mass and, to some

---

[1] The 1962 act restricting entry from Commonwealth countries was passed following concerns from the Home Office that unrestricted migration would lead to social unrest. Anti-migration feeling led the Labour government in 1964 to introduce stricter immigration rules, which were consolidated in the 1968 and 1971 Immigration Acts. The new conservative era was also marked by the increasing importance of migration in the political debate, with immigration and asylum being issues in the 1992 national and 1994 European elections (Spencer 2011).
[2] The British Brothers' League, active in East London in the early years of the twentieth century, is one of the most prominent examples of anti-migrant movements organized in the UK.

N. Montagna (✉)
School of Law, Middlesex University, London, UK

© The Author(s) 2018
J. Mulholland et al. (eds.), *Gendering Nationalism*,
https://doi.org/10.1007/978-3-319-76699-7_15

extent, unexpected migration, has changed the demography of the country with a dramatic increase in the foreign-born population. In this mutated context, recent migration is perceived as a "threat" by large portions of British society who perform menial and unskilled jobs, have few educational qualifications, and feel they are not represented by traditional parties (Wodak 2015). Second, it is taking place in a context of growing scepticism about multicultural policies and attempts to accommodate different ethnic groups on the basis of mutual recognition. According to some, including influential figures on the left, the multicultural model has failed, as the frequent conflicts involving ethnic and religious minorities demonstrate, and is no longer able to deal with growing migration flows (Goodhart 2013). Criticism of multiculturalism is often associated with the sustainability of migration either in terms of integration into the British system of values or in terms of the number of migrants putting pressure on the welfare system.

Third, anti-migrant feelings are often paralleled by hostility towards the EU, which is blamed for its free mobility regime and its effects on the UK. The EU is the catalyst for complaints concerning unrestricted immigration, welfare that privileges foreign nationals against UK citizens, the decline in sovereignty, and the perceived loss of control over the country's borders. In this respect, Brexit brought together and interpreted these two intersecting dimensions, showing how anti-European nationalism is linked to hostility to migrants. Fourthly, while past politicization was fundamentally managed between the two main parties, the Conservatives and Labour, the current debate has led to the growth of a nationalist right that is disputing this bipolar system. The nationalist right has now become a key player in the British political landscape and, even if its electoral results are still poor and its membership limited in number, it is heavily influencing the country's agenda, and its opposition to migration is a key element in its success (Ford and Goodwin 2014).

By focusing on female activists in movements of the nationalist right, this chapter examines how such women frame migration and turn it into a political issue. In particular, it looks at four dimensions: the perception of migration in terms of "mass migration", and the associated threat to national identity; the pressure on the welfare system; the impact of migrants on the labour market; and migration in relation to the EU. These dimensions are examined with an emphasis on the gender perspective, that is, on the ways nationalist women activists assess the implications of migration for women in these areas.

The chapter draws on 36 in-depth semi-structured interviews with female activists from the United Kingdom Independence Party (UKIP), the British National Party (BNP), and the English Defence League (EDL) and on observational ethnographic work associated with attendance at three EDL rallies (Tower Hamlets, Slough, and Peterborough).[3] Although there are significant differences between the support bases of these three organizations, the socio-economic background of participants was mainly lower and working class. Only four out of 36 had a degree and two more had an A-level; 25 per cent were homeowners, a percentage that is significantly below the national average, while occupations were mainly secretarial, supervisory, and caring. In terms of age, the bulk of the interviewees (58%) were between 40 and 60, while the rest were equally divided between those below and above this age range. The participants' social composition mirrors what Ford and Goodwin (2014) define as "the left behind", identifying both those who are in a weaker position in the labour market and with respect to globalization processes and who have been forgotten by left-wing and former working-class parties. They are the most exposed to migrant competition in the labour market and feel that foreign nationals are illegitimate beneficiaries of resources and welfare provision that should belong to the natives, therefore anti-migration politics are more attractive to them. Contrary to what is a common belief, women in nationalist parties perceive these organizations as an opportunity for them to participate in politics and to have their rights represented again. In a context where women's rights are framed as under threat by a growing presence of migrants, perceived as mostly coming from Muslim countries or with a Muslim background, the nationalist right is seen as a

---

[3] The interviews were part of the research project *Women in nationalist movements in the UK*, funded by the British Academy/Leverhulme, aiming to explore the nature and quality of women's support for the nationalist right in the UK, comparing women supporters of three variably positioned representatives of the nationalist right, which were the main groups in the UK at the time of the project: the United Kingdom Independence Party, the British National Party, and the English Defence League. The project was carried out by a research team based in the Department of Criminology and Sociology, School of Law, Middlesex University, London, that involved Dr. Jon Mulholland, Dr. Nicola Montagna, and Dr. Erin Sanders-McDonagh.

new chance to preserve the social and political position they have conquered in Western societies (for more details on the methodology, see Mulholland—this volume).

The three organizations from which our participants were recruited share in common an opposition to mass immigration, where the latter is often pictured as a chaotic and uncontrolled invasion. There are differences however in how the three organizations frame immigration. While the anti-immigration politics of the BNP relies on the biological racism of traditional fascism, UKIP's anti-immigration stance is associated with their rejection of the European Union project and its implications for the sovereignty of the UK. It is populist in the very sense of the term. Opposition to migration is linked to an opposition to the political elite, represented by both the big business and the EU. Finally, the EDL's anti-immigration stance appears more orientated towards the protection of national culture and values. Migration as a whole is conflated with Muslim immigration, with Islamophobia and xenophobia often overlapping in their discourse. Britain is thought of as a community of value that is undermined by the arrival of migrants whose values coincide with Islam.[4] During the interviews, migration was a recurrent theme, and a source of concern for most of the participants, although these differences among the activists of the three groups did not emerge clearly. Migration was often linked to issues of Europe and the EU, women's rights, national identity, and the threat migrants pose to the welfare state and services relating to women's needs.

To investigate female nationalists' views on migration, this chapter is divided into two parts. The first explores the gendering of the parties of the nationalist right and the role played by migration issues. The second is based on the data from the fieldwork and is subdivided into four sections which examine perceptions of the impact of migratory flows on the country, the labour market, the welfare state, and how migration is perceived in relation to the EU. The chapter will show that migration is more than a general issue and that female activists of nationalist groups find in the anti-migrant agenda an answer to their concerns as women.

---

[4] See, for example, the "12 questions and answers" on migration on the EDL official website: http://www.englishdefenceleague.org.uk/12-questions-and-answers/ (accessed on 25 September 2017).

# Women in Nationalist Parties and the Migration Issue

The role of women in the nationalist right and nationalist movements generally is growing across Europe, contradicting the electoral and membership trends that still show a "gap" between men and women in size of participation and number of votes for the nationalist right (Immerzeel et al. 2015). In France, Marine Le Pen has not only become leader of the party and candidate in the presidential elections, but she has renewed the party's agenda, making it more appealing to larger constituencies and seriously challenging the mainstream parties the leadership of the country. In Italy, some female leaders have become key figures of the nationalist right, while in Germany, Frauke Petry, the leader of Alternative für Deutschland, has made the nationalist right a serious contender in the national elections after decades of marginality. Although nothing similar has happened yet in the UK, there are signs of change. Among the fragmented and, so far, electoral minoritarian nationalist spectrum, UKIP is possibly the party in which women could be said to have risen to key roles, with Diane James, who won an overwhelming victory in the leadership race *in September 2016. Her resignation a couple of weeks after, citing a lack of "sufficient authority" in the party*, shows that it is, however, too early to say if these signs represent significant change.

While the paternalist and misogynistic character of nationalist parties and movements may put off women (Ford and Goodwin 2014) and explain the gender gap in members and votes, the growing importance of gender issues in the domain of immigration and integration policies may be a key to understanding their increasing interest and roles in them. (Akkerman 2015). Research has shown that nationalist parties and movements across Europe owe much of their support to harsh anti-migration positions (Mammone et al. 2012; Mammone et al. 2013; von Mering and McCarty 2013) and "immigration scepticism (i.e. wanting to reduce immigration) is among the principal factors for predicting who will vote for a radical right wing party" (Rydgren 2008). In the UK, support for nationalist movements is driven by the concern that mass migration is a threat to the nation and native groups and, therefore, that control over borders should be reinstated more firmly. Although there are differences between parties and their positions may vary according to the circumstances, migration is used as a catch-all explanation for unacceptable and rapid social change that leaves many people behind and as a symbol of the failure of the traditional parties and the liberal elite to govern the country (Malik 2014).

In relation to gender issues, two main areas may play a role in women's consent to nationalist movements. First, women who participate in nationalist politics see these movements as a trench in the "clash of civilizations" between the Christian West and Islam, with which migrants are often associated (for a more in-depth analysis of the reasons behind this framing, see Mulholland—this volume). Adherence to nationalist politics, therefore, is partly a defence of women's rights; the relatively emancipated condition of women in the West is counterposed to the lack of rights and freedoms in the countries where most foreigners are believed to be coming from. Since women are framed as the major victims of Islam, opposition to migration becomes a way to stop what the participants call the "Islamization" of the West and the threat that Muslim migration represents to their rights and security. The rights that women enjoy in Western societies are not only the clearest sign of the irreconcilable difference between Western civilization and Islam, they are also the main reason to oppose migration. In this sense, the engagement of female activists in nationalist organizations may be perceived as empowering and emancipatory—not so much from Western patriarchy, as was the case in the past (see Blee 1996), as from the world of migrants' culture that they regard as narrow and hostile towards women (Farris 2017).

Second, the roots of women's participation in nationalist politics are in their socio-economic background. They see these movements as a defence against the challenge that migrants pose over welfare provision and the labour market in both state and private sectors. Migration is generally framed as a source of economic competition, a pressure on social services and the functioning of the welfare state. In a context of economic crisis and austerity, women are among the most vulnerable and are those who suffer most from the restructuring of welfare resulting from recent government policies. As has been noted (Gillies 2013: 106), "Women make up the largest proportion of the public sector workforce and as a consequence have been most vulnerable to cost cutting redundancies. At the same time, reduced childcare subsidies and changes to tax credit benefits are forcing working mothers on low incomes back into the home". By diverting responsibility for the withdrawal of state services and resources for parents and children from public spending cuts to migrants, the nationalist right and its anti-globalization politics are seen as defending the welfare state from the threat of migration. In this sense, a politics of "welfare chauvinism" that supports the welfare state for native citizens but rejects open immigration policies and the ready access to social programmes for foreigners (Banting 2000) may become a mobilizing factor and appeal to female voters.

These positions on migration form much of the nationalist narrative and are likely the main drivers of women's support. The following sections will mainly focus on the second dimension by exploring how the participants in the project perceive migrants as a threat to the "nation" and as competitors in the labour market and for welfare provision.

## Women and Migration: Several Sources of Concern; "they arrive in thousands"

For the female activists who participated in the project, regardless of their affiliation, the size of current migratory flows is an increasingly important concern. They compare migration with either natural cataclysms, through metaphors such as flood and swamp (Allen and Blinder 2013), or with military operations. Migration is represented as an "invasion" of people who "are infiltrating our country" and "taking us over". When the focus shifts to numbers, these are never supported by clear figures. Rather, people who migrate are "too many", "arrive in thousands", and "overcrowd" the UK in "huge influxes". Not only have these "high numbers" been changing the demography of the country, they have also transformed its urban landscape and therefore its identity. The main threat comes from Muslims and Eastern Europeans:

> I think most of the Muslims in the west of Europe are immigrants. There are a lot of Somalians [sic], a lot of Pakistanis. In Germany they have

> Turkish Muslims. Why do they move here? Because they're trying to take over the world? It's just Nazism all over again. (EDL 21)
>
> You're over-run with the Poles and they've opened Polish shops in the town and they speak in Polish and they've got Polish shops and you're thinking, 'Hang on, this was a beautiful, historic English border town. What's happening?', you know. That's what it's about. It's just too much taking our identity away because there's too many. (UKIP 29)

However, as is the case in other European countries, migrants are not all racialized in the same way by the UK's nationalist female activists (Copsey 2010; della Porta et al. 2012; Mayer 2013). While those from Eastern Europe are seen as competing for welfare benefits, jobs, and other redistributive resources, Muslim migration is perceived as a threat to women's rights and more generally to national identity (on this point, see Mulholland—this volume). Concerns about being "pushed out", and becoming a cultural minority, as well as feelings of estrangement and being foreign in their own country, are equally widespread among the participants across the three groups:

> …that's not right, not to the loss of our identity and it's slowly being stripped away (…) Let them come here, let them feel comfortable but don't you dare take away my identity just to make an immigrant feel comfortable. I'm sorry I just don't want that. (UKIP 12)
>
> It's like you're permanently on holiday, like you've gone abroad and when you're abroad you're the only English-speaking person and everybody else is talking a foreign language. But you expect that because you're abroad but you don't expect it when you're at home and nobody is speaking English. (UKIP 19)

Migration is only accepted if it contributes to the British economy in the respect of the national identity and the traditions of the country. In the words of this UKIP member, cultural defence and the preservation of social stability become conflated:

> This is what I know, we can't take everybody, we're full (…) Migrants are only welcome, in my opinion, if they are going to add something to the

country. If they are going to live by our laws, by our standards, and not object to our traditions which are our Christian beliefs or our, you know, traditions that have gone on in this country for hundreds of years. 'If you're going to come in and complain about them, then go away. (UKIP 30)

## "They seem to have taken over the jobs, houses…"

Research across Europe has also shown that nationalist parties are mostly supported by voters who are more likely to be confronted by competition from immigrants over public services and other scarce resources such as houses, jobs, and welfare benefits (Koopmans et al. 2005; Rydgren 2007). They are often white, poorly educated, and unskilled workers who occupy similar segments of the labour market and compete for the same jobs as most migrant groups. These voters are in a weaker position in the labour market and share the same type of public services and resources—for example, in the health and education sectors. They therefore feel the competition from foreign workers more keenly and are correspondingly more sensitive to migration than other social strata (Bulli and Tronconi 2012). In the next two sections, I will focus on how the participants perceive the threat of migrants in the labour market and welfare system. As is happening in the urban context where, according to the participants, the opening of new Eastern European shops have been dramatically changing the cityscape of British towns, the labour market is also seen as being progressively taken over by Eastern European migrant workers. The competition is particularly felt in the labour-intensive, low-paid, and gendered employment sectors such as hospitality and care:

> I mean, where I am now it's all, mostly, hospitality positions, jobs, you know; people in hotels and breakfast, it's all that sort of thing out here. And I'd say nine out of ten of the staff are now Polish and yet they work hard, you know, and they talk to you and they keep themselves clean and they're alright, fine. But they have taken the jobs that the young out here should have because there's nothing else for them out here. (UKIP 12)

> I was working in a hotel at the time, not front of house, I was doing laundry and things like that and we had a Polish girl came to work and because

she was willing to work all the hours God sends, we got our hours cut. She was taking over the work. Out in Poland, apparently, she was a medical secretary. She didn't have the right qualifications to do that job here. Here she just carried on cleaning or whatever – and because of the subsidy that the hotel was getting to employ her – and I just thought 'this is wrong'. (BNP 3)

When female activists communicate their concerns about work, they assume a gender perspective and look at the impact migration has on women, particularly in their roles as mothers or grandmothers. They express a maternalistic point of view, and their fears over migrant competition, whereas real or imaginary, are often related to their children and grandchildren: "I want my kids to have a future in a job like I used to walk into a job" (BNP 24), and "This is the future of my kids, really. As we live now, it's hard to get into a job and the way I'm feeling, it's getting overcrowded" (UKIP 10).

The negative impacts of immigration on the labour market include earnings. Participants in this project reiterate the widespread belief that migration drives down wages, particularly for less-skilled workers. What seems to be unfair competition may well bring social tensions and eventually conflict between natives and foreign nationals:

> Well, at the moment they all get on fine but I think once it gets, it gets too many, I think there'll probably be resentment, you know, because the Polish will probably will take the jobs that the English people feel that they should be being paid more for, you know, because that's what it's all about isn't it […] it'll get worse, won't it?, you know, because the wages'll go down and down because people are prepared to work for less so it's not going to improve is it? So I think everybody's going to get less and less. (UKIP 29)

Hostility to unskilled migrants is paradoxically reinforced by a more open and flexible approach to other forms of migration, notably where there is a shortage of skills in the upper end of the labour market:

> I mean, fair enough, if we've got a shortage in, you know, say, doctors or something, fine, let them few people come through, that's fine. I don't have an issue with that. But stop the floodgates. (BNP 17)

"So that if we have a shortage of doctors then, yes, people coming in who want to be a doctor in this country, fine. Give them the clearance to come in. But if they're coming in and they have no job to go to, then sorry you stay out." (UKIP 30)

As we can see, feelings towards migrants vary according to the position that migrant workers have in the labour market. Whereas unskilled British workers and migrants compete in the same segment of the labour market, with an impact on job opportunities and wages, skilled migration is seen favourably, particularly in sectors such as health assistance—a safety net and traditional source of pride and identity for working-class people and the British in general, as clearly showed by our participants.

## "But they don't spend their money over here": Migration, Sustainability, and Welfare Chauvinism

Another area of concern for our participants across the three groups is welfare provision and the negative impact that mass migration may have on its functioning. This research identifies three main sensitive issues for female nationalist activists. First, migrants are frequently seen as people who "abuse" the British welfare state, resulting in fewer state-subsidized services for natives. Although this complaint involves different areas of service provision, it is probably in the healthcare sector that our participants most feel the pressure. In the participants' rhetoric, migrants "take advantage of the health service" (BNP 3) and move to the UK because "their countries aren't like England; they don't get benefits, they don't get health benefits – they have to pay for it". (BNP 7). This is the "benefit-scrounger" rhetoric, which is very similar to the tabloid portrayal of migrants as the undeserving recipients of welfare benefits and which reinforces another widespread narrative, that of the Briton as victim:

> Yes, because I think Labour and Conservatives have let too many immigrants in the country and I think the English people are suffering, schools and hospitals and, you know, benefits – they're paying a lot more benefits out – and I think that's ruined the country. (BNP 6)

Second, participants emphasize the issue of the welfare state's sustainability. Migrants arrive in Britain in great quantities, attracted by the welfare system, and grow numerically much faster than the British:

> The majority have only had 2.4 children because they want to keep the population of the country down and the resources, you know, look after the resources. And then this lot are coming in and having ten kids and more, eight wives, you know. (UKIP 29)

The pace of migrants' numerical growth is not sustainable and threatens the welfare state. These feelings are often gendered and it is often perceived pressure from foreign nationals on maternity or women's healthcare services that raises most concern:

> (…) the NHS is being overworked. The maternity services, they're being, well, they're being exhausted because of this, you know. There's far too many people in England, well, shall we say Derby. Most of the women who come to Derby or who are in my area in maternity services, I'd say six out of ten of those are non-British nationals. (BNP 7)

The view that the pressure migrants place on the system is unsustainable is reinforced by the distorted feeling that, unlike elderly people (the British pensioners) who retire and live abroad and who put their savings "into the system and keeping the local businesses going" (UKIP 19), the migrants who live and work in the UK "are not giving a lump sum to the country, they're coming to make money in the country they've chosen to live in" (UKIP 19).

Migrants are, therefore, portrayed as a cost to British welfare while their economic contribution either as workers and tax-payers or as consumers goes unacknowledged. Even when migrants are welcomed as hard workers with genuine intentions, and not regarded as wanting to live on benefits and take advantage of the generosity of the British welfare system, their contribution to the country's economy is disputed by our participants. Migrant workers may bring some benefits to the country's economy, but overall they still "screw it" or "put a burden" on it, in expressions widely used by nationalist activists:

You know the problems with education, with jobs, with housing, with the NHS, all of those things are made worse by mass immigration. The more people that come into this country, the more of a burden there's going to be on the resources that supply all of those things, you know. (UKIP 10)

Third, the participants express what has been defined as "welfare chauvinism" (Kitschelt 1995: 22). They regard the welfare state as an exclusive system of social protection for natives against migrants who do not belong to the British community and whose presence endangers the welfare of the national in-group. Therefore, the allocation of public spending and its beneficiaries becomes another field of conflict between competing interests that widens the crack between "us" and "them", between the ethnically homogeneous natives and all the "others". Participants turn Gordon Brown's phrase: "*British jobs* for *British* workers" into the claim, "British welfare for British people".

If you read the newspapers today, there's an elderly lady in Swaffham who's lost her doctor because the doctor is no longer able to (quote) 'cope with the number of immigrants' and they are having to sign up on the books. So you can see why they have a problem. And so the position is not anti-immigrant. It is controlled immigration, immigration that can be absorbed and the various support services can tolerate. (UKIP 32)

## "Britain, to be honest, has become Europe's dumping ground"

Anti-EU feelings are widespread among nationalist parties that see the EU as a supra-national Leviathan that rules over the nation-states and represents a threat to national sovereignty. As research has repeatedly shown (Giovannini 2015), the anti-EU stance is common to all nationalist right movements across Europe, and constitutes a significant part of its popularity, particularly among the lower strata of society. Even among the participants to this project, hostility to the EU figures high in their agenda and hostility to the EU and migration are understood as two faces of the same coin. The EU serves as an overarching and integrating motif that effectively brings together multiple other but related political themes.

The European question, and migration, often become conflated, particularly where migration comes from Eastern European countries:

> I have two issues. One is Europe and the other is mass immigration, the Open Door policy that this country has because of Europe and I am quite worried about Eastern Europe, about the amount of people coming in from Eastern Europe. (UKIP 5)

Similar to migration, the EU threatens the country's identity, and what some participants see as British distinctiveness. One of the most frequently expressed anxieties is that through EU membership, Britain will lose its distinctiveness and become merely one part of a broader European identity:

> I understand. I don't want to join the Euro, I don't want to lose the monarchy, I don't want to have an armed force of Europe. I want us to keep our armed forces, our monarchy and our currency. I don't want to be ruled by Brussels. That is the end line for me. (UKIP 27)

For others, hostility to Europe is more practical and has to do with the daily life effects of being part of the Union, particularly with regard to migration. Being part of the EU is often associated with a lack of control over the UK's borders. The government is framed as powerless against the EU, unable to either control who enters the country, or to deport undesired people (e.g. suspected terrorists and undocumented migrants):

> And people say we're being racist. We're not, we're trying to manage our borders by doing that but unfortunately the EU says we can't manage our own borders. They say we have to let everyone in, even if they're the poorest people in the world and they're going to be coming to live on our welfare. (UKIP 5)

Across the three groups, our participants commonly linked uncontrolled migration, and access to the welfare system, to the UK's obligations regarding freedom of circulation and border policy within the EU. If migrants exploit the generosity of the British system, and the

British people are victimized by foreign nationals, this is because of the agreements the UK has with the EU:

> Well, I just think Britain, to be honest, has become Europe's dumping ground. That's my view. It's now Europe's dumping ground. None of the other… You know, France won't tolerate it, Belgium doesn't tolerate it, you know, and they all flood here because of the benefit state and, you know, even if they're not claiming, you know, benefits and they are actually working, they're still getting health care, you know, so they're still getting something out of us. (BNP 17)

> Yes, I do, yes. I mean, I think the general consensus is being part of the EU a lot of people that don't live here – yes, I understand the free movement between the EU, I understand that but a lot of them come here thinking, you know, 'basically we can go over there and we can get free benefits'. (EDL 18)

The combination of mass immigration, and the UK's membership of the EU, was seen to impact significantly on the NHS, and we have already noted how central the NHS is to nationalist activists' concerns. The NHS is a distinctive institution for generations of British people. Although it is still working and providing excellent services in the view of our participants, the pressure from the EU, either coming from migrants or the demands from Brussels, is putting its functioning and existence under risk:

> [The NHS] is still a great organization and to see it misused because of Europe, you know, because if you're spending millions of pounds on people who have not paid into it then it's other parts of the NHS are going to be compromised and that bothers me, morally. (UKIP 5)

In the narratives of our participants, the diverse themes reviewed in this chapter intersect and mutually reinforce. Migrants arrive *en masse* to take advantage of the generosity of the welfare state, and to the point that the system that was established for the benefit of the British people is on the verge of collapse. Within this context, the EU serves is a catalyst for multiple complaints and resentments, uniting multiple themes under the single banner. The EU's free movement policy renders foreign nationals and UK citizens equally entitled to enjoy the benefits of the British system. In times of economic crisis and diminished resources, however, this is problematic and difficult to accept.

## Concluding Remarks: Gendering Hostility to Migration

This chapter has shown how migration and migrants are a contentious issue for nationalist female activists. In particular, it has focused on the perception of migratory flows and their size and the consequences these have on the identity of the country, on the labour market, and on the welfare system. These areas of concern for female activists show the ways in which migration is a major issue that explains their participation in nationalist parties. Is there a gender dimension in these views? Is there a specifically female perspective? Although our project investigated the views of female activists without comparison to male activists, this chapter has shown that migration is more than a general issue. Rather, it is often framed within a gender perspective, and female activists find in the anti-migrant agenda an answer to their concerns as women. When nationalist female activists refer to migration, they assume a gendered point of view. Their concern for what they perceive as mass migration is over the consequences that this may have on women's rights and on women's ability to access welfare provisions as in the past, before the Labour and the Conservative party "opened the floodgates for millions of immigrants" (BNP 17). When it comes to work, they assume the role of mothers and grandmothers and of female workers who work in labour-intensive, low-paid and gendered sectors, such as hospitality and care, in which there is competition from migrant workers, particularly from Eastern Europe. Similarly, their hostility to migration is justified with regard to the state of the welfare system and its sustainability in the face of growing pressure from migrants—particularly with regard to gendered provisions such as maternity services. Gender issues may, therefore, be a further potential cleavage in nationalist politics, and a more targeted agenda may attract more female support than is currently the case and narrow the gender gap between men and women's electoral support for nationalist parties. Similarly, how female nationalist activists perceive the migration threat to welfare provisions and labour market may be an area which needs to be further investigated.

# References

Akkerman, Tjitske. 2015. Gender and the Radical Right in Western Europe: A Comparative Analysis of Policy Agendas. *Patterns of Prejudice* 49 (1–2): 37–60.

Allen, William, and Scott Blinder. 2013. *Migration in the News: Portrayals of Immigrants, Migrants, Asylum Seekers and Refugees in National British Newspapers, 2010 to 2012*. Migration Observatory report: COMPAS, University of Oxford.

Banting, Keith G. 2000. Looking in Three Directions: Migration and the European Welfare State in Comparative Perspective. In *Immigration and Welfare: Challenging the Borders of the Welfare State*, ed. Michael Bommes and Andrew Geddes, 13–33. London: Routledge.

Blee, Kathleen. 1996. Becoming a Racist: Women in Contemporary Ku Klux Klan and Neo-Nazi Groups. *Gender and Society* 10 (6): 680–702.

Bulli, Giorgia, and Filippo Tronconi. 2012. *Regionalism, Right-wing Extremism, Populism: The Elusive Nature of the Lega Nord*. In *Mapping the Far Right in Contemporary Europe. Local, National, Comparative, Transnational*, ed. Andrea Mammone, Emmanuel Godin, and Brian Jenkins, 78–92. Abingdon: Routledge.

Copsey, Nigel. 2010. *The English Defence League: A Challenge to Our Country and Our Values of Social Inclusion, Fairness and Equality*. London: Faith Matters.

Farris, Sara. 2017. *The Name of Women's Rights: The Rise of Femonationalism*. Durham: Duke University Press.

Ford, Robert, and Matthew Goodwin. 2014. *Revolt on the Right: Explaining Support for the Radical Right in Britain*. London/New York: Routledge.

Gillies, Val. 2013. Personalising Poverty: Parental Determinism and the Big Society Agenda. In *Class Inequality in Austerity Britain. Power, Difference and Suffering*, ed. William Atkinson, Steven Roberts, and Mike Savage, 90–110. Basingstoke: Palgrave Macmillan.

Giovannini, Eva. 2015. *Europa Anno Zero. Il Ritorno dei Nazionalismi*. Padova: Marsilio Editore.
Goodhart, David. 2013. *The British Dream: Successes and Failures of Post-War Immigration*. London: Atlantic Books.
Immerzeel, Tim, Hilde Coffé, and Tanja van der Lippe. 2015. Explaining the Gender Gap in Radical Right Voting: A Cross-National Investigation in Western European Countries. *Comparative European Politics* 13 (2): 263–286.
Kitschelt, Herbert. 1995. *The Radical Right in Western Europe: A Comparative Analysis*. Ann Arbor: University of Michigan Press.
Koopmans, Ruud, Paul Statham, Marco Giugni, and Florence Passy. 2005. *Contested Citizenship: Immigration and Cultural Diversity in Europe*. Minneapolis: University of Minnesota Press.
Malik, Kenan. 2014. Preface. In *European Populism and Winning the Immigration Debate*, ed. Clara Sandelind. Falun: ScandBook.
Mammone, Andrea, Emmanuel Godin, and Brian Jenkins, eds. 2012. *Mapping the Extreme Right in Contemporary Europe: From Local to Transnational*. London: Routledge.
———, eds. 2013. *Varieties of Extreme Right-Wing Extremism in Europe*. London: Routledge.
Mayer, Nonna. 2013. From Jean-Marie to Marine Le Pen: Electoral Change on the Far Right. *Parliamentary Affairs* 66: 160–178.
von Mering, Sabine, and Wyman McCarty. 2013. *Right-Wing Radicalism Today. Perspectives from Europe and the US*. London: Routledge.
della Porta, Donatella, Manuela Caiani, and Claudius Wagemann. 2012. *Mobilizing on the Extreme Right: Germany, Italy, and the United States*. Oxford: Oxford University Press.
Rydgren, Jens. 2007. The Sociology of the Radical Right. *Annual Review of Sociology* 33: 241–262.
———. 2008. Immigration Sceptics, Xenophobes or Racists? Radical Right-Wing Voting in Six West European Countries. *European Journal of Political Research* 47 (6): 737–765.
Spencer, Sarah. 2011. *The Migration Debate*. Bristol: Policy Press.
Wodak, Ruth. 2015. *The Politics of Fear. What Right-Wing Populist Discourses Mean*. London: Sage.

# 16

## 'Narrations of the Nation in Mobility Life Stories: Gendered Scripts, Emotional Spheres and Transnational Performativity in the Greek Diaspora'

Anastasia Christou

## Introducing Actors, Approaches and Interactive Affective Contexts in Researching Greek Mobilities

The joys and perils of international migration are historically part and parcel of the phenomenon. As a historical phenomenon, migration is enduring and continues to shape contemporary social life, public and political debate. Politically contested and socially complex, migration is one of the most pervasive forces of a globalized world under multiple crises, closely related to notions of displacement and emplacement, belonging, in/exclusion and identity. Multiple power dynamics are involved in both migrant and migration stories, as with inter-/intra-generational relations which are often challenged by diverging perspectives on gender and sexuality. Hence, not only wider challenges of societal

A. Christou (✉)
Department of Criminology and Sociology, School of Law,
Middlesex University, London, UK

© The Author(s) 2018
J. Mulholland et al. (eds.), *Gendering Nationalism*,
https://doi.org/10.1007/978-3-319-76699-7_16

incorporation place strain on identities and relations, often migrant communities themselves are constrained by struggles over ethnic group cultural values and norms that may lead to friction, fraction and trauma.

This chapter examines some of these liminal spaces of fragility and fracture that members of the Greek diaspora experience, especially as they negotiate first- and second-generation identities in understanding how ethnic/national consciousness impacts on family relations and personal aspirations. While my investigations of the Greek diaspora have involved multi-sited, multi-method, comparative ethnographic research with several migrant generations on varying mobilities (e.g. ancestral homeland return migration, homecoming visits, transnational mobilities, etc.) and settlement in Greece, Cyprus, Germany, Denmark and the United States, this chapter will draw primarily from narrative material (for details on methodological and theoretical context, refer to respective studies in Christou 2006; Christou 2011a, b; Christou and King 2014), mostly focusing on *second-generation* biographical (life history) portrayals.

While personal identities are continuously developed, reflected and shaped through their inner dialogue (cf. Archer 2000), the methodological tool of using life stories and narrative accounts to elicit responses on identity construction is useful in stimulating reflexive inner dialogic processes whereupon participants can sift through emotions, social roles, memories and stories to develop further awareness of their sense of self (Christou 2009). Conceptually, as Faist (2010) suggests, the concepts of diaspora and transnationalism have served productively for the past decades as analytic lenses through which to view the outcomes of mobilities and shifting borderscapes. While at times both concepts are either used interchangeably or erroneously conflated to denote the same, it is pertinent to note their distinction for a productive study of social and cultural transformations during cross-border movements. In the case of the Greek migrant samples, the research confirmed that beyond its Greek etymological origin, phenomenologically and empirically, the Greek case was a pronounced *diaspora* in fulfilling most of the conditions that Safran (1991), Brubaker (2005), and Cohen (2008), among others, have advanced in explaining the diasporic condition and consciousness. Parallel to this and integral are the transnational activities and identities that the Greek diaspora exhibit which are no doubt linked to the former.

To reiterate what has been already endorsed in King and Christou (2010), while the classical definition of diaspora such as the one advanced by Cohen (2008) encompasses a multiplicity of flows and mobilities, such as counter-diasporic returns to the ancestral homeland by the second generation, there is a conceptual trap involved here since the protracted meaning of diaspora can also become conflated with other notions such as transnational social fields and varying ethnic communities. Hence, it is important to underscore that, 'what distinguishes the diasporic condition from contemporary international migration and transnational communities…is historical continuity across at least two generations, a sense of possible permanence of exile, and the broad spread and stability of the distribution of populations within the diaspora' (King and Christou 2010, 172). What makes the second generation an even more fascinating case study as discussed in this chapter is the fact that their sense of 'possible permanence of exile' as described above continues to manifest despite their relocation to the ancestral homeland, and, hence the 'unbearable' nation/state (cf. Christou 2014) with its overbearing 'nationness' as presented through the discussion of the narrative extracts that follow.

The Greek diaspora offers an interesting case for examining affective[1] interactions and confrontations as regards identity construction where rigid ethno-national and religious norms are often in antagonistic opposition to lifestyle choices, personal and sexual identities (Christou 2016). The disjuncture that exists between the 'gendered/sexed self' and the 'ethnic self' is one that often triggers heteronormative hegemonies of the nation as expressed and experienced by those diasporic Greeks who feel compelled to conceal their gay identities (Christou and King 2014; Christou 2016). The disjuncture exists precisely because the institutions of family and marriage are powerful cultural markers re-configuring migrant offspring lives, especially in the case where heteronormativity engrained within the 'ethnic self' clashes with lifestyle choices of same-sex relationships/marriages.

---

[1] Affective interactions here capture the visceral context of such through feelings, emotions, everyday life experiences, moods and so on, in a sensorial, embodied and experiential framing, as, for instance, discussed in Zheng et al. 2016 or Christou 2011a, b.

Additionally, patriarchal practices are frequently reproduced in conservative ethnic enclave behaviours in diasporic settings where migrants unveil extreme fascinations with morality and the safeguarding of women's bodies and choices (Christou 2011a, b; Christou and King 2011). Thus, it is imperative to go beyond earlier historical accounts that underscore the Greek diaspora family as a source of support, guidance and comfort and to recognize the existence of contemporary works that have critically examined the more complex and traumatic aspects of diasporic families. In such accounts of those family relations, there is clear and extensive evidence of patriarchy, tension, domestic violence and intolerance to offspring interactions with other ethnic groups, as well as fierce opposition to female independence and to a range of alternative sexualities (cf. Christou and King 2010).

Hence, any discussion on *gendering nationalism* should acknowledge the intersections of diaspora and gender by addressing the centrality of performative aspects of experiences in challenging traditional gender ideologies and relations where the prevailing norms are anchored in specificities of 'cultural authenticity' of the nation while denying migrant agency (cf. Al-Ali 2010).

## Scripted Lives, Gendered Emotional Spheres and Performative Social Practices

One of the pervasive forces of the nation is its implication in the creation of invisible scripts that control our lives. The mythological power of the nation lies in its very narrative as a myth of authenticity and purity of identity that is at once real and imaginative but above all acts to connect those seeking membership in it through a sense of belonging (cf. Anderson 1983). The nation is also a signifier of honour and shame expressive in its ideals of cultural purity and religiosity (cf. Willert Stauning 2014). The encounter of my participants with such austere perceptions is recurrent and a source of frustration and trauma for most participants but even more pronounced for the women participants in the study. In the narrative extract below, Nicole's depiction of this is quite intense:

Very old-fashioned and conservative behavior, especially with their daughters. They don't let them be free and independent. They police the girls but they don't mind if their boys fuck every woman in sight, and they don't even make the connection that those girls are somebody's daughters, instead they are proud of their sons and they don't care about the daughters of others as long as their daughter is a virgin. Such stereotypical morality of hypocrisy, very old-fashioned, honor and morality, idiotic and it really bothers me that sons have more value than daughters even today and I see it loud and clear in my own family. Pure inequality, and they don't want to admit it as hypocritical Greeks but as a Greek-Danish woman, I can see it, they do it in my own family, my aunts, uncles, everybody. (Nicole, 38 years old, Greek-Danish female)

The extract above clearly demarcates parallel but differing lives for male vs. female Greek migrant offspring—the former enjoying ample freedom (to indulge in acceptable heteronormative sexualities) and the latter enduring constraint (to protect their morality by restricting pre-marriage sexual encounters) as practised by Greek family norms. Interestingly, Nicole invokes the nation in juxtaposition here by self-identifying as a 'Greek-Danish' woman and being aware of the inequalities and the cultural distinctions that she perceives as hypocritical. In a sense Nicole's conscious reflexive deployment here is one of 'hybridity' and its functionality as a filter to understanding the meanings and modalities of ethnic life. While debates on 'hybridity' have been insightful and stimulating (e.g. Papastergiadis 2000; Brah and Coombes 2005; Stewart 2011), the concept itself has also been critiqued for its limitations (Werbner 2001; Acheraïou 2011). Hence, I do not wish to ground the narrative analysis here on the concept of hybridity but rather to draw attention to the productive elements of participant agency in reflecting on the very messiness or mixedness that cultural politics entail.

At the same time, it is important to note that the exclusions and constraints faced by my study participants do extend to male migrant participants. This underscores that patriarchy impacts both women and men in significant and similar ways. Andrew's lengthy narrative excerpt below is full of intense feelings of hatred as he discloses painful childhood memories and the emotively traumatic articulations of extreme suffering in oppressive and unbearable conditions of the ancestral and family context.

I have plenty of regrets. I have encountered numerous difficulties in adjusting to having Greek parents and they are far too multifarious to list here. To be brief, Greece is a poor, backward nation and one of my greatest masturbatory fantasies is to see their beloved homeland evaporate.... Calling Greece a nation that I would feel at home is an insult to my education and sense of self. Suffice it to say that I come from a degenerate race of miserable, self-serving troglodytes. I have had many, many opportunities to learn more about my debased race. I have very little pride on the gigantic accomplishments of the Hellenes since the birth of Jesus. The outstanding or salient elements of the Greek character are: a sense of ignorance; an amazing ability to lie to oneself; a desire to relax and do little or nothing. I would rather kill myself than think of myself as one of these miserable barbarians. We speak Greek when we talk about simple, everyday matters. If I had my way, we would drop Greek in favor of a civilized tongue. I would like to demur on this point of loving, caring parents who sacrifice their lives for their children. The most challenging part of our relationship (for them) must be that I hate them and this place (Greece) and everything it stands for. For me, I would like to be less angry, and I wish I didn't let them see it sometimes. If I could, I would stand time and nature on their respective heads, murder God and Jesus, and live through even such an experience to escape and survive. (Andrew, 43 years old, Greek-American male)

Andrew is very vocal about his anger above and his explicit rejection of elements of 'Greekness', be that the Greek language, history, religion, social norms. Contrary to what Brubaker (2010, 76) claims when he states that, 'migration is as old as human history, and so too are questions of membership and belonging. The development of the modern nation-state fundamentally recast both migration and membership, subjecting both to the classificatory and regulatory grid of the nation-state', the excerpt above appears to reflect a different expression of belongingness. As a unit of analysis, the nation is evidently central in the lives of participants in the research on the Greek diaspora (cf. Christou and King 2014) and the fragmentation and discontent it triggers is exemplified in the emotive language that Andrew employs to describe some of the deeply affective impacts it has on the psychosocial well-being of diasporics. It is also apparent that 'movement beyond the nation-state is currently recasting migration and membership again in a postnational mode, but there is little evidence for such an epochal shift' (ibid 2010, 76), since identities continue to be shaped, among other signifiers, through national consciousness. Andrew's position is clearly an indication of a postnational modality when he vehemently wishes to sever ethnic ties. In this context a postnational modality of identity or citizenship would reflect one that is defined as post-territorial (refer to Sassen 2002 on notions of postnational and denationalized citizenship). As astonishing as it may appear to those migrants eager to claim a sense of homing and belonging, Andrew evidences a rejection of both. Moreover, while he did not want to speak on the record about his personal circumstances in relation to his private and intimate life, the sexualized imaginary he offers above concerning his ancestral 'backward nation' is equated with one of his 'greatest masturbatory fantasies' to see his parents' 'beloved homeland evaporate'. In a sense, the nation, the ancestral homeland becomes both the oppressor and liberator of repressed sexuality as Andrew equates his climaxing with freedom from the constraints of his ancestry.

In the next section, we will discuss how transnational performativity of both ethnicity and identity is stimulated and dismantled from the very inception of the nation as 'tribe' on a grand scale a la Anderson's (1983) 'imagined communities', but the strong bonds of which may turn into restraint of individual agency. Hence, as Andrew illustrates, the nation is experienced as the ultimate oppressor of autonomy, thus its erasure signifies agentic liberation from the constraints imposed on social actors. In (re)telling his life, Andrew is (re)scripting a livelihood of freedom from the otherwise oppressive limitations that a life anchored in the nation entails. For Andrew the 'happiness script' is one that obliterates the nation, evaporates roots and removes any traces of religiosity and family ancestry.

# Transnational Performativity: The Nation in Ruins and the Self Under Construction

One of the core tenets of diasporic life is that of transnational relations and indeed transnational identities in the making between the 'here' and 'there' of the respective country of birth for the offspring (usually the host country for the first generation) and their ancestral homeland. The pioneering work associated with the transnational turn in migration studies over two decades ago (i.e. Glick Schiller et al. 1995; Smith and Guarnizo 1998) focused on the migrants as social agents of mobility empowered and acting from below while engaged in activities spanning two or more nation-states encompassing cultural transfer, social remittances, kinship networks, political engagements and even business entrepreneurship (Faist 2010). To a certain degree this transnationality may seem refreshing and sustaining of one's creativity and multidirectionality of experiences, but often it is also a source of tension and contestation when it comes to norms, values, morals and lifestyle choices. At the same time, the idea of 'freedom' and 'escape' (cf. Ahmed 1999) seems to be a salient feature in narratives of mobility and return when it comes to both first- and second-generation diasporans (cf. Blunt 2005).

So, for instance, Anna who is a second-generation Greek-German discusses the exclusions that her mother experienced in the homeland attributed to her activist leftist practices and ideologies during an era of authoritarianism in Greece. The episode below and similar ones conveyed to Anna by her mother made a huge impression on her:

> She was being followed and her life was made difficult, she was forced to leave, wanting never to return again. Even today when she narrates this incident it is a very emotional moment and she bursts into tears when talking about these stories. …In this way I too, as a young child, experienced the reality concerning our existence as Greeks in a foreign country, the search for a cultural identity. (cited in Christou 2011a, b, 156)

The stigma of exile that Anna's mother experienced was one where the magnitude of the nation as a unit of collective belonging is dismantled and replaced by a container of fear, trauma and intense emotionality that has remained intact for many decades. Such affective encounters are also ingrained into the developmental trajectories of the second generation, and, as a result, the search for a sense of cultural belonging and a sense of identity can be exacerbated (cf. Damousi 2015).

In that sense, Anna then narrates her own search for an identity through her mother's traumatic past experiences in the homeland, marked by the unbearable feeling of marginalization and the agonizing moments of surveillance due to her political beliefs. It is somewhat astonishing that given such an ingrained family narrative of exclusion by the very nation that is supposed to embrace its members in the veil of an imagined community, Anna's search for a sense of place and self is characterized by a strong pull toward that same homeland:

> I had a great liking to Greece, I loved Greece very much, the Greek culture which I imagined in the way I wanted to and knew about and at a certain point in time, after having lived in Germany… I experienced the two cultures intensely. I was greatly influenced I would say half and half, not more or less – I felt the powerful desire to return and so I am here today. (cited in Christou 2011a, b, 157)

Anna talks about the intensity that one experiences when immersed in a life of two cultures, often at the polar opposites of practices and social norms. And, here, she quantifies those influences as being 'half and half', as other participants often refer to percentages in articulating their cultural selves. At the same time, Anna describes the potent emotionality of return as a desire of self-actualization and hence a life plan, the relocation to the ancestral homeland, in her case, moving from Germany to Greece, the latter being the place that became a catalyst for her mother's relocation to Germany. If there is an analytic point to underscore here, it is one that encapsulates both the emotional spheres and the gendered scripts that transnational performativity generates in the mobility pathways that both the first and second generations experience. Here, we realize that despite the trauma and sense of exile that Anna's mother had experienced as we discovered earlier in her extract, Anna herself makes an agentic break from any predisposed life script and decides to immerse herself in both cultures in experiencing them fully and intensely. The emotionality of return migration is also underscored as a 'powerful desire' for Anna who makes the even more serious life decision to relocate to her mother's country of birth and her ancestral homeland. But, how does the ancestral homeland figure in terms of participants' mobility pathways and identities? Here, it is crucial to revisit the emotional spheres of personal and social suffering when patriarchy is aligned to national belonging.

As Walby (2011) brings our attention to 'gender regimes' to acknowledge the persistence of patriarchy in following a critical and political edge to our analysis of social relations, it is important to note that both women's and men's social lives are shaped by the kind of socio-cultural, structural, heteronormative patriarchal regimes that find anchor in the discourses of the nation, evident above, among others, in both Nicole's and Andrew's narrations. Even trauma in such cases becomes a pathway, albeit a painful one, to developing one's identity and coming to grasps with the fragments of such gendered identification processes as curtailed or cultivated by national consciousness and experiences. Thus, 'not only do social practices produce and reproduce norms of masculinity and femininity but the reconfigurations of everyday life as constrained or shaped by migration can further pronounce such categorizations' (Mavroudi and Christou 2015, 2). Hence, diasporic identities involve processual entanglements (cf. Mavroudi 2007) with roots/routes, post/nationalist and emotive parameters (cf. Herzfeld 1997).

Such identities are confined and transgressive, contested and contesting of nationness and ultimately in seeking inclusion may experience and exert exclusion. Therefore, as paradoxical as it may appear at surface, the painful experiences of patriarchy and oppression with all the trauma associated in coping and making life choices, may collectively create new life scripts and a revisiting of one's sense of identity and belonging. It is important to understand such processual entanglements when conducting narrative research on topics that trigger powerful emotional responses. Moreover, it is appropriate to keep in mind that researchers should maintain proximity with nuanced and critical (collective and personal) critiques as a pathway to potentially alter practices of power. This (feminist) awareness is one which understands power to be continually 'becoming' (Browne 2008, 146). It is relevant here to note that trauma plays a particular social role as regards how the nation prescribes collectivity in the name of shared values or ideals that appear to be greater than the nation and are conflated under notions of 'authenticity' and 'morality'.

## Concluding on Narrations of the Nation in Greek Migrant Lives

If there is such a thing as a feminist utopia, it should be principled on a plight to resisting hegemony, eradicating patriarchy as a form of hegemony and advancing alternative frameworks for equitable, socially just and ultimately happy collective and individual lives. Hegemony is manifested as social, cultural, ideological and political power that flows through and within the boundaries of the nation which maintains its own normalization in enforcing the respective values and norms that sustain it. The nation operates as social container of power. This kind of hegemony is found in the practices of patriarchy that the participant excerpts referred to in earlier sections. As membership in the nation implies implementation of its core values and principles, those social actors who adhere and embrace those ethno-cultural values fulfil their role which at the same time sustains their sense of belonging. It would be a logical fallacy to assume that those who disobey such ethno-national norms and values would continue to enjoy acceptance, tolerance and membership in this context. Hence, more specifically, as the ethno-religious parameters demarcate such spheres, it is evident to understand as Whitehead et al. (2013, 127) argue that 'religions have already decided on what constitutes the gender and sexual identities of men and women; such identities are embedded for all time and for all to access in their respective scriptures. Those who read, learn, believe, and promote such readings are, willingly or not, co-opted into a larger hegemonic project around gender power'. This exemplifies the view of many feminist scholars (e.g. Daly 1985) of the patriarchal conditions that religions operationalize to oppress women and to reinforce their marginalization across a number of social spheres. If 'patriarchy has God on its side' (Millet 2005, 51), then, it becomes clear that as Kantsa (2014, 827) demonstrates, 'same-sex desiring women often feel the need to hide their sexual choices from their kin and relatives in order not to endanger their relations. But also in ever-growing cases where women engaged in same-sex relationships feel "brave" enough to come-out to their parents, it is usually the parents who negate, this time, the act of "coming-out", by refusing to talk about the issue, and warn their daughters that they should remain silent on their sexual preferences. Since kin and family relations are still important in Greek society, this is their way of sustaining and preserving the relationship with their daughters'.

At the same time, for those who cherish a sense of ethnic identity but who do not wish to conform to the exclusionist principles of such may experience a dichotomized identity and further struggles to belong compounded by deep feelings of alienation. That kind of particular understanding of the ethnic self cannot be adequately grasped when such an identity rejects the reproduction of cultural norms and seeks to reinvent a self that is crafted by choice and agency (cf. Kirtsoglou 2004; Pavlou 2009; Yannakopoulos 2010; Kantsa 2014). If we reflect on the narrations articulated by participants in earlier sections in this chapter, we sense that Greekness is confronted by an eroding of hermetically sealed traditional notions of identity, and, as a result, breaks down and dismantles gendered and sexed stereotypes that accompanied it in the past. In particular, the agency expressed in the case of same-sex sexualities highlights that issues of gender, family, kinship and sexuality in Greece have shifted narrations around practices of desire and the scripted stories around them through the lens of choice that participants articulate. Irrespective of the enduring and unbearable hegemony of the ethno-cultural signifiers that the nation exerts on diasporic identities, such diasporic identities are agentic albeit saturated by the particular emotive and performative spheres that participants move through.

It is apparent throughout the discussion of the empirical findings from research with the Greek diaspora that this is a case where the heteronormativity and the hegemonic patriarchy exemplified in participant narrative accounts underscore how strong the national idea remains in lived personal and social experience. In other cases the nation can be seen as embracing forms of home-nationalism whereupon choice of gender and sexual scripts becomes enlisted as the 'national ideal'. Caution should be raised in not categorizing the Greek diasporic case as one fitting a 'traditional' end of the spectrum and hence as an exemplar of the nation more generally, while in other ethnic contexts the national imaginary may have seen significant shits (however circumscribed and problematic such a generalization may appear) as reflective of more 'progressive' accounts. So, for instance, at the time of finalizing this chapter, the United Kingdom is at the same time marking the 50th anniversary of the Sexual Offences Act 1967, which partially decriminalized gay sex, yet has one of the worst records on gender equality at work.

In this chapter I have explored some of the dimensions of how the nation is narrated through mobility life stories of Greek diasporics and how such life scripts are shaped by gender, emotion and transnational experiences. Some of the findings highlight the compartmentalized practices of social expectations where the dynamics of sexuality, intimacy and gender render belonging to the nation as untenable. Clearly, as notions of contemporary families and attributes of identities are resisting stereotyped behaviours, in mirroring more progressive understandings of the role of the nation in people's lives, it is hoped that a new schema will develop that critically reflects on the plurality of identities that hold equal acceptance to those that mirror primordial perceptions of the national self.

Gender and sexuality are contested concepts and have been transformed through contingent processes in social relations and social divisions. A range of innovative, pluri-methodological and comparative insights on a spectrum of geographical regions and historical periods have tried to make sense of such inequalities, marginalizations and exclusions stemming from sexual and gender social politics. Narrative, biographical and ethnographic research aim to explore oppressions and lived experiences in understanding the personal and the political as inscribed on bodies marked by differing degrees of power. Such analyses and findings have in turn enriched academic activism in combining conceptualizations with praxis.

# References

Acheraïou, Amar. 2011. *Questioning Hybridity, Postcolonialism and Globalization*. London: Palgrave Macmillan.
Ahmed, Sara. 1999. Home and Away: Narratives of Migration and Estrangement. *International Journal of Cultural Studies* 2 (3): 329–347.
Al-Ali, Nadge. 2010. Diasporas and Gender. In *Diasporas: Concepts, Identities, Intersections*, ed. Kim Knott and Sean McLoughlin, 118–122. London: Zed Books.

Anderson, Benedict. 1983. *Imagined Communities: Reflections on the Origin and Spread of Nationalism.* London: Verso.

Archer, Margaret. 2000. *Being Human: The Problem of Agency.* Cambridge: Cambridge University Press.

Blunt, Alison. 2005. Cultural Geography: Cultural Geographies of Home. *Progress in Human Geography* 29 (4): 505–515.

Brah, Avtar, and Anne Coombes. 2005. *Hybridity and Its Discontents: Politics, Science, Culture.* New York: Routledge.

Browne, Kath. 2008. Power and Privilege: (Re)Making Feminist Geographies. In *Feminisms in Geography: Rethinking Space, Place and Knowledges*, ed. Pamela Moss and Karen Falconer Al-Hindi, 140–148. New York: Rowman & Littlefield Publishers.

Brubaker, Rogers. 2005. The 'Diaspora' Diaspora. *Ethnic and Racial Studies* 28 (1): 1–19.

———. 2010. Migration, Membership, and the Modern Nation-State: Internal and External Dimensions of the Politics of Belonging. *Journal of Interdisciplinary History* 1: 61–78.

Christou, Anastasia. 2006. *Narratives of Place, Culture and Identity: Second-Generation Greek-Americans Return 'Home.* Amsterdam: Amsterdam University Press.

———. 2009. Telling Diaspora Stories: Theoretical and Methodological Reflections on Narratives of Migrancy and Belongingness in the Second Generation. *Migration Letters* 6 (2): 143–153.

———. 2011a. Narrating Lives in (E)motion: Embodiment and Belongingness in Diasporic Spaces of Home and Return. *Emotion, Space and Society* 4: 249–257.

———. 2011b. Translocal Spatial Geographies: Multi-sited Encounters of Greek Migrants in Athens, Berlin and New York. In *Translocal Geographies: Spaces, Places, Connections*, ed. Katherine Brickell and Ayona Datta, 145–161. Farnham: Ashgate.

———. 2014. Ageing *'Phantasmagorically'* in Exile: The Resilience of Unbearable and Unattainable Homelands in the Jewish and Cuban Imagination. In *Re-thinking Home: Transnational Migration and Older Age*, ed. Katie Walshand Lena Nare, 176–187. London: Routledge.

———. 2016. "Ageing Masculinities and the Nation: Disrupting Boundaries of Sexualities, Mobilities and Identities." *Gender, Place and Culture: A Journal of Feminist Geography,* 23, 6: 801–816.

Christou, Anastasia, and Russell King. 2010. Movements Between 'White' Europe and America: Greek Migration to the United States. In *Diasporas: Concepts, Identities, Intersections*, ed. Kim Knott and Sean McLoughlin, 181–186. London: Zed Books.
———. 2011. Gendering Diasporic Mobilities and Emotionalities in Greek-German Narratives of Home, Belonging and Return. *Journal of Mediterranean Studies* 20 (2): 283–315.
———. 2014. *Counter-Diaspora: The Greek Second Generation Returns 'Home*. Cambridge: Harvard University Press.
Cohen, Robin. 2008. *Global Diasporas: An Introduction*. London/New York: Routledge.
Daly, Mary. 1985. *Church and the Second Sex*. Boston: Beacon.
Damousi, Joy. 2015. *Memory and Migration in the Shadow of War: Australia's Greek Immigrants After World War II and the Greek Civil War*. Cambridge: Cambridge University Press.
Faist, Thomas. 2010. "Diaspora and Transnationalism: What Kind of Dance Partners"? In *Diaspora and Transnationalism: Conceptual, Theoretical and Methodological Challenges*, ed. Rainer Bauböckand and Thomas Faist, 9–34. Amsterdam: Amsterdam University Press.
Herzfeld, Michael. 1997. *Cultural Intimacy: Social Poetics in the Nation-state*. New York: Routledge.
Kantsa, Venetia. 2014. The Price of Marriage: Same-sex Sexualities and Citizenship in Greece. *Sexualities* 17: 818–836.
King, Russell, and Anastasia Christou. 2010. Diaspora, Migration and Transnationalism: Insights from the Study of Second-Generation 'Returnees'. In *Diaspora and Transnationalism: Conceptual, Theoretical and Methodological Challenges*, ed. Rainer Bauböckand Thomas Faist, 167–183. Amsterdam: Amsterdam University Press.
Kirtsoglou, Elizabeth. 2004. *For the Love of Women. Gender, Identity and Same-Sex Relations in a Greek Provincial Town*. London/New York: Routledge.
Mavroudi, Liz. 2007. Diasporas as Process: (De)constructing Boundaries. *Geography Compass* 1: 467–479.
Mavroudi, Liz, and Anastasia Christou. 2015. Introduction. In *Dismantling Diasporas: Rethinking the Geographies of Diasporic Identity, Connection and Development*, ed. Anastasia Christou and Liz Mavroudi, 1–11. Farnham Surrey: Ashgate.
Millet, Kate. 2005. *Sexual Politics*. New York: Doubleday.

Papastergiadis, Nikos. 2000. *The Turbulence of Migration: Globalization, Deterritorialization and Hybridity*. Oxford: Polity Press.
Pavlou, Miltos. 2009. Homophobia in Greece. Love for Equality. County Report for i-RED (Institute for Rights Equality & Diversity). http://www.red-network.eu/resources/toolip/doc/2011/11/25/i-red_homophobia_in_greece2009--6.pdf. Last accessed 13 Dec 2016.
Safran, William. 1991. Diasporas in Modern Societies: Myths of Homeland and Return. *Diaspora: A Journal of Transnational Studies* 1 (1): 83–99.
Sassen, Saskia. 2002. Towards Post-national and Denationalized Citizenship. In *Handbook of Citizenship Studies*, ed. F. Engin Isin and Bryan S. Turner, 277–291. London: *Sage*.
Schiller, Glick, Linda Basch Nina, and Cristina Szanton. 1995. From Immigrant to Transmigrant: Theorizing Transnational Migration. *Anthropological Quarterly* 68 (1): 48–63.
Smith, Michael P., and Louis Guarnizo, eds. 1998. *Transnationalism from Below*. New Brunswick: Transaction Publishers.
Stewart, Charles. 2011. Creolization, Hybridity, Syncretism, Mixture. *Portuguese Studies 27 (1)*: 48–55.
Walby, Sylvia. 2011. *The Future of Feminism*. London: Polity Press.
Werbner, Pnina. 2001. The Limits of Cultural Hybridity: On Ritual Monsters, Poetic Licence and Contested Postcolonial Purifications. *Journal of the Royal Anthropological Institute* 7: 133–152.
Whitehead, Stephen, Anisa Talahite, and Roy Moodley. 2013. *Gender and Identity: Key Themes and New Directions*. Oxford: Oxford University Press.
Willert, Trine Stauning. 2014. *New Voices in Greek Orthodox Thought Untying the Bond between Nation and Religion*. London: Routledge.
Yannakopoulos, Kostas. 2010. Cultural Meanings of Loneliness: Kinship, Sexuality and (Homo)sexual Identity in Contemporary Greece. *Journal of Mediterranean Studies* 18 (2): 265–282.
Zheng, Wang, Fangzhu Zhang, and Wu Fulong. 2016. Affective Neighbourly Relations Between Migrant and Local Residents in Shanghai. *Urban Geography* 38 (8): 1182–1202.

# Part IV

Institutional Mediations Past and Present: Understanding the Conditions for Women-Friendly Nationalisms

# 17

# 'Gender Diversity' and Nationalisms in Multiple Contexts

## Jill Vickers

Feminist scholars of nationalism focus on demonstrating the existence of 'gender diversity'[1] and how it affects gender equality and national projects.[2] Most 'mainstream' scholars consider 'gender' irrelevant to explaining the origins of nations and the rise, spread, and intensity of nationalism—questions they consider most important. As a political force, nationalism has its own history characterized by gender diversity, but it also shows variability in gender/nation relations in different contexts that some gender scholars attribute to a country's location in colonial or anti-colonial contexts (Yuval-Davis 1997). Kaplan (1997) demonstrates that the history of Europe's 'modern' nation-states involved women's coercive privatization, although in several cases (Finland, Norway) women were active participants in anti-imperialist independence movements with contexts similar to anti-colonial movements.

---

[1] While much of the text focuses on 'gender regimes' produced by family law codes that assume a heterosexual norm, 'gender diversity' includes sexual minorities.
[2] 'National projects' include nationalist movements, nation-state formation, and nation-building. Included are formal and informal institutions, practices, discourses/ideologies.

J. Vickers (✉)
Department of Political Science, Carleton University, Ottawa, ON, Canada

© The Author(s) 2018
J. Mulholland et al. (eds.), *Gendering Nationalism*,
https://doi.org/10.1007/978-3-319-76699-7_17

To make sense of the various patterns of gender/nation relations, the text compares the effects of 'gender diversity' in different contexts, specifically in *modernizing* and *anti-modern* national projects, in different historical waves and in *colonial* and *anti-colonial/imperial* contexts.

Studies of women's current involvements in national projects reflect the histories of gender/nation relations. First, 'membership in the nation…[was] powerfully gendered … through the denial of the franchise … silencing and [legal] disabilities, barring.. [women] from property, education, and politics' (Ely 2000, 32). This resulted from nationalism originating where male dominance was already well established. But while nationalization increased men's status, power, literacy, education, and military skills (Wiesner 2000), women's privatization reduced their status and power through more repressive family law, sustained by 'separate spheres' ideologies and violence. Even when women's legal exclusion ended, a century or more of disabilities remained embedded as historical legacies in the institutions, practices, and discourses of most European nation-states. One question of interest is the effects such legacies have on women's current engagements with national projects. Cases in which women participated actively in national projects occurred when nationalist elites had to mobilize whole communities to achieve independence from European empires. Comparing gender/nation relations in 'modernizing' 'great powers' with cases in which women were active participants suggests several hypotheses: first, that in modernizing 'great powers', nationalists mobilized young men to capture state institutions, but privatized women to ensure men's sexual access and control of women's reproductive capacity and property; second, that in anti-imperial/colonial contexts, mobilizing women to win independence often resulted in their gaining the vote when men did. But the subsequent political and legal trajectories for women differ in the two scenarios, suggesting other things also affected long-term outcomes. Case studies suggest it mattered if women were organized sufficiently to resist privatization (Vickers 2006). Moreover, long-term outcomes are most often 'women-friendly when a positive ideological 'fit' exists between nationalists' and feminists' conceptions of women's political roles. Cockburn (1997) conceptualizes nationalist ideologies as 'inclusive' or 'exclusionary' depending on their vision of 'the people'; that is? if women are included. An important research question, therefore, is how women's active participation, absence, or symbolic presence affect national projects. Participation by individual women is less likely to influence national projects than participation by organized women. Although little systematic research exists, some feminists (e.g. de Sève 2000) speculate from their own experience that organized women's active participation may reduce nationalist movements' propensity for violence, as in post-1960 Quebec.

The text has four parts. Part one outlines concepts, frameworks, and research questions used to study 'gender diversity' in various contexts. Part two explores approaches to systematic comparison. Part three examines comparisons of gender/nation interactions in the French and American revolutions; that is, in modern nationalism's first 'wave', different manifestations of similar nationalist ideologies, different stages of Greek nation-state development, and colonial and anti-colonial/imperial contexts. The conclusion asserts the value of systematic comparisons in locating gender in theories of the rise, spread, and intensity of nationalism, and in several long-term outcomes including the contemporary effects of historical gender/nation interactions.

## Concepts, Frameworks and Research Questions

The text uses these key concepts. First—*gender/nation interaction*—combines 'gender' and 'national projects'; that is, 'nations', nationalist discourses and movements, and nation-state-seeking, founding, and consolidation (together 'nation-state making'). Second are short- and long-term *outcome*s of such interactions. Third, *gender regimes* are the stable patterns of sex/gender power relations in state institutions or across societies. Fourth, *gender diversity* identifies men's and women's different experiences with national phenomena as in gender/nation interactions at various stages of nation-state making. The fifth is *contextual analysis*, an approach that rejects positivists' idea of general laws but also dismisses postmodernists' skepticism that meaningful generalizations are possible (Goodin and Tilly 2006). Instead it offers an intermediate approach based on comparing how contexts affect gender/nation interactions and short- or long-term outcomes. It locates nationalist and feminist phenomena in historical contexts; that is, times and places, adopting robust causal mechanisms to explain differences. Finally, *active participation* designates *organized* women's political actions in national projects, notably in state-seeking nationalist movements. This contrasts with women's absence or 'presence' as individuals, or as passive symbols of national identity.

Ely (2000, 32) thinks women were excluded from *all* 'emergent national contexts' in Europe, but some feminist scholars have identified diversity as a key characteristic of gender/nation interactions. Vickers (2006, Figure 1) mapped 15 cases in different contexts. Organized women active participants, with simultaneous male/female citizenship in one third. In the other ten cases, women were not active participants, although some individual women participated. The long-term outcomes mostly were negative. Jayawardena (1986) mapped 12 cases in anti-colonial contexts, with organized women participating actively and gaining the vote simultaneously with men in all 12. But women often couldn't parlay their votes into long-term, positive outcomes, for example, by getting family law reform which made it difficult to achieve autonomous organizations. Moreover, despite initial support for reforms, most men resisted the greater freedom within families that women needed to make them effective citizens able to advocate on their own behalf. In some anti-colonial cases, nationalist leaders recruited women to 'modernize' the public sphere *symbolically* by their presence. Nationalist elites often believed modern cultural identities require women's public participation, but few wanted to democratize the family which they considered a site for reproducing traditional values.

Elites presenting women as symbols of 'modernity' in the public sphere, but resisting equality in the family, is a pattern that occurs in anti-colonial/imperial contexts in which foreign rule makes the family the safest site for preserving traditional values and languages.

What causes *gender diversity* and what effects does such diversity have in different contexts? Yuval-Davis (1997) and Joseph (1997) attribute different patterns of gender diversity to a country's location in relations of colonialism. Jacoby (1999, 513) theorizes that while 'non-western' feminists merge feminism and nationalism, making nationalist movements sites for women's emancipation, 'western feminists …reject nationalism as an emancipatory framework'. Tohidi (1994, 110) thinks this is because 'western feminists have a greater capacity for autonomous organizing [after their] fierce struggle to extend...democratic and civil rights'. But this doesn't explain national projects in Europe in which organized women participated actively in national projects, for example, in the Nordic countries that have high levels of political representation of women today— long-term positive outcomes from historical legacies. Countries display different patterns for example: while women had legal rights in the communist countries and rates of (quota-based) political representation higher for the period than in Western Europe, families weren't democratized and few of the rights persisted after capitalism was introduced. Moreover, organized women hadn't enough clout to influence nationalist movements, although some women supported even violent national projects.

Anthias and Yuval-Davis (1989, 7) developed a much-used framework that categorizes women's presence in national projects: as biological and boundary reproducers; ideological reproducers of cultures and collectivities; signifiers of national/ethnic differences; and participants in national, economic, political, and military struggles. (Except in the last category, women's roles are usually passive.) While it shows how national projects are 'gendered', the framework can't explain gender diversity, nor what conditions make women active participants. An insight of feminist institutionalism is that women's 'absence' from participation because of privatization becomes embedded in the institutions and discourses of new nation-states. Such historical legacies shape current gender/nation relations and help explain their diversity.

Other frameworks conceptualize nationalism as occurring in historical 'waves' that relate to ideological 'imaginings' of the nation (e.g. Anderson 1991) or relate them to iterations of modernity (Hearn 2006). This suggests the importance of distinguishing between 'anti-modern' and 'modernizing' nationalisms. Feminist activism also is conceptualized as occurring in 'waves' that relate to advances in women's literacy, education, organization, rights, and freedoms in public and private spheres. Decades of gender/nation case studies provide insights into gender diversity, but few 'western' feminists consider nationalist projects as sites of emancipation. Nonetheless, gender scholars who focus on anti-colonial national projects in peripheral, minority nations (Catalonia, Scotland, Quebec) have different perspectives. Moreover, case studies show that some women are attracted to right-wing, populist nationalisms. Finally, most case studies of European national projects assume they are violent, with negative outcomes for women. These biased analyses assume all women are alienated from nationalism.

## Approaches to Comparison

This text draws on three different approaches to comparison: *theoretical comparisons* that compare abstracted ideal types to their theorized opposites, for example, civic and ethnic nationalisms; *historical comparisons* that situate phenomena in different times and places; and comparisons of *ideologies* or discourses. The text 'genders' Hearn's 'wave' framework (2006, 13) by incorporating feminist mobilizations. Hearn organizes the 'conventional historical narrative about the rise and spread of nationalism' into seven 'waves' from 'the Age of Revolutions' to the anti-/post-communist 'wave' of separatist and irredentist movements after the collapse of the USSR and Yugoslavia. He speculates that nationalism's interactions with changing iterations of 'modernity' will generate more 'waves' when new forms and uses of 'nationalism' emerge, as with current right-wing populisms in Europe and the white nationalisms of Brexit and Trump.

Mainstream theorists ignore gender/nation scholarship believing it 'diverts attention from the central debates on nations and nationalism' (Hutchinson and Smith 1994, 12) and lacks 'a comprehensive causal analysis of…[how] …gender… contribute[s] to the formation of nations and the spread and intensity of nationalism' (Smith 1998, 10). Maxwell (2016, 1) thinks gender/nation scholars, reacting to being ignored, 'focus…disproportionately on documenting the experiences of women… to show…[they] can and do participate in nationalist politics'. While most theorists of nationalism consider 'modernity' a single 'stable state', Hearn (2006, 8) thinks each historical 'wave' focuses on 'a different iteration of modernity..,[and] generates new nationalisms' that relate to different gender regimes. In this light, Europe's 'great powers' were considered 'modern', yet their private, sex/gender relations stayed mainly 'traditional' until the mid-twentieth century.

How do different patterns of gender diversity relate to historical and ideological 'waves' and various iterations of 'modernization' or anti-modernization? All 'modern' 'nation-states' are structured around a public/private 'divide', although the extent to which family law privatizes women differs. However, in all of them, women were (and are) expected to mediate between the 'modern' and 'traditional', and the 'secular' and the 'spiritual' (Canovan 1996). In anti-colonial/imperial contexts, women were recruited to be visible in the public sphere to establish that the dominated culture deserved independence (Chatterjee 1989). Nonetheless, male dominance and traditional gender relations persisted after independence, denying women greater freedom in family relations, and political agency. After the First World War, when some European women had political rights, 'anti-modern' nationalists were determined to re-traditionalize private spheres and rescind women's political rights. Albanese (2006, 186/7) theorizes that all nationalists want to keep the private sphere traditional, but in anti-colonial/imperial contexts, women often develop a feminist consciousness and organize *within* nationalist movements, becoming conscious nationalists who reproduce their nations physically and socially by choice and participate in shaping institutions to advance their interests. Since women's reproductive capacity is basic to nation-state making, the main difference is between nations that coerce women and nations in which they act freely.

## Empirical Comparisons of Gender Diversity

This section compares patterns of gender diversity, iterations of 'modernity' and national projects in different contexts and 'waves'. Comparisons include: different patterns of gender diversity in the French and American revolutions; 'extreme', 'anti-modern' nationalisms' in different 'waves' and global regions; changes in women's participation through stages of Greek nation-state making; and the effects of women's active participation in independence struggles in anti-imperial or anti-colonial contexts.

## Colonial Versus Anti-colonial Contexts

The French Revolution's invocation of universal rights inspired women's eventual inclusion as citizens of modern nation-states, but full citizenship eluded French women until 1944. The new, post-revolutionary nation-state established 'a sexually differentiated public/private divide [and] … constitutional formalization of citizenship…[based on] women's legal exclusion from the nationally defined, bourgeois public sphere' (Sluga 1998, 93). Despite some women's participation in the revolutionary struggle, they all were forced out of public affairs by Jacobins suspicious of activist women. Moreover, their participation wasn't required for the revolution's success. Repressive family law, that is, the *Napoleonic Code*, established women's privatization, along with other laws denying women freedom of speech, association, and assembly. A 'separate spheres' ideology legitimized women's privatization. Consequently, 'nationalists implicated gender in the organization of the state…[making] gender difference a significant site of national identification' (Sluga 1998, 93). When monarchy was re-established, repressive laws and women's privatization remained part of French institutions for almost two centuries.

The American revolution also was 'a watershed in … popular perceptions of women's relationship to the state' (Zagarri 2007, 22). From the 1760s, 'leaders realized …women's support…would be critical to the resistance movement and the course of the war…and…[women had] to be won over to the cause' (22). Women defended their homes and families and pursued literacy in order to follow events. Post-revolutionary opportunities for girls' education increased substantially. Moreover, in the republic's early decades, women influenced state politics in numerous ways. In New Jersey, unmarried, propertied women could vote. But the institutionalization of representative government, mainly through the formalization of parties, pushed women out. Since states retained English common law, *coverture* denied married women legal and economic rights, though they had more civil rights than European women, and five decades after the revolution, a national women's movement emerged. In France, political activism for women included participating in subsequent violent uprisings.

Comparing patterns of gender diversity in two revolutions in Hearn's 'first wave' of nationalism is a 'parallel demonstration of theory' (Skocpol and Somers 1980), *revealing different features in seemingly similar cases.* The contexts in which the two revolutions occurred differed: France was a colonial power; America a fragile federation of 13 colonies that took decades to develop a central state. American women's participation in the revolution won them respect and civil rights, while French women were considered 'monstrous' and 'disorderly' if they spoke or acted in public. Equating women's participation in public affairs with treachery and reaction became deeply embedded in France's national institutions as historical legacies with 'women's exclusion… increasingly premised on the identification of "femininity" with the private sphere' (Sluga 1998, 90). The French model of a 'modern' nation-state based on women's exclusion from public affairs was spread by the Napoleonic 'system' across Europe and by colonization. This pattern of gender diversity characterized 'modernity' in a colonizing 'great power', *but other patterns emerged on Europe's periphery.*

Smith (1998) considers early 'nationalism …an inclusive and liberating force', ignoring women's privatization and loss of status and power during and after the French Revolution. But American women who participated actively in the revolution were considered citizens, were freer, and had more opportunities for literacy and education while politics remained informal. But the development of formal party and electoral systems finally excluded women not yet organized *as* women, or able to resist when President Jackson established 'universal' suffrage for white men only (1828). The resulting representative democracy gave party elites control over elections and policy-making, while the (white) women who tried to enter party politics experienced a backlash. Nonetheless, they retained informal connections to decision-makers by canvassing, petitioning, and forming voluntary associations that eroded the public/private divide and promoted a new civil society. A trope of 'republican motherhood' existed in both countries. In France it signified women's sexual availability and reproductive roles, while in America it was considered a political role that legitimized women's citizenship (Zagarri 2007) and (white) girls' right to education.

Are there contemporary manifestations of the historic legacies from founding gender/nation interactions? To establish this, it would be necessary to consider subsequent interactions to assess the importance of the founding 'wave'. So, while (white) women developed more civil society organizations to influence American politics through interactions related to slavery, the civil war, 'whites-only nationalism, and non-white immigration, Black and populist nationalisms also have an effect. The argument for path dependence is stronger for France. But the most significant difference is between the colonizing 'great powers' and state-seeking, anti-imperial nations. Long-term outcomes of initial gender/nation interactions are evident in Finland, where *organized* women actively participated in the struggle for national independence and creating social democracies (Vickers 2006). Late industrialization and the formation of women's political organizations before parties developed resulted in Finnish women's early incorporation as active citizens before independence. Subsequently, they now have *the highest rates of political representation globally*, gender parity cabinets by law, women as president and prime minister—sometimes both—and progressive 'women-friendly' policies and programs. Norway shows a similar trajectory since women organized their own referendum to show they wanted Norway to be independent of Sweden. The common element is *women's sense that they are co-creators of their nation-state,* not alienated from it.

## Comparing Within Types of Nationalist Ideologies

This section considers gender diversity in '*extreme*' *nationalisms* that usually are *anti-modern*, with fascist (Italy, Germany), authoritarian (Hungary, Spain, Greece), religious (India), populist (Argentina, USA), and militarist (Chile, Japan) ideologies. While some gender scholars (e.g. Albanese 2006) consider all nationalisms victimizers of women, many conflate types of nationalism and fail to recognize that not all women are victims of nationalisms. Some ethnic German women supported Nazi 'purification' policies to eradicate Jews, gypsies, homosexuals, and people with disabilities. They also supported 're-traditionalizing' sex/gender relations (Koonz 1987). This makes it important to differentiate among types of nationalisms.

Eatwell (2003) considers 'extreme' nationalism a societal reaction to severe shocks; that is, war defeats, democratization, and modernizing gender relations that traditionalists consider 'pollution' and the cause of societal breakdown. In the 1930s, anti-modern nationalists determined to 'purify' and 'regenerate' their nations by restoring pre-modern traditions and rescinding women's political rights. However, not all 'extreme' nationalisms are 'anti-modern' in this way: for example, the populist Peronist regime in Argentina enfranchised women, who became its main supporters, and Trump hasn't suggested disenfranchising women. 'Extreme' Hindu nationalism (*Hindutva*) also empowers high-caste women to lead actions against Muslims, thereby encouraging their political activity despite the traditionalist content of the nationalism. Moreover, many Hindu women demand a single family law code, rejecting the legal pluralism that enables larger minorities (Muslims, Christians) to have 'personal laws' that differ from the purportedly secular code. While most feminists oppose this demand, Hindu nationalist women claim it is necessary for their equality. Therefore, women who are part of a society's dominant culture may participate in 'extreme' nationalist movements that harm minority women and benefit from the former's participation. In Europe, 'anti-modern' variants of 'extreme' nationalism 're-traditionalized' gender relations, for example, through fascist family policies in Italy and Germany (Albanese 2006, 186), and more traditional religious codes in Greece, Spain, and Portugal. While such policies didn't alter reproductive behaviour or aggregate fertility levels in the long term, minority women experienced forced abortions and sterilization, and women generally were denied access to reliable contraception and safe abortion, fostering women's alienation from nationalism in these countries.

A key difference between modern and anti-modern nationalisms is the *voluntary* or *involuntary* nature of motherhood, and how it affects women's citizenship. Cockburn (1998, 39) relates this to 'inclusive' and 'exclusionary' conceptions of 'the people', positing a continuum ranging from exclusionary nationalisms that force women to reproduce the nation or ethnic group at one end, to inclusive nationalisms that treat women's reproduction as voluntary at the other. 'Extreme' nationalisms are usually associated with involuntary reproduction, privatization, and passive citizenship. 'Inclusive' nationalisms support voluntary reproduction and active citizenship.

## Comparing Stages of Nation-State Development

When nationalists ended Ottoman rule in territories populated by ethnic Greeks, Europe's 'great powers' recognized Greece as a nation-state (1832), but it was many decades before a stable nation-state existed. Smith (1986, 146) claims the history of Greek nation-state development involves 'a conflict of two ideas of the nation, the territorial and the ethnic…civic and genealogical-cum-religious'. But during this period, nationalist elites applied four different models of 'Greekness', each with different gender regimes: *liberal civic, moderate ethno-cultural, extreme ethnic*, and, currently, *democratic civic*. Vickers and Vouloukos (2007, 502) found that women successfully used themes from all of these, except extreme ethnic nationalism. For example, women established their claim to citizenship by fighting in the War of Independence, and when the new state legislated compulsory education (1833), it included girls. Both occurred when the *liberal civic model* based on women's privatization was employed by nationalist elites imitating the French. But a later identity crisis made elites adopt a moderate *ethno-cultural model* that built on women's earlier familial roles in promoting Greek ethnic identity and language under Ottoman rule. Under it, elites were more open to women's participation and gave literate women the right to vote locally. In the 1930s, an *extreme ethnic model* was introduced by several dictators who rescinded women's political rights, re-traditionalized sex/gender relations, banned women's organizations, and criminalized their political activity. Half a century and a civil war later, a *democratic civic* model based on equal citizenship rights was established, although women still struggle for inclusion.

Why are there so many models of 'Greekness' and patterns of gender diversity? Greek nationalism was a mass movement before a Greek state developed, and under Ottoman rule, 'Greekness' was produced both by the Orthodox church and by women in families. So, while 'western' women 'struggled to be included in the definition of the public nation, [as]… equal citizens' (Hearn 2006, 159), Greek women first joined the struggle to create a nation-state. Greek national identity was 'dynamic and constantly in evolution…[as]…the borders of the national community…[were] renegotiated, reorganized and reaffirmed repeatedly' (Triandafyllidou 2005, 177). To incorporate ethnic Greeks still under Ottoman rule, nationalist leaders recruited unmarried, literate women to teach them Greek. Women also supported the (successful) movement to make demotic Greek the national language.

The secular, individualist constitution (1844) that emphasized continuity with Ancient Greece denied women political rights. Under Ottoman rule, 'Greekness' had been mainly a religious identity, but nationalist elites favoured secularism, blaming the Orthodox church for Greeks' long, humiliating subordination. They also promoted 'western' dress, making urban women objects of conspicuous consumption, and excluding their rural sisters. When some 'western' scholars declared modern Greeks 'Eastern Slavs', Greek nationalists began to stress their Byzantine heritage and Orthodox Christianity's role in the Eastern Roman empire. With this 'ethnic turn', Greeks stopped imitating 'westerners', and nationalists adopted a *moderate ethno-cultural model* that glorified women as 'Guardians of Greekness' and 'bearers of an oral tradition free of external influences' (Varikas 1993, 271–2). Women teachers were considered agents of national regeneration, representatives of the 'spiritual realm', and repositories and transmitters of authentic Greek culture and language. In reaction, the increasingly powerful Orthodox church insisted that women limit their reproduction of 'Greekness' to being mothers. But a strong women's movement, formed within the nationalist movement, declared *motherhood a voluntary act* and demanded full political rights and family law reform, with some success.

But in the late 1930s, the dictatorship enacted a more repressive family law code and re-traditionalized gender relations, legitimized by an *extreme ethnic nationalism* that attacked minorities and forced teachers and other professionals to portray Greece as ethnically homogeneous. When a *democratic civic model* eventually was established, many women's groups first aligned with the socialist government (PASOK), and a new constitution (1976) re-instated political rights women had gained in a brief democratic interlude (1952). But the repressive family law code remained in force until 1983, limiting women's ability to exercise their citizenship.

Eventually, an autonomous feminist movement won its repeal and won reproductive freedom based on access to contraception and to first trimester abortion. However, the women's movement's momentum quickly dissipated, leaving feminist activists increasingly detached from Greek nationalist politics.

## Women's Participation in Anti-colonial and Anti-imperial Contexts

Historically, 'civic' nations in Europe's colonizing 'great powers' denied women full citizenship and nationality rights for long periods after their founding, and as most national institutions are path-dependent, the effects of this historical legacy persist. So while European women are now part of 'the general body of citizens', they still remain subject to 'rules, regulations and policies …specific to them' (Yuval-Davis 1997, 24). (Examples include laws governing abortion and infanticide.) Virtually every nation-state using civil or common law has laws governing infanticide, prostitution, and abortion that only apply to women. Where women were active participants in independence struggles, and gained political rights when men did, they often used such rights to promote family law reforms and make governance more democratic. This also occurs in recently resurgence minority nationalisms (e.g. Catalonia, Scotland) and in most anti-colonial contexts. West's (1997) concept of 'feminist nationalism' identifies positive ideological alliances found between feminists and nationalists in Quebec, Puerto Rico, Hawai'i, and the Philippines, among others.

Women are most often active participants in national projects in anti-imperial/colonial struggles in which *whole communities must be mobilized* to win independence. Feminist scholars have emphasized cases in which participation and positive outcomes were short-lived, for example, Algeria and Ireland. They also emphasized cases in which such outcomes are long term, for example, Finland and Norway. Other conditions associated with long-term positive outcomes include an on-going need for women's participation, for example, in nation-building; a well-organized women's movement; and a good ideological 'fit' between nationalists' and feminists' conceptualizations of women's roles. Other variables that may make women's participation more effective are literacy and education.

# Conclusion

This text provides fresh insights about nationalism, opens up new dimensions for analysis, and expands established categories. It also shows that many gender scholars' beliefs that nationalist projects invariably exclude women need reconsideration given much evidence of women's participation in anti-imperial/colonial movements. The text makes an original contribution to nationalism scholarship by showing the importance of context in understanding the current effects of long-established historical legacies and the value of systematic comparison in studying women's roles in national projects and their outcomes. The comparison between the French and American revolutions in the same historical 'wave' of nationalism but in different contexts shows the effects of context—for example, colonial and anti-colonial—on patterns of gender diversity. It also shows how 'modernization' and 'nationalization' promoted French men's status, literacy, and education, but caused women's to deteriorate. While nationalization 'modernized' many men's lives, women remained privatized and unable to shape their own lives through political agency. The repressive laws and 'separate spheres' ideologies that sustained women's privatization were embedded in state institutions and nationalist discourses as historical legacies until the mid-twentieth century with effects persisting today. Masculinizing nationalist movements made recruiting and militarizing men easier; and men's monopoly over the benefits of mobilization intensified their attachment to nationalism and, arguably, national projects' propensity for violence.

The comparisons reveal different patterns of gender diversity in colonial and anti-imperial/colonial contexts. So while women's political participation in the French and American revolutions seem similar, there were important differences, for example: America's revolutionary generations acknowledged women's contributions to independence and in teaching their children republican value; while in France, women's political participation was considered dangerous and subversive. The conception of 'republican motherhood' also varies. In France, it refers to women's sexual and reproductive roles and women's privatization as 'passive' citizens without political agency, for whom formal education was not needed. In America, it refers to women's political role in transmitting republican values to their children, for which women were seen to need formal education. This 'contrast of contexts' shows how apparently similar cases in the same historical 'wave' differ because their contexts differ and offer contrasting opportunities for organizing and participating.

The text also reveals that elites may use different models of the nation at different stages and that different visions of 'the nation', and women's role in it, may be in competition. The model based on women's privatization embeds male dominance into national institutions, making it hard to overcome men's monopoly on national politics after women gained legal and political rights. But where women participate in successful independence struggles, women's movements use memories of women participants to 'feminize' nationalist discourses today. Comparing ideologies across multiple cases, and different iterations of 'modernity' or 'anti-modernity', shows how nationalism and feminism interact. Before the Second World War, most 'extreme', 'anti-modern nationalisms wanted gender relations 're-traditionalized', and used the 'disorderly women' trope to argue the 'unnaturalness' of women's political participation and its potential damage to the nation. But after the tipping point when women could vote in most countries, some 'extreme nationalists' granted women the vote (Argentina). In India, 'extreme' Hindu nationalism legitimizes high-caste women's violent campaigns against Muslim women and casteless people. This also reveals problems of 'gendering' definitions of 'modernity', since most 'modern' nation-states privatized women historically, often for centuries, and excluded them from active participation in national projects.

Incorporating evidence about gender diversity into narratives about nationalism reveals new ways of addressing the 'big questions' posed by nationalism theory, for example, by asking how women's presence or absence affects nationalist mobilizations. This text's approaches also help formulate 'big questions' that have long escaped nationalism theorists, such as by introducing sex/gender into Hearn's claim that 'modernity' has multiple forms. Historically, colonizing 'great powers' made claims about being 'modern' to justify their rule over people they maintained were 'backward', partly on the basis of how they treated 'their' women. Today, dominant nationalists use claims that internal 'others'—immigrants, Muslims, blacks—oppress 'their women' in ways unacceptable in 'modern' societies, to justify excluding and oppressing them. This text suggests many avenues for further theorizing, for example, by analysing race/nation interactions and interactions that relate 'nation' to forms of diversity in addition to 'ethnicity' and language. It also suggests the value of new empirical research and of comparing existing cases to generate fresh theoretical insights.

# References

Albanese, Patrizia. 2006. *Mothers of the Nation*. Toronto: University of Toronto Press.
Anderson, Benedict. 1991. *Imagined Communities*. London: Verso.
Canovan, Margaret. 1996. *Nationhood and Political Theory*. Cheltenham: Edward Elgar.
Chatterjee, Partha. 1989. Colonialism, Nationalism and the Colonized Woman. *American Ethnologist* 16: 622–633.
Cockburn, Cynthia. 1998. *The Space Between Us*. New York: St.Martin's Press.
Eatwell, Roger. 2003. *Fascism*. London: Chatto and Windus.
Ely, Geoff. 2000. Culture, Nation and Gender. In *Gendered Nations*, ed. Ida Blom, Karen Hagerman, and Catherine Hall, 27–40. London: Bloomsbury Publishing.
Goodin, Robert E., and Charles Tilly. 2006. *Handbook of Contextual Political Analysis*. Oxford: Oxford University Press.
Hearn, Jonathan. 2006. *Rethinking Nationalism*. Basingstoke: Palgrave Macmillan.
Hutchinson, John, and Antony Smith. 1994. *Nationalism*. Oxford: Oxford University Press.

Jacoby, Tami A. 1999. Feminism, Nationalism and Difference. *Women's Studies International Forum* 22 (5): 511–523.
Jayawardena, Kumari, ed. 1986. *Feminism and Nationalism in the Third World.* London: Zed Press.
Joseph, Suad. 1997. The Public/Private—The Imagined Boundary in the Imagined Nation. *Feminist Review* 57: 73–92.
Kaplan, Gisela. 1997. Comparative Europe: Feminism and Nationalism. In *Feminist Nationalism*, ed. Lois A. West, 3–40. London: Routledge.
Koonz, Claudia. 1987. *Mothers in the Fatherland.* New York: St. Martin's.
Maxwell, Alexander. 2016. *Gender and Nationalism: A Friendly Exchange.* H-Nationalism website, June 8. https://networks.h-net.org/node/3911/discussions/129163/gender-and-nationalism-friendly-exchange
de Sève, Micheline. 2000. Women's National and Gendered Identity. *Journal of Canadian Studies* 35 (3): 61–79.
Skocpol, Theda, and Margaret Somers. 1980. The Uses of Comparative History in Macro-social Inquiry. *Comparative Studies in Society and History* 22: 174–197.
Sluga, Glenda. 1998. Identity, Gender, and the History of European Nations and Nationalisms. *Nations and Nationalism* 4 (1): 87–112.
Smith, Anthony D. 1986. *The Ethnic Origins of Nations.* Oxford: Blackwell.
———. 1998. *Nationalism and Modernism.* London: Routledge.
Tohidi, Nayereh. 1994. Modernity, Islamization and Women in Iran. In *Gender and National Identity*, ed. Valentine M. Moghadam, 110–147. London: Zed Books.
Triandafyllidou, Anna. 2005. When, What and How Is the Nation? In *When Is the Nation: Towards an Understanding of Theories of Nationalism*, ed. Atsuko Ichijo and Gordano Uzelac, 177–198. London: Routledge.
Varikas, Eleni. 1993. Gender and National Identity in Fin de Siecle Greece. *Gender and History* 5 (2): 269–283.
Vickers, Jill. 2006. Bringing Nations In. *International Feminist Journal of Politics* 8 (1): 84–108.
Vickers, Jill, and Athanasia Vouloukos. 2007. Changing Gender/Nation Relations. *Nationalism and Ethnic Politics.* 13 (1): 501–538.
West, Lois A., ed. 1997. *Feminist Nationalism.* London: Routledge.
Wiesner-Hanks, Merry E. 2000. *Women and Gender in Early Modern Europe.* 2nd. ed. Cambridge: Cambridge University Press.

Yuval-Davis, Nira, and Floya Anthias. eds. 1989. Introduction. *Woman-Nation-State*. London: Routledge.
Yuval-Davis, Nira. 1997. *Gender and Nation*. London: Sage.
Zagarri, Rosemary. 2007. *Revolutionary Backlash: Women and Politics in the Early American Republic*. Philadelphia: U. of Pennsylvania Press.

# 18

## Territorial Autonomy, Nationalisms, and Women's Equality and Rights: The Case of the Hong Kong Special Administrative Region

### Susan J. Henders

Decentralized state architecture and multilevel governance (MLG) is often accompanied by conceptions of territorialized political community and collective identities infused with what David Campbell (1998, 143) terms a "nationalist imaginary". The present chapter explores how nationalist-infused formal, meso-level autonomy arrangements affect women's rights and equality, or as Vickers (2013, 1) puts it, how "different state architectures affect and are affected by interactions between territorial and non-territorial interests and identities". The focus is the Hong Kong Special Administrative Region (HKSAR), whose meso-level autonomy arrangement aims to reconcile People's Republic of China (PRC) government nationalist claims to Hong Kong with claims of a distinct

---

Eliza Lee, Jill Vickers, and the volume editors and reviewers provided invaluable comments on a chapter draft. The author is also grateful for conversations with Staci Ford, Puja Kapai, Eliza Lee, and Lisa Moore and a visitorship at the Hong Kong Institute for the Social Sciences and Humanities, the University of Hong Kong, during the research. The chapter's viewpoints and weaknesses are solely the author's responsibility.

S. J. Henders (✉)
York University, Toronto, ON, Canada

© The Author(s) 2018
J. Mulholland et al. (eds.), *Gendering Nationalism*,
https://doi.org/10.1007/978-3-319-76699-7_18

territorial political identity in the latter. In 1997, Hong Kong became part of the PRC under the 1984 Sino-British Joint Declaration (JD), which promised the former British colony considerable autonomy and self-rule for 50 years except in foreign affairs and defense.

Hong Kong's experience affirms that devolving authority to meso-level governments can both advance and inhibit gains in rights and equality for women (Ortbals et al. 2011), depending on structural, institutional, and ideational factors. The pre-1997 negotiations and preparations for the HKSAR caused a political legitimacy crisis that opened up wider constitutional reforms, creating opportunities for feminist activists to promote women-friendly laws and policies. Feminist concerns did not impel devolution, but its timing and political conditions facilitated limited women-friendly outcomes. However, after the 1997 handover, the autonomy arrangement became a power base for conservative elites who supported patriarchal social relations and resisted women-friendly policies. Nationalist politics have blocked democratization, supported the institutionalization of laissez-faire capitalist norms and social relations, and normalized racialized and ethnicized othering, harming progress on women's equality and rights.

## Nationalist Politics, Territorial Autonomy Arrangements, and Women's Equality and Rights

The claims based on fused territorial identity and political groupness that characterize nationalist politics often aim at legitimating political actions. They assume that nation-like entities are the "basic constituents of social life, chief protagonists of social conflicts, and fundamental units of social analysis" (Brubaker et al. 2006, 7, 9). Gender is central to nationalist claims in multiple ways explored in the present volume. Fundamentally, by ignoring or minimizing internal differences based on gender, nationalist claims create gendered silences and exclusions. These are experienced intersectionally, as gendered individuals are differently situated in mutually reinforcing fields of power related to class, ethnicity, race, nation, and citizenship status, among other cleavages often erased by nationalism (see Hill Collins 2000, 18). While nationalist claims are often "state-led" or "state-seeking" (Peterson 2000, 55), they may also legitimate demands for meso-level territorial autonomy. Whether the "group" concerned is deemed a nation, a minority community, or another territorial political entity, the associated nationalist claims "misrepresent the diversity … within the borders it names", encoding it in exclusionary silences that harm many women in intersectional ways (Eisenstein 2000, 35). Thus, meso-level autonomy arrangements are important sites for examining the consequences for women of interactions between decentralized state architectures and claims of nationalist-infused identities and interests at the meso- and state-levels.

Elsewhere, I argued that meso-level autonomy arrangements often create legal and institutional frameworks denying rights and equality to many women and other vulnerable residents because they entrench exclusionary understandings of territorial identities and values in the institutions, discourses, and practices of autonomy (Henders 2010, 23–24, 224–228). However, autonomy arrangements also protect the identity and values of minority territorial communities within states in ways that can advance women's citizenship. As Kabeer (2005) argues, it is through community claims and obligations that individual women achieve many basic material and identity needs; the political challenge is protecting collective identities in ways that see patriarchy, classism, racism, and other exclusion as equally damaging to a minority community as state-imposed majority preferences. Understanding the conditions that promote this outcome requires comparative case analysis, while individual case studies help identify and test explanatory propositions.

The literature on gender, decentralized state architecture, and MLG offers findings useful for studying Hong Kong. This is despite case-specific attributes that complicate its use in theory-building. First, the literature mainly focuses on federalism, MLG, and meso-level devolution in established or emerging liberal democratic states.[1] However, the PRC is a unitary state, with decentralized features somewhat akin to federal states (Henders 2013). It is also an authoritarian state that, nevertheless,

---

[1] Exceptions include Haussman et al. 2010.

allows the territory's 7.3 million residents comparatively extensive liberal rights and freedoms while blocking democratically accountable government. Further, the literature mainly concerns the outcomes for women of *decentralization within existing states*, whereas Hong Kong's arrangement came about to facilitate *its incorporation into the PRC* after more than 150 years of British rule (see Henders 1997, 526–528). There have been sharp tensions between state nationalist claims aimed at legitimating PRC sovereignty and influence in the territory, and nationalist-infused Hong Kong identity claims aimed at legitimating the territory's political autonomy and, recently, demands by a minority of residents for the community's self-determination and independence.

How has this affected women's rights and equality? According to the gender and state architecture literature, a key issue is whether a meso-level autonomy arrangement becomes a permanent power base for conservative elites (Vickers et al. 2010, 233–234). It also matters *when* meso-level autonomy arrangements are established: Vickers (2013, 2) and Sawer and Vickers (2010, 9), drawing on Haussman (2005) and Mackay (2010a), argue that meso-governments in older federations often have impeded women-friendly reforms, while those in recently federalizing states have sometimes expanded opportunities for increasing women's descriptive representation and activism. This is partly because of the changing MLG context—international legal and political norms have become more favorable to women's rights and equality in recent decades. Sawer and Vickers (2010, 7, 10–12) also argue that MLG contexts in Europe and liberal democratic federations may provide more sites for women's representation and participation, enabling women's groups to choose a more hospitable policy venue when confronting meso-level barriers. According to research on Scotland, Wales, and Northern Ireland (Chaney et al. 2007), the constitutional reforms accompanying meso-level devolution also can create political opportunities for women activists successfully to push for women's equality and rights.

Comparative study of liberal democratic, democratizing, and non-democratic contexts suggests that non-democracy decreases opportunities for women's groups to challenge discriminatory and exclusionary policies and processes, even if formal democracy does not necessarily prevent autonomy arrangements from becoming conservative power bases

(Henders 2010, 224–228). For instance, Mackay (2010b, 157, 160) argues that strong sub-state social-democratic values have helped prevent this in Scotland since devolution. Ortbals et al. (2011, 21) suggest "stable leftist governance" in the central state can be a key factor. Taking the analysis to a non-democratic context, the analysis of the HKSAR below explores how nationalist-infused politics have interacted with institutional, ideational, and structural factors identified in the literature, as well as the political economy context, to produce gains, but also barriers to advancing women's equality and rights.

## The Transition to 1997 and Women's Equality and Rights

Until the 1990s, the British Hong Kong government, backed by a conservative business community and local Chinese elites, largely resisted recognizing women's rights and equality, arguing it had to respect local customs and maintain a laissez-faire capitalist economy. Lack of democracy facilitated this, as did reliance on ruling the mostly ethnic Chinese local population by co-opting largely male conservative business and rural elites, who mediated the political representation of women's concerns (Lam and Tong 2006, 10). Further, until the 1980s, elite white expatriate and middle-class ethnic Chinese women dominated the women's movement. Focused mainly on charitable activities and service provision, the movement sidelined progressive demands for rights and equality as well as many livelihood concerns of the poor majority (Lam and Tong 2006, 10; Ng and Ng 2002, 21).

The 1984 JD, and the autonomy arrangement it promised, ushered in significant political change and a political crisis that eventually increased women's formal rights and equality. The crisis owed much to how the arrangement institutionalized capitalist and nationalist claims and norms: it aimed to facilitate Britain's honorable departure while legitimating Hong Kong's "return to the motherland" and ending China's "century of humiliation" under Western and Japanese imperialism; it also tried to ensure continuation of Hong Kong's liberal, capitalist economy, institutions, and way of life after the territory became part of the PRC, an authoritarian state still experimenting with marketization and opening to the world economy. The PRC government claimed to be decolonizing and re-nationalizing Hong Kong, but many Hong Kong people felt excluded from decision-making about their future and unsettled by the JD's vague promise to elect the Chief Executive and legislature with no method or date specified.

Consequently, the 1984–1997 period saw a strengthened sense of a shared territorial identity distinct from the PRC, helping precipitate the legitimacy crisis. Historically, Hong Kong people had largely resisted strong identification with a state, culture, or place, instead identifying with the global market; hard work and luck; and self-sufficient families (Mathews et al. 2008, 12; Lee 2003, 8), the latter dependent on women's social reproductive labor. Now residents were increasingly directed to turn their primary political identity and loyalty toward the PRC. Many local business elites aligned themselves with the PRC state as patronage, and economic opportunities in China's rapidly expanding economy became "a backdoor route to nationalism" (Mathews et al. 2008, 1, 15, 18). Other people demanded stronger guarantees for civil rights and freedoms as well as democratization to protect collective values and sometimes greater social citizenship for the poorer majority. Questions about the legitimacy of the 1997 handover and the ability of the autonomy arrangement to protect Hong Kong's distinctness peaked with the brutal suppression of the 1989 Tiananmen Square protests in Beijing. The British Hong Kong government introduced constitutional reforms to try to quell fears. Crucially for women, the colonial legislature passed a historic *Bill of Rights Ordinance* in 1991, making international human rights norms directly enforceable through Hong Kong law and introducing the first directly elected Legislative Council seats.

Although not impelled by government feminist commitments (Fischler 2003, 48, 54–55; Ng and Ng 2002, 13), the reforms opened the way for advances in women's formal rights. Previously the constitution failed to recognize women's legal right to equality (Lam and Tong 2006, 11), and local laws did not prohibit sex discrimination or harassment. The British government had ratified the Convention on the Elimination of All Forms of Discrimination Against Women (CEDAW), but not extended it to

Hong Kong. The equality rights provisions of the main international human rights covenants were unenforceable in local courts. Now, the *Bill of Rights Ordinance* explicitly recognized that men and women were equally entitled to civil and political rights (Art. 1), if initially only in the public sphere. In 1994, the government also repealed a long-standing law prohibiting female rural land inheritance in the New Territories district of Hong Kong, while the 1995 *Sex Discrimination Ordinance* forbade discrimination based on sex, marital status, and pregnancy (Petersen 2003, 23, 29; Lim 2015, 45–50). Then, in 1996 an Equal Opportunities Commission (EOC) was established to enforce the ordinance, although feminists criticized its weakness (Ng and Ng 2002, 15, 22–24). In 1996, the UK government finally extended CEDAW to Hong Kong and made its first report on its implementation to the United Nations (UN) CEDAW Committee.

The constitutional reforms enabling these women-friendly advances created new channels for influencing policy favoring women. The introduction of directly elected legislative seats alone did achieve this, especially as the new political parties were largely male dominated, and even those supporting democratization and human rights reforms did not prioritize nor always recognize gender issues (see ibid., 22–23). However, organized women and individual feminists used the ground-breaking 1991 election campaign to press gender issues, alongside sympathetic directly elected as well as government-appointed women legislators (Petersen 2003, 23–25; Lim 2015, 36–44).

Consistent with gender, state architectures, and MLG literature findings, the timing of devolution and specific MLG arrangements contributed to women's gains in Hong Kong.[2] Preparations for establishing the HKSAR occurred at a time of more women-friendly international norms and processes. The extension of CEDAW and other international human rights treaties to Hong Kong, by the British and then the PRC government, established a relatively women-friendly international political space in which local women's groups could lobby for change in the territory. From the late 1990s, Hong Kong women's groups and non-governmental

---

[2] Due to space limitations, the effects in Hong Kong of central state women's policies are not examined here.

organizations used the fora provided UN human rights treaty-bodies to criticize weak implementation of treaty obligations by the British and, after 1997, the PRC governments (Petersen 2003, 42). These treaty-bodies lack authority over states, so they rely on "naming and shaming" governments to improve compliance. Nevertheless, the CEDAW Committee was instrumental in pushing the HKSAR government to establish the Women's Commission in 2001, after years of lobbying by women's groups (Lim 2015, 44–45). With a mandate to advance women's opportunities, status, and rights and mainstream these in policy processes, the Women's Commission has drawn criticism from women's groups claiming it is conservative and has weak authority (Kennett et al. 2013, 94–95).

# Women's Rights and Equality Since Establishment of the HKSAR

During the transition to the 1997 handover to the PRC, therefore, converging factors brought women's issues onto the political agenda and helped advance limited formal equality rights. However, substantive political and socioeconomic inequalities for women continued, including after the handover. The post-1997 autonomy arrangement did not cause this outcome but enabled it. Its non-democratic and laissez-faire capitalist norms and practices institutionalized the power of conservative elites and a gendered political economy while supporting resistance to women-friendly reforms in government, business, and wider society. Nationalist-infused norms, practices, and politics helped legitimate the arrangement, harming most women while normalizing an ethnic hierarchy particularly damaging to racialized minority women. Before detailing these arguments, the section outlines some key indicators of women's political and socioeconomic inequality since 1997.

## Substantive Inequality in Post-1997 Hong Kong

Since the establishment of the autonomy arrangement, women have remained under-represented in formal political decision-making and

HKSAR government administration. The proportion of women legislative councilors increased to a peak of 18 percent but then fell to 14 percent after the 2016 election (Women's Commission 2011, 31; Legislative Council 2016). Two women were among six legislators disqualified for taking the oath of office in insufficiently nationalist ways represented by authorities as insulting the PRC or not clearly affirming the legitimacy of PRC sovereignty over Hong Kong (Chung and Lau 2017). Until recently, women rarely led political parties (DeGolyer 2013, 125). In 2007, women were just 13.6 percent of the Election Committee that nominates the Chief Executive, for appointment by the central government (CEDAW 2012, para 7.5). Since 1997, two women have served as Chief Secretary (the civil service head), and the proportion of women in government directorate-level posts has increased, but only to 31 percent as of 2009. In 2011, women held 21.4 percent of Executive Committee (cabinet) seats not held by civil servants (Women's Commission 2011, 31). In 2014, women made up just over 32 percent of government-appointed advisory and statutory bodies (Equal Opportunities Commission 2015, para 12; CEDAW 2012, para 7.12). There has never been a woman judge on the Court of Final Appeal (Court of Final Appeal 2014).

Women's socioeconomic equality also continues and has worsened since 1997 by some measures. Near equality in educational attainment has not translated into equal employment opportunities, remuneration, or work conditions (Lee 2003, 5; DeGolyer 2013, 13; Kennett et al. 2013, 88). By 2015, 53.7 percent of the poor were women and a full two-thirds of the working poor (Oxfam 2016, 2–3, 14). Women suffer disproportionately from the HKSAR government's minimal adoption of international labor standards, such as for minimum wages, regulated working hours, and anti-workplace discrimination for mothers and pregnant women (Kennett et al. 2013, xii, 52–55, 100; Wu, Alice 2016a, b). A residual approach to public social protection disadvantages women, not least because policies gear the limited benefits available to the lifetime paid employment patterns typical of men and of women with working spouses (Leung Lai-ching 2004, 164–166). Gendered exclusion has also been accentuated by poor public social protection for old age (elderly women are the largest group of poor individuals), unemployment, maternity, and work-related injury, despite some government-subsidized housing and healthcare (see Kennett et al. 2013, xii, 40–45, 52–55). The exclusion experienced by racialized minority women is detailed later.

## Nationalism, Capitalism, and Non-democracy

Since 1997 state nationalist claims and policies have intensified, aiming to legitimate the autonomy arrangement, which, in turn, institutionalizes PRC sovereignty and ethno-nationalist claims to Hong Kong. This creates barriers to the advancement of women's substantive equality. Alongside the economic and status-based incentives that foster PRC nationalism in Hong Kong, mentioned earlier, state nationalism infuses the territory through such means as PRC flags on official buildings, media, and government discourses, policies and laws. Hong Kong identity claims infused with nationalist understandings of the coincidence of identity, territory, and political community have also increased. Many residents emotionally identify with a Chinese nation, but not necessarily the Chinese state or government (Mathews et al. 2008, xv). Many have publicly protested state nationalist-infused policies such as proposed curriculum reforms, new national security laws, and the blocking of democratization for Hong Kong. Since 2009, the increase in residents' self-identification with Hong Kong and declining PRC identification has been steep, and "localist" movements and political parties have emerged amid a sense of mounting threats to Hong Kong's distinctness from PRC and HKSAR government policies, mainland migrants and tourists, and economic development. Even establishment elites and HKSAR officials have sometimes used localist claims to legitimate policy (Ping and Kwong 2014, 1088–1089, 1100). In 2016, localist parties elected six legislative councilors, one amassing the territory's highest vote numbers. This triggered intensified state nationalist claims; the disqualification of six legislators because of how they took their oaths of office, noted earlier; and government assertions that demanding self-determination and/or independence for Hong Kong threatened PRC sovereignty and security.

These competing state and sub-state nationalisms have complicated and sharpened the already polarized political atmosphere in which women's organizations operate. Like most political parties and civil society groups, most women's organization align themselves (or are seen as aligned) with two opposing camps defined by central-local tensions, orientations, and political issues: the pro-PRC establishment camp and the pro-democracy opposition. This division weakens women's groups' cooperation to advance women's equality and rights. Groups oriented to the two camps often differently respond to PRC claims of "nation" and "Chineseness" in relation to gender issues, symbols, and discourses; have unequal material, social resources, and class positions; and take divergent stances on feminism (Fischler 2003, 55, 58). The camp centered on the Hong Kong Federation of Women has been characterized as "middle class, non-feminist, [and] pro-Beijing" (Lam and Tong 2006, 13). Critics accuse it of weak leadership and failing publicly to challenge the patriarchal, PRC government created and Hong Kong statutory bodies (e.g., the EOC and Women's Commission) where its members sometimes hold appointments. Women's groups allied with the pro-democracy camp have less policy influence and fewer resources and are disadvantaged in competitions for government funding. Their members rarely hold positions on statutory or PRC bodies (ibid., 13–14, 21–22; Lee 2012, 547–548). Pro-PRC groups often stress consensus politics and social harmony, "loyalty and service" to the PRC, and "unity" and "stability". To opposition-oriented women's groups, these stances reinforce the very social order that impedes women's substantive equality and rights (Fischler 2003, 69; Lam and Tong 2006, 26).

When the central and HKSAR governments block democratization in the name of sovereignty and national security as well as political and economic stability, they also limit women's descriptive and substantive representation and opportunities to challenge the prevailing gendered, classed political economy (Kennett et al. 2013, 84–85; Lam and Tong 2006, 7). The gendered, classed Election Committee, discussed earlier, exists because the central government and establishment interests block democratic direct election of the Chief Executive. Their unwillingness to allow a fully directly elected Legislative Council also especially marginalizes women and poorer residents. The 30 traditional functional constituency seats in the 70-seat body are chosen by occupational, social, and political sectors where conservative business, professional elites, and other pro-PRC interests dominate. This determination of "function" disenfranchises those doing precarious work or unpaid social reproductive labor or who are unemployed (Hong Kong Women's Coalition for Beijing

'95 1997; Young and Law 2004; Migrants Rights International 2003). As such, few women have ever held traditional functional constituency seats, faring better in polls for the 35 directly elected seats. Women held no functional constituency seats after the 2012 and 2016 elections.

If pro-democracy and localist political parties and movements have been comparatively open to women's representation and issues, they still conceptualize democratization and human rights—as well as the collective values of Hong Kong—with little attention to sex/gender specificities, including gendered, classed, and racialized socioeconomic inequalities (see Fischler 2003, 65, 68; Lim 2015, 129). The demands of the mostly male-led 2014 Umbrella/Occupy Central Protests focused on directly electing the Chief Executive. However, after incidents of sex/gender-based violence against female protesters by some opponents, some women protesters held a SlutWalk and used street art to denounce rape culture as well as non-democracy (Wu, Rose 2016b, 98–100; Kuo and Timmons 2014).

State nationalism and dominant discourses of Hong Kong identity that stress its capitalist ethos (see Lau and Kuan 1988) also legitimate the laissez-faire capitalist values entrenched in the autonomy arrangement, thereby undermining women's socioeconomic equality. The Basic Law of the HKSAR requires government to maintain "expenditure within the limits of revenue", low taxes, prudent fiscal reserves, and Hong Kong's free-port status (BL 107, 108, 111, 114); it provides for a land-lease system that supports property-based wealth inequalities (BL 120–123). The quasi-constitutional status of these norms delegitimizes the demands of women's and other civil society groups for government economic intervention and policy changes to improve social citizenship. Establishment discourses of Hong Kong belonging stress reliance on families, neighborhoods, and communities for care and social protection, sometimes associating this with ethnic "Chineseness"; such norms disproportionately rest on women's unpaid, precarious, and underpaid work (Lee 2003, 4–5; Kennett et al. 2013, 37).

## Racialization and Gender

The claimed *ethnic Chineseness* of the Hong Kong identity fostered by the autonomy arrangement, as a state-nationalizing and laissez-faire capitalist project, has particularly harmed poorer, racialized women not ethnicized as Chinese or as Hong Kong belongers. White expatriate women often benefit from residual high status from colonial times and experience less socioeconomic and legal marginalization (Law and Lee 2012, 121–122). The result is what Sautman (2004, 115) has called a "quasi-ethnocracy"— a political order largely favoring Hong Kong ethnic Chinese but that is also gendered, classed, and racialized. Within its foundation are PRC nationality norms, which prescribe and normalize the BL's ethnic, classed, and racialized criteria for access to permanent residency, HKSAR passports, and high public office (ibid., 111–112).

Many recent mainland PRC women immigrants are marginalized by such nationalist-infused norms, policies, and laws. Hong Kong residents often presume mainland newcomers are cultural inferiors and an economic burden on society, even though most territorial residents have Chinese ethnicity and come from families originally from the mainland, and even though many mainland women are married to or have long-term relationships with Hong Kong men. Newcomer mainland women experience high levels of unemployment, precarious employment, and poverty due to exclusion and stigma in the job market and in workplaces and when seeking public services and social protection. Those who are single parents or married with children are additionally disadvantaged because of childcare shortages, social program residency requirements, and immigration policies restricting family reunification (Sautman 2004, 113; Kennett et al. 2013, 110–111, 120–123; Pun and Wu 2004; Law and Lee 2012). Meanwhile, government immigration and citizenship policies favor wealthier, better-educated, mostly male mainland immigrants as creators of transnational capital (Wu 2003, 136, 141; Lam and Tong 2006). The HKSAR government claims the stability and prosperity of Hong Kong justify such policies, deploying exclusionary discourses (Pun and Wu 2004, 127–133). In recent years, some localist groups have othered mainlanders too, sometimes using verbal and physical attacks.

Also marginalized by the quasi-ethnocracy are more than 340,000 mostly female foreign domestic workers, largely from the Philippines and Indonesia. Their political participation, social inclusion, and economic security are undermined by ethnically based policies denying them residency rights even if they have lived in Hong Kong for more than seven years, the usual qualification. They also lack adequate employment rights and protection (Leung and RainLily 2015, 4, 9–10).

Additionally, a smaller population of racialized ethnic minority women experience substantive inequality and rights deficits because of discrimination based on ethnicity/race, class, as well as gender. Many are Hong Kong born but denied PRC nationality. In her meta-study of the territory's ethnic minorities, Puja Kapai (2015) shows that these women have been less likely than other residents to participate in public and political life, get a university education, or hold managerial, professional, or administrative positions. They were also more likely to be poor and unable to access social programs and government, legal, and first responder services. While ethnic minority men also experience considerable disadvantage and prejudice, women suffered disproportionately. While many factors contributed to their exclusion, intersectional, racialized, gendered prejudices were the primary causes (ibid., Chap. 3, 13–17, Key Observations and Recommendations, 4).

If racialized women are excluded by the autonomy arrangement, with its ethno-nationalist-infused, gendered, and classed politics, some residents have been pushing for change. Kapai's meta-study points to the possibility of a discursive shift conducive to a more inclusive citizenship for racialized minority women. Such a shift is evident in the high-profile 2015 film "Ten Years", which portrays a localist movement that includes a Hong Kong-born woman of Pakistani heritage.[3] Further, the manifesto of the localist political party, Demosisto, states that Hong Kong's character "[embraces] multiplicity" based on gender, class, ethnic, national, and other cleavages (Demosisto 2016).

## Conclusions

The Hong Kong case suggests that the affects of meso-level autonomy arrangements on women's equality and rights depend on the nature of state- and meso-level nationalist-infused politics as well as how this politics interacts with the timing and processes of the arrangement's adoption, MLG,

---

[3] Thanks to Eliza Lee for this observation.

political institutions including state- and meso-level regime type, *and* the political economy. Comparative case study research could identify generalizable patterns in how these interconnected factors influence whether autonomy arrangements become permanent power bases for conservative elites supportive of patriarchy. In Hong Kong, women's formal equality improved under the constitutional reforms trigged by the pre-1997 political legitimacy crisis, supported by propitious timing with respect to the UN-based MLG context. However, the post-handover autonomy arrangement impeded improvements in women's substantive political and socio-economic equality by institutionalizing non-democracy, laissez-faire capitalist norms, and the dominance of a central state-business alliance. Nationalist-infused state- and meso-level identity claims, politics, and norms legitimate this outcome. They normalize the political dominance of the pro-PRC/pro-democracy cleavage, with its emphasis on central-local relations and contestation over formal democracy and civil and political rights and sideline issues of women's substantive exclusion. Nationalisms have also reinforced ethnically based understandings of self and other harmful to racialized minority women. Yet, given the centrality of community for individual women's identity and livelihoods, getting rid of the autonomy arrangement is no answer. Rather, it is to move toward a politics and understanding of meso-level collective identities and values that prioritize reducing patriarchy, classism, and racialization as much as creating meaningful, formally democratic self-government for Hong Kong as a whole.

This case study points to two more questions needing comparative case study research on other non-democratic and democratizing contexts. First, is formal democratization necessary if meso-level autonomy arrangements are to advance women's equality and rights, both formal and substantive? Under what conditions do such arrangements encourage meso-level collective identity claims supportive of these goals? The experience of established democracies suggests that formal democracy and associated liberal rights and freedoms alone do not guarantee woman-friendly meso-level arrangements and that the nature of nationalist politics is a key conditioning factor. This suggests that, in Hong Kong, formal democratization alone would not bring a substantively more woman-friendly autonomy arrangement without a reduction in exclusionary state and substate nationalist politics that electoral competition itself has often enflamed. However, formal democratization could likely also open more channels for women to challenge interconnected gendered, classed, and ethnic and racialized exclusion, including in the laws, policies, and political economy of the autonomy arrangement and its associated understandings of collective identity and values. Nevertheless, with democratization unlikely in Hong Kong in the short term, women's groups need additional strategies to push for change too.

# References

Brubaker, Rogers, Margit Feischmidt, Jon Fox, and Liana Grancea. 2006. *Nationalist Politics and Everyday Ethnicity in a Transylvanian Town*. Princeton: Princeton University Press.

Campbell, David. 1998. *National Deconstruction: Violence, Identity, and Justice in Bosnia*. Minneapolis: University of Minnesota Press.

CEDAW. 2012. Consideration of Reports Submitted by States Parties under Article 18 of the Convention on the Elimination of All Forms of Discrimination Against Women, Combined Seventh and Eighth Periodic Reports of States Parties, Hong Kong, China (UN Doc. CEDAW/C/CHN-HKG/7-8), 20 January. http://www2.ohchr.org/english/bodies/cedaw/docs/CEDAW-C-CHN-HKG-78_en.pdf Accessed 15 Oct 2016.

Chaney, Paul, Fiona Mackay, and Laura McAllister. 2007. *Women, Politics and Constitutional Change: The First Years of the National Assembly for Wales*. Cardiff: University of Wales Press.

Chung, Chris and Kimmy Lau. 2017. Court Ruling Disqualifying Hong Kong Lawmakers over Oath-taking Controversy 'A Declaration of War'. *South China Morning Post*. July 14. Updated July 15, 2017. http://www.scmp.com/news/hong-kong/politics/article/2102609/four-more-hong-kong-lawmakers-disqualified-over-oath-taking. Accessed 29 Aug 2017.

Court of Final Appeal. HKSAR. 2014. *The Judges*. Hong Kong: HKSAR Court of Final Appeal. http://www.hkcfa.hk/en/about/who/judges/introduction/index.html. Accessed 15 Oct 2016.

DeGolyer, Michael E. 2013. *The Changing Faces of Hong Kong Women in the Community and National Context, 1994–2010*. February. Hong Kong: Civic Exchange and the Women's Foundation.

Demosisto. 2016. *Mission: Self-Standing: Shaping the Character of Hong Kong and Embracing Multiplicity*. Hong Kong: Demosisto. https://www.demosisto.hk/mission?lang=en. Accessed 9 Oct 2016.

Eisenstein, Zillah. 2000. "Writing Bodies on the Nation for the Globe." In *Women, States and Nationalism: At Home in the Nation?*, edited by Sita Ranchod-Nilsson and Mary Ann Tétreault, 35–53. London: Routledge.

Equal Opportunities Commission. HKSAR. 2015. Office of the High Commissioner for Human Rights, United Nations Equal Participation in Political and Public Affairs in Hong Kong Submission from the Equal Opportunities Commission, Hong Kong. Jan. Geneva: Office of the High Commissioner for Human Rights. United Nations. http://www.ohchr.org/Documents/Issues/EqualParticipation/contributions/EOC-HKSAR.pdf. Accessed 15 Oct 2016.

Fischler, Lisa. 2003. Women's Activism During Hong Kong's Political Transition. In *Gender and Change in Hong Kong: Globalisation, Postcolonialism and Chinese Patriarchy*, ed. Eliza W.Y. Lee, 49–77. Vancouver: University of British Columbia Press.

Haussman, Melissa. 2005. *Abortion Politics in North America*. Boulder and London: Lynne Rienner.

Haussman, Melissa, Marian Sawer, and Jill Vickers, eds. 2010. *Federalism, Feminism, and Multilevel Governance*. Farnham: Ashgate.

Henders, Susan J. 1997. Cantonisation: Historical Paths to Territorial Autonomy for Regional Cultural Communities. *Nations and Nationalism* 3 (4): 521–540.

———. 2010. *Territoriality, Asymmetry, and Autonomy: Catalonia, Corsica, Hong Kong, and Tibet*. New York: Palgrave Macmillan.

———. 2013. Assessing Hybridity in the People's Republic of China: The Impact of Post-Mao Decentralization. In *The Routledge Handbook on Regionalism and Federalism*, ed. John Loughlin, Wilfried Swenden, and John Kincaid, 371–386. New York: Routledge.

Hill Collins, Patricia. 2000. *Black Feminist Thought*. 2nd ed. New York: Routledge.

Hong Kong Women's Coalition for Beijing '95. 1997. Alternative Report on Women in Hong Kong. In *EnGendering Hong Kong Society: A Gender Perspective of Women's Status*, ed. Fanny M. Cheung, 385–394. Hong Kong: Chinese University Press.

Kabeer, Naila. 2005. Introduction: The Search for Inclusive Citizenship: Meanings and Expressions in an Interconnected World. In *Inclusive Citizenship: Meanings and Expressions*, ed. Naila Kabeer, 1–29. London: Zed.

Kapai, Puja. 2015. Status of Ethnic Minorities Report, 1997–2014. Hong Kong: Zubin Foundation and Centre for Comparative and Public Law, Faculty of Law, University of Hong Kong. http://www.law.hku.hk/ccpl/pub/EMreport.html. Accessed 5 Oct 2016.

Kennett, Patricia, Chan Kam Wah, Chung Kim Wah, Pun Ngai, and Lucille Lok Sun Ngan. 2013. Governance and Citizenship in East Asia: Beijing, Hong Kong, Taipei, and Seoul. *Research Report Series* 20. Hong Kong: Centre for Social Policy Studies, Department of Applied Social Sciences, Hong Kong Polytechnic University, June.

Kuo, Lily and Heather Timmons. 2014. The Umbrella Movement Marks a Coming of Age for Hong Kong's 'Princess' Generation. *Quartz*. Nov 14. http://qz.com/285345/the-umbrella-movement-marks-a-coming-of-age-for-hong-kongs-princess-generation/. Accessed 15 Sept 2016.

Lai-Ching, Leung. 2004. Engendering Citizenship. In *Remaking Citizenship in Hong Kong: Community, Nation, and the Global City*, ed. Agnes S. Ku and Ngai Pun, 157–173. London: Routledge.

Lam, Wai-Man, and Irene L.K. Tong. 2006. Political Change and the Women's Movement in Hong Kong and Macau. *Asian Journal of Women's Studies* 12 (1): 7–35.

Lau, Siu-Kai, and Hsin-Chi Kuan. 1988. *The Ethos of the Hong Kong Chinese*. Hong Kong: Chinese University Press.

Law, Kam-Yee, and Kim-Ming Lee. 2012. The Myth of Multiculturalism in 'Asia's World City': Incomprehensive Policies for Ethnic Minorities in Hong Kong. *Journal of Asian Public Policy* 5 (1): 117–134.

Lee, Eliza W.Y. 2003. Introduction: Gender and Change in Hong Kong. In *Gender and Change in Hong Kong: Globalisation, Postcolonialism and Chinese Patriarchy*, ed. Eliza W.Y. Lee, 3–22. Vancouver: University of British Columbia Press.

———. 2012. The New Public Management Reform of State-Funded Social Service Nonprofit Organizations and the Changing Politics of Welfare in Hong Kong. *International Review of Administrative Sciences* 78 (3): 537–553.

Legislative Council. HKSAR. 2016. Members Biographies. Hong Kong: HKSAR Legislative Council. http://www.legco.gov.hk/general/english/members/yr16-20/biographies.htm. Accessed 17 Oct 2016.

Leung Lai-Ching and RainLily. 2015. The Effectiveness of the "We Stand Program for Female Migrant Workers and Ethnic Minority Women": A Research Report. April. Hong Kong: RainLily.

Lim, Adelyn. 2015. *Transnational Feminism and Women's Movements in Post-1997 Hong Kong: Solidarity Beyond the State*. Hong Kong: Hong Kong University Press.

MacKay, Fiona. 2010a. Descriptive and Substantive Representation in New Parliamentary Spaces: The Case of Scotland. In *Representing Women in Parliament: A Comparative Study*, ed. Marian Sawer, Manon Tremblay, and Linda Trimble, 171–187. London: Routledge.

———. 2010b. Devolution and the Multilevel Politics of Gender in the United Kingdom: The Case of Scotland. In *Federalism, Feminism, and Multilevel Governance*, ed. Melissa Haussman, Marian Sawer, and Jill Vickers, 155–168. Farnham: Ashgate.

Mathews, Gordon, Eric Kit-wai Ma, and Tai-lok Lui. 2008. *Hong Kong, China: Learning to Belong to a Nation*. London: Routledge.

Migrants Rights International. 2003. MRI and Migrant Forum in Asia (MFA) Symposium, "Asian migrant workers: Issues, needs and responses." Parallel Event of the 59th Session of the Commission on Human Rights, Palais des Nations, Geneva April 7. http://www.migrantwatch.org/mri/whats_new/mri_mfa_symposium.htm. Accessed 6 June 2005.

Ng, Catherine W., and Evelyn G.H. Ng. 2002. The Concept of State Feminism and the Case for Hong Kong. *Asian Journal of Women's Studies* 8 (1): 7–37.

Ortbals, Candice D., Meg Rincker, and Celeste Montoya. 2011. Politics Close to Home: The Impact of Meso-level Institutions on Women in Politics. *Publius* 29 (1): 1–30.

Oxfam, Hong Kong. 2016. Report on Women and Poverty (2001–2015), September. Hong Kong: Oxfam. http://www.oxfam.org.hk/(X(1)S(10wxlvysadhico55fkeseq55))/content/98/content_30227en.pdf. Accessed 15 Oct 2016.

Petersen, Carole J. 2003. Engendering a Legal System: The Unique Challenge of Postcolonial Hong Kong. In *Gender and Change in Hong Kong: Globalisation, Postcolonialism and Chinese Patriarchy*, ed. Eliza W.Y. Lee, 23–48. Vancouver: University of British Columbia Press.

Peterson, V. Spike. 2000. Sexing Political Identities/Nationalism as Heterosexism. In *Women, States and Nationalism: At Home in the Nation?* ed. Sita Ranchod-Nilsson and Mary Ann Tétreault, 54–80. London: Routledge.

Ping Yew Chiew, and Kwong Kin-Ming. 2014. Hong Kong Identity on the Rise. *Asian Survey* 54 (6): 1088–1112.

Pun, Ngai, and Wu. Ka-Ming. 2004. Lived Citizenship and Lower-class Chinese Migrant Women: A Global City Without Its People. In *Remaking Citizenship in Hong Kong: Community, Nation, and the Global City*, ed. Agnes S. Ku and Pun Ngai, 139–154. London: Routledge.

Sautman, Barry. 2004. Hong Kong as a Semi-ethnocracy: 'Race,' Migration and Citizenship in a Globalized Region. In *Remaking Citizenship in Hong Kong: Community, Nation, and the Global City*, ed. S. Ku Agnes and Pun Ngai, 115–138. London: Routledge.

Sawer, Marion, and Jill Vickers. 2010. Introduction: Political Architecture and Its Gender Impact. In *Federalism, Feminism and Multilevel Governance*, ed. Melissa Haussman, Marian Sawer, and Jill Vickers, 3–18. Farnham: Ashgate.

Vickers, Jill. 2013. Is Federalism Gendered? Incorporating Gender into Studies of Federalism. *Publius* 43 (1): 1–23.

Vickers, Jill, Melissa Haussman, and Marian Sawer. 2010. Conclusion. In *Federalism, Feminism and Multilevel Governance*, ed. Melissa Haussman, Marian Sawer, and Jill Vickers, 229–238. Farnham: Ashgate.

Women's Commission. HKSAR. 2011. Hong Kong Women's Development Goals. Hong Kong: Women's Commission. http://www.women.gov.hk/mono/en/research_statistics/report_on_women_development.htm. Accessed 15 Oct 2016.

Wu, Ka-Ming. 2003. Discourse on *Baau Yih Naai* (Keeping Concubines): Questions of Citizenship and Identity in Postcolonial Hong Kong. In *Gender and Change in Hong Kong: Globalisation, Postcolonialism and Chinese Patriarchy*, ed. Eliza W.Y. Lee, 133–150. Vancouver: University of British Columbia Press.

Wu, Alice. 2016a. Be Wary of Effusive Praise for Women's Achievements – Gender Inequality is Still Entrenched in Hong Kong. *South China Morning Post*. May 8. http://www.scmp.com/comment/insight-opinion/article/1941696/be-wary-effusive-praise-womens-achievements-gender. Accessed 30 June 2016.

Wu, Rose. 2016b. Radical Inclusion in the Umbrella Movement: Interstitial Integrity and the New Pentecostal Rebirth of Hong Kong. In *Theological Reflections on the Hong Kong Umbrella Movement*, ed. Justin K.H. Tse and Jonathan Y. Tan, 87–106. New York: Palgrave Macmillan.

Young, Simon N. M., and Anthony Law. 2004. *A Critical Introduction to Hong Kong's Functional Constituencies*. Hong Kong: Civic Exchange. http://www.hkhrm.org.hk/resource/A_critical_introduction_to_HK_FC.pdf Accessed 20 Oct 2016.

# Index[1]

## A

A2 nationals, 271
Abdullah, Nesrîn, 160
Abedi, Amir, 207
*Abnegada*, 134
Aboriginal, 39, 42
  nations, 15
  women, 15, 188, 196, 197
Abortion, 118, 330
Abraham, Linus, 272
Abu-Lughod, Lila, 242
Acheraïou, Amar, 303
Açık, Necla, 148
Active citizenship, 153
Active participation, 320
Activism, 17
Activists, 20
*Adevarul*, 269
Adoni, Hana, 102

Affective, 301, 306
Afghan cameleers, 34
Afghanistan, 22
African Women, 10
Agentic liberation, 305
Age of Revolutions, 322
Ahmed, Sara, 74, 75, 244, 306
AIDS, 21, 99
  crisis, 97
Akkaya, Ahmet Hamdi, 154, 154n11
Akkerman, Tjitske, 6, 22, 166, 170, 179, 204, 208, 216, 242, 285
Albanese, Patrizia, 323
Albania, 214
Albert, Edward, 97
Albizu Campos, Pedro, 129, 130, 132, 137, 140, 141
Algeria, 330
*Al HaMishmar*, 94

---

[1] Note: Page numbers followed by 'n' refer to notes.

© The Author(s) 2018
J. Mulholland et al. (eds.), *Gendering Nationalism*,
https://doi.org/10.1007/978-3-319-76699-7

*Alleanza Nazionale*, 250
Allsopp, Harriett, 151
Almog, Oz, 91
Alsema, Adriaan, 119
Alter, Joseph S., 58
Alternative für Deutschland, 285
Altman, Dennis, 73, 78, 83
Alt-Right, 2n2, 23
Amar, Paul, 73
American Park movement, 94
American revolution, 324
Amin, Idi, 9
Amnesty, 250
Amnesty International, 9–10
Ancestral homeland, 301, 305–307
    return migration, 300
Ancient Sumer, 153
Anderson, Benedict, 130, 149, 155, 224, 253, 305
Anderson, Bridget, 225
Anthias, Floya, 8, 20, 130, 133, 225, 231
Anti-colonial
    context, 149, 318, 320, 323, 330–331
    feminism, 149
    movement, 141
    nationalisms, 11
    nationalist movement, 134, 135
Anti-egalitarian, 23
Anti-elite, 181
Anti-EU feelings, 293
Anti-European nationalism, 282
Anti-feminist backlash, 118
Anti-Homosexuality Act, 4
Anti-immigration, 208, 243
    campaign, 269
    ideology, 17
    politics, 244, 284
Anti-imperial
    contexts, 318, 320, 323, 330–331
    colonial movements, 331
    nations, 326
Anti-imperialist independence
    movements, 317
Anti-ISIS, 146
Anti-Islam, 6, 182
Anti-Islamic politics, 3
Anti-LGBT, 72
Anti-libertarian, 23
Anti-migration, 285
Anti-modern and modernizing
    nationalisms, 321
Anti-modernization, 323, 332
Anti-modern nationalists, 323
Anti-Muslim, 6, 182
Antiracism, 196
Antiretroviral therapy, 22
Anti-Roma discourses, 18
Anti-same-sex marriage
    campaign, 115
Anti-Semitism, 23
Anti-statist, 152
Anti-workplace discrimination, 345
Anxiety, 32, 38, 39, 42
Appadurai, Arjun, 77
Arabs, 13, 92, 157, 195
Arameans, 157
Archer, Margaret, 300
Ardizzoni, Michela, 169
Argentina, 110, 114, 116, 326, 327, 332
Armenians, 157
Arrangements, 338–341
Asceticism, 91
Askola, Heli, 228, 230
Assimilation, 111, 156

Assumptions, 131
Assyrians, 157
Atchison, Jennifer, 34
AustLit, 34
Australia, 12, 22, 31–39, 41, 44, 114, 120
　national identity, 31
Australian, 31, 33, 34, 36, 37, 40, 42–44
　colonies, 31, 41
　government, 32
　nation, 31–33, 44
　national imaginary, 12, 31–45
　national mythology, 40
Australian Associated Press 2013, 31
Australian Capital Territory (ACT), 120
Australian Federation, 35
Australian Labor Party, 121
Authenticity, 302
Autodétermination et solidarité avec les femmes autochtones, 197
Autonomous organizations, 320
Autonomous women's movement, 14
Autonomy arrangement, 348, 350
Avanza, Martina, 248
Ayala, César J., 136, 138
Ayboğa, Ercan, 148, 153n10
Ayoroa Santaliz, José Enrique, 138n17
Azulay, Orly, 96


B

Bacchetta, Paola, 243
Bachchan, Amitabh, 55
Backlash sentiments, 171
Backward marriages, 16
Badgett, M.V. Lee, 122
Badinter, Elizabeth, 175
Baev, Nikolai, 79
Balabanova, Ekaterina, 263
Balaji, Murali, 51
Balch, Alex, 263
Bale, Tim, 204
Ballarat (Victoria), 36, 39
Bandyopadhyay, Sekhar, 56
Banerjee, Sikata, 12, 52
Banting, Mark, 72
Barcan, A., 34, 41
Bashan, Tal, 96
Basic Law (BL), 348
Baum, Dalit, 111
Beauchamp, Colette, 193
Beauvoir, Simone de, 112
Beciu, Camelia, 261, 270
Bélanger-Campeau Commission, 194n14
Bell, Duncan, 32
Belonging, 8, 299, 302, 304, 305, 307–309
Benford, Robert, 264
Bergoglio, Cardinal Jorge, 117
Berlusconi government, 245
Bernabe, Rafael, 136, 138
Bernstein, Mary, 111
Bettio, Francesca, 249
Bhabha, Homi, 77, 92
Bharatiya Janata Party (BJP), 12, 56, 63, 64
Bible, the, 92
Bigo, Didier, 76
Bill 63, 189
Bill 101, 192
*Bill of Rights Ordinance*, 342
Biological racism, 284

## 360   Index

Bird, Michael, 259
Birrell, Ralph W., 38, 39, 41
Black and minority ethnic (BME), 171
Black and populist nationalisms, 326
Black feminism, 149
Blacks, 333
Blackton, Charles S., 34, 42
Blagoi, Ivan, 68, 75
Blainey, Geoffrey, 36, 38–41
Blair House, 138, 140n25
Bledsoe, Caroline H., 230
Blee, Kathleen M., 20, 21, 242, 286
*Bloc Identitaire*, 23
Blood ties, 155
BNP, *see* British National Party
Bodily life, 17, 224
Bogan, 38
Bogayski, Yuval, 100, 101
Boia, 277
Bollywood, 51, 53–56, 61, 62
Bolsonaro, Jair, 116
Boltanski, 261
Bonizzoni, Paola, 16, 228, 229
Bonjour, Saskia, 225, 227
Bookchin, Murray, 154n11
Border crossings, 16
Borders, 286
Borderscapes, 300
Bosia, Michael J., 70, 73
Bosque-Pérez, Ramón, 136
Bossi-Fini Act, 250
Bourgeoisie, 151
Boyarin, Daniel, 90
Bracke, Sara, 242
Bragg, Bronwyn, 227, 227n1, 232
Brah, Avtar, 303
Brazil, 114, 115, 117, 118
Brexit, 322
Brexit referendum, 281
Bride price, 158
Bristol, 1–3
Britain, 16
Britain United Under One Law For All, 209–210
British, 34, 38, 44, 176, 210, 260, 262
British Academy/Leverhulme Trust, 167
*British and Immigrants United Against Terrorism*, 1
British colonies, 33
British culture, 205, 209
British Hong Kong government, 341, 342
British journalists, 18
British Mandate, 92, 96
British National Party (BNP), 2n2, 15, 18, 165–168, 170–174, 179–183, 206, 283
Britishness, 208, 212, 215, 216
British parliament, 33
British values, 16, 43, 210, 216
British way of life, 211
British welfare, 292
Brown, Lucy, 2n2
Browne, Kath, 308
Brownfield-Stein, Chava, 91n3
Brubaker, Rogers, 300, 304, 338
Bruno, Miñi Seijo, 130, 138
Bruno, Seijo, 140n25
Bucharest, 259
Bulgoromanians, 269
*Bulletin, The*, 33, 34, 43
*Bulletin de liaison FLFQ*, 191
Bulli, Giorgia, 289

Bunzl, Matti, 6, 169
Buonanno, Gianluca, 246
Burkas, 175, 214
Bush, 33, 34
Bushman, 34, 43
Bushrangers, 33
Butler, Judith, 78, 99, 155


C

Cadetes, 138
Cadwalladr, Carole, 259
Caffentzis, George, 251
Caiani, Manuela, 288
Calhoun, Craig, 78, 224
California Gold Rush, 38
Cameron, David, 114, 117, 270
Campbell, David, 337
Canada, 10, 120, 190
Canales, Blanca, 134, 137, 138
Cancel Miranda, Rafael, 129, 140
Canovan, Margaret, 323
Cansiz, Sakine, 151
Capitalism, 152
Capitalist modernity, 153
Capitalist norms, 338
*Carabinieri*, 3, 4, 8
Carbonnier, Jean, 116
Care, 16
   and domestic work, 249
Caring mothers, 242
Carpenter, John, 266
Carter, Elisabeth, 168
Carter, Jimmy, 130n2
Casey, Nicholas, 119
Castañeda, Heide, 229
Castles, Stephen, 260
Catalonia, 321, 330

Catholic Church, 115, 117, 199
Catholic society, 117, 119, 134
Çayan, Mahir, 151
Cenî, 149
*Centre des femmes*, 187n1, 191
Century of humiliation, 341
Chakrabarty, Dipesh, 49
Chaldeans, 157
Chaney, Paul, 340
Channel One, 71, 75, 78
Charsley, Katharine, 226
Charter of Fundamental Rights
   (CFR) of the European
   Union, 110
Charter of the French Language,
   192n10
Charter of the Social Contract, 157
Chasin, Alexandra, 111
Chatterjee, Partha, 130, 323
Chauncey, George, 95
Chauvin, Sébastien, 225
Chavez, Leo R., 229, 231
Chechen region, 13
Chechens, 157
Chechnya, 12, 67–69, 80–82
Cheregi, Bianca, 17
Chicago, 136
Childbearing, 16, 229
Childcare, 209
Child marriage, 158, 210
Chile, 326
China, 36, 43, 341
Chinese miners, 34
Chineseness, 347, 348
Chinese women, 341
Christian, 111, 121, 327
   duty, 135
Christian Right, 10

Christian West, 286
Christianity, 114, 178
Christian-majority countries, 114
Christou, Anastasia, 18, 300–302, 304, 306–308
Chung, Chris, 345
Ciorbea, Victor, 269
Citizens, 16, 320
Citizenship, 17, 90, 155, 305
Civic nation, 330
Civil Code, 115
Civilization, 6, 154
Civilizational conflict, 177
Civil marriage, 116
Civil rights, 342
Civil war, 328
Claire, Marie, 21
Clarke, Harold, 207, 209
Clash of civilizations, 22, 169, 172, 183, 286
Class, 43, 152
Classism, 339
CNN, 5
Cockburn, Cynthia, 318, 327
Coenders, Marcel, 205
Cognitive structures, 264
Cohen, Robin, 300, 301
Cole, J. Michael, 115
Coleman, Renita, 272
Colombia, 114, 117, 118
Colonial and anti-colonial/imperial contexts, 318
Colonial and post-colonial cultural, 12
Colonial governments, 31
Colonial *vs.* anti-colonial contexts, 19, 324–326
Colonialism, 9, 150–152, 320

Colonies, 33, 35, 37, 39, 42
Colonizing 'great powers', 326, 330, 333
Coming-out, 309
Communes, 153, 159
Communist era, 321
Communitarian, 265
Communities of value, 225
Community, 8, 17, 149, 351
Comparative analysis, 20
Comparative ethnographic research, 300
Comparisons of ideologies, 322
Compassionate inclusion, 232
Conjugal duty, 112
Connell, Rae Wynn, 52
Conradi, Alexa, 197
Conservative gender, 168
Conservative Party, 207, 296
Conservative values, 114
Conservativism, 170
Constable, Nicole, 227n1, 230
Consumerism, 153
Content analysis, 265
Contextual analysis, 319
Convention on the Elimination of all Forms of Discrimination Against Women (CEDAW), 342, 343
Convention on the Rights of the Child (CRC), 109
Coombes, Anne, 303
Copsey, Nigel, 166, 288
*Corriere della Sera*, 4
Cosmopolitan, 265
Counter-diasporic returns, 301
Counterpublic, 89–103
Coverture, 324

Critical discourse analysis (CDA), 94
Critical feminist studies, 147
Critical race approaches, 11
Croatia, 148
Cross-border lives, 16
Cruising, 95
Cult, 180
Cultural authenticity, 302
Cultural belonging, 306
Cultural boundaries, 13
Cultural fundamentalism, 172
Cultural identity, 149
Cultural minority, 288
Cultural transfer, 306
Culture and values, 210
Curthoys, Ann, 34, 36
Cutts, David, 165, 207

D

Dagestan, 80
*Daily Express*, 268
*Daily Mail*, 268
Daly, Mary, 309
Daniel, Tallie Ben, 111
Danilin, Pavel, 78
D'Aoust, Anne-Marie, 226
*Davar*, 94
Davidson, Raelene, 34, 36
Deakin, Alfred, 33
Decentralization, 153
Decentralized state architectures, 339
Declaration of Independence (1948), 93
Defence of Marriage Act in 1996, 22
Defense Service Law, 91
DeGolyer, Michael E., 345
De Hart, Betty, 225, 229

Delph, Edward Williams, 95
Delphy, Christine, 113
Demir, Arzu, 148, 158, 159
Democracy, 149, 152
Democratic Autonomous Regions of Afrin, Jazira and Kobane, 157
Democratic autonomy, 153, 157
Democratic civic model, 328
Democratic civilization, 153
Democratic confederal model, 154
Democratic confederalism, 146, 152–154
Democratic Federalism, 157
Democratic federal system, 157
Democratic modernity, 153
Democratic nation, 14, 147, 150, 153, 155–157, 160
Democratization, 20, 147, 150, 338, 346, 348, 351
Demosisto, 350
Denationalized citizenship, 305
Denmark, 120
Desai, Radhika, 51
De Sève, Micheline, 319
Despotism, 150
Development, 32
Devolution, 338
Devolution projects, 19
Dhruvarajan, Vanaja, 20
Diachronic dimensions, 94
Diaspora, 301, 302
Diasporic experiences, 18
Diasporic mobilities, 18
Diasporics, 302, 304, 305, 310
Dictatorship, 150
Digby, Anne, 37
Direct action, 156
Direct democracy, 159

Direct participation, 159
Dirik, Dilar, 14
*Dirty Business: How mining made Australia*, 35
Disabled people, 9
Disorderly women, 332
*Disparaître*, 192
Displacement, 299
Diversity, 23, 156, 317
DNA, 113
Domestic and sexual labor, 113
Domestic violence, 158, 216, 302
Dominant civilization, 153
Dominijanni, Ida, 8
Doncaster, 208
Donovan, Catherine, 111
Dos Santos, Sara Leon Spesny, 229
Douglas, Bruce, 115, 116
Drabble, Laurie, 168, 206
Drovers, 33
Drywood, Eleonor, 231
Duggan, Lisa, 111
Dumbrava, Costica, 230
Duncan, Peter J. S., 79
Durham, Frank D., 266

E

Eastern Europe, 214, 247
Eastern European, 289
  immigrants, 212
Eastern Roman empire, 329
Eastern Slavs, 329
Eatwell, Roger, 327
Ecology, 153
Economic competition, 18
Economic frame, 267
Economic security, 349
Eden, Michal, 102

Edenborg, Emil, 12, 22
Educational frame, 267
*Egalité*, 117
Eggebø, Helga, 225, 226
Eisenstein, Zillah, 148, 339
Ekho Moskvy, 67
Ekman, Kajsa, 113
Election Committee, 347
Electoral systems, 325
Elite, 284
Ely, Geoff, 318, 320
Emancipation, 321
Emancipatory, 286
Emasculate, 148
Emasculated male, 199
Embodied identity, 149
Emergent national
  contexts, 320
Emotion, 311
Empire, 36
Emplacement, 299
Employment frame, 18, 44, 267
Employment rights, 350
Empowering, 286
Enchautegui, Maria E., 232n4
Encounters, 306
*Enfermera*, 134, 137
English common law, 324
English Defence League (EDL), 1, 7, 18, 206, 283
Enlightenment, 112, 178, 216
  values, 214
Entman, Robert, 262, 264, 265
Equal Opportunities Commission (EOC), 343, 345
Equality, 19, 122, 195, 344–350
*Esclavage*, 113
*États généraux du féminisme*, 196, 197, 199

Ethnic, 171
　Chinese, 341, 348
　communities, 301
　enclave, 302
　identity, 310
　minority men, 350
　national consciousness, 300
　and racialized exclusion, 352
　self, 301, 310
Ethnicity, 6, 8, 156, 333
Ethno-cultural signifiers, 310
Ethnodemographic inversion, 171
Ethnographic, 17
　research, 311
Ethno-national norms, 309
Ethno-racial groups, 122
Eureka Lead, 39
Eureka Rebellion, 39, 40
Europe, 16, 22, 169, 170, 179, 204, 205, 217, 284, 317, 320–322, 325, 327, 328, 330
European, 169, 178
Europeanization, 169
European nation-states, 318
European Parliament, 165
European societies, 17
European Union (EU), 8, 207, 209, 276
　migrants, 271
　policy, 18
Evans, Geoffrey, 207
Evelev, John, 95
Even, Uzi, 102
Excessive, 16
Exclusion, 10
Exile, 13, 301
Extreme and populist radical right (PRR), 167, 169, 171, 174, 183

Extreme ethnic model, 328
Extreme ethnic nationalism, 326, 328, 329
Extreme nationalism, 6
Extreme politics, 21
Extreme right, 166, 179
　organizations, 168
　party, 165n1

F
Facebook, 206
Face-to-face democracy, 154
Fair, Linda S., 227
Fairclough, Norman, 243n4
Faist, Thomas, 300, 306
Families, 300–302, 307, 311
Familistic culture, 244
Family, 35–37, 41, 43, 109, 111, 113, 116, 117, 121, 123, 140, 155, 195, 320
　law codes, 317n1
　migration, 209, 229
　migration management, 16
　relations, 310
　reunification, 349
　values, 92, 111, 119
Fanghanel, Alexandra, 174
Fanon, Frantz, 190
Farage, Nigel, 203, 270
Farooqui, Mahmood, 49
Far-right, 16, 207
　millennials, 21
　politics, 20
Farris, Sara R., 7, 17, 170, 174, 243, 286
Fascism, 150, 284
Fascist, 165, 326
Fascist family policies, 327

Fassin, Éric, 227
Father's rights, 209
Fazira-Yaccobali, Vazira, 51, 56
FBI, 130, 136n12, 139, 140n26
Federalism, 157, 339
Federal Russian government, 68
Federal states, 339
Federation, 33–35, 38–42
*Fédération des femmes du Québec*, 187n1
*Fédération nationale Saint-Jean-Baptiste*, 187
Fekete, Liz, 22, 169, 172, 180
Female Genital Mutilation (FGM), 209
Female participation, 20
Feminicidal, 14, 146
Femininity, 11, 14, 35, 37, 134, 308, 325
Feminism, 15, 150, 194, 200, 320, 332, 347
Feminists, 111, 113, 131, 148, 175, 309, 317–319, 321, 342, 343
 activism, 321
 consciousness, 323
 institutionalism, 321
 institutionalist framework, 19
 literature, 8
 mobilizations, 322
 nationalism, 330
 radical democracy, 150–155
 scholars, 320
 values, 215
Femonationalism, 11, 174
Femoprotectionism, 113
Femoprotectionist, 111
Ferguson, Sam, 266
Fernandes, Leela, 51

Fernandez, Nadine T., 227
Ferrao, Luis Angel, 133, 134n9, 134n10
Ferretti, Andrée, 189n3
Fertilities, 16, 327
Female genital mutilation (FGM), 210
Figueroa Cordero, Andres, 129
Filiation, 112
Film, 12
Finland, 120, 317, 326, 330
Finnish women, 326
First World War, 323
Fischler, Lisa, 342, 347
Five Year Plan, 53, 54, 62, 63
Flach, Anja, 148, 151, 153n10
Florence, 3, 4
Flores, Irvin, 129
Forced marriages, 158, 227
Ford, Robert, 165, 166, 207, 209, 282, 283
Foreigner, 9
Forest, Maxime, 122
*Forum pour un Québec féminin pluriel*, 192, 193
Foucault, Michel, 71
Fougeyrollas-Schwebel, Dominique, 189
Frames of migration, 17
Framing, 262
France, 114–116, 119, 214, 325, 332
Francophone majority, 15
*Fraternité*, 117
Free Associated State, 132, 137, 140
Freedom, 150
 problem, 154
Free movement of labor, 17

Free World, 132
French and American revolutions, 319, 323, 331
French Declaration of the Rights of Man, 110
French McGill, 189
French Revolution, 324, 325
Friedman, Sara L., 227n1
*Front de libération des femmes du Québec*, 15, 187n1, 189
*Front de Libération du Québec*, 189n3
*Front National*, 241
Fryberg, Stephanie A., 266
*Fuerzas Armadas Revolucionarias de Colombia* (FARC), 118

G

Gaby, 102
Gallo, Ester, 249
Gamson, William A., 264
Gandhi, Mohandas Karamchand, 50, 61, 63
*Gândul*, 269
Gandy, Oscar, 265
Garcés-Mascareñas, Bianca, 225
Gatekeepers, 227
Gates, Gary J., 120
Gay, 89–103
　children, 116
　community, 90
　counterpublic, 101, 102
　couples, 118
　identities, 301
　and Lesbian Association, 100
　and lesbian Catholics, 118
　and lesbian inclusion, 13
　male parents, 113

marriage, 14, 122
media, 90
men, 13, 94–95, 98–99, 101–103
men and lesbians, 122
minorities, 111
pride, 5, 103
rights, 7, 111, 118, 119
GayRussia, 77, 81
*Gays Against Sharia*, 1, 5
Genç, Yüksel, 149
Gender, 5, 9–11, 15, 16, 18, 19, 21, 23, 32, 34–38, 43, 137–141, 148, 166–171, 182, 203–217, 284, 299, 302, 311, 317
　conservatism, 6
　diversity, 319, 320, 331
　divisions, 137
　egalitarianism, 6
　equality, 6, 14–15, 17, 158, 178, 225, 241, 317
　gap, 285
　identities, 6
　injustice, 15
　interactions, 19
　justice, 178
　nation interactions, 319, 326
　nation relations, 317
　nation scholarship, 322
　perspective, 290
　political culture, 6
　prejudices, 350
　regimes, 308, 319, 322
　relationships, 16
　roles, 110
　scripts, 307
　and sexed stereotypes, 310
　and sexual identities, 309
　and sexualized borders, 11

Gender (*cont.*)
    and sexualized identities, 19
    sexual liberation, 169
    and sexual scripts, 310
    and sexual traditionalism, 23
    white backlash, 178
Gender-based discrimination, 158
Gender-neutral, 13
Gender-undifferentiated
    participation, 20
General Assembly Declaration on the
    Elimination of Violence
    Against Women, 113
*Génération Identitaire*, 23
Generations, 300
Geneticization, 230
Genocide, 145
Gerhards, Juergen, 22
German women, 326
Germany, 285, 307, 326
Gezmiş, Deniz, 150
Gibbs, Leah, 34
Gibson, Chris, 34, 36
Gilboa, Nir, 97
Gillies, Val, 286
Gilman, Sander L., 90
Giovannini, Eva, 293
Gisby, William, 263
Globalization, 20, 49–52, 55, 56, 73, 78, 79, 201
Global mobility, 229
Global South, 9, 247
Goffman, Erving, 264
Gold, 31, 42
Goldfields, 31, 35, 36, 38
*Gold Fields Management Act 1852*, 39
Gold license system, 40
Gold mining, 41
Gold-rushes, 32, 35, 36, 38, 41–43
Gonzales, Roberto G., 231
Good migrants, 251–254
Goodhart, David, 282
Goodin, Robert E., 319
Goodwin, Mathew J., 165, 166, 168
Goodwin, Metthew, 207, 209, 282, 283
Gordinenko, Irina, 67, 82
Gouges, Olympe de, 112
Governance, 17
Governmental technology, 32
Gramscian, 153
*Grande noirceur*, 191
Grassroots-democratic
    mobilization, 160
Grattan, Hartley, 34
Grayzel, Susan R., 148
Great Britain, 17
Great Depression, 132
Greater London Assembly (GLA), 165, 166
Great power, 20, 328
Greece, 10, 304, 306, 307, 310, 326, 329
Greeks, 300, 303, 304, 306, 310, 328
    culture, 307
    culture and language, 329
    diaspora, 300, 310
    ethnic identity, 328
    family norms, 303
    migrant, 18, 309–311
    national identity, 328
    nationalist politics, 330
    nation-state, 319, 323
Greek, Annie, 2n2
Greekness, 304, 310, 328, 329
Grimshaw, Patricia, 37

Grishin, Aleksandr, 77
Grooming, 173, 180
*Guardian, The*, 21, 276
Guarnizo, Louis, 306
Guilbault, Diane, 201
Guillaumin, Colette, 113
Güneş, Cengiz, 151
Gutekunst, Miriam, 228
Gypsies, 326

## H

*Haaretz*, 94
Habsburg Empire, 90
Hagelund, Anniken, 242
Hannah Papanek, 148
Happiness of the Next Generation Alliance, The, 115
Hardt, Michael, 149
Harper, Mark, 270
Harteveld, Eelco, 181, 205
Have-nots, 166, 171
Hawai'i, 330
Hawley, George, 23
Hayton, Richard, 207
*Hazman Havarod*, 94, 97, 99, 100
Healey, Dan, 72, 81
Hearn, Jonathan, 321, 322, 325, 333
Hegelian, 152
Hegemony, 11, 12, 157, 309, 310
  masculinity, 58, 61
Heinemann, Torsten, 230
Henders, Susan J., 19, 339, 340
Hertog, James, 265
Heteronormativity, 13, 33, 41, 43, 44, 89–103, 199, 216, 301, 308, 310
  families, 99
  hegemonies, 301
  patriarchal norms, 19
  values, 92
Heterosexual
  couples, 113, 115
  divorce rate, 122
  marriage, 122
  norm, 317n1
Heterosexual-only marriage, 119
*Hevjiyana azad*, 156
Hewitt, Roger, 171
Hickman, Mary J., 94
Higgs, David, 95
High Court of Australia, 121
Hill Collins, Patricia, 339
Hindu, 54, 57
  nationalism, 54, 56, 59, 327, 332
  women, 327
Hindu Indian, 12
Hindutva, 54, 56, 57, 327
Hipkins, Danielle, 148
Historical and feminist institutionalism, 11
*Historical comparisons*, 322
Historical 'waves', 321
HIV, 22
Hong Kong Special Administrative Region (HKSAR), 341, 343, 345, 347, 348
Hochberg, Gil Z., 103
Holocaust, 98
Homecoming visits, 300
Homeland, 133
Homonationalisms, 11, 23, 70, 103, 111, 169, 310
Homonationalist, 81
Homonormativity, 13, 111
Homonorms, 118

Homophobia, 13, 68–70, 74, 80–83, 111, 113
  policies, 94
Homophobic (Muslim) Chechnya, 69
Homophobic Russia, 68
Homoprotectionism, 13, 111, 113
Homosexual acts, 4
Homosexuality, 9, 21, 97, 103, 114, 115
Homosexual propaganda, 78, 80, 82
Homosexual propaganda law, 68
Homosexuals, 5, 111, 326
Homosocial institutions, 91
Hong Kong, 11, 19, 337, 339, 342, 343, 346, 348, 350, 351
  ethnic Chinese, 349
  statutory bodies, 347
Hong Kong Federation of Women, 347
Hong Kong Special Administrative Region (HKSAR), 19, 337
Hong Kong Women's Coalition for Beijing, 347
Honor, 148, 156, 302
  killings, 158
Honor-based violence, 210
Hooper, Charlotte, 52
Hope Not Hate, 23
Horowitz, Nizan, 100
Horsti, Karina, 231
House of Representatives Standing Committee on Regional Australia, 36
Housewifization, 154
Howard, John (Prime Minister), 120
Human rights, 348
Hungary, 326

Hutchinson, John, 322
Huysseune, Michel, 248
Hybridity, 303

Ideal migrant, 225
*Identitäre Bewegung*, 23
Identities, 32, 299, 300, 308
  *vs.* alterity, 260
*Idle No More*, 197
Illegal migrants, 251
Imaginary, 89
Imagined communities, 149, 305, 307
Imaginings of the nation, 321
Immerzeel, Tim, 205, 285
Immigrants, 333
Immigration, 15, 18, 195, 208
  and citizenship policies, 349
  policies, 349
Immorality, 35
Imperial cosmopolitanism, 156
Imperialism, 152
Imperialist, 10
Inclusion, 10, 13
Independence Park, 99, 101–103
Independence struggles, 330, 332
*Independent, The*, 276
*Independentistas*, 131
India, 11, 326, 332
Indian middle-class, 12
India Poised Campaign, 55, 56, 63
Indigenous, 8, 205
Indigenous women, 211, 214
Indonesia, 349
Industrialization, 326
Industry, 32, 33, 40, 42

Infanticide, 330
Inferiorization, 173, 174
Insiders, 17
Institutional structures, 19
Institutionalist framework, 19
Interactions, 301
International Covenant on Civil and Political Rights (ICCPR), 109
International Covenant on Economic, Social and Cultural Rights (ICESCCR), 109
International human rights treaties, 343
International labor standards, 345
Inter-national mobilities, 11
Intersected identities, 19
Intersectionality, 149, 176, 183, 339, 350
Intimate, 224
Intimate lives, 223
Intra-EU migration, 266
IPSOS Mori, 207
Iraq, 22, 145, 152
Ireland, 114, 330
Irish Constitution, 117
Irvine, Jill A., 148
ISIS-controlled areas, 142
Islam, 6, 7, 11, 15, 16, 20, 22, 24, 167, 170, 177–180, 182, 205, 209, 211, 215
Islamic faith, 213
Islamic opposition to 'women's rights, 22
Islamic patriarchal norms, 16
Islamic State (ISIS), 14, 142, 145, 157, 159
Islamic Ummah culture, 156
Islamization, 286
Islamophobia, 168, 169, 172, 174, 179, 180, 284
Israel, 11, 13, 22, 89, 91–94
Israeli, 89
  civil society, 91
  law, 92
  masculinity, 99
  military service, 91
  nationalism, 101–103
Italy, 10, 326
*Izvestiya*, 76

J

Jackson, Andrew (President), 325
Jacobins, 324
Jacoby, Tami A., 320
Jaikumar, Priya, 56
James, Diane, 285
Janus-faced, 7, 79, 166, 170
Japan, 326
Japanese imperialism, 341
Jayawardena, Kumari, 320
Jayuya, 134, 137, 138, 140n25
Jensen, Lars, 36
Jensen, Tina, 227
Jewish community, 13
Jewish immigrants, 91
Jewish people, 93
Jewish settlers, 92
Jews, 326
Jihadists, 145
Jiménez de Waggenheim, Olga, 130, 136, 139
Jinga, Ion, 270
Joan of Arc, 138
Jongerden, Joost, 154, 154n11

Joseph, Suad, 320
Judeo-Christian, 169
Juntas Municipales, 135
*Jurnalul National*, 269, 272

K

Kabeer, Naila, 339
Kadyrov, Ramzan, 68, 69, 82
Kalgoorlie (Western Australia), 36
Kaltwasser, Cristóbal Rovira, 6, 166, 170, 181, 182
Kampala, 5
Kantsa, Venetia, 309, 310
Kanyas, Yoav, 13, 22
Kapai, Puja, 350
Kaplan, Gisela, 317
Karimi, Faith, 4
Kato, David, 5
Keating, Christine (Cricket), 111, 113
Kelly, Michael, 23, 117
Kennett, Patricia, 344, 345, 349
Khan, Shahnaz, 49, 56
Khoo, Siew-Ean, 228
Kilkey, Majella, 233
Kimmerling, Baruch, 91
Kin, 309
King, Russell, 300–302, 304
Kin-Ming, Kwong, 346
Kinship, 155
Kinship networks, 306
Kirchner, Cristina, 116
Kirtsoglou Elizabeth, 310
Kitschelt, Herbert, 208, 293
Klanderman, Bert, 20
Knapp, Michael, 148, 153n10, 159
Knox, Malcolm, 36
Kobane, 14, 145, 160

Kofman, Eleonore, 225, 228
*Komsomolskaya Pravda*, 71
Kon, Igor, 72
Koonz, Claudia, 326
Koopmans, Ruud, 289
Kosicki, Gerald, 264
Kost'uchenko, Elena, 67
Köttig, Michaela, 21, 166
Kraler, Albert, 225, 227
Krause, Elizabeth L., 230
Kuan, Hsin-Chi, 348
Kundnani, Arun, 178
Kuntsman, Adi, 75
Kuo, Lily, 348
*Kurdayetî*, 151
Kurdish, 145, 151, 157
    freedom movement, 14, 146, 148, 160
    struggle, 149–150
    women, 14, 146, 148
    women fighters, 149
Kurdish Stalingrad, 146
Kurdish Supreme Council, 158
Kurdistan, 11, 146n3, 150, 155, 157
Kurdistan Regional Government, 152
Kurdistan Workers' Party (PKK), 146, 150, 151, 155
Kurds, the, 151

L

Labor/Labour, 31–45, 261, 296
    exploitation, 39
    market, 38
    migration, 265
Labour Party, 207
Laclau, Ernesto, 149
Lai-ching, Leung, 345
*Laïcité*, 117

Laissez-faire capitalist economy, 341
Laissez-faire capitalist norms, 338, 344, 351
Lakoff, George, 266
Lam, Wai-Man, 341, 342, 347, 349
Lamoureux, Diane, 15, 190, 200n22
Lan, Pei-Chia, 226, 227n1, 229
Lanctôt, Martine, 190
Langue maternelle, 199
Lapidus, June, 118
*Las Enfermeras de la República*, 134
Latin America, 11, 119
Lau, Kimmy, 345
Lau, Siu-Kai, 348
Law, Anthony, 347
Law, Kam-Yee, 349
Lawson, Henry, 33, 34, 40, 43
Le Pen, Marine, 285
Lebanon war, 93
Lebrón, Lolita, 129, 139, 140
Lee, Catherine, 224, 226
Lee, Eliza W. Y., 342, 345, 347
Lee, Kim-Ming, 349
Left behind, the, 283
Left-wing, 283
Lega Nord, 17, 241
Legitimacy, 16
Leinonen, Johanna, 232
Lemke, Thomas, 230
Lennon, Stephen, 7
Leonard, Diana, 113
Lesbian, 118
Leung, Lai-Ching, 350
Lévesque, René, 189n3
Levy, Yagil, 91
Lewis, Jane, 233
LGBT, 69–73, 75–78, 80–83, 89, 91, 93, 97, 100, 103
 community, 4–5, 9, 10
 counterpublic, 99, 100
 population, 21
 rights, 12, 22, 93
LGBT Association, 98, 100–102
LGBTI, 111, 116
LGBTQ, 7
LGBTQI, 194
Liberal civic model, 328
Liberal democracy, 22, 112
Liberal-democratic, 170
 federations, 340
 nations, 13
 states, 339
Liberal-feminism, 179
Liberal feminist, 174
Liberal rights and freedoms, 351
Liberal values, 216
Liberation, 15
 of women, 14
Liberatory (non-)nationalisms, 14
Libertarian ideals, 156
*Liberté*, 117
Liberty GB, 2n2
Lichtner, Giacomo, 56
Life stories, 300
Lilly, Carol S., 148
Lim, Adelyn, 343, 344
Lim, Jason, 174
Liminality, 19
Liminal spaces, 300
Linden, Annette, 242
Lissak, Moshe, 91
Liversage, Anika, 227, 228
LN, 17
Localist, 346
 movement, 346, 350
 political parties, 348

Lokodo, Simon, 5
*Los Cadetes de la República*, 134
Low quality human capital, 16
Luibhéid, Eithne, 224, 229
Lundberg, Thomas Carl, 207
Lykke Lind, Peter, 5
Lynch, Philip, 207

M

*Maariv*, 94
Macfarlane, Ingereth, 34
Mackay, Fiona, 340
Madeleine Parent, 191, 191n7, 196
*Magaim*, 94
Maidan, 76
Maillé, Chantal, 198
Mainstream feminism, 198
Majumdar, Ruby, 49
Male activism, 20
Male body, the, 12
Malik, Kenan, 286
Mammone, Andrea, 20, 285
Manchester, 2
Mane, Sherril, 102
*Mangal Pandey: The Rising*, 12, 49, 50, 52, 53, 55–57, 61, 62
Manhood, 156
*Manifeste des femmes québécoises*, 190
Manifesto, 189
*Männerparteien*, 166, 182
*Marche du pain et des roses*, 191n7, 194
Marchesi, Milena, 230
Marcus, Aliza, 151
Marian, Sawer, 340
Maroni, Roberto, 250
Marrero, Mildred Rivera, 139n22

Marriage, 110
Marriage Amendment Act, 120
Marriage Equality Act, 120–121
Marriage-and-family demographic, 122
Married lesbians, 120
Martial culture, 91
Martial family, the, 13
Martin, Diarmuid, 117
Marxist-Leninist, 147, 150, 152
Masculine, 130
Masculine movement, 142
Masculinism, 14, 23
Masculinist, 10, 20, 168
 assumptions, 21
 heterosexuality, 116
 paradigms, 21
 rhetoric, 247
Masculinity, 11–13, 22, 24, 31–45, 49–64, 89–103, 150, 156, 308
Masculinizing nationalist movements, 331
Mass immigration, 216
Mass migration, 18, 285
Massad, Joseph, 90
Mathews, Gordon, 342
Matrilinearity, 113
Mavroudi, Liz, 308
Mawby, Rob C., 263
Maxwell, Alexander, 90, 322
May, Theresa, 270
Mayer, Nonna, 20, 204, 288
Mayer, Stephanie, 170, 180, 182
Mayer, Tamer, 52
Mayes, Robyn, 38
McAleese, Mary, 117
McCarty, Wyman, 285
McClintock, Anne, 21, 50

McDonald, Paula, 38
McGill University, 190
McLeod, Douglas, 265
Media, 276
  discourses, 264
  frames, 262
Mediatization, 260
Melamed, Shaham, 89, 92
Melbourne, 36
Mellon, Jon, 207
Memmi, 190
Men, 20, 35, 36, 38, 39, 42–44
Menjívar, Cecilia, 227n1, 228, 232n4
Merla, Laura, 233
Meso-level autonomy arrangements, 19, 337, 350, 351
Meso-level territorial autonomy, 339
Messaris, Paul, 272
Mexico, 141
Meyer, Michael, 94
Meyers, Diana Tietjens, 148
Middle-class, 12, 32–44
Middle-class men, 34
Middle East, 11, 148, 149, 153, 155, 157
  politics, 160
Mies, Maria, 148, 154
Migrants, 7, 36, 171, 275, 300, 303
  care-givers, 17, 244, 253
  domestic and care workers, 253
  men and women, 17
  women as carers, 249
Migrants Rights International, 348
Migration, 16, 20, 43, 281, 299, 304, 308
  control, 16, 224
  studies, 306

Migration Watch, 270
Milashina, Elena, 67, 82
Militarism, 49, 91, 149
Military self-defense, 14
Millbank, Jenni, 111
Millennial, 24
Miller, Mark J, 260
Millett, Kate, 112, 309
Miners, 31, 32, 34–36, 38–44
Miners Rights, 40
Minimum wages, 345
Mining, 12, 31–45
  industry, 32, 35, 43
Mining Affairs Department, 41
Mining Boards, 41
Minister for Mines, 41
Minority, 273
  nationalisms, 330
  territorial communities, 339
Miramare, 3
Misogynist, 242
Misogyny, 8, 113, 213, 215
Mixed-status families, 230
MLG, *see* Multilevel Governance
Mobility, 17, 300, 301, 306
Moderate ethno-cultural model, 329
Modernity, 152, 320, 322, 332, 333
Modernization, 323, 331
Modernizing and anti-modern national projects, 318
Modernizing great powers, 11, 318
Moffitt, Benjamin, 204
Mojab, Shahrzad, 148
Monarchy, 324
Monroe, Kristen Renwick, 71
Montagna, Nicola, 18, 283n3
Morality, 31–45
Moral-political society, 153

Moral values, 37
Morgentaler Affair, 194
Morrissey, Belinda, 148
Moscow, 72, 73, 79
Mozes, Alun. T, 95
Mosse, George L., 72, 90
Mosul, 145
Motherhood, 327, 329
Mouffe, Chantal, 149
Mudde, Cas, 6, 166, 170, 171, 179, 181, 182, 204, 216, 241n1
Mugabo, Délice, 197
Mulholland, Jon, 15, 16, 22, 283n3, 284
Mulinari, Diana, 242
Multiculturalism, 171, 193, 282
Multicultural policies, 282
Multi-ethnic military alliance, 157
Multilevel Governance (MLG), 337, 340, 343, 350
Muñoz Marín, Luis, 132, 137, 140
Munshi, Shobha, 50
Muscular, 53
   nationalism, 11, 12, 53, 55, 59, 60, 62
Museveni, Yoweri (President), 4, 9
Muslim, 6, 7, 11, 13, 15–17, 68, 73, 80–82, 166, 167, 169, 170, 173–177, 179, 180, 182, 195, 283, 327, 333
   civilization, 182
   colonization, 6
   extremism, 209
   femininity, 176
   grooming gangs, 173
   homophobia, 71
   majority, 13
   masculinity, 176
   men, 15
   migrants, 212
   patriarchy, 15, 171–175, 177, 178, 182
   women, 15, 16, 200, 201, 215, 216, 332
Muslim-minority nations, 11
Muslim Other, 16, 22, 23, 111
Muslim world, 169
Mustasaari, Sanna, 231
Myths, 32, 34, 35, 43

Nagel, Joane, 7, 53, 90
Nandy, Ashis, 54
Napoleonic system, 325
Napoleonic Code, 324
Narrations, 309–311
Narrative accounts, 300
Narrative analysis, 303
Nartova, Nadya, 70
Nation, 6, 8, 9, 12, 15, 17, 19, 21, 32, 36, 42, 43, 110, 116, 148, 152, 155, 302, 305, 306, 309, 310, 317, 332
Nation building, 89, 91, 155
Nation in Arms, 89–103
National Action, 23
National Action Committee, 191n7
National community, 8
National consciousness, 305, 308
National Front, 165
National Guard, 138
National ideal, 310
National identity, 8, 16, 18, 20, 34, 43, 44
National imaginary, 31–35, 39, 40, 42, 44, 89

# Index

Nationalism, 5, 6, 10, 11, 14, 15, 20, 21, 23, 49, 50, 52–53, 55–57, 60–62, 91, 130, 141, 152, 155, 156, 167–169, 194, 317, 320, 325, 332, 346
   scholarship, 331
Nationalist, 33, 34, 57, 138, 151, 152, 166–169, 318
   agenda, 20
   discourses, 9, 148
   elites, 320
   ideas, 13
   ideologies, 318
   imaginary, 337
   movements, 11, 14, 15, 285, 317n2, 319
   parties, 18
   politics, 148, 338–341
   projects, 10, 321
   protest, 2
   rhetoric, 130
   right, 18, 282
   women, 131, 140
Nationalist-infused norms, 344
Nationalist-infused policies, 346
Nationalist-infused politics, 341, 350
Nationalist Party, 129, 133–137, 139, 140
Nationalist Party Juntas, 134
Nationality norms, 349
Nationalization, 331
National labor market, 18
National liberation, 151
National liberation movements, 130, 154
National myth, 43
National press, 18
National pride, 33
National projects, 19, 317n2
National regeneration, 329
National Resistance Movement (NRM), 9
National self, 311
National struggle, 14
National values, 277
Nation-builder, 35
Nation-building, 37, 43, 317n2
Nation-gender interactions, 19
Nationhood, 14, 155, 156
Nationness, 16, 19, 301, 308
Nation-state, 13, 16, 19, 153, 155–156, 160, 195, 304, 306
Nation-state formation, 317n2
Native, 178, 180
   culture, 16
   women, 16
Nativism, 11, 16, 23, 203–217
Nativist attitudes, 205
Nativist ideas, 16
Naturalization, 224
Nature, 110
Nazi, 326
Neergard, Anders, 242
Negri, Antonio, 149
Nehru, Jawaharlal, 50, 61, 63
Nehruvian, 54
Neo-communitarian, 224
Neoliberal, 15
Neo-liberalism, 19
Netherlands, 122
Neuberger, Benyamin, 93n5
New Jersey, 324
New South Wales, 33, 35, 36, 38, 39
   government, 38
New York City, 136
New York Nationalist Party, 140

NHS, 259, 295
Nickels, Henry C., 94
9/11, *see* September 11, 2001
Non-democracy, 340, 346–348, 351
Non-indigenous, 16
Non-Muslim, 177
Non-Muslim world, 169
Non-nationalistic social coherence, 160
Non-normative sexualities, 6, 11
Non-stateness, 160
Nordic countries, 321
North America, 10
Northern Ireland, 340
Norway, 317, 326, 330
Nuclear family model, 111

O

Obergefell, Jim, 120
Öcalan, Abdullah, 146, 147, 149, 151, 153–155
Oceania, 11
Öcolan, 14
O'Connor, Erin E., 135
Ohana, Etay, 99
O'Hare, C.W., 39
Okin, Susan, 175
Okiror, Samuel, 5
O'Leary, Véronique, 190
Oliver, Marcia, 9
Olmsted, Fredrick Law, 94, 95
O'Neill, Luke, 120
Onger, Richie, 102
Ophir, 38
Oppression, 214
Oppressors, 15, 17, 167
*Option Québec*, 189n3
Orientalist perspective, 92

Ortbals, Candice D., 338, 341
Orthodox Christianity, 329
Orthodox church, 328, 329
Orthodox Jews, 92
Osborne, George, 33
Oslo Accords, 93
Osmani, Farida, 193, 196
Othering, 15, 16, 170
Otherness, 10
Ottoman Empire, 155
Ottoman rule, 328
Outsiders, 17
Oza, Rupal, 50

P

Padania, 244, 248
Padanian cultural heritage, 248
Pain, Emil, 77
Pakistani immigrants, 212
Pakistanis, 287
Palestine, 92, 111
Palestinian, 13, 91
    occupation, 93
Pallares, Amalia, 230
Pan, Zhongdang, 264
Panofsky, Erwin, 265
Papastergiadis, Nikos, 303
Paralitici, Che, 132
Parallel demonstration of theory, 325
Parameswaran, Radhika, 50
Parenthood, 16
Parenting, 229
Parker, Margot, 209
Parkes, Henry, 33
Parliament, 32
Parody, Gina, 119
*Partenaires de la souveraineté*, 194n14
*Partij voor de Vrijheid*, 241

*Parti Québécois*, 189n3, 202
PASOK, 329
Pasquinelli, Sergio, 249
Passarelli, Gianluca, 244n5
Pateman, Carole, 112
Patriarchy, 14, 112, 119, 131,
  150, 156, 159, 160,
  167–169, 172, 174, 182,
  183, 286, 302, 303,
  307–310, 339, 351
  narratives, 148
  nationalist agenda, 20
  oppression, 177
  social relations, 338
  violence, 146
Patrilinearity, 113
Patriotic mothers, 148
Patriotism, 211
Patriots, 215
Patterson, Banjo, 33, 43
Patterson, Molly, 71
Pavlou, Miltos, 310
Payette, Lise, 192
Pearse, Guy, 31
Pedophilia, 116
Pegida, 2
Peled, Yoav, 93
Pellander, Saara, 226, 231, 232
People's Defense Units (YPG), 146
People's Republic of China (PRC), 337, 339, 342, 343, 346, 347, 349, 350
Pereira, Michaela, 120
Perez, Carmín, 139
Performative, 11, 18
  aspects of experiences, 302
  spheres, 310
Peronist regime, 327
Persson, Emil, 70

Petersen, Carole J., 343, 344
Peterson, V. Spike, 339
Petry, Frauke, 285
Pew Research Center, 55
Phenomenon, 31
Philippines, 330, 349
Phrygian cap, 115
Picard, Isabelle, 197
Pijpers, R., 263
Ping, Yew Chiew, 346
Pini, Barbara, 38
Pinkwashing, 103, 111
Plain, Gill, 148
Plevneliev, Rosen, 270
Pluralism, 116
Podosenov, Sergei, 76
Poland, 8
Poles, 8, 288
Polish, 288
Political and religious
  conservatism, 13
Political correctness, 181, 213
Political enfranchisement, 12
Political frame, 267
Politically literate, 154
Political mobilization, 149
Political participation, 349
Political rights, 330
Politics of belonging, 263
Politics of inclusion, 6
Polygamy, 158, 210
Ponce Massacre, 139
Ponta, Victor, 270
Pope Francis, 118
Popular Democratic Party (PPD), 132, 136
Populist, 284
  and extreme right, 180, 181
  nationalism, 11

Populist Radical Right (PRR) parties, 6, 16, 17, 165n1, 181, 203–217, 241
Porto Alegre, 196
Portugal, 327
Post-colonial contexts, 21, 148
Postcolonial feminist theories, 198
Post-colonial nationalisms, 11
Post-colonial process, 13
Post-colonial theory, 11, 198
Post-enlightenment, 112
Post-Fordist, 208
Postmodernist, 319
Postnational, 304
Post-struggle societies, 148
Post-territorial, 305
Power, 32, 37, 40–43, 311
Power, Margaret, 14, 243
PRC, *see* People's Republic of China
Press, 260
Private sphere, 323, 325
Pro-democracy, 347
Progressive Christians, 121
Propaganda, 70, 71, 73, 76, 77, 82
Prostitution, 114, 180, 330
PRR, *see* Populist Radical Right parties
Puar, Jasbir K., 20, 21, 70, 73, 77, 81, 83, 103, 111, 179
Public/private divide, 323
Public security frame, 18, 267
Public social protection, 345
Public space, 89
Puerto Rican, 129, 130, 135
 independence, 131, 141
 independence struggle, 131
 nationalism, 141
 nationality, 133
 police, 136, 138
 women, 139
Puerto Rican Nationalist Party, 130
Puerto Rico, 11, 131, 132, 136, 138, 140, 330
Pun, Ngai, 349
Purification, 326
Purity, 302
Putin, Vladimir, 13, 68, 69, 73, 75, 76, 78, 80–82

Q

Quasi-ethnocracy, 349
Quebec, 15, 187, 195, 198, 200, 319, 321, 330
 feminists, 188, 190
 nationalism, 194
Quebec national liberation, 188
Quebec Native Women, 194, 197
*Québécois de souche*, 188
*Québécoises de souche*, 192
*Québécoises deboutte*, 187n1
*Québécoises toujours deboutte*, 187n1
Queensland, 33

R

Race/nation interactions, 333
Race purity, 23
Racial, 171
 sexual, and economic violence, 149
Racialization, 7, 11, 348–350
 of sexism, 7, 170, 243
Racialized ethnic minority women, 350
Racialized minority women, 344
Racialized Other, 245

## Index

Racialized women, 350
Racism, 23, 207, 269, 339
Racist, 168, 180, 269
  registers, 17
Radical democracy, 150, 153
Radicalisation, 21
Radical nationalist groups, 189
Raghuram, Parvati, 225
Rai, Amit S., 83
Rainbow families, 13, 110, 113, 114, 122
RainLily, 350
Ram, Uri, 93n5
Randall, Margaret, 132
Rape, 7, 113, 153, 174
  culture, 348
  gangs, 180
Raqqa, 157
*Rassemblement national*, 189n3
Read, C.R., 37
Rebellion, 39, 40
*Rebel Media, The*, 2n2
Reese, Stephen D., 264
Referendum, 15
Refugees, 7
Regional democratic autonomy, 152–153
Religion, 92
Religious doctrines, 9
Religious minorities, 179
Repressive family law code, 324, 329
Reproductive, 224
  practices, 223
Republican motherhood, 325, 332
Republic of Ireland, 110, 117
Resentment, 166
Residency rights, 349
Residents, 16

Resistance, 149
Respectable, 35–37
Re-traditionalized sex/gender relations, 326, 328, 329
Return migration, 307
*Revanche des berceaux*, 199
Reverse-discourse, 155
Revolution, 154
Revolutionary people's war, 152
Rhodes, James, 166, 171, 179, 182
RIA Novosti, 77
Riabov, Oleg, 74
Riabova, Tatiana, 74
Rich, Adrienne, 198n18
Richardson, Eileen H., 226
Rights, 13, 93, 110
Right-wing parties, 18, 217
Right-wing press, 259
Right-wing, populist nationalisms, 322
Rimini, 3
Robertson, Caolan, 2n2
Robinson, Tommy, 2, 7
Roggeband, Conny, 266
Rojava, 153n10, 157, 159, 160
Rojava-Northern Syria, 157
Rojava Revolution, 146, 157, 158
Roma, 18, 275
Romania, 10, 259, 275
Romanian, 259, 262
  media, 17
  migrants, 18
  people, 18
Romano, David, 151
Rosado, Isabel, 139, 141
Rosado, Marisa, 130, 137
Rose, Wu, 348
*Rossiyskaya Gazeta*, 71

Rotbard, Sharon, 96
Roussef, Dilma, 115
Rural, 34
Russia, 10, 12, 77, 82
Russian, 13
  mass media, 72
  media, 13, 71, 75–78, 81, 82
  nation-state, 13
Russian Federation, 22, 67–69
Rydgren, Jens, 285, 289
Rydstrom, Jens, 122
Rytter, Mikkel, 227

S

Sacred duty, 134
Sacrificing, 134
Safran, William, 300
Salcido, Olivia, 228
Salvini, Matteo, 245
Same-sex, 309
  couples, 110, 113, 119, 121
  divorce rate, 122
  marriage, 13, 110, 111, 113, 114, 116, 118–120, 122
  partnerships, 208
  relationships, 309
Same-sex-couple-headed families, 113
San Juan, 138, 139
Sanders-McDonagh, Erin, 16, 44, 168, 283n3
Santos, Juan Manuel (President), 119
Sasson-Levi, Orly, 91, 91n3, 101
Sautman, Barry, 349
Savarkar, Vinayak Damodar, 56, 57, 64
Saviors, 15
Şaylemez, Leyla, 151n9

Scenarios, 318
Schemata of interpretation, 264
Schengen, 260
Scheufele, Dietram, 265
Schifirneţ, Constantin, 262
Schiller, Glick, 306
Schinkel, Willem, 224, 226
Schultz, Stanley K., 94
Scotland, 321, 330, 340
Scott, Joan W., 83
Scrinzi, Francesca, 7, 17, 170, 174, 242, 243, 248, 249
Scripts, 302, 310
*Sección femenina*, 133
Second-generation, 18, 300, 301, 306, 307
  identities, 300
Second World War, 332
Secular, 323
Secularism, 178
Secularization, 116
Secular national values, 117
Security, 267
Self-actualization, 307
Self-determination, 340
Self-governance, 157
Self-governance system, 146
Semantic network analyses, 265
Semiotics, 11
Sénac, Réjane, 122
Separate spheres ideology, 318, 324
September 11, 2001, 21, 201, 209
Serbia, 148
*Servage*, 113
*Sexage*, 113
Sex discrimination, 342
Sexism, 7, 17, 243
Sex slavery, 145

Sexual citizenship, 224
Sexual cosmopolitanism, 3, 6
Sexual crime, 7
Sexual democracy, 227
Sexual freedom, 178
Sexual identities, 301
Sexual intimacy, 225
Sexuality, 5, 9–11, 15, 18, 21–23, 90, 166–171, 182, 299, 305, 311
Sexuality rights, 11
Sexualization, 16, 168
  of Islamophobia, 11
  of racism, 17, 170, 174, 243
Sexualized double-standard, 17
Sexualized imaginary, 305
Sexual liberalism, 7
Sexual minorities, 10, 23, 317n1
Sexual non-conformity, 7
Sexual Offences Act 1967, 311
Sex work, 34–36, 42, 44
Shafir, Gershon, 93
Shame, 302
Shapiro, Michael J., 74
Sharia Law, 2, 212
*Sharia Watch UK*, 2n2
Sharma, Jyoti, 55
Shengal, 145
Shkandrij, Myroslav, 79
Silvestri, Sara, 94
Sinjar, 145
Sino-British Joint Declaration (JD), 338
Sirriyeh, Ala, 227
Skilled migration, 291
Skilton, Nick, 12
Skocpol, Theda, 325
Skype, 206

Sluga, Glenda, 324, 325
Slutwalk, 348
Smith, Anthony D., 155, 322, 325, 328
Smith, Michael P., 306
Smooha, Sami, 93n5
Snow, David A., 264
So, Alvin, 227n1
Social and sexual drama, 171–182
Social benefits, 18, 267
Social coherence and citizenship, 14
Social Contract for the Democratic Federalism System of Northern Syria, 158
Social democracies, 326
Social democrats, 154
Social Ecology, 154n11
Social imperialism, 9
Social inclusion, 349
Social justice, 110, 122
Social order, 37, 38, 42
Social Progress Index, 120
Social remittances, 306
Social reproducers, 242
Social reproduction, 16, 224, 251
Social values, 37
Socialism, 150, 152
*Société Saint-Jean-Baptiste*, 189n3
Sodomy, 5, 92, 93
Solina, Carla, 149
Somalians, 287
Somers, Margaret, 325
Sotomayor, José Pepe, 139
South Africa, 110
South East Asian, 11
Sovereigntist, 195
Sovereignty, 154, 346, 347
Soviet Union, 152

## Index

Spain, 326
Spanish-American war, 132
Spierings, Niels, 6, 7, 182, 204
Spirescu, Victor, 260, 261
Spivak, Dori, 201
Srivastava, Neelam, 49
Stand Up To Racism, 2
State architectures, 337
State-business elite, 19
State homophobia, 73
State-led, 339
State nationalism, 348
State-sanctioned homophobia, 11
State-seeking, 339
State-seeking nationalist movements, 320
*Statesman, The*, 21
State-sponsored violence, 13
Status of Women, 191n7
Staver, Anne, 227
Stella, Francesca, 70, 73
Stewart, Charles, 303
Strasser, Elisabeth, 226
Stricovsky, Alon, 100
Stuart Hall, 149
Suffrage, 40
*Sun, The*, 260, 273
Surrogacy, 113
Swagmen, 33
Sweden, 326
Symons, Jonathan, 73, 78, 83
Syria, 145, 160
Syrian Democratic Forces, 157


Tabet, Paola, 114
Tabloids, 261
Taiwan, 114

Tankard, James, 265
Tasmania, 33, 36
Taubira, Christiane, 116
Taylor, Verta, 111
Tel Aviv, 13, 102
   city council, 95, 98
   Independence Park, 89, 94
Ten years, 350
Territorial autonomy, 338–341
Territorialized political community, 337
Territory, 8
Theocratic patriarchy, 176
Theoretical comparisons, 322
Thin centred-ideology, 204
Third World countries, 200
Third World liberation movements, 190
Thomas, Lyn, 94
Thompson, Nick, 4
Thorleifsson, Cathrine, 208
Tiananmen Massacre, 342
Tilly, Charles, 319
Timmons, Heather, 348
Tissot, Sylvie, 246
Titus Corlățean, 270
Tlostanova, Madina, 79, 80
Tohidi, Nayereh, 321
Tommy English, 1
Tong, Irene L. K., 341, 342, 347, 349
Toomey, Simon, 204
Torah, 92n4
Torres, Benjamín J., 130
Torresola, Angelina, 134
Torresola, Doris, 139
Torresola, Griselio, 140
Toupin, Louise, 190
Towns, Ann, 242

Traditional values, 12, 69, 70, 73, 74, 78, 79, 81, 82
Translocal mobilities, 18
Transnational, 18, 148
 communities, 301
 experiences, 311
 identities, 260, 305
 migration, 264
 and migration theory, 11
 mobilities, 300
 performativity, 305, 307
 relations, 305
 social fields, 301
Transnationalism, 18
Transnationality, 233, 306
Transsexual, 4
Trauma, 302, 308
Tremblay *vs.* Daigle, 194
Triandafyllidou, Anna, 329
Tribal affiliations, 155, 156
Tribe, 305
Tronconi, Filippo, 289
Truman, Harry S. (President), 138
Trump, Donald John, 116, 322, 327
Tufail, Waqas., 173
Tuorto, Dario, 244n5
Turkish, 150
Turkish Muslims, 288
Turkmen, 157
Turner, Bryan S., 223, 226
20th century, 20
Tyranny, 180

U

Udmurtia, 81
Uganda, 4, 9
UK, *see* United Kingdom
UK Against Hate, 2

UK Independence Party (UKIP), 2n2, 16, 18, 203
UKIP, 205–207, 209, 216
Ukraine, 76
Ukrainian, 76
Ultra-nationalist, 166
Umbrella/Occupy Central Protests, 348
Uncontrolled migration, 8
UN Convention on the Elimination of all forms of Discrimination Against Women (CEDAW), 112
Undesirable migrants, 254
Undocumented migrants, 294
Unfairness, 15, 166, 167, 171, 179, 183
UN human rights treaty-bodies, 344
United Kingdom (UK), 10, 16, 117, 166, 167, 174, 176, 178, 179, 182, 183, 311
United Kingdom Independence Party (UKIP), 283
United Nations (UN), 132, 145, 343
United Russia, 73
United States National Guard, 138
United States of America (USA), 11, 21, 114, 116, 133, 136, 325, 326, 332
Uniting Church, 121
Universal Declaration of Human Rights (UDHR), 109
Universal suffrage, 325
Unproductive burdens, 232
Unskilled migrants, 290
Upper-class, 35, 39, 42
Uribe, Álvaro (President), 119
"Us" and "Them", 260
US Census bureau, 120

US colonialism, 129, 141
US colonial rule, 130, 134–135, 138, 139
US Congress, 137, 140
US Constitution and Bill of Rights, 110
US government, 136, 139
US-led Global Coalition, 145
US military, 136
US repression, 132
US Senate, 21
US Supreme Court, 120
USA, *see* United States of America
USSR, 322
Üstündağ, Nazan, 159, 160
Utuado, 138

V

Values, 34, 35, 41, 42
Van Bruinessen, Martin, 155
Van Der Brug, Wouter, 204
Van Gorp, Baldwin, 264, 265
Van Hooren, Franca, 250
Van Houdt, Friso, 224, 226
Van Spanje, Joost, 204
Varikas, Eleni, 329
Vatican, 117
Velvet triangle, 195
Verkhovskii, Aleksandr, 77
Vickers, Jeanne, 148
Vickers, Jill, 19, 20, 318, 320, 326, 328, 337, 340
Victims, 14, 15, 17, 167, 174
Victoria, 33, 35, 39, 40
Victorian *Act to Restrain by Summary Proceedings Unauthorised Mining on Waste Lands of the Crown 1852*, 39
Victorian colony, 36
Victorian goldfields, 39
*Victorian Mining Statute*, 41
*Victorian Royal Commission on Goldfield Problems and Grievances*, 40
Victorian-era, 32–37
Vieques, 133
Violence, 113, 149, 152, 159, 176
 against women, 118
Vliegenthart, Rens, 266
von Mering, Sabine, 285
Vouloukos, Athanasia, 328
*Vrem'a*, 71
Vulnerable non-Muslim women, 15

W

Walby, Sylvia, 308
Wales, 340
Wang, Sean H., 229
War, 8
War of Independence, 95, 328
War on terror, 22
Ward, Russel, 34
Warner, Michael, 90
Warren, Carol A., 95
Washington D.C. police, 140
Waters, Anne Marie, 2n2
Webb, Paul, 204
Weber, Max, 155
Weininge, Otto, 90
Weiss, Meredith L., 70, 73
Welfare benefits, 289
Welfare chauvinism, 287
Welfare dependency, 16
Welfare State, 195
Welfare system, the, 18
Wentz, Sarah, 119

Werbner, Pnina, 303
West, 6, 7, 9, 13, 167, 169
  *vs.* the Rest, 110, 111
West, Lois A., 330
Western, 169
  feminists, 320
  nationalisms, 15
  nations, 21
Western Europe, 321
Westrheim, Kariane, 149, 151
Wetland, Kurt, 204
Whitaker, Richard, 207
White backlash, 166, 170–171, 182
  thesis, 166, 167, 183
White expatriate women, 349
White men, 34
White solipsism, 197
White supremacism, 23
Whitehead, Stephen, 309
Whites-only nationalism, 326
Wiesner-Hanks, Merry E., 318
Wigstock, 99, 102
Wigstock riots, 100
Willert, Trine Stauning, 302
Winter, Bronwyn, 13, 22, 111, 115, 122
Wodak, Ruth, 94, 243n4, 282
Woman-friendly outcomes, 20
Womanhood, 14, 141
Women, 9, 10, 14, 19–21, 35–37, 42, 44, 137–141, 166, 167, 169
  active engagement, 20
  autonomous organization, 160
  bodies, 8
  citizenship, 327
  confederalism, 154, 158
  emancipation, 320

equality and rights, 337–341, 347, 351
formal equality, 351
freedom, 158
immigrants, 349
justice systems, 158
liberation, 147, 150, 154, 159
liberationist, 152
liberationist paradigm, 146
nationalists, 18, 141
participation, 330–331
relationship to nationalism, 133
representation and participation, 340
reproductive capacity, 323
reproductive rights, 118
revolution, 153
rights, 17, 19, 112, 344–350
sexual availability, 325
Women-friendly international norms, 343
Women-friendly outcomes, 338
Women-friendly policies, 338
  and programs, 326
Women-friendly reforms, 340
Women's Commission, 344, 345, 347
Women's Defense Units (YPJ), 146, 160
Wong, Lee L., 227, 227n1, 232
Wong, Penny, 121
Working-class, 34, 36–39, 42–44
  masculinities, 12
  mining men, 32
World March of Women (WMW), 191n7, 196
World Social Forum, 196
World War II, 132, 136

Wray, Helena, 226, 229
Wright, Clare, 36, 37
Wu, Ka-Ming, 349
Wu, Rose, 345

## X

Xenophobia, 168, 207, 284
*Xwebûn*, 156

## Y

Yahav, Dan, 96
Yannakopoulos Kostas, 310
Yardley, Jim, 51
*Yediot Ahronot*, 94
*Yediot Iriat Tel Aviv*, 94
Yezidi-Kurdish, 145
Yezidis, 145

Young , Simon N. M., 347
Young women, 21
Yugoslavia, 322
Yuval-Davis, Nira, 8, 20, 130, 133, 148, 155, 225, 230, 242, 263, 317, 320, 330

## Z

Zagarri, Rosemary, 324, 325
Zaslove, Andrej, 182, 204
Zelizer, Barbie, 273, 277
Zheng, Wang, 301n1
Zionism, 90
Zionist, 92, 103
Zorkin, Valerii, 80
Zúquete, José Pedro, 6, 169, 170, 172
Zwickel, Jean, 138

CPSIA information can be obtained
at www.ICGtesting.com
Printed in the USA
LVHW04*1244280518
578668LV00005B/10/P